'MORE FRUITFUL THAN THE SOIL'

'MORE FRUITFUL THAN THE SOIL'

Army, Empire and the Scottish Highlands, 1715–1815

ANDREW MACKILLOP

TUCKWELL PRESS

First published in Great Britain in 2000 by
Tuckwell Press
The Mill House
Phantassie
East Linton
East Lothian EH40 3DG
Scotland

Copyright © Andrew Mackillop, 2000

ISBN 1 86232 161 2

British Library Cataloguing in Publication Data

A catalogue record for this book is available
on request from the British Library

The right of Andrew Mackillop to be identified as the author of this work has been
asserted by him in accordance with the Copyright, Design and Patent Act 1988

Typeset by Hewer Text Ltd, Edinburgh
Printed and bound by The Cromwell Press, Trowbridge, Wiltshire

Contents

Tables	vii
Abbreviations	ix
Glossary	xi
Acknowledgements	xiii
Introduction	1
1 The Emergence of a British-Highland Military, 1715–46	13
2 Imperial Specialisation: the British-Highland Military, 1746–1815	41
3 The Annexed Estates: Improvement, Recruitment and Re-settlement, 1746–1784	77
4 The Campbells of Breadalbane: Recruitment and Highland Estate Management, 1745–1802	101
5 Military Recruiting and the Highland Estate Economy, 1756–1815	130
6 The Military and Highland Emigration, 1763–1815	168
7 Military Service and British Identity in the Highlands, 1746–1815	204
Conclusion	234
Appendices	245
Bibliography	251
Index	267

Tables

1. Military Officers, their Relations and the Scottish County Electorate, 1788 — 52
2. Officers and Half-Pay Officers of Highland Regiments, 1740–1784 — 62
3. Origin and Social Profile of Military Personnel, Annexed Estates, 1763–4 — 93
4. Social and Tenurial Origins of Glenorchy and Netherlorne Recruits, 1759 — 108
5. Percentage of Hired or Family Recruits, Perthshire Estate, 1795 — 117
6. Relative Cost of Rent and Hired Recruits, Breadalbane Estate, 1793–5 — 117
7. Structure of Perthshire Estate, 1793 and Social Origins of Recruits, 1793–5 — 119
8. Structure of Argyll Estate, 1788 and Social Origins of Recruits, 1793–5 — 120
9. Lewis Kelp Production, 1794–1799 — 135
10. Impact of Recruiting upon Manpower and Farm Structure, 1778–1799 — 140
11. Social Origins of Recruits from Atholl and North Uist Estates, 1778–1799 — 143
12. Half-Pay Officers on Highland Estates, 1768–1804 — 148
13. Military Officers and the Sutherland Estate, 1802 — 149
14. Chelsea Pensioners from Highland Counties and Battalions, 1740–1800 — 150
15. Chelsea Pensioners and Highland Estates, 1764 — 151
16. Military Earnings Relative to Rent, Lochbuie Estate, Mull, 1795–1796 — 152
17. Volunteer Pay Relative to Rent in the West Highlands and Islands, 1795–1802 — 153
18. Type of Land Promise to Highland Soldiers, 1790s — 162
19. Half-Pay and Exchange Rates, 1766 — 173
20. British and Highland Half-Pay Officers Reduced in 1763 — 177
21. Men Raised in England, Ireland and Scotland under the Additional Act and Enlisting in the Regular Army, June 1804–December 1805 — 228

Abbreviations

A.U.L.	Aberdeen University Library
B.A.M.	Blair Atholl Muniments
B.L.	British Library, London
C.D.T.L.	Clan Donald Trust Library, Armadale, Skye
D.C.M.	Dunvegan Castle Muniments
D.H.	Dumfries House
F.E.P.	Forfeited Estate Papers
G.C.A.	Glasgow City Archive
G.U.B.R.C.	Glasgow University Business Records Centre
G.U.L.	Glasgow University Library
H.M.C.	Historical Manuscripts Commission
H.R.A.	Highland Regional Archive, Inverness
J.R.L.	John Rylands Library, Manchester
M.L.	Mitchell Library, Glasgow
N.L.S.	National Library of Scotland, Edinburgh
P.R.O.	Public Record Office, Kew, London
S.R.O.	Scottish Record Office, Edinburgh (now National Archives of Scotland)

Glossary

Baile	A farm township
Bolls	A Scottish weight measure not exceeding six bushels
Duthchas	The heritage of a clan, usually conceived of as favourable access to land and resources
Fencible regiment	Unit raised for service only within Scotland. After 1794 extended to Ireland and Europe
Grassum	Customary one-off payment by tenants over and above annual rents to the landlord upon receiving or renewing a tack
Line regiment	Regular army unit with no geographic restrictions on service destination
Mail land	Unit assessing farm productivity and rent levels
Merkland	Unit of land assessed for taxation purposes at 13 shillings 1/3d sterling.
Na Daoine	'The Men'. Lay religious preachers
Off reckonings	Payments made to a regimental colonel for recruiting and maintaining his men
Rouping	An auction
Steelbow	Credit, often in the form of seed, stock or farming equipment, from landlord to tenant
Souming	Assessing or fixing the number of tenant stock on a farm's common grazing
Wadset	A mortgage – a farm and rental assigned to a creditor as method of interest payment

Acknowledgements

In writing this work I have become indebted to a significant number of people and institutions. As the bulk of my research was completed at these two repositories I would first like to register my sincere appreciation to the staff of the National Archives of Scotland (formerly the Scottish Record Office) and National Library of Scotland. I would also like to thank the following people or institutions for allowing me access to the collections in their possession: Atholl Estates, the Duke of Buccleuch, the Dumfries family, Mr. John Macleod and the Clan Donald Trust. I would especially like to thank Mr Donald Stewart, until recently archivist at Dunvegan, for his friendly welcome and extremely helpful approach to my requests for documents.

This work is an extended version of my thesis on Highland recruitment, which I completed at the Scottish History Department at Glasgow University. Ironically, I was first nudged towards this subject by Dr. Lionel Glassey of the Modern History Department. In helping me decide that recruiting, or, to be more precise, its socio-economic effects, was an obviously neglected area worthy of examination, Dr Glassey not only spared himself the ordeal of perhaps having to tutor me but unselfishly provided a rather unfocused student with some sense of purpose. When I first started my research I benefited from the expertise of Allan Macinnes, who not only brought home to me the worth of Highland history within a Scottish context, but also encouraged me to view the region as very much a part of the evolving British Empire. Despite his departure to Aberdeen he was good enough to review certain aspects of the last chapter and suggest some additional lines of argument, for which I am grateful. Dr. Colin Kidd was typically generous not only in offering general support and friendly criticism, but also in immediately suggesting appropriate articles for many of my queries, no matter how apparently obscure. Similarly, I would like to express my warm thanks to the external examiner of my thesis, Don Withrington, who characteristically dissected the all-too apparent weaknesses in my work. A special thank you is also required to Professor Ted Cowan, who supervised the final years of my Ph.D. As well as providing much needed criticism and review of my work, his mixture of forthright encouragement, broad contextual analysis and injections of humour helped me enormously. I do hope I have persuaded him that the issue of recruitment entails more than 'buttons and brass' military history.

A three-year postdoctoral research fellowship at the Scottish History Department at St Andrews provided me with invaluable time and material security to mull over and develop some wider ideas regarding the role of the Highlands within the eighteenth-century British Empire. I would like to express my thanks not only to my departmental colleagues there, but also to Grant Distillers and Dr. Sandy Grant-Gordon, in particular, for providing me with that opportunity. Regrettably, it appears I was the last Glenfiddich Research Fellow in Scottish History, and I, as much as the Department at St Andrews, regret the loss of a research post that provided one of the few means whereby those studying Scottish history could go on to broaden their areas of knowledge and interest. [I would, moreover, like to express my appreciation to John and Val Tuckwell for agreeing to tackle the whole sordid story of the Highlands and The 'Fiscal-Military State']

I would also like to say cheers to the following people who made the experience of studying Scottish history at Glasgow so intellectually rewarding and enjoyable: Ronnie, Fiona and John for providing what I can only describe as the very best in pub argument, friendly support and commentary. Similarly, my deepest thanks to Ewen Cameron, who also ploughs the furrow of Highland history, for his advice, encouragement and considerable support, which I have deeply appreciated. Outside of history I feel I must mention: Nom', Murch, James, Calum, Pick, Wilbur and Joe for reminding me that reading the private mail and affairs of people who have been dead for several hundred years does not necessarily constitute, to external observers at least, a particularly useful or even reputable career. I shall in light of their advice, often expressed in distinctly unchristian and drunken language, remember that all historians are apparently little better than 'jumped up story tellers'. I would also like to especially thank Moira, my mother, Neil and Norman my brothers, and Morag my sister for their support and encouragement, despite obvious concerns that I apparently appeared happy to remain a student for the rest of my life. Finally, my deepest debt and thanks go to Carol, whose very real and significant sacrifices in her own career, not to mention near-suicidal trips driving back and forth along the M8, enabled me to stick with history and complete this work. Having now finished it, all I can really do is express my deepest gratitude and all my love.

Introduction

The impact of British army recruiting within the Scottish Highlands during the period from approximately 1715 to 1815 has been described by a prominent commentator in the following terms: 'The issue was perhaps the most explosive single element in the entire history of the Highland clearances'.[1]

Despite the importance attributed in that instance to such military activity, there has been curiously little in-depth analysis of the motives for and impact of regiment raising in the region. Any attempt to explain why there has been such a dearth of academic study of this particular subject needs to bear in mind the present image and reputation of Highland regiments. They constitute in many respects one of Scotland's most immediately recognisable but controversial cultural icons. To some they represent a distorted and, indeed, distastefully jingoistic hangover from Scotland's imperial past. More crucially, they also appear to be of little or no actual relevance to the wider processes which shaped modern Scotland, be it demographic, industrial, or agricultural change. Partly for these reasons the academic community seems to have concluded that the examination of Scotland's distinctive contribution to Britain's imperial military is somewhat politically incorrect, and best left to purely military historians and antiquarians. Indeed, whatever the validity of claims voiced by one English historian regarding Ireland's historiographic blindness to its role within eighteenth- and early nineteenth-century British imperialism, it is an accusation that undoubtedly has a ring of truth with respect to Scotland.[2] One specific result of this situation has been that these regiments and the processes that created them have been all but buried under a whole corpus of material from both the nineteenth and twentieth centuries which can generally be described as regimental histories. This literature has overly romanticised such levies; indeed, in the case of some Victorian examples it descends into almost racial stereo-typing of the Gael as an enthusiastic, undisciplined warrior whose natural fighting genius only found full expression once contained within the disciplined framework of the British army. Generally, this genre emphasises the direct Highland connections and traditions of such regiments and ensures that the whole issue is

---

1. E. Richards, *A History of the Highland Clearances: Agrarian Change and the Evictions, 1746–1886*, vol. 1 (London, 1982), p. 147.
2. C.A. Bayly, *Imperial Meridian: The British Empire and the World, 1780–1730* (London, 1989), pp. 12–13.

represented largely from the army's perspective, with little or no reference to the wider social and economic context. Often written by army or ex-army officers, such regimental histories continue to reinforce an interpretation that many would describe as at best historically inaccurate and, at worst, as conveying a false and twee image of the Highlands and Scotland as a whole.[3]

This book, then, is an attempt to rectify the lack of a broad political, socio-economic study of recruitment in the Highlands. Its aim has been to try and understand its origins and impact and to examine the process through all its stages, from its role within eighteenth-century British imperialism to its consequences for the various tenant groups residing upon Highland estates. The approach has been to examine as wide a variety of sources as possible. Highland history has traditionally been dogged by controversy over the extent to which reliance upon one particular source, be it estate records or Gaelic poetry, somehow invalidates the findings of those who use it.[4] The book makes no apologies for deploying government and, above all, estate records in an effort to understand why recruitment occurred to the extent it did. Yet, in order to understand how estate populations reacted to their involvement, whether voluntary or otherwise, in this process, a deliberate research strategy has been to examine tenant petitions and memorials in an attempt to shed some light on what the expectations and agenda of Gaels actually were. Obviously, such a source is far from perfect: petitioning inevitably involved tenantry deferring to proprietary authority and tempering their opinions in order to avoid alienating either the factor or the laird. Nonetheless, such material provides an invaluable insight into the actual, specific demands of individuals, and has the additional benefit of not being influenced by hindsight. Above all, this study is based upon what seems, to its author at least, the common sense premise that particular sources are best used when they appear to be most appropriate. Thus, for example, government and estate records form the bulk of research material for chapters on the origin and tenurial consequences of military recruiting, while Gaelic poetry forms part of the assessment of how if at all military service moulded the Gaels' sense of their own identity.

Nothing better illustrates the need for a fuller understanding of military

3. For typical examples, see F. Burgoyne, *Historical Record of the 93rd Sutherland Highlanders* (London, 1883); R.P. Dunn-Pattison, *History of the 91st Argyll Highlanders* (London, 1910); T.A. Mackenzie and J.S. Ewart, *Historical Records of the 79th Queen's Own Cameron Highlanders* (London, 1887); J.S. Keltie, *A History of the Scottish Highlands, Highland Clans and Highland Regiments*, vol. 2 (Edinburgh, 1875). For modern works that show relatively greater sensitivity to the socio-economic context, see D.M. Henderson, *Highland Soldier: A Social Study of the Highland Regiments, 1820–1920* (Edinburgh, 1989), specifically Chapters 1 and 2. Also L. MacLean, *The Raising of the 79th Highlanders* (Inverness, 1980), p. 11.
4. J. Hunter, *The Making of the Crofting Community* (Edinburgh, 1976), p. 4; E.A. Cameron, *Land for the People? The British Government & the Scottish Highlands, c. 1880–1925* (East Linton, 1996), pp. 9–15.

recruitment than the importance accorded to it in the historiography of the Highland Clearances. The publication of David Stewart of Garth's *Sketches of the Character, Manners and Present State of the Highlanders of Scotland*, and, later, the deeply influential *Gloomy Memories* by Donald Macleod helped ensure recruitment emerged as a vital component within the wider high-profile debate surrounding land and population in the region. In what was for the Victorians one of the most emotive and cogent arguments against the estate management policies of Highland proprietors, Macleod contended that: 'The children and nearest relations of those who sustained the honour of the British name in many a bloody field – the heroes of Egypt, Corunna, Tolouse, Salamanca and Waterloo – were ruined, trampled upon, dispersed, and compelled to seek an asylum across the Atlantic'.[5]

There is little doubt that the recruitment issue intensified dispute over the status and rights of Gaels. It insured the profound sense of betrayal, absent with respect to the rest of Scotland, that characterised discussion of land use and agricultural change in the region. Its impact upon perceptions of the Sutherland Clearances is typical in this respect. The mass evictions in Sutherland in the first two decades of the nineteenth century have for some time been accepted as unusual in terms of the numbers involved and amounts of capital deployed. Yet it is not merely the matter of scale that explains the unusually intense passions aroused by the Sutherland Clearances. The Sutherlands were in fact the last landlord family from the region to raise a proprietary regiment for the British army, and that fact alone goes a long way towards explaining the particularly bitter folk memories associated with them. In Alexander Mackenzie's immensely popular book, *The History of the Highland Clearances*, first published in 1883, particular attention was paid to the irony of military service and British patriotism being rewarded with eviction. Mackenzie's book gave detailed accounts regarding the lack of Highland men for the Crimean War. He directly contrasted this poor response to the large number of men that late Victorian society firmly believed had been recruited under the clan system during the French and Napoleonic period.[6] This military dimension to the wider debate on the Highlands thus proved vital in the development of popular views of the region in the second half of the nineteenth century. Above all, it ensured that, unlike other areas such as Ireland, Highland depopulation came to be seen as a matter of British national interest. The betrayal of a people that many firmly believed to be the nation's finest soldiers moved the debate onto an entirely different level, away from property and legal rights, and onto moral and even patriotic grounds. Furthermore, it undoubtedly assisted the process whereby landlords were

5. D. Macleod, *Gloomy Memories in the Highlands of Scotland versus Mrs. Harriet Beecher Stowe's Sunny Memories* (Glasgow, 1892), p. 1.
6. A. Mackenzie, *A History of the Highland Clearances* (Glasgow, 1966), pp. 49, 67, 105–106.

put on the moral and political defensive by the 1880s. It was thus noted of the region's proprietors:

> Alas, for the blush that would cover their faces if they would allow themselves to reflect that, in their names, the fathers, mothers, brothers, wives, of the invincible '78th' had been remorselessly driven from their native soil. But we tell Highland proprietors that were Britain some twenty years hence to have the misfortune to be plunged into such a crisis as the present, there will be few such men as the Highlanders of the 78th to fight her battles [and] if another policy towards the Highlanders is not adopted, that sheep and deer, ptarmigan and grouse, can do but little to save it in such a calamity.[7]

In essence, the landlords stood accused of acting against the nation's defence and security interests. It is worth noting at this point that such an analysis was in fact a substantial distortion of Britain's real military situation in the 1880s. Though the number of Highlanders recruited had been prone to exaggeration during the eighteenth century itself, it was even more the case that by the last decades of the nineteenth century Gaels could in no way be described as a vital element in Britain's recruiting strategy or a decisive factor in her military strength. Indeed, contrary to popular understanding, Highlanders, and Scots in general, did not make up a particularly strong numerical element within the British army after the 1830s. They were, for example, proportionally outnumbered by the Irish, who undoubtedly constituted the best British recruiting ground relative to population.[8] However, the legends surrounding Highland regiments ensured that recruiting retained its position as an important issue determining wider attitudes to the region. Indeed, military service had given additional legitimacy to the land claims of Highland populations since before the beginning of the nineteenth century. That this moral aspect had been noticeably unsuccessful until the 1880s should in no way detract from the fact that it consistently formed a sub-theme within the whole question of land and population in the region. Thus it was that in the spring of 1813, in one last attempt to avoid removal, the population of Kildonan in Sutherland deployed the military card. They stated 'that they were *loyal* men, whose brothers and sons were now fighting Bonaparte and they would allow no sheep to come into the country'. Even more telling was the fact that when the tenantry organised a petition to Elizabeth, Countess of Sutherland, they deliberately chose William Macdonald, a pensioner from the 93rd Sutherland Highlanders. By choosing an ex-soldier the population

7. A. Mackenzie, *op. cit.*, pp. 168–169.
8. For discussion respecting the over-emphasis on the number of Highlanders in military service evident by the 1790s, see J.E. Cookson, *The British Armed Nation, 1793–1815* (Oxford, 1997), p. 129; H.J. Hanham, 'Religion and Nationality in the Mid-Victorian Army', in M.R.D. Foot (ed.), *War and Society: Historical Essays in Honour and Memory of J.R. Western, 1928–1971* (London, 1973), pp. 163–167.

were attempting to create a context where the reality of their economic redundancy was clouded, and former obligations to them were suddenly remembered.[9]

The influence of the military dimension in broadening the scope of the land question can thus be traced to within the period of first-phase clearance itself. However, it was during the time of the Napier Commission that the true legacy of the whole historiographical treatment of the recruiting issue can be seen at its most important. During the inquiry into conditions in the Highlands, the liberal character of the government produced ideological anxieties over what amounted to intervention in the property rights of landlords. It became necessary, therefore, to construct unique characteristics for Highland society that justified such interference. The result was that the Commission sought to clarify the issue of how, and by what means, land came to be held in the region.[10] It was at this particular juncture that recruiting assumed an importance that belied its rapid decline in the region seventy-odd years previously. In Assynt the commission was informed of the betrayal of tenurial security and legitimacy won through military service:

> The great majority joined the army on the distinct understanding that the parents would be kept in their holdings; but upon the return of the survivors, they found their parents huddled together on the seashore and their former holdings converted into so many sheep walks. I have seen some of the soldiers when they came home going to the stances where their fathers lived and shedding tears and saying they would go and pull down Dunrobin castle.[11]

This tradition, the Commission noted, had also been cited in Lewis and Skye. On the latter island the question was put directly as to why government should intervene in the area. Crofters replied that favourable government protection would bring about a return of the large-scale recruiting which had been evident during the wars of the later eighteenth and early nineteenth centuries. The Commissioners noted that the concept of sons for land was an 'extremely interesting one' – betraying, perhaps, their desire to find a legitimate excuse for their involvement. That the question of recruitment played a part in justifying intervention can be seen from the comments of the *Highlander* newspaper ten years after the commission had sat. In May 1893 the paper published original judicial documentation from a 1790 case regarding the Macleod estate in Skye. They charted the contested eviction of soldiers who had enlisted for Lieutenant Colonel Norman Macleod of Dunvegan during the American War of Independence. The case of these

9. R.J. Adam, *Sutherland Estate Management, 1802–1816*, vol. 2 (Edinburgh, 1972), pp. 180–188.
10. E.A. Cameron, *op. cit.*, pp. 32–3.
11. Parliamentary Papers, 1884, XXXII, *Report of H.M.'s Commissioners of Inquiry into the Condition of the Crofters and Cottars in the Highlands and Islands of Scotland*, pp. 1738–1740.

soldiers, the paper argued, 'Provide[s] what Lord Napier and Ettrick was so anxious to find proof of, namely, that the land in the Highlands was largely held for military service rendered by the people to their chiefs'.[12]

Although recruiting was vital in determining external attitudes to the region, it is also the case that much of the historiography respecting the development of Highland regiments exhibits major flaws and weaknesses. One such example is the tendency for military recruiting to be seen as a direct extension of the culture and social norms of pre- 1745 Highland society. This presumed link between British military service and clanship has proved so durable because it actually emerged very early on in the evolution of Highland regiments. During the 1745 Jacobite uprising, Adam Ferguson, chaplain to the 42nd Highland Regiment, preached a sermon best remembered as an exhortation to its soldiers to 'play the men for our people'. In one sense the troops were being assigned a role which has been ascribed to Highland soldiery ever since. In essence, they were to represent the cutting edge of the region's reconciliation with the wider British union. Yet more subtle still is the impression given by Ferguson's sermon that these men were innately representative of Highland society, and that as regular, full-time soldiers of the British Crown they were involved in an activity which was both a privileged and yet entirely natural function of a militaristic northern population.[13]

Regimental histories have reinforced the idea that the continuance of military service through the medium of the British army was based on old clan values and attitudes. Perhaps the most important work in this respect is that of David Stewart of Garth. In his book, published in the early 1820s, Stewart explicitly linked the series of eighteenth- and early nineteenth-century Highland battalions to the influence of residual clanship. He argued that these regiments were a product of a unique set of social arrangements. Indeed, Stewart constructed a whole socio-cultural framework to explain to his wider British readership what the French wars had largely confirmed for them: namely, the supposedly innate bellicosity of the Highlander. He argued that 'In forming his military character the Highlander was no more favoured by nature, but by the social system under which he lived'.[14] The substantial nineteenth-century expansion in regimental histories merely served to consolidate this analysis. Though for obvious reasons they tended to concentrate on the operational histories of their respective regiments, devoting only a few pages in the opening chapter to the actual process of obtaining men, the

---

12. Parliamentary Papers 1884, XXXIII, *Report of H.M's Commissioners of Inquiry into the Condition of the Crofters and Cottars in the Highlands and Islands of Scotland*, pp. 28, 63, 957; *The Scottish Highlander & North of Scotland Advertiser*, 11 May 1893, p. 4.
13. A. Ferguson, *A Sermon Preached in the Erse Language to His Majesty's First Highland Regiment of Foot* (London, 1746), p. 3.
14. D. Stewart, *Sketches of the Character, Manners and Present State of the Highlanders of Scotland*, vol. 1 (Edinburgh, 1822), p. 218.

impression given by such literature was that recruitment in the post-Culloden period was completed by the same means and under the same conditions as had been evident prior to 1746. Thus, in 1800 the 93rd Sutherland Highlanders were raised by 'clan attachments and through this instinct'. The Reay Fencibles were similarly raised when the government 'made appeals to their noblemen to arm their clansmen'.[15]

However, such analysis manifestly fails to explain why the region's militarism continued and, indeed, expanded while clanship itself rapidly collapsed. Another reason to be cautious of suggestions that large-scale British army recruiting can be explained in such terms lies in the fact that clanship's military *raison d'être* has itself been somewhat prone to exaggeration. It has been noted, for example, that in the first half of the eighteenth century there were 'large numbers of clansmen, many of whom knew little else but making war'. This modern scholarly quote is indicative of a general trend which, until recently, disregarded the noticeable commercial changes in early eighteenth-century Highland society and their effects upon clan militarism. The last military action arising from an essentially private clan feud was in fact fought in August 1688 at Mulroy in Lochaber, and only took place because one side – the Mackintoshes – had government troops amongst its ranks. Likewise, a list of manpower in Blair Atholl and Glen Tilt from as early as 1702 shows that only 46% were armed in some way, while only one in five was equipped with both a sword and musket. A similar list from 1705 detailing a total of 649 men from the Grant estate in the parishes of Cromdale, Inverallen, Duthill, Abernethy and Rothiemurchus shows that only 36% had a weapon of any kind, while a mere 12% had the full accoutrements of sword and gun. Clearly, the military aspects of clanship had been in long-term decay since well before the end of the seventeenth century.[16] This does not mean, however, that the military capabilities of the region should be underestimated: many clansmen had, for instance, received training in the armies of France and the Dutch Republic. Moreover, in an ironic twist, the growing British army presence in the region between 1715 and 1745 helped to externally buttress the military capability of certain clans. The presence of independent companies in the region, especially after 1725, allowed chiefs like Simon Fraser of Lovat, by rotating service amongst his ordinary tenantry, to build up large numbers of clansmen with a working knowledge of up-to-date military techniques and hardware. Thus, while the Highlands undoubtedly maintained considerable military potential, it is important to clarify the precise nature of the processes that preserved militarism in the region. In a sense, army employment and, in the case of Jacobitism, state-sponsored insurrection, helped disguise the fact

15. A.E.J. Cavendish, *An Reismeid Chataich* (published privately, 1928), p. 10; J. Mackay, *The Reay Fencibles* (Glasgow, 1890), pp. 9, 13.
16. J.M. Hill, *Celtic Warfare, 1595–1763* (Hampshire, 1993), pp. 14–15, 150; A.I. Macinnes, 'Repression and Conciliation: The Highland Dimension 1660–1688', in *Scottish Historical Review*, vol. 55 (1986), p. 195; B.A.M., Box 44/III/c; S.R.O., Seafield Muniments, GD 248/38/2/2.

8   *'More Fruitful than the Soil'*

that privately motivated clannish violence was largely a thing of the past by the Act of Union.[17]

Appreciable decline in clan militarism warns against the assumption that the later high-profile Highland presence within Britain's imperial military was in some way natural and inevitable. Reinforcing this is the fact that clanship was not structurally designed for the constant large-scale wars in which Highland regiments later took part. At the turn of the seventeenth century the Macleods of Dunvegan and Macdonalds of Sleat engaged in a protracted feud which, given their close proximity, forced the constant retention of military manpower to secure their agricultural sectors from raiding. These powerful clans found that within three years their struggle could not be sustained because of the needs of the labour-intensive arable sector. Likewise, devastation inflicted during the Covenanting era upon clans like the McLeans of Duart meant that, even after a generation, almost 25% of their arable resources could not be cultivated because of a lack of manpower. The Macleods of Dunvegan suffered hundreds of casualties at the Battle of Worcester in 1651, which produced a legacy of military caution that survived until 1745. Even where the military characteristics of clanship were retained in a permanent way, as in the case of the Camerons of Locheil, it was usually in order to protect vital agricultural resources and farms.[18] Military activity under clanship was in fact designed primarily to complement and buttress the agricultural sector. The influence of continental techniques and logistics, while allowing clans to retain themselves in the field for increasing periods of time, was nonetheless undermined by the overriding priority given to agrarian concerns. After Prestonpans in 1745, for example, desertion from the Jacobite army increased significantly. This was by no means a demoralised force, yet to many rank-and-file the campaign had been completed. Meanwhile, the harvest cycle was well advanced and the needs of domestic economy began to take precedence over notions of sustained and prolonged military campaigning.[19]

This economic and social context of clan service has not received the comment and analysis that it undoubtedly deserves. Yet it is crucially important in that it strongly suggests that the type of military activity at which clanship proved particularly adept did not necessarily mean erstwhile clansmen were the ideal soldiery for the global conflicts of the post-Culloden

17. S.R.O., Campbell of Stonefield Papers, GD 44/18, 'Political state of the Highlands, 1744'; *The Parliamentary History of England from the Earliest Period to the Year 1803*, vol. 14 (London, 1813), pp. 743–4.
18. I.F. Grant, *The Macleods: The History of a Clan, 1200–1956* (London, 1959), p. 195; A.I. Macinnes, 'The Impact of the Civil Wars and Interregnum: Political Disruption and Social Change within Scottish Gaeldom', in R. Mitchison & P. Roebuck (eds.), *Economy and Society in Scotland & Ireland, 1500–1939* (Edinburgh, 1988), pp. 60–1.
19. F.J. McLynn, *The Jacobite Army in England* (Edinburgh, 1983), pp. 18–19, 24. For a highly perceptive discussion of the localism inherent in Scottish concepts of military service, see J.M. Bulloch, *Territorial Soldiering in the North East of Scotland during 1759–1814* (Aberdeen, 1914), xvi, xxx–xxxvii.

period. After all, Britain, in common with its European counterparts, found itself routinely capable of maintaining an army of over 100,000 men for the best part of a decade, and in theatres as diverse as North America and Bengal. The nature of war was thus completely different from that which characterised the campaigns of Highland clans. Indeed, one of the most important commentaries on the whole subject of Highland military recruiting recognises this fundamental difference, and explains a paradox whereby the supposedly martial Highlander seemed to despise and mutiny against particular forms of British military service.[20]

While current analysis of Highland recruitment is certainly open to question, it is also the case that a re-examination of the topic is overdue in light of recent developments in the fields of British, Scottish and Imperial history. The lack of detailed studies on the subject is in a sense all the more surprising, given the now well-established emphasis placed on the army's role in bringing about both Scottish and Highland assimilation with the British state. An early form of this argument was that regiment-raising by the descendants of prominent Jacobite chiefs erased the sins of their families and facilitated their acceptance into the Anglo-British political elite. More generally, in a seminal study of the eighteenth-century origins of British national identity, war, and especially imperial war, has been assigned a central and all-important role. Military conflict with European and Catholic powers, it has been argued, proved to be one of the most effective mechanisms whereby Scots were able to fully participate on the British stage and to avail themselves of the wealth and material security generated by imperial expansion. From this perspective Highland regiments can be viewed as perhaps the most significant factor dictating the course and pattern of the region's identification with the British state, and, more generally, as an important Scottish dimension within the ongoing and extremely topical debate on the nature, strengths and weaknesses of Britishness.[21]

This debate on identity is paralleled by recent investigations of the nature and impact of early modern state formation. Concepts of a British 'fiscal-military state', for example, provide a new and innovative perspective through which Highland recruitment can be evaluated. It has been argued that the moral, legal and budgetary authority of this fiscal-military polity was such that it exerted considerable centralising influence while simultaneously being 'colonised' by those who wished to direct its actions and benefit from its protection.[22] This raises the issue of how far recruitment was symptomatic

20. J. Prebble, *Mutiny: Highland Regiments in Revolt, 1743–1804* (Harmondsworth, Middlesex, 1975), p. 232.
21. B.P. Lenman, *Jacobite Clans of the Great Glen, 1650–1784* (London, 1984), p. 178; L. Colley, *Britons: Forging the Nation, 1707–1837* (London, 1994), pp. 3–6.
22. J. Brewer, *The Sinews of Power: War, Money and the English state, 1688–1783* (London, 1989), xxi, pp. 191–2; J. Brewer, 'The Eighteenth Century British State: Contexts & Issues', in L. Stone (ed.), *An Imperial State at War: Britain from 1689–1815* (London, 1994), p. 66.

of the state's growing authority within the Highlands; and, for that matter, how far regiment-raising was in fact part of the region's own particular method of state colonisation. This analysis can be extended to include the question of how far recruitment constitutes an important Scottish example of interacting links between what has been usefully conceptualised as a British 'metropolitan core' and its 'provincial' component parts. In this sense recruitment is a case study of how Scotland, as both part of the core and of the periphery, adjusted to inclusion within the British Empire. In addition, it provides a more focused framework within which to compare Scotland with other 'provincial' societies, most obviously Ireland. Thus, while the success of Scottish elites in the private, entrepreneurial and commercial sectors is relatively well known, there remain questions over the extent to which the lack of an indigenous Parliament disadvantaged Scots in their competition for imperial patronage against the Irish, and, indeed, whether disproportionate colonisation of the army was in fact indicative of an inability to break into more lucrative sectors of the fiscal-military or domestic British state.[23]

Such questions ultimately tie into broader issues regarding the nature of Scotland's Britishness and its interaction with the empire. For example, there has been a growing debate as to whether the empire did in fact exercise a unifying effect or was simply a framework in which various 'provincial' groups defined their own distinctive interests, strategies and priorities. A particularly useful aspect of this line of thought is the idea that a single British imperial vision simply did not exist. Instead, various metropolitan and provincial ideologies promoted their own particular vision of what the empire was and should be all about. Imperialism emerges less as an all-embracing centralising agency inducing cultural, social and economic uniformity, than as an interactive process in which peripheries constructed their own particular agendas and links with the metropolitan core, while being both influenced by and, in turn, influencing the empire's development.[24] An issue that will therefore form an important, central theme within this study is how far the Highlands' high-profile involvement within Britain's imperial military can be seen as one such distinctively 'provincial' approach to empire.

23. S.J. Connolly, 'Varieties of Britishness: Ireland, Scotland and Wales in the Hanoverian State', in A. Grant & K. J. Stringer (eds.), *Uniting the Kingdom? The making of British History* (London, 1995), p. 201.
24. B. Bailyn and P. D. Morgan (eds.), 'Introduction', in *Strangers within the Realm: Cultural Margins of the First British Empire* (London, 1991), pp. 1, 7; N. C. Landsman, 'The Provinces and the Empire: Scotland, the American colonies and the development of British provincial identity', in L. Stone (ed.), *An Imperial State at War: Britain from 1689 to 1815* (London, 1994), p. 260. For an earlier discussion that argues 'provincial' areas were more receptive and prone to cultural, political and social assimilation, see J. Clive & B. Bailyn, 'England's Cultural Provinces: Scotland and America', in *William and Mary*, vol. 9, 3rd series (1954).

In addressing these wider issues, however, this study also centres on the eighteenth-century Scottish Highlands. Examination of recruitment's impact upon the region is helped immeasurably by the excellent state of health in which academic study of the Highlands finds itself. As controversial as always, debate has broadened out beyond mere polemical writings on the brutality of the landlord or the 'laziness' of the Highlander, into studies of the region's increasing connections with and integration into a wider British economy. Within this new historiography the Clearances are now to some extent understood as symptomatic of a whole range of forces, from commercial subordination to demographic determinism. These arguments have focused less on the landlords than on structural differences and connections with stronger central and industrialising economies.[25] Yet this method of assessing Highland history has in no way deflected examination of the proprietary class. Analysis of their role and impact remains one of the most important elements within Highland historiography. Indeed, while the role of the wider economic background has been increasingly acknowledged, the significance attached to estate management practices and elite strategies has not diminished, but, instead, has complemented the wider framework of market forces and socio-economic change.[26] Within these various debates, however, government, except during and immediately after the 1715 and 1745 uprisings, has been viewed as exercising minimal influence in the region. This clearly was not the case with regard to recruitment, and this book will address the question of whether a reliance upon military employment formed one facet of a statist strategy by Highland proprietors struggling to deal with the myriad of social and economic problems that increasingly afflicted the area.[27]

This overview has attempted to highlight some of the weaknesses in our current understanding of mass military recruitment in the Scottish Highlands during the period from 1715 to 1815, and to suggest that the subject has a much wider relevance than might at first seem the case. If military service was

25. M. Gray, *The Highland Economy, 1750–1850* (Edinburgh, 1957), pp. 57–8; R.H. Campbell, 'The Scottish Improvers and the Course of Agrarian Change', in L.C. Cullen & T.C. Smout (eds.), *Comparative Aspects of Scottish and Irish Economic and Social History, 1600–1900* (Edinburgh, 1977), pp. 207–212; E. Richards, *A History of the Highland Clearances: Emigration, Protest, Reasons*, vol. 2 (London, 1985), pp. 132–133, 138–139, 156–57.
26. T.M. Devine, 'Landlordism and Highland Emigration' in T.M. Devine (ed.), *Scottish Emigration and Scottish Society* (Edinburgh, 1992), p. 85; A.I. Macinnes, 'Land ownership, Land Use and Elite Enterprise in Scottish Gaeldom; from Clanship to Clearance in Argyllshire, 1688–1858' in T.M. Devine (ed.), *Scottish Elites* (Edinburgh, 1994), p. 2; J. Hunter, loc. cit., p. 5.
27. A.I. Macinnes, 'Scottish Gaeldom: The First Phase of Clearance', in T.M. Devine & R. Mitchison (eds.), *People and Society in Scotland, 1760–1830*, vol. 1 (Edinburgh, 1988), p. 82; T.M. Devine, 'Social Responses of Agrarian "Improvement": The Highland and Lowland Clearances in Scotland' in R.A. Houston & I.D. Whyte (eds.), *Scottish Society, 1500–1800* (Cambridge, 1989), pp. 150–51.

simply a thread of continuity from the era of clanship, then it is necessary to explain why more men were produced in the 1790s, when its influence was appreciably less, than in 1745. Part of the reason why this question has not been fully addressed is that scholars have tended to examine the issue of military levying with one eye on the fact that clanship was undergoing a process of rapid, terminal collapse. Thus, if military recruiting was merely residual clanship, there is a certain logic to the assumption that it would quickly follow the fate of the mechanism that allowed it to occur. It is necessary, however, to avoid such narrow parameters and examine the contemporary political, economic and social factors that maintained and expanded the military experience of the Highlands. This approach needs to be extended into an examination of the recruiting methods used, and the impact of this activity on the various social groups upon Highland estates. This, in turn, involves charting the reasons why landlords, despite their determination to commercialise their estates, nonetheless continued to levy their tenantry for military purposes, and how far this decision then prevented the coherent and undiluted imposition of Lowland-style 'improvement'. Further down the social scale, its impact will be highlighted within the context of inter-tenantry relations as opposed to the more traditional land-lord-versus-tenant framework.

More generally, this study attempts to clarify some over-simplifications regarding recruiting. Rather than assume that men were obtained in the post-Culloden period in traditional clannish fashion, analysis will concentrate instead on whether clanship's actual importance arose from the fact that it evolved into a form of provincial 'lobbying' rhetoric that lubricated Highland and, later, Scots colonisation of Britain's imperial-military. After all, powerful though British government was, it was not necessarily well informed or even aware of the complicated decline of clanship and the emergence in its stead of purely commercial relations between landlords and Highland tenantry. What governments knew was the military capacity of the region. This had been convincingly demonstrated in 1745. This work will, therefore, attempt to reassess the impact of the last Jacobite campaign in terms of its effect upon metropolitan perceptions of the Highlands, rather than dwelling upon its lack of influence on the course and scale of economic change in the region. In summary, Highland regiments need to be treated as a phenomenon of the post-Culloden age, much like sheepfarming and kelping, and seen as a factor which significantly shaped the changes that occurred in the Highlands during the hundred years between Sheriffmuir and Waterloo.

CHAPTER ONE

The Emergence of a British-Highland Military, 1715–46

The thirty years between the major Jacobite uprisings of the '15 and the '45 have been seen within the context of the Scottish Highlands as a relatively undramatic period during which the balance between integrative Hanoverian pressures and particularist Jacobite tendencies fluctuated constantly, but remained roughly in an overall equilibrium. From its apogee in 1715 Scottish Jacobitism seemed to decline in the 1720s into instances of localised Highland violence, or fitful, uncoordinated and poorly supported skirmishes, again confined to the north of Scotland. Over-reliance on foreign powers inconsistently hostile to the United Kingdom failed to provide the basis for a coherent long-term strategy and left those seeking the restoration of the Stuarts vulnerable to the deep anti-French and anti-Catholic sentiments that pervaded both Scotland and England. However, these undoubted weaknesses served to induce complacency within the factious Argathelian and Squadrone Whig interests that controlled Scotland and who remained bitterly divided throughout the 1715–1746 period. Thus, while forces of social and economic change slowly eroded clanship from within, no clear or consistent government policy of assimilating the Highlands emerged in this period. Conversely, Jacobitism retained important ideological coherence through the influence of entrenched Episcopalianism and gained additional sympathy from ongoing nationalist resentment stemming from imagined and real abuses of the Act of Union.[1]

This political stalemate formed the backdrop to the emergence in May 1725 of the first post-Union Highland independent companies. While these military units appeared to constitute just another strand in the largely static balance of support between Jacobite and Hanoverian causes, they in fact entailed the beginning of a proactive relationship between the Highland periphery and a manifestly centralised British military. Although created

1. For discussion of socio-economic change and political continuity, see E. Cregeen, 'The Changing Role of the House of Argyll in the Scottish Highlands' and R. Mitchison, 'The Government of the Highlands, 1707–1745', in N.T. Phillipson and R. Mitchison (eds.), *Scotland in the Age of Improvement: Essays in Scottish History in the Eighteenth Century* (Edinburgh, 1996), pp. 6, 10, 15–16 & 35–8; W.A. Speck, *The Butcher: The Duke of Cumberland and the Suppression of the '45* (Caernarfon, 1995), p. 18; B.P. Lenman, *The Jacobite Clans of the Great Glen, 1650–1784* (London, 1984), pp. 95, 100–103.

initially to undermine Jacobitism and expedite political and economic integration, the development of a military establishment which guaranteed regionally specific patronage, for Hanoverian Highlanders at least, represented a conspicuous acknowledgement by the British state of its own internal diversity at a time when other areas of Scottish society were experiencing considerable albeit inconsistent assimilative pressures.[2] The emergence of such a customised institution was symptomatic of the state's increasingly sophisticated managerial practices, and of its willingness to use a variety of often paradoxical methods to ensure the integration or, more immediately, containment of the north of Scotland. Military commissions represented one such mechanism and were seen as a relatively abundant political resource that could generate wider loyalties to the British state. The decision in September 1706, for instance, of John Campbell, second Duke of Argyll, to throw his interest behind the Union bill was expedited by the promise of a major-general's commission, and demonstrated clearly how the army could be deployed in a Scottish context to supplant or at least circumvent older loyalties.[3] In this broader sense independent companies were never limited to a wholly insular policing agenda, although, initially, the predominance of whig personnel underlined their immediate objective of destroying Highland disaffection and, in the longer term, clanship in general.[4] Attention has, however, usually dwelt on their failure in this particular regard rather than on the longer-term implications for the region's assimilation arising from the creation of an institution which appeared to entrench so many local and distinctive aspects of Highland society.[5] Indeed, the emergence of these initially insignificant companies – not more than 270 to 315 men in 1725[6] – raises much broader issues

---

2. J. M. Simpson, 'Who Steered the Gravy Train, 1707–1766?', in N.T. Phillipson and R. Mitchison (eds.), *Scotland in the Age of Improvement: Essays in Scottish History in the Eighteenth Century* (Edinburgh, 1996), pp. 54–55; D. Hayton, 'Constitutional Experiments and Political Expediency, 1689–1725', in S.G. Ellis & S. Barber (eds.), *Conquest & Union: Fashioning a British State, 1485–1725* (London, 1995), pp. 290–93, 300; J.S. Shaw, *The Management of Scottish Society, 1707–1764* (Edinburgh, 1983), pp. 88–92.
3. K. M. Brown, 'From Scottish Lords to British Officers: State Building, Elite Integration and the Army in the Seventeenth Century', in N. Macdougall (ed.), *Scotland and War, AD 79–1918* (Edinburgh, 1991), pp. 145–48, 149, 152. For the eighteenth century, see B.P. Lenman, *op. cit.*, pp. 178 & 186; A. Murdoch, *The People Above': Politics and Administration in Mid-Eighteenth Century Scotland* (Edinburgh, 1980), pp. 124–5; L. Colley, *Britons: Forging the Nation, 1707–1837* (London, 1992), pp. 120, 126–7 & 129.
4. P. Simpson, *The Independent Highland Companies, 1603–1760* (Edinburgh, 1996), pp. 110–112, 117.
5. R. Mitchison, *loc. cit.*, pp. 28–9, 43; B.P. Lenman, *op. cit.* pp. 103, 135.
6. S.R.O., Mitchell Papers, RH 2/5/12, pp. 15–16. Wade's scheme, presented to the King in April 1725, called for three companies at a strength of 60–70 men under three captains, as well as another three companies commanded by lieutenants at a strength of 30–35 men.

including how, exactly, the relationship between clanship and a 'civilising' and centralised Hanoverian military worked in practice. Moreover, the direct development of Highland regiments from these independent companies poses questions regarding the coherence of the assimilative political forces operating on Highland society, and the issue of how far the region's strong particularisms brought adjustments within the process of integration itself.

Companies and Criminals, 1715–1745

Justification for the re-establishment of Highland independent companies in 1725 revolved around two main constituent strands of a perceived 'Highland problem': namely, 'barbarity', expressed largely in the form of endemic criminal lawlessness, and, second, the region's historic record of deep-rooted political disaffection and military insurrection. However, the neat coherence implied in such an all-encompassing phrase as 'Highland problem' should not be accepted uncritically. Despite Whig propaganda that portrayed banditry and political disaffection as one and the same, the region in fact suffered from legal and criminal problems that were often quite separate from the wider issue of military insurgency.[7] The emergence of these new companies, therefore, took place within a disparate framework riddled with misconceptions and inconsistencies that were, ironically, vital in determining the nature and development of the region's subsequent contribution towards Britain's imperial army. A fundamental inconsistency within the notion of a 'Highland problem' sprang from the fact that issues of lawlessness and military insurrection divided primarily, though by no means absolutely, along local and central perspectives. Within the Highlands and on its Lowland periphery independent companies were seen primarily as reasonably effective instruments of social law and order. Albeit that Simon Fraser of Lovat's lobbying in 1717 for the re-establishment of recently disbanded pre-Union companies centred upon the political issue of Jacobitism's military containment, subsequent pressure for new units in the mid-1720s actually came from localities suffering from repeated small-scale cattle raiding. In February 1724 gentry and tenants in the parishes of Kilearn and Buchanan in Stirlingshire compiled rates of cattle loss since 1717 in order to provide information for Scottish M.P.s lobbying for new companies. These essentially local, legal and proprietorial concerns were reflected closely in the memorial submitted by the Court of Session judge and former Lord Justice Clerk, James Erskine, Lord Grange, at the end of 1724. Given his own legal background, it was not at all surprising that these apprehensions over ineffective judicial protection of

---

7. For an interpretation that points to a 'government' as opposed to a 'Highland' problem, see A.I. Macinnes, *Clanship, Commerce and the House of Stuart, 1603–1788* (East Linton, 1996) p. 124.

property were echoed by Archibald Campbell, Earl of Ilay and later third Duke of Argyll, who surmised that the lack of impartial justice in the Highlands formed 'the very essence of their barbarity'.[8] While the initiatives of 1724–5 are generally accepted as the highest pre-Culloden point of government interest in the Highlands, London's concerns were in fact centred upon the subtly different objective of military pacification and containment. Official memorials, for instance, exhibited a tendency to list the effective strength of clan manpower, quoted at between 24,100 and 22,100 men, as opposed to the equally problematic if somewhat more complex issue of legal jurisdictions and private, partial justice in the region.[9] General George Wade in his 1727 report to the King exemplified these specific, military aims when he noted that the bearing of arms by Highlanders undoubtedly had unfortunate criminal and violent consequences, but that 'the greatest inconveniency was their being proper and ready instruments [for] the Pretender'.[10] Ilay, despite his concerns over legal conditions in the region, highlighted these very different local and central government agendas when he noted to Grange that the largely administrative and legalistic tone of his report had resulted in delay of its consideration in London, adding, 'for all those views here are at present suspended, excepting the disarming [sic] the disaffected Highlanders which you will recommend as of the last consequence to the government in case of any new disturbance at home or abroad'.[11]

Ilay's advice not only demonstrated the conscious subordination of law and order issues in government circles to that of military affairs, but also that, as in the seventeenth century, few Scottish politicians consequently found it in their interest to distinguish between purely criminal violence and political and armed disaffection. Only by drawing attention to the latter could concerned officials in Edinburgh get Westminster to consider policies to deal with the former. Nor indeed was this a practice limited to managerial elites in Edinburgh and London. Particular cases of disorder continued to be used freely for political advantage by chiefs themselves, be they Jacobite or Whig. Thus, while many senior members of Scotland's legal establishment conceded that clan feuding had become a thing of the past, the deliberate misrepresentation of disorder reinforced metropolitan perceptions that robbery and 'private scuffles' kept Highlanders accustomed to arms in such a way that, under entirely different circumstances, they could then be deployed to devastating effect in a wider political

---

8. S.R.O., RH 2/4/313, ff. 200–201; S.R.O., Montrose Muniments, GD 220/5/1008/16; S.R.O., Mar & Kellie Papers, GD 124/15/1263/3; R. Mitchison, *loc. cit.*, p. 35.
9. For a 1719 and 1724 estimation of the clans' effective fighting men see, S.R.O., Miscellaneous Broadstairs Papers, GD 1/616/46; S.R.O., Mitchell Papers, RH 2/5/12, pp. 13–14
10. S.R.O., Mitchell Papers, RH 2/5/12, p. 48.
11. S.R.O., Mar & Kellie Papers, GD 124/15/1262/1&3.

crisis.[12] Indeed, manipulation of the region's reputation for disorder and disaffection had become something of a standard political mechanism in Scotland, applicable within even a wholly Lowland context. At the height of the malt tax riots during the spring and summer of 1725, Wade, whilst deploying an additional English regiment to subdue Glasgow, avoided further provocation of Scottish sensibilities by announcing that his action was not an attempt to overawe the population of the city but was in direct response to a rumour, entirely unsubstantiated, that Russian arms had been landed on the Isle of Lewis.[13] Albeit that in January 1744 the Camerons and Lochaber MacDonnells did use the need to settle outstanding cases of mutual cattle loss as a pretext to congregate for Jacobite activity, it was also just as likely that Highlanders themselves would not baulk at playing upon Lowland suspicion of Highland disorder.[14] In September 1739 the imminent outbreak of war between Britain and Spain provided the Ross and Munro interest in Ross-shire with an opportunity to discredit Sir Alexander Mackenzie of Coul. While in fact a representative of an erstwhile Jacobite family, Mackenzie's growing Whig credentials in Argathelian circles threatened to undermine the electoral supremacy of the Ross and Munro alliance. Poinding and counter-poinding of cattle by parties of armed men deployed by Coul and then by Ross of Balnagown ensured that Ross of Pitcalnie, together with Captain George Munro of Culcairn, commander of one of the independent companies, eventually intervened against the Mackenzie laird. The result was an appeal to Edinburgh by the Ross interest that couched what was essentially a local incident in terms more likely to solicit a positive response from the legal establishment in the south. Mackenzie of Coul was accused of sedition and of convening 200–300 men, armed with Spanish weapons and intent on acting against the national interest. That the charge was accepted and Coul arraigned at the Court of Justiciary demonstrates how the issue of law and order in the Highlands could be manipulated for political ends. The episode, however distorted, was typical in that it served to reinforce perceptions at the centre of criminal and political disorder in the region.[15]

12. For the seventeenth century, see A.I. Macinnes, 'Repression and Conciliation: The Highland Dimension 1660–1688', in *Scottish Historical Review*, vol. 55 (1986), pp. 173–5; R Clyde, *From Rebel to Hero: The Image of the Highlander, 1745–1830* (East Linton, 1995), pp. 12–15; S.R.O., Mar & Kellie Papers, GD 124/1263/1, pp. 2–4.
13. S.R.O., RH 2/4/318, f. 262; S.R.O., Mitchell Papers, RH 2/5/12, p. 24.
14. N.L.S., Fletcher of Saltoun Papers, Ms 16596, f. 60; Ms 16597, f. 15; N.L.S., Haldane Papers [uncatalogued]; letter dated Inverie, 13 January 1744 from Aeneas and Coll MacDonnell to Locheil; letter dated Edinburgh, 25 February 1744 from John Macleod-Donald Cameron of Locheil; letter, 1744, Mr Thomas Montford to John Baillie, Writer to the Signet; N.L.S., Yester Papers, Ms 7060, ff. 60 & 79. I am grateful to Professor Allan Macinnes for the Haldane references.
15. S.R.O., Mackenzie of Coul Papers, GD 1/1149/19(1–2). For an assessment of Coul's political stance by the Argylls, see S.R.O., Campbell of Stonefield Papers, GD 14/18.

It was unfortunate for the Highlands' reputation throughout the rest of Scotland that such smear tactics formed a crucial aspect of lobbying for Hanoverian patronage. Most infamously, Simon Fraser of Lovat's memorials to King George I in 1717 and 1724 played upon all the usual negative perceptions of the region.[16] While any attempt at gaining government favour usually involved exposing some legal, financial or political irregularity, applications for company commissions, given the nature of their intended duties, invariably involved relating instances of extreme local violence. In September 1742 Mackenzie of Coul informed John Hay, fourth Marquis of Tweeddale and Secretary of State for Scotland, that parties of armed 'loose men' were terrorising Ross-shire even though independent company detachments were stationed within the county. In the spring of 1739, whilst attempting to counter accusations of their corrupt and ineffectual operations against thieves in Inverness and Ross-shire, both Lovat and Sir Duncan Campbell of Lochnell were seriously undermined by a memorial from Kenneth Mackenzie of Seaforth that requested and justified further local commissions in view of ongoing localised robbery and violence.[17]

Nor should it be assumed that, once in the region, independent companies brought an automatic and constant peace. The biased involvement of Munro of Culcairn in the Balnagown-Coul dispute highlights how the theoretical 'civilising' influence of the companies actually operated in practice to compound local differences and particular clan tensions. Likewise, both Culcairn and Simon Fraser of Lovat used their companies at burgh and county elections to intimidate and restrict voters. Indeed, Lovat's aggressive use of his soldiers at a by-election in Nairn in 1735 was only one particular charge that eventually ensured the loss of his commission in October 1739. During elections of the Provost of Dingwall in October 1740 Culcairn's soldiers, in a blatantly political manoeuvre, arrested several Mackenzie members of the town council. This resulted in a fight with armed Mackenzie clansmen and the subsequent death of two people when Munro's soldiers fired upon an assembled crowd. Just how far the company had deviated from its peacekeeping role can be sensed from the remark of a contemporary in Edinburgh that: 'All here blame the council for bringing the forces to be present at an election . . . this looks something like another Porteous affair'.[18] Aside from involvement in atypical, highly charged electoral contests, the companies often institutionalised or

16. S.R.O., Mitchell Papers, RH 2/5/12, pp. 2–4. For the attempt in 1717 by Lovat to retain his company by heightening fears of a new Jacobite uprising as opposed to crime prevention, see S.R.O., RH 2/4/313, ff. 68 & 196.
17. S.R.O., Robert Craigie of Glendoick Papers, GD 1/609/2/37a–c, 44b; S.R.O., Seafield Muniments, GD 248/97/1/2; GD 248/97/2/47, 51–52, 77 & 79. For the impact of Seaforth's memorial, see W. Fraser (ed.), *The Chiefs of Grant*, vol. 2 (Edinburgh, 1883), pp. 374–76, 381; S.R.O., Seafield Muniments, GD 248/97/4/6.
18. S.R.O., Seafield Muniments, GD 248/97/2/75, 81; W. Ferguson, 'Dingwall Burgh Politics and the Parliamentary Franchise in the Eighteenth Century', in *Scottish Historical Review*, vol. 38 (1959), pp. 91–94; *Scots Magazine*, vol. 2 (Edinburgh, 1740), pp. 484–485; N.L.S., Mackenzie of Delvine Papers, Ms 1140, f. 38.

legitimised more mundane, if highly suspect, local practices. Coll MacDonnell of Barrisdale's influence over company detachments brought additional security and sophistication to his surprisingly large-scale blackmail operations. Relations between James Murray, second duke of Atholl, and Macgregors from Rannoch Moor, meantime, had become badly strained in 1742 on account of the latter's extensive reiving activity. Atholl's chamberlain noted that the Macgregors' confidence arose from the fact that the company charged with arresting local thieves was commanded by Captain James Grant-Colquhoun: neither he nor his soldiers, it transpired, were prepared to move against the Macgregors on account of close kin association.[19]

Yet, in contrast, the active deployment of soldiers in local property disputes also served to exacerbate existing tensions. Sustained cattle raiding into Kintail by Macphee kinsmen of Cameron of Glendessary throughout the 1730s finally provoked Mackenzie tenantry into demanding a detachment of company soldiers to assist their own efforts at recovering stolen stock. An earlier attempt in 1735 by Macleod of Dunvegan's largely disarmed Glenelg tenantry to recover cattle without official backing had resulted in one fatality and several grave injuries. Confident that the presence of six company soldiers gave it official authority, the Kintail expedition ended in July 1742 in an ambush at Locharkaig, and the severe wounding of several Mackenzies by a party of 80 Cameron clansmen: wisely, the Glendessary men avoided injuring the soldiers. Without official military backing it was unlikely that the Kintail tenantry would have considered such a provocative strike against a distant and united kindred. Despite raising local expectations, the army's failure was compounded by the fact that later retaliatory raiding by the Camerons resulted in the death of a servant appointed by Mackenzie of Fairburn to guard cattle against just such an eventuality. The increasingly sour relations between the Camerons and Mackenzies continued to deteriorate and eventually culminated in the destruction of Mackenzie of Lentron's house in the early summer of 1743.[20]

This suggests that, at one level at least, analysis of army patronage and its effect on localities is in need of revision. Traditional emphasis had focused on how the companies served to extend the actual presence of the Hanoverian state within the Highlands, contain if not prevent local disorder, and imbue a greater sense of integration amongst those with wavering political loyalties. While certainly valid in itself, sole emphasis on the 'civilising' effects is only a partial analysis. Ultimately, the process of awarding commissions was a two-way relationship that influenced both recipient and dispenser. Thus, an indirect consequence of Highland elites actively lobbying for Hanoverian patronage was the entrenchment in Edinburgh and London of perceptions

---

19. A.J. Youngson, *After the Forty-Five: the Economic Impact on the Scottish Highlands* (Edinburgh, 1973), pp. 18–20; B.A.M., Box 46/15/41, 47–8.
20. S.R.O., Seafield Muniments, GD 248/171/2/48; S.R.O., Robert Craigie of Glendoick Papers, GD 1/609/2/37b–c; N.L.S., Yester Papers, Ms 7056, f. 122.

that stressed not only the 'barbarity' of the region but also its ongoing distinctive condition and problems. The crucial, longer-term importance of this constant and, indeed, increasing reinforcement of traditional images of the region was that it generated a willingness at the political centre to create and retain specific and distinctive forms of remedial military organisation for the Highlands at a time when the rest of the British army was experiencing heightened centralisation and regulation.[21]

The Development of a British-Highland Military

Despite their decidedly ambiguous impact upon social disorder, the independent companies reconstituted by Wade have emerged with a remarkably favourable reputation. Indeed, their departure to join the regular army in Flanders in 1743 has been viewed as an important factor in the substantial loss of Hanoverian authority within the region that later ensured the largely uncontested outbreak of the '45.[22] However, their limited effect upon the social and criminal dimensions of the 'Highland problem' stands in direct contrast to their emergence as part of the wider British military. This raises the issue of how such distinctively Highland units, catering to unique conditions within the region, were, nevertheless, transformed into an integrated part of the army whilst largely retaining their original, particularist character.

From their very inception in 1725 central government had placed a subtle but unmistakable emphasis on the companies, envisaging a wider, more expressly military role that centred initially upon the disarming and containment of militant Jacobitism. As early as 1715 a scheme by Macpherson of Killihuntly for preserving peace in the region noted that pacification could be achieved through the presence of independent companies or a regiment 'modelled for that purpose'.[23] The inclusion of a regimental mechanism as a solution for social disorder confirmed that the exact status and nature of Highland involvement within the army had already become blurred, imprecise and thus, significantly, open to flexible and changing interpretation. It is also suggestive that Wade, widely considered as unusually attuned to conditions in the Highlands, conspicuously treated the companies formed in 1725 as a regular component of his wider Scottish command. Thus, despite assertions that the companies' removal from the Highlands in the spring of 1743 represented a dramatic break with the understanding they were to be deployed only within the north, their wider use within Scotland had in fact been evident from their establishment. In the summer of 1725 two of the new Highland levies joined a containment garrison left in Edinburgh by Wade

---

21. A. Bruce, *The Purchase System in the British Army* (London, 1980), pp. 22–26.
22. R. Mitchison, *loc. cit.*, pp. 37–8; B.P. Lenman, *op. cit.*, p. 100; P. Simpson, *loc. cit.*, p. 121.
23. B.A.M., Box 42/1/(1)/64.

while he took the bulk of his forces into Glasgow in order to support Duncan Forbes of Culloden, the new Lord Advocate, in his attempts to restore order and apportion blame in the aftermath of the malt tax riots.[24] Moreover, Wade's insistence on regular reviews and company encampments ensured their ability to work as a larger military unit, but detracted from their local policing duties. Likewise, Forbes, Lord President from 1737, cautioned against the use of companies to seize prominent Lochaber and Brae Atholl Jacobites. Such overt military actions by local, policing units, he argued, would leave areas loyal to the government exposed to direct retaliation or, as was more likely, opportunistic raiding.[25]

The companies' deployment against those recruiting for the French and Prussian armies was also symptomatic of this broader military agenda. Prevention of such activity was motivated by the recognition that it not only offered a focus for exiled Jacobites but also that it undermined the growth of a genuine and deep-rooted sense of British identity in the region. Indeed, the depth of Hanoverian anxiety was such that it lead to attempts to sever Scottish commercial and trading links with certain areas of Europe. Thus, in 1740 James Steuart of Dalguise, from Highland Perthshire, found that the Swedish East India Company had begun to dismiss the Scots in its service in direct response to concerns expressed by King George II.[26] The general exception to the attempted curtailment of non-British patronage was the Scots-Dutch Brigade. Its three regiments represented a quasi-Scottish contribution to the defence of the Dutch Republic against France, and were thus an integral part of the Hanoverians' overall strategy for maintaining the balance of power in Europe. The whole phenomenon of foreign service was undoubtedly, though not exclusively, linked to both long- and short-term economic conditions.[27] The winter of 1739–40, for example, was intensely cold; this caused economic hardship and forced many to enter the British, Dutch or wider European militaries. Poor conditions certainly assisted Scots-Dutch recruitment in Perthshire throughout 1740: while in July 1745 Nor-

24. S.R.O., Seafield Muniments, GD 248/97/2/75 & 93; J. Prebble, *Mutiny: Highland Regiments in Revolt, 1743–1804* (Harmondsworth, Middlesex, 1975), pp. 32, 34–5, 37–9, 44 & 48; P.W.J. Riley, *The English Ministers and Scotland, 1707–1727* (London, 1964), p. 284; S.R.O., Mitchell Papers, RH 2/5/12, p. 24; S.R.O., Abercairny Muniments, GD 24/1/464/D/43–44. As early as the 1690s Highland companies had been attached to specific army regiments and actually assimilated with forces sent to Ireland, see P. Simpson, *loc. cit.*, pp. 89–90.
25. W. Fraser (ed.), *op. cit.*, vol. 2, p. 381; S.R.O., Seafield Muniments, GD 248/97/1/57 & 94; GD 248/97/4/8; J. Prebble, *op. cit.*, p. 39; S.R.O., Mitchell Papers, RH 2/5/12, p. 46; N.L.S., Yester Papers, Ms 7066, ff. 147 & 174.
26. S.R.O., Seafield Muniments, GD 248/97/2/25, 52; *Scots Magazine*, vol. 5 (Edinburgh, 1743), p. 49; R. Mitchison, *loc. cit.*, p. 38; S.R.O., Steuart of Dalguise Muniments, GD 38/2/6/30 & 70.
27. S.R.O., Seafield Muniments, GD 248/97/2/25 & 52; N.L.S. Miscellaneous Small Collections, Ms 3648, ff. 35–6.

man Macleod of Macleod noted that there were 'shoals of Skye men in [Dutch] service for lack of bread'.[28]

Figures for the drain of men, especially to French battalions, remain unknown and may never have been on a particularly large scale; nevertheless, this export economy to non-British destinations served to rationalise hostile political attitudes towards the region and harden perceptions regarding the real and imaginary disaffection of the Highlands. Not only did this act as justification for entrenching the companies' military priorities, but subsequent pressure from the King and Cabinet ensured that whilst the region's civil administration was increasingly paralysed as a result of Whig division, the issue of foreign recruiting received uncharacteristically prompt and decisive attention.[29] Albeit that attempts to curtail theft (the limited number of men meant companies were curative rather than preventative) remained an aspect of the companies' remit, such tasks continued to be undermined right up until the '45 by the priority given to the prevention of foreign recruiting.[30]

The inexact nature of the companies' duties could be dismissed as simply a logical response to a multifaceted 'Highland problem'. Yet the importance of this ambiguity within their remit should not be under-underestimated, nor, indeed, analysed from a purely Highland perspective. This mixture of local policing and mainstream military responsibilities was central to the development and character of the region's subsequent contribution towards the army. In direct contrast to American provincial regiments raised in 1740, for instance, where a combination of colonial and British officer personnel was preferred, it was conceded that British-Highland units required an exclusively Gaelic profile to operate locally. The Highlands were thus, from an early stage in the eighteenth century, presented with a potentially less competitive environment than American colonists when it came to accessing army patronage. Moreover, whilst considering new commissions for the Highland regiment in Flanders, Lord Advocate Robert Craigie expressed a wider assumption that this particularly specialised deployment of Gaels ought to apply even if Highland companies transferred their duties into the regular army. He noted: 'In the first case they will fall to be disposed off as other military employments, for promoting the power and influence of the

---

28. J. Ferguson (ed.), *The Scots-Dutch Brigade in the service of the United Netherlands, 1572–1782* (Edinburgh, 1899), introduction; *Scots Magazine*, vol. 2 (Edinburgh, 1740), p. 42; S.R.O., Steuart of Dalguise Muniments, GD 38/2/6/14 & 41; D.H., Loudon Papers, A/1001, f. 21.
29. D. Warrand (ed.), *More Culloden Papers*, vol. 5 (Inverness, 1930), p. 25; N.L.S., Fletcher of Saltoun, Ms 16593, f. 61; Ms 16596, f. 60; *Scots Magazine*, vol. 3 (Edinburgh, 1741), p. 49; vol. 7 (Edinburgh, 1745), pp. 246 & 296; N.L.S., Yester Papers, Ms 7045, f. 94; Ms 7058, ff. 26 & 28; Ms 7063, f. 23; S.R.O., Robert Craigie of Glendoick Papers, GD 1/609/2/14, 24–25 & 27.
30. S.R.O., Robert Craigie of Glendoick Papers GD 1/609/2/14, 27; GD 1/609/3/5; S.R.O., Seafield Muniments, GD 248/171/3/81, 83; N.L.S., Culloden Papers, Ms 2968, f. 203; N.L.S., Yester Papers, Ms 7055, f. 83; Ms 7056, ff. 11 & 19; Ms 7063, f. 130; Ms 7066, ff. 113, 145–47.

administration, only it were to be wished they were Highlanders . . . but if they are employed in the Highlands they must be people of interest in the several countries they are to be stationed'.[31] Although never a uniform practice, the tendency to focus patronage on Highland personnel was pronounced, and it was sometimes denied to even the most prestigious Lowland families as a result. Refusing his own son Henry, Andrew Fletcher, Lord Milton added in May 1745: 'As to the Highland regiment I never asked it . . . because I knew it a fixed rule that none but those who had a Highland family interest would be named, as you see is the case'.[32]

In this respect a comparison with Ireland is also instructive. Numbering 12,000 men, the 'Irish establishment' represented arrangements finalised in 1699 whereby a certain number of regiments were paid for and maintained by the Irish parliament. The Lord Lieutenant of Ireland had semi-autonomous control over appointments to these battalions; and while restricted to junior commissions, both he and his deputy, the Lord Justice, claimed rights of priority for higher posts.[33] Overall, Ireland's distinctiveness seemed to be reflected in this arrangement, and the separateness of the Irish establishment was undoubtedly unique within the structure of the British army. Nevertheless Ireland's particular military contribution was also riven by paradox. The Lord Lieutenant, for instance, was often constrained by involvement in English politics and exposed to non-Irish calls on his favour as a result. More crucially, regiments that formed the basis of his patronage were frequently moved on and off the establishment and out of his jurisdiction, preventing the emergence of units with a comprehensive Irish officer profile. Indeed, battalions consisting exclusively of Irish officers and men were precisely what the Irish establishment attempted to avoid. Deeply hostile towards the recruitment of Catholics, and concerned to maintain the security of the 'Protestant interest', British military elites from 1715 until at least the mid-1750s remained deeply sceptical and suspicious of enlisting large numbers of Irishmen, and certainly had little intention of retaining and institutionalising distinctive Irish regiments within Ireland. In 1724, just as the need for a distinctive Highland contribution to the army was being conceded by, ironically, an Irishman, George Wade, his fellow countrymen were being discharged from the Irish establishment and replaced with recruits brought

---

31. In 1740 the British raised 3,000 Americans for service against the Spanish. While the Colonel, the Captains and half the Lieutenants were American, the cabinet insisted that the Lieutenant-Colonel, the Major and half the Lieutenants were Britons with previous military experience. R.H. Harding, 'The Growth of Anglo-American Alienation: The Case of the American Regiment, 1740–1742', in *Journal of Imperial and Commonwealth History*, vol. 17 (1989), p. 165; N.L.S., Yester Papers, Ms 7063, f. 68.
32. N.L.S., Fletcher of Saltoun Papers, Ms 16513, f. 77.
33. K. P. Ferguson, 'The Army in Ireland from the Restoration to the Act of Union' (Trinity College, Dublin, Ph.D., 1980), pp. 54–55, 64–65; J. W. Hayes, 'The Social and Professional Background of the Officers of the British Army, 1714–1763' (University of London, M.A. Thesis, 1956), pp. 18–22.

over from Britain. Not until the conflict of 1756–63 did recruitment of Irishmen from both religious camps receive reluctant unofficial sanction; moreover, frequent drafting in whole or in part to other British regiments continued to fragment and disperse the undoubtedly disproportionate contribution made by Irish officers and men.[34] The distinctive arrangement in Ireland, therefore, was not intended to generate highly particular and distinguishable centres of Irish involvement within the regular army. If such concentrations did occur, as indeed was to be the case within the army of John Campbell, fourth Earl of Loudon, in America during 1756–57, it was through simple weight of numbers and not as a result of conscious policy.[35] Comparisons between different sectors of the British army, therefore, reveal that attitudes towards the question of distinct regional contributions varied considerably, and that as early as 1725 a distinctive approach had been adopted in the Highlands that differed markedly from the arrangements imposed elsewhere in Ireland and America. The genesis of this radically different policy, with its deliberate concentration of Highland personnel, both in terms of soldiers and officers, lay in the fact that contemporaries believed policing of the region's social disorder was fully compatible with and complementary to the containment of its political and military disaffection. In effect, the new imperial Highland military owed much of its structure and character to the relatively old 'Highland Problem'. Overall, the duality within independent companies was vitally important in that it particularised initial Highland involvement within the army while at the same time holding open the possibility for a slide into more generalised and regular participation within Britain's military machine.

This possibility became a reality on 19 October 1739 when Walpole's declaration of war against Spain ended the longest period of peace Britain was to experience in the eighteenth century. Britain's first international conflict since the companies' re-establishment prepared the ground for a decisive alteration in the overall balance between local and integrated duties which had characterised their role within the British military up to that point. Indeed, it is testimony to the rapid reappraisal of their intended role that a mere six days after the declaration of hostilities the

---

34. K. P. Ferguson, op. cit., pp. 58, 70–73, 99–100; R.B. McDowell, *Ireland in the Age of Imperialism and Revolution* (Oxford, 1991), pp. 59–63; A.J. Guy, 'The Irish Military Establishment, 1660–1776', in T. Bartlett & K. Jeffery (eds.), *A Military History of Ireland* (Cambridge, 1996), pp. 217–219; J. Brewer, *The Sinews of Power: War, Money and the English state, 1688–1783* (London, 1989). p. 32. For Scots lobbying the Lord Lieutenant of Ireland, see N.L.S., Fletcher of Saltoun Papers, Ms 16511, ff. 94, 98, 142; J.R.L., Bagshawe Muniments, B. 5/1, pp. 51, 80 & 100; S.R.O., Campbell of Barcaldine Papers, GD 170/1179/3.

35. If a regiment was stationed in Ireland for a sufficient period, the Lord Lieutenant's control over appointments could result in relatively large concentrations of Irish officers. See P.J. Marshall, 'A Nation defined by Empire, 1755–1776', in A. Grant & K. J. Stringer (eds.), *Uniting the Kingdom? The Making of British History* (London, 1995), p. 210.

companies were re-constituted as the 43rd Highland Regiment.[36] This alteration in official status confirms how the idea of fully integrating the region's military potential was already largely accepted within the thinking of political elites in Edinburgh and London. Indeed, the idea of forming line regiments from Highland manpower had a long, if undistinguished, history. As early as the summer of 1685, and again in 1690, John Campbell, first Earl of Breadalbane, mooted the idea of retaining 4,000 clansmen to act as both a garrison within the Highlands and as a relatively cheap army of reserve for use within Scotland as a whole. In February 1692, Breadalbane resurrected the scheme and intelligently tailored his proposals to suit William's European preoccupations by including a suggestion that a regiment drawn from these 4,000 men be deployed in foreign service. Though never implemented in the fashion proposed by Breadalbane, regiments formed from Whig clans did eventually serve on the continent during the war of 1688–97.[37] Proposals that regular regiments be constructed from companies initially instituted for policing reasons were also apparent in a memorial sponsored by the Atholl family in 1703: an idea resurrected in 1717 when Breadalbane's scheme was again highlighted as an attractive option for the Crown:

> His Majesty may therefore ballance ye exterminating of ye Highlanders at long runn by trouble, expence and noise on ye one hand, wt ye advantage of a present totall settlement on ye other and if some of ye clanns should serve His Maj'tie in Flanders, it would show how farr Britain is reduced to a totall obedience.[38]

Such thinking reveals how a sophisticated, if cynical, rationale justifying the recruitment of Highlanders had germinated during the immediate pre- and post-Union period. Wade himself confirmed the realisation that Highlanders could readily form a regular contribution to the army when, in February 1727, in response to a Spanish invasion scare he suggested that companies be expanded so that 'these, including officers might on occasion be formed into a battalion of 525 men'.[39] In 1737 a scheme was circulated proposing that two battalions, commanded by Fraser gentry, be raised in the region. A year later, whilst rumours abounded concerning the regimentation of the six existing

36. N.L.S., Mackenzie of Delvine Papers, Ms 1136, f. 103; P. Simpson, *op. cit.*, pp. 202–203.
37. P. Hopkins, *Glencoe and the End of the Highland War* (Edinburgh, 1986), pp. 103–4, 270, 330. For the original proposal in early 1692, see J. Dalrymple, *Memoirs of Great Britain & Ireland from the dissolution of the last parliament of Charles II until the sea battle of La Hogue*, vol. 2 (London, 1773), pp. 217–20; J. Prebble, *op. cit.* p. 21.
38. B.A.M., Box 42/I/(1)/47: Proposals for a regiment, c. 1703; S.R.O., RH 2/4/313, ff. 192, 194–95, Proposals Regarding the Highlanders, 1717. For a similar proposal in 1715, see A.I. Macinnes, *Clanship, Commerce and the House of Stuart*, p. 236, n. 14.
39. S.R.O., Mitchell Papers, RH 2/5/12, p. 44.

companies, Forbes himself suggested the creation of four or five new Highland battalions.[40] Indeed, given the number of occasions on which Highland regiments were either proposed or widely rumoured, the surprising aspect of the companies' eventual regimentation was not that it happened over six years before Culloden, but that it had not in fact occurred much earlier.

From 1739 until the end of 1741, the war with Spain was largely maritime and colonial. As a result, expansion and active deployment of the military was largely restricted to naval and marine forces.[41] By 1743, however, the nature of the war had changed and with it the likelihood that the Highland Regiment would remain in the region. George II's favourite in the administration formed in February 1742, John Granville, first Earl of Carteret, espoused a more radical involvement in Europe and a direct linking of Britain's interest with the recognised balance of power between France and Austria. Often portrayed as a 'grey water' policy, the continental focus of Carteret's strategy meant that by 1743 a British army of 16,000 had been sent to Flanders to demonstrate the new administration's commitment. This more radical anti-French policy inevitably meant a broadening of the war, and it was in order to reinforce this relatively small British army that the Highland Regiment was ordered onto the continent in the spring of 1743.[42]

It is not altogether surprising that analysis of the Austrian War of Succession has focused on its role as a catalyst for the events of the '45. Yet this apparently distant conflict was also a landmark in defining the nature of the region's connection with the army. From London's perspective, heavy commitments against the French entirely justified the overseas deployment of Highland manpower. Indeed, despite certain reservations, even Carteret's Squadrone allies asserted that if France were heavily defeated on the continent its willingness to support a Jacobite campaign in Scotland would be seriously weakened.[43] That foreign support for an uprising was in

40. S.R.O., Society of Antiquaries Collection, GD 103/2/371: 'List of Fraser Gentlemen as may be regimented for His Majesty's service', c. 1737; P. Simpson, *op. cit.*, p. 123; S.R.O., Seafield Muniments, GD 248/97/4/52. On 10 February 1740 Aeneas McDonnell of Scothouse noted to Lovat: 'I minde some years agoe, there was a rumour that all the independent companies were to be regimented'.
41. J. Brewer, *op. cit.*, p. 30; *The Caledonian Mercury*, 5 February 1740; *The Scots Magazine*, vol. 2 (Edinburgh, 1740), pp. 352–3; S.R.O., Clerk of Pencuik, GD 18/3229/1.
42. J. Black, 'Foreign Policy and the British State, 1742–1793', in J. Black (ed.), *British Politics and Society from Walpole to Pitt, 1742–1789* (London, 1990), pp. 147–148; R. Browning, *The Duke of Newcastle* (London, 1975), pp. 101–115; J. Black, *Pitt the Elder* (Cambridge, 1992), pp. 40 & 44; S.R.O., Seafield Muniments, GD 248/172/1/18.
43. J. Prebble, *op. cit.*, pp. 42–3, 57; G. Menary, *The Life and Letters of Duncan Forbes of Culloden* (London, 1936), pp. 188–92; D. Warrand (ed.), *op. cit.*, vol. 3, pp. 150–152, 184–85; N.L.S., Culloden Papers, Ms 2968, f. 217; W.A. Speck, *op. cit.*, pp. 16–17; N.L.S., Yester Papers, Ms 7056, ff. 11, 122; Ms 7057, f. 101; Ms 7058, f. 18; S.R.O., Robert Craigie of Glendoick Papers, GD 1/609/2/34; GD 1/609/3/2.

fact far more likely under precisely these conditions of French military defeat or stalemate not only revealed the naiveté and incompetence of the Squadrone administration, but also ignored the question of what alternative arrangements if any were to be constructed for the peace and security of the north of Scotland.

The search for an alternative to Wade's garrison policy in the years prior to the '45 was hindered by deep division between the Argathelian and the Squadrone interests.[44] Given Campbell dominance within the Highlands, Tweeddale, despite the technical primacy of his office, found that his relatively weak control over Scotland as a whole was magnified when it came to constructing policies for the region. Despite later attempts by Duncan Forbes to act as an intermediary, Ilay and Tweeddale's mutual distrust prevented any progress on new disarming legislation, or on Forbes's own proposals to control the area. Indeed, Forbes, primarily as a result of his close alliance with the second Duke of Argyll, was seen by the Squadrone as part of the wider Argathelian network. Thus in May 1744, despite the serious Jacobite scare of the early spring, Craigie suggested that the Lord President was deliberating exaggerating unrest in the region simply to inflate his own importance and gain new company commissions for allies and close family 'creatures'.[45]

Initially, the case for new independent companies seemed waterproof. Such units had formed a primary mechanism in Wade's apparently successful strategy for the disarming and containment of the region. Likewise, Forbes, the man most closely associated with the now officially favoured policy of creating Highland line regiments, stressed that the deployment of Gaels in overseas service was only wise if implemented in tandem with a strong, ongoing company presence within the region.[46] Although Tweeddale, Craigie and Solicitor-General Robert Dundas of Arniston agreed, they remained extremely reluctant to hand additional patronage over to the Argyll interest – an attitude reinforced in September 1744 when, upon hearing of a proposal to raise two companies of 70 men, the third Duke assumed the privilege of naming half the officers.[47] Unsurprisingly, Tweeddale was not prepared to lobby for such a company. Nevertheless, the French invasion scare of early spring 1744 disabused, if only partially, both the administration in London and Scotland of the notion that successful British campaigning on the continent would prevent domestic rebellion. Notwithstanding continuous efforts throughout 1744, it was not until February 1745, with the re-emergence of Argyll through

44. R. Mitchison, *loc. cit.*, pp. 29–45.
45. G. Menary, *op. cit.*, pp. 73, 91–92, 260, n. 1; S.R.O., Robert Craigie of Glendoick Papers, GD 1/609/2/25 & 29; N.L.S., Fletcher of Saltoun Papers, Ms 16591, ff. 61, 94; N.L.S., Yester Papers, 7062, ff. 39, 97, 142–3.
46. N.L.S., Yester Papers, Ms 7057, ff. 101, 113; Ms 7058, f. 18.
47. N.L.S., Yester Papers, Ms 7055, f. 85; Ms 7056, f. 122; Ms 7063, f. 147; Ms 7064, f. 17.

his alliance with the Pelhams, that three new Highland companies were established.[48]

Yet the effectiveness of new companies within the region was undermined by the continual debate surrounding their character and deployment. Attempts, for instance, to secure clear safeguards for their domestic policing role within the Highlands were undermined by interpretations which stressed that any new units could also, if necessary, operate outside the region as a fully integrated part of the army in Flanders. These conflicting objectives simply mirrored, only now more explicitly, the central and local concerns that had been evident since 1717 with respect to the role of Highland units. As before, initial pressure for new companies came almost exclusively from chiefs and gentry like Sir Robert Gordon of Gordonstoun, John Campbell, Lord Glenorchy and Archibald Campbell of Stonefield, all of whom were primarily motivated by concern for property protection or domestic political security. Highlighting this local agenda, Glenorchy noted in July 1744 'the expense and trouble we are at to protect ourselves and the state of war in which we have been since the Highland Reg't left us'. Following some early optimism, however, it transpired that any new commissions were in fact to arise from two more companies added to the Highland Regiment operating in Flanders. It proved extremely difficult therefore for even Tweeddale to clarify whether any new Highland companies would be used exclusively within the region or simply drafted onto the continent.[49]

This prevented a truly sustained containment of the region's social and political uncertainties. As early as May 1743, as the Black Watch marched out of the region, Dundas noted to Tweeddale that companies 'will always be useless if wanted by the government [abroad]'. Likewise, in July 1744, Craigie noted the relatively enthusiastic response within the Highlands at the prospect of new commissions, but added: 'it will make the matter more difficult if it's understood they are designed for foreign service'.[50] The possibility of overseas deployment seriously undermined the potentially positive impact of the three companies secured in early 1745. Welcomed by the likes of Glenorchy and Atholl as long overdue recognition of government neglect, these new units were seen by others, like Robert Craigie and Thomas Hay, brother to Tweeddale, primarily as recruiting nurseries for the Highland Regiment in Flanders – a prospect that naturally drew a hostile response from chiefs suffering from repeated cattle losses.[51]

48. N.L.S., Yester Papers, Ms 7060, ff. 50, 55; Ms 7061, f. 22; Ms 7064, f. 89; D. Warrand (ed.), *op. cit.*, vol. 3, pp. 229–30; N.L.S., Culloden Papers, Ms 2968, ff. 254 & 273; N.L.S., Fletcher of Saltoun Papers, Ms 16596, f. 60; *Scots Magazine*, vol. 7 (Edinburgh, 1745), p. 98. W.A. Speck, *op. cit.* p. 29.
49. S.R.O., Macpherson of Cluny Papers, GD 80/631/20; B.L., Hardwicke Papers, Add Ms 35450, f. 20; N.L.S., Fletcher of Saltoun Papers, Ms 16597, f. 17.
50. S.R.O., Mackay of Bighouse, GD 87/1/5; B.A.M., Box 46/17/35; N.L.S., Yester Papers, Ms 7056, f. 122; Ms 7063, ff. 40 & 42.
51. N.L.S., Yester Papers, Ms 7063, f. 130; Ms 7064, f. 54; Ms 7065, f. 86; N.L.S., Mackenzie of Delvine Papers, Ms 1327, f. 9.

Created, initially, as an acknowledgement of the Highlands' distinct political and social circumstances, the region's policing establishment was thus evolving into a decidedly mainstream part of the army; the result, moreover, was an increasing neglect of the local conditions which had given rise to the companies in the first place. Yet failure to secure replacement companies with a wholly internal remit was not simply the result of Whig political division; it was also symptomatic of a fundamental wartime reappraisal by the state which witnessed a shift from containment of the region's distinctive problems to an increasingly proactive securing of a surplus of military manpower. The establishment, in May 1745, of a second Highland Regiment (the 54th regiment), to be commanded by the Earl of Loudon, confirmed such a reappraisal and the consolidation of a British-Highland military very much focused on regular, overseas service. Despite the fact that the regiment's historic reputation rests on its ineffectual attempts at countering Jacobitism in the northern Highlands during the '45, it was in fact commissioned in direct response to Britain's heavy defeat at Fontenoy, and was in no way an internal security measure for the Highlands. From its very inception it was a line regiment and not, as Forbes continued to hope, a social and political police force. Ironically, however, its intended overseas destination slowed its recruitment rate which ensured that, beyond the 210 men of the three additional companies, another Hanoverian levy was actually in the region when the Jacobite uprising erupted in late July 1745.[52]

Jacobitism and Military Patronage

The emergence of a second Highland regiment demonstrates how large-scale military recruitment in the region was in fact a pre-1745 development. Indeed, compared to the limited and relatively static number of political, legal and administrative posts available in Scotland, the growth in military patronage was striking – and seen as such by contemporaries. By 1745 the Scots-Dutch had expanded to over 5,000 men: Tweeddale assiduously manipulated the additional posts brought about by this expansion in order to counter the control exercised by his Argathelian opponents over British military commissions.[53] Despite the maintenance of Dutch outlets for Highlanders, however, the early 1740s were especially characterised by a more general involvement of Scots within the British military. Evidence that imperial opportunities were being consciously offered to Scots can be seen in the 1740 expedition to the West Indies led by Charles Cathcart, eighth Lord Cathcart. Ilay's secretary noted that 'there are three regiments to be raised in ye plantations & Lord Cathcart has got the nominating ye Lieutenants, which he had already done,

52. N.L.S., Fletcher of Saltoun Papers, Ms 16597, ff. 17, 20; Ms 16604, f. 187; Ms 16605, ff. 33, 48, 50, 54, 169; Ms 16610, f. 57.
53. B.L., Hardwicke Papers, Add Ms 35509, f. 309; N.L.S., Fletcher of Saltoun Papers, Ms 16596, f. 105; N.L.S., Yester Papers, Ms 7045, f. 119; Ms 7064, f. 89; N.L.S., Culloden Papers, Ms 2968, f. 254.

and I am told they are all Scotsmen who served as cadies [cadets] in other regiments'.[54] India was also increasingly prominent as a source of patronage. Through his influence with its shipping committees, the financier John Drummond of Quarrell ensured from as early as 1724 that East India Company posts were consciously deployed to bring disaffected families, especially in Perthshire, the North-East and Ross-shire, into a more stable relationship with the Whig establishment.[55] It cannot, therefore, be assumed that Gaels were seriously excluded from involvement in British imperial service simply because a large number of Highland regiments did not exist.[56] Indeed, clan gentry proved to be both flexible and astute at maximising opportunities within the army. The Frasers of Farraline and Ardochy surmounted the problem of limited availability of commissions in specifically Highland units by installing their sons as volunteers in Lowland or English regiments commanded by Scottish colonels such as John Campbell of Mamore. Likewise, the placement of younger members of families such as the Grants within Highland companies was often seen as a temporary prelude to subsequent promotion into line regiments. In this sense, the wider importance of the companies lay as much in their function as a regional funnel into the wider British military as in their role of policing the Highlands.[57]

Over-emphasis on the limited number of Highland units has been compounded by a failure to distinguish between the dispensation of domestic patronage to reliable Whigs and the separate use of overseas commissions. This has masked the extent to which imperial patronage was increasingly seen as a method of undermining disaffection. Indeed, security concerns over arming Jacobite personnel within Scotland actually helped ensure that overseas as opposed to internal patronage became the government's preferred avenue when distributing offices to Highlanders. Regimentation of the companies in the autumn of 1739, for example, was promoted by senior Scottish politicians in order to prevent the companies being disbanded on charges that certain captains had trained their clansmen for future Jacobite mobilisation. Once a regular component of the army and deployed overseas, it was argued, a switch of allegiance would be impossible.[58] Such specific

---

54. S.R.O., Clerk of Pencuik, GD 18/3229/1; N.L.S., Culloden Papers, Ms 2968, f. 137. For evidence of Highlanders operating in a military capacity in British Georgia, see R.H. Duff (ed.), *Culloden Papers* (London, 1815), p. 155 and A.W. Parker, *Scottish Highlanders in Colonial Georgia: the Recruitment, Emigration and Settlement at Darien, 1735–1748* (Athens, Georgia, 1997), pp. 20, 38–51.
55. G.K. McGilvray, 'East India Patronage and the Political Management of Scotland, 1720–1774' (Open University Ph.D., 1989), pp. 121, 147–9; D.C.M., 4/110–111.
56. A.I. Macinnes, *Clanship, Commerce and the House of Stuart*, p. 194.
57. N.L.S., Miscellaneous Small Collections, Ms 3648, ff. 35–6; W. Fraser (ed.), *op. cit.*, vol. 2, p. 379; S.R.O., Seafield Muniments, GD 248/97/4/3.
58. N.L.S., Mackenzie of Delvine Papers, Ms 1136, f. 98; N.L.S., Fletcher of Saltoun Papers, Ms 16710, f. 84; W.C. Mackenzie, *Simon Fraser, Lord Lovat: His Life and Times* (London, 1908), pp. 309–10, n. 3.

anxieties also meant that when particular clan gentry were refused commissions in Highland companies, automatic exclusion from regular regiments did not necessarily follow.[59] James Fraser of Foyers is just such an example. His failure to obtain an independent company commission in 1736 sprang from Ilay's unease over the political leanings of clan Fraser; yet even Lovat conceded that the exclusion of his gentry from domestic patronage in no way prevented their future access to line regiments. Ilay confirmed the existence of this distinctive patronage policy when he secured a commission for Foyers in Jamaica. Much to Lovat's dismay, Foyers refused the appointment, describing West Indian conditions as a poor substitute for the opportunity to steadily accrue wealth through local service in the Highlands. That Fraser was offered but in fact refused imperial service and later became a prominent Jacobite underlines the complexities of Highland disaffection, and serves to caution us against assuming that the growth of the empire meant the inevitable extinction of Highland particularism. Nevertheless, it is significant that Lovat clearly believed the best opportunity for politically disadvantaged clans lay in commissions within regular regiments. Indeed when he requested an ensigncy in September 1739 for the financially stricken Mackinnon family, he specifically highlighted line regiments as opposed to Highland companies as a natural avenue for many elite families.[60]

The idea that military service represented an answer to Jacobitism also ensured the continual resurrection of proposals for new Highland regiments. High expectations were certainly evident by the early 1740s. In March 1741 Lord George Murray, the Jacobite commander in 1745–6, informed his pro-Hanoverian brother that the arrival of full-scale war made further regiments inevitable, and that the Atholl family could expect to be the natural beneficiaries. Indeed, by March 1744 his half-brother Lord John Murray was confident he had obtained a new battalion; while on the Island of Skye the two main chiefs noted 'a talk of raising more Highland reg'ts'. Such rumours persisted, and as late as June 1745 Argyll informed Norman Macleod of Macleod that if Loudon's regiment was completed quickly, further opportunities for additional patronage would be secured.[61]

Forbes had previously linked the distribution of overseas commissions with the erosion of Jacobitism, and argued in 1743 that conditions had never been more opportune. Contrary to later historical interpretation, which has stressed the region's political continuities, he contended that the Highlands had in fact changed radically since 1715 and that despite areas of solid support, Jacobitism was a severely weakened force. Both he and Archibald

59. T.M. Devine, *Clanship to Crofters' War: The Social Transformation of the Scottish Highlands* (Manchester, 1994), p. 27.
60. N.L.S., Fletcher of Saltoun Papers, Ms 16597, f. 30; S.R.O., Seafield Muniments, GD 248/97/1/7; GD 248/97/2/19,83,92–3, 97–8.
61. A.I. Macinnes, *Clanship, Commerce and the House of Stuart*, p. 194; L. Leneman, *Living in Atholl – a Social History of the Estate, 1685–1785* (Edinburgh, 1986), p. 144; B.A.M., Box 46/17/23 & 35; D.C.M., 4/120, 159.

Campbell of Stonefield highlighted the growing divisions amongst previously Jacobite families; these included the Mackenzies, the Macleods, the Macdonalds of Sleat, the ducal house of Gordon, the Macphersons, the Mackintoshes and the Macleans.[62] Although there were divisions within clans of both political persuasions, Jacobitism does emerge as the main casualty with roughly a 30% fall in support between the '15 and the '45.[63]

It is within this context of less stable, more fluid clan support for both the Whig and Jacobite positions that the operation and expectation of military patronage as a whole, and British-Highland commissions in particular, need to be placed. Moreover, military posts represented only one measure deployed by the Argathelians against disaffection. Although obviously less flexible, another strategy was to renew the terms of feudal superiority on the estates of various forfeited families. However, the arbitrary alienation of wadsetting capability on Stewart of Appin's property and the retention of all mineral rights on Locheil's estate undermined any realistic hope that this policy would 'make them gratefull and servicable to yr Grace and the government'.[64] By contrast, the opportunities offered by army patronage appeared to inspire an unusual level of both optimism and realism in government circles. While Jacobite chiefs later claimed the creation of the 54th Regiment meant that the Hanoverians had 'formed a scheme of hooking all the Highland chieftains into their military service', there was not in fact any real attempt to direct commissions towards solidly disaffected clans like the Camerons or the Lochaber MacDonnells. The limitations of army patronage were in fact well understood; indeed, where commissions had failed to curtail Jacobitism, as with Lovat, they were summarily rescinded by London.[65] Instead, posts were quite deliberately offered to families who already appeared either neutral or susceptible to co-operation. Prominent recipients of this selective policy included Aeneas Mackintosh, Norman Macleod of Macleod, Sir Alexander Macdonald, Lord Charles Gordon, Ewan Macpherson of Cluny, Malcom Ross, Younger of Pitcalnie, and Duncan Robertson of Drumachuine.[66]

Though by no means a comprehensive success, the use of military com-

62. S.R.O., Campbell of Stonefield Papers, GD 14/18; N.L.S., Fletcher of Saltoun Papers, Ms 16596, f. 60; Ms 16604, f. 187; Ms 16605, ff. 27 & 41.
63. A.I. Macinnes, *Clanship, Commerce and the House of Stuart*, pp. 180–81, 190–191.
64. N.L.S., Mackenzie of Delvine Papers, Ms 1136, f. 103; D.C.M., 4/124; N.L.S., Fletcher of Saltoun Papers, Ms 16596, f. 60; Ms 16604, f. 165.
65. N.L.S., Mackenzie of Delvine Papers, Ms 1136, f. 103; S.R.O., Seafield Muniments, GD 248/97/4/35. For similar removal of commissions from suspected personnel in 1727, see S.R.O., Mitchell Papers, RH 2/15/12, p. 46.
66. J. Browne, *History of the Highlands and of the Highland Clans*, vols. 3 & 4 (Glasgow, 1838), pp. 112, 239–240; S.R.O., Seafield Muniments, GD 248/97/4/35; G. Menary, *op. cit.*, p. 238. For an initially positive reaction amongst Robertson gentry to involvement in the army until denied commissions by Argyll, see N.L.S., Mackenzie of Delvine Papers, Ms 1327, ff. 12, 24.

missions to engender loyalty should not be dismissed by an over-emphasis on Pitcalnie, Lovat and Cluny's dramatic switch back to Jacobitism during the '45. The Jacobite recruiting of Malcom Ross, nephew to Forbes, despite his ensigncy in Loudon's battalion, represented a serious reverse but also served to entrench the Hanoverian sympathies of his father. Lovat, meanwhile, had been broken six years earlier, and the transfer of his company into regular service ensured the loss of over 70 men from his own reserves of around 700. Cluny was without doubt the most spectacular failure, especially given his earlier co-operation over the issue of law and order and his acceptance of a captaincy in the second Highland battalion. Yet his switch to Jacobitism was noticeably tardy; and, earlier, in August 1745, he had actually moved to support General John Cope in his march north to Inverness. Indeed, had Loudon's Regiment been completed and deployed on the continent as intended, there is every reason to believe Cluny would have remained loyal to the Hanoverians. This would certainly have been the case with Aeneas Mackintosh who was unable to prevent his company's desertion to his wife's clan regiment, but whose refusal to condone his kindred's support for Charles Stuart weakened the overall mobilisation of Clan-Chattan.[67]

Failure to inculcate loyalty often sprang from the incoherent nature of government policy, inter-clan tension, simple geography, and luck. Thus, while Forbes of Culloden endeavoured to influence the Macphersons, similar attempts to repeat the process with the Mackintosh and Gordon families simply drove Cluny, who deeply resented their respective claims to feudal superiority in Badenoch, into a closer relationship with the Frasers and Camerons. Furthermore, sandwiched between his Jacobite kin, the Farquharsons, and the Lochaber MacDonnells, any effort on the part of Cluny to remaining loyal would have been rendered impracticable by the realities of his extremely exposed situation. Likewise, co-ordination of the deployment of commissions with other aspects of government policy was often nonexistent. The use of Forbes' influence in the Court of Session to obtain recognition for Duncan Robertson of Drumachuine to the Strowan estate in early 1745, for instance, actually undermined the positive impact that could have arisen from Argyll's offer of a lieutenancy in Loudon's, which Robertson had earlier seemed determined to accept in order to secure the property.[68]

67. N.L.S., Miscellaneous Small Collections, Ms 3648, ff. 37–40; S.R.O., Seafield Muniments, GD 248/97/4/35; W, Fraser (ed.), *op. cit.*, vol. 2, p. 402; N.L.S., Fletcher of Saltoun Papers, Ms 16609, f. 278. The Mackintosh family had already developed strong links with the British military; see D. Warrand (ed.) *op. cit.*, vol. 3, p. 129; I.H.M. Scobie, 'The Independent Companies of 1745–7', in *Journal of the Society of Army Historical Research*, vol. 20 (1941), p. 11. For the reactions of Ewan Macpherson of Cluny and Aeneas Mackintosh to the outbreak of the '45, see B.P. Lenman, *op. cit.*, p. 126.
68. S.R.O., Campbell of Stonefield Papers, GD 14/18; D.C.M., 4/124; N.L.S., Fletcher of Saltoun Papers, Ms 16596, f. 60; Ms 16609, f. 278; N.L.S., Mackenzie of Delvine Papers, Ms 1136, f. 149; B.A.M., Box 46/(1)/26; J. Browne, *op. cit.*, pp. 239–240.

Army patronage could also be as much an irritant as a balm in the Highlands. Disproportionately bestowed upon Campbells, it inevitably alienated those whose requests for rank were denied as a result. Failure to obtain commissions in Lord Loudon's battalion estranged George Mackenzie, third Earl of Cromartie, as well as the sons of Maclean of Torloisk. Meanwhile, Robertson of Drumachuine, safely assured of his succession in Strowan, was actually insulted by the offer of a lieutenancy after being promised a higher rank.[69] The political wrangling amongst Whigs that prevented coherent government within Scotland as a whole also impaired the ability of Argyll and others to consistently distribute commissions with a long-term anti-Jacobite agenda in mind. The most disastrous example of this was in May 1743 when the Squadrone John Dalrymple, second Earl of Stair, Commander-in-Chief of the British army in Flanders, ordered the 43rd Highland Regiment onto the continent. Though obviously part of the wider European war, a subtext to his actions was that, once in Flanders, commissions in the regiment fell under his remit as opposed to being controlled largely by Ilay in Scotland. As third Duke of Argyll, Ilay likewise exhibited these overtly political concerns. Although appointments in Loudon's Regiment showed Argyll's willingness to accommodate suspected Jacobites, it also included eleven Campbells out of a total of thirty-eight officers. Not surprisingly, Robert Craigie noted that 'the officers in the new Highland regiment, all said to be nominees of His Grace the Duke of Argyll rivetts [sic] a dependence that will not be easily pulled up in this country'.[70]

There were however some successes. The inclusion of Lord Charles Gordon in the new Highland Regiment not only secured support from elements of the House of Gordon, but also ensured that the Jacobite recruiting of his brother, Lord Lewis, was hampered to some extent.[71] The most decisive success was in Skye where the normally ambiguous position of the Macleods of Dunvegan, and the profoundly anti-Argathelian attitude of the Macdonalds of Sleat, were turned into substantial mobilisation for Hanover. Forbes and Argyll were fully aware that Norman Macleod was more susceptible to overtures of co-operation than Sir Alexander Macdonald. Macleod accordingly received assurances of patronage and by January 1745 was pressing Macdonald to accept any future offer of commissions from Argyll. In May 1745 Norman's son, John, received a captaincy in Loudon's battalion, whilst Macdonald simultaneously agreed to use the Laird as a means of requesting patronage from the Campbell interest.

69. S.R.O., Seafield Muniments, GD 248/47/5/31; N.L.S., Yester Papers, Ms 7066, f. 67; N.L.S., Fletcher of Saltoun Papers, Ms 16609, f. 257; J. Browne, *op. cit.*, pp. 239–240.
70. D.C.M. 4/123; N.L.S., Culloden Papers, Ms 2968, f. 217; N.L.S., Fletcher of Saltoun Papers, Ms 16604, ff. 181, 190; Ms 16605, ff. 16, 27.
71. N.L.S., Fletcher of Saltoun Papers, Ms 16604, f. 187; Ms 16513, f. 34; A.J. Youngson, *The Prince and the Pretender: Two Views of the '45* (Edinburgh, 1996), p. 123.

Thus, when the '45 commenced in late July both clans were conspicuously committed to Loudon's Regiment, making their customary caution and prevarication less of an option and dangerously obvious. As a result, around 1,600 men were either denied to or indeed deployed against Charles Stuart – a total that represented as much as 20% of the clan manpower raised by the Jacobites. Beyond this substantial loss of military muscle, the real importance of the Hanoverian coup in Skye lay in the subsequent restrictions imposed upon the Jacobites' ability to recruit freely in Inverness-shire.[72]

Clanship's Indian Summer

The consolidation of strategies that largely equated the military contribution of the Highlands with regular, overseas service left the question of internal protection for the region unanswered. Regardless of political faction, it had become increasingly clear during 1742–3 that the collapse of Wade's garrison strategy meant a fundamental rethink of methods to control the region was not only desirable, but necessary. Possible solutions were: new independent companies, renewed disarming legislation and, perhaps most surprising of all, a return to local, clan-based methods.[73] The growing prospect of regular army service made any new additional companies a partial and unreliable solution at best. Removal of clan weaponry had been an explicit priority of the remedial programme instituted by Wade, and formed a central objective of 'civilising' Hanoverian theory. The ultimate importance of disarming is underlined by the fact that the final, clinching accusation against Lovat that resulted in the withdrawal of his company was his apparent unwillingness to implement disarming legislation in Glenmoriston.[74] Yet, ironically, without a large garrison and an effective intelligence capability in the shape of Highland companies, not only was further disarming impossible but, indeed, tacit acceptance of rearming amongst previously de-militarised clans became, of necessity, an increasingly noticeable feature of government policy. Robert Dundas of Arniston, although extremely critical of any notion that clanship should continue as an *ad hoc* form of judicial management, revealed this reappraisal in October 1743 when he noted: 'I was certainly informed when in the Highlands that there were 500 stands of arms brought from Liverpool to the Isle of Skye this last Spring, I do not believe with any intention against the government, but really to defend themselves'. A year later Macleod sought additional protection, and officially

---

72. S.R.O., Seafield Muniments, GD 248/172/1/61; D.C.M., 4/120, 123, 127; S.R.O., Campbell of Stonefield Papers, GD 14/18; N.L.S., Mackenzie of Delvine Papers, Ms 1136, f. 150. For estimates of Macleod and Macdonald manpower as well as their strategic importance, see S.R.O., Miscellaneous Broadstairs Papers, GD 1/616/46; *Scots Magazine*, vol. 7 (Edinburgh, 1745), pp. 540 & 588.
73. N.L.S., Yester Papers, Ms 7054, f. 38; Ms 7055, ff. 65, 83–5; S.R.O., Robert Craigie of Glendoick Papers, GD 1/609/2/33; GD 1/609/3/2.
74. W. Fraser (ed.), *op. cit.*, vol. 2, p. 381.

requested arms from the government. The application was refused; yet it is indicative of how far chiefs understood the change in government attitudes that Macleod felt he could even ask.[75]

Acceptance of the necessity for some clan-based arrangements was further evident when both Dundas and Lieutenant-General Joshua Guest agreed that a large conference held in February 1744 between Lochaber MacDonnells and Sir James Grant's tenantry had concentrated on an attempt to settle disputes over cattle, and had in no way posed a general threat to the public.[76] Undoubtedly, this tolerance of local methods of defence and legal process sprang from the Crown's realisation that its position in the region was at its weakest since the '15 uprising. Nevertheless, the turnaround in deeply hostile attitudes towards militarised clanship is striking. While in February 1739 a new, comprehensive disarming bill had been widely anticipated, subsequent alterations in international circumstances and the departure of the Highland Regiment not only halted such legislation but, indeed, witnessed active government opposition to further attempts at Highland de-militarisation. Thus Tweeddale noted in August 1742:

> It is confidently asserted here that they [disaffected clans] are now better armed than ever and I know there was a new Bill prepared and intended to have been brought in last session of Parliament for disarming the Highlands, which I, with some difficulty prevented. I must acknowledge I have not observed any good effects from the previous two bills for disarming that country.[77]

Official policy had thus changed radically from the era of Wade when the paramount importance of disarming had been rigorously asserted. Active prevention of disarming is not normally associated with Hanoverian governments, and such a change of priorities emphasises how the relationship between pre-Culloden administrations and the Highlands should not be seen purely in terms of the Scottish legal elite's hostility towards clanship.[78] Clearly, the process of British military and imperial expansion helped deflect immediate attention from legislation which sought to deal with clanship and, instead, induced a slowing down in the process of eliminating the region's particularist features. Assisting this largely pragmatic position was the knowledge that independent companies had never been sufficiently powerful or plentiful to allow a total abandonment of kin-based methods of local

75. N.L.S., Yester Papers, Ms 7058, f. 147. For local attempts by Macleods and Macdonalds to protect their droving economy, see B.P. Lenman, *op. cit.*, Ch. 7; D. Warrand (ed.) *op. cit.*, vol. 4, p. 10.
76. N.L.S., Mackenzie of Delvine Papers, Ms 1143, f. 159; N.L.S., Yester Papers, Ms 7060, ff. 79 & 113.
77. W. Fraser (ed.), *op. cit.*, vol. 2, p. 376; S.R.O., Robert Craigie of Glendoick Papers, GD 1/609/2/27.
78. C. Kidd, *Subverting Scotland's Past: Scottish Whig Historians and the Creation of an Anglo-British Identity, 1689-c. 1830* (Cambridge, 1993), pp. 153–156.

management. Lovat, not admittedly a trustworthy commentator, confessed he had required the assistance of 'country gentlemen' to maintain order in his area: an uncharacteristically candid stance which was nevertheless given credence by his use of clansmen as opposed to company soldiers to defend his own woods from raids by Grants of Glenmoriston in 1738.[79] Indeed, both Craigie and Dundas surmised that Forbes of Culloden's suggestion of local watch commissions for lairds and clan gentry represented the only realistic alternative to independent companies, the Solicitor-General concluding that 'I know not whither you have any thoughts of arming any men in the Highlands, but I do not think the President's scheme bad'. Accordingly, he urged Tweeddale to formalise clan arrangements through the resurrection of a system of government payments and sureties practised previously by the Squadrone administration of John Kerr, first Duke of Roxburghe.[80]

The re-adoption of clan-based methods of property protection in the years immediately prior to Culloden was in fact noticeably comprehensive. In Argyll, Colin Campbell of Glenure was informed in May 1743 that the third Duke risked severe cattle losses if he failed to support Glenshira and Glenorchy tenantry in their efforts to form private watch companies. In May 1742, John Campbell, second Earl of Breadalbane, eschewed the deployment of a private watch as a result of the proximity of company troops at Taybridge. Instead, he levied a cess of one shilling and six pence per merkland to finance prosecutions made possible by the apprehension of thieves by the soldiers. Such enthusiasm suggests that the companies' inconsistent performance in dealing with crime notwithstanding, there might indeed have been a long-term shift towards Crown justice had they remained in the region. However, by July 1744 circumstances had changed. Lord Glenorchy informed Lord Chancellor Hardwicke that his father's estate desperately needed a new independent company. Yet rather than getting any positive response he was forced to re-deploy his own clansmen who, in turn, seemed to be implicated in thieving against local Macintyre tenantry. The need for clan alternatives was also evident in Atholl. Having earlier dismissed the watch of Aeneas MacDonnell of Lochgarry upon the arrival of company troops in Rannoch, the second Duke of Atholl was forced in 1743 to lobby Alexander Robertson of Strowan to secure his influence in preventing renewed depredations. Summarising, explicitly, the direct connection between war and the need for the re-establishment of stable arrangements based on kin association, Atholl's agent noted, 'It will prove no broken reed to those who rely on it altho' the nation be something loose'.[81]

Local protection schemes proliferated across the Highlands. Alexander

---

79. W. Fraser (ed.), *op. cit.*, vol. 1, p. 381; S.R.O., Seafield Muniments, GD 248/97/3/92.
80. N.L.S., Yester Papers, Ms 7061, f. 53; Ms 7054, f. 38; Ms 7055, ff. 85, 122.
81. S.R.O., Campbell of Barcaldine Papers, GD 170/939/6; GD 170/940/5–6; B.L., Hardwicke Papers, Add Ms 35450, f. 20; B.A.M., Box 46/15/48; B.A.M. Box 46/15/58, 60.

Mackenzie of Fairburn and then Mackenzie of Lentron supervised schemes in Wester Ross which, as already noted, resulted in conflict with Cameron kindreds. Such was the increased reliance on clan methods to combat Lochaber reivers that Lentron 'resolved not to compound any, but to bang them force for force'.[82] In May 1745 Commissioners of Supply in Sutherland raised £280 for a watch on the passes of Corriecainloch, the east end of Lochshin and the Kyle of Sutherland; whilst in 1741 James Graham of Glengyle agreed with local gentry in Highland Stirlingshire to protect their cattle in return for payments calculated at 4% of their rents.[83]

The best example of this resurgence of clan methods was Ewan Macpherson of Cluny. In May 1744 he offered to maintain a private watch of seven men, and to repay persons who suffered losses while under his protection. Despite the obvious blackmail, contracts were drawn up with the tenants and landlords of the estates of Airlie, Invercauld and Culloden. In May 1745, a similar plan seemed doomed to failure in Moray and Elgin following the withdrawal of subscriptions by lairds who viewed the additional companies being raised for the Highland Regiment as an alternative to Cluny's arrangements. However, Robert Gordon of Gordonstoun noted the lack of guarantees that such army companies would be kept in the area, adding, 'I cannot help that the government do not interpose in such a manner as I could wish'. Noting the effectiveness of Macpherson's efforts, he urged heritors like Grant of Rothiemurchus and Campbell of Cawdor to join the scheme. Indeed, this clan arrangement was so welcome locally that Norman Macleod of Dunvegan informed Cluny that a request to government for an official subsidy was not altogether out of the question. Given the earlier discussions between Dundas, Craigie and Tweeddale, the notion was hardly fanciful. Macleod added cautiously that he believed government wished to see watch schemes introduced systematically and regulated by legislation, which suggests some lairds believed that established methods of protection based on kinship, as opposed to disarming, would be entrenched by law.

The Indian summer of traditional clan methods for keeping the peace had thus become generalised across the Highlands – from Sutherland, through Wester Ross and Eastern Inverness-shire, to Atholl and Argyll. Nor was this level of reliance on local association and influence restricted merely to the prevention of social crime. In February 1744 Tweeddale approached George Gordon, third Duke of Gordon, and asked that he assume responsibility for the peace and security of Badenoch and districts of the Eastern Highlands under his influence. Nor was this renewal of kinship as a method of government confined to vague notions of magnate authority. Whilst recon-

---

82. N.L.S., Mackenzie of Delvine Papers, Ms 1327, f. 10; N.L.S., Yester Papers, Ms 7056, f. 122.
83. H.R.A., S.C./1: 1/1, pp. 38–39; D.J. Withrington and I.R. Grant (eds.), *The Statistical Account of Scotland*, vol. 9 (Wakefield, 1978), pp. 401–406.

stitution of Lord Lieutenancies had been avoided in 1727 from a 'dislike of putting power into the hands of the heads of clans', by 1744 Lord Reay was proposed as a new Lord Lieutenant for Caithness precisely because his clan had retained their military effectiveness through sustained involvement with the Scots-Dutch.[84]

Changed attitudes towards clanship's overall utility had thus cut across the judicial and administrative positions of government. Most crucially, the conspicuous revival of kin association as a defence mechanism ensured that any new commissions within the British-Highland military, despite its increasingly overseas and integrated deployment, nonetheless continued to be assessed and perceived almost exclusively in terms of clan influence. Thus Robert Dundas concluded that 'tho the immediate business be to prevent stealing, to be sure such a number of those who are or have the name of being employed ought to be at the call of the government upon any inland service'.[85] An obvious indication of clanship's direct influence on the emergence of the region's distinctive military was the tendency for new commissions to be awarded to lairds deemed to have supervised efficient and responsible watch schemes. Although better remembered for their subsequent Jacobitism, both Cluny and the Lochgarry family were prominent recipients of army patronage in the months leading up the '45 precisely because they had shown themselves to be responsible managers of their clan resources: nothing can better illustrate how a direct relationship had evolved under wartime conditions between clanship and the British army.

Conclusion

Given the wider political paralysis and indifference that characterised attempts to assimilate the Highlands through judicial and administrative reform in the period from 1715 until 1746, the emergence and development of a distinctive regional military is all the more surprising. Indeed, the reconstitution and growth of Highland companies represented the most proactive and innovative area of government policy in the region during this period. Moreover, though army commissions never proved to be the missing panacea for Highland Jacobitism, it is important to move beyond detailed examination of the origins of the '45 and re-evaluate the pivotal

84. S.R.O., Robert Craigie of Glendoick Papers, GD 1/609/2/33; N.L.S., Culloden Papers, Ms 2968, f. 250; R. Mitchison, *loc. cit.*, p. 40; S.R.O., Campbell of Stonefield Papers, GD 14/18; N.L.S., Yester Papers, Ms 7061, f. 99.
85. N.L.S., Yester Papers, Ms 7054, f. 38. Another example of the connection between private watches and regular commissions was Alexander Mackenzie of Fairburn. His earlier involvement in cattle protection made him and others believe he was a natural candidate for any army commissions awarded to the Mackenzies, though he later refused a company intended for use against local Jacobites. See G. Menary, *op. cit.*, p. 239; N.L.S., Mackenzie of Delvine Papers, Ms 1327, f. 10.

relationship between disaffection, clanship and the formation of the British Highland military. This involves a change of perspective at several levels. First, the relationship between clanship and the army was complex in the extreme. Though increased involvement by Highlanders in the army was officially implemented in 1725 to assist the decline of the region's distinctive social arrangements, clanship was later re-evaluated in the 1740s by political elites in London as both a short-term solution to local law and order problems and as a long-term framework that, in their eyes, served to organise increasingly valuable concentrations of Highland manpower within the regular army. This re-evaluation was expedited by the shift from Walpole's peaceful strategy of the 1720s and 1730s to the aggressive imperial and continental aggrandisement of the 1740s.[86]

Second, while analysis has dwelt on the particular practices that served to integrate the Highlands into the United Kingdom, examination of the policies that helped create independent companies and Highland regiments underlines how regional distinctiveness, in itself, could sometimes influence the process of assimilation. In 1725 perceptions of the region remained wholly dominated by the threat of military insurrection on the part of Highland Jacobites. This helped ensure the creation of a customised military establishment that ironically sought to reflect and increasingly utilise the very same social features it was attempting to destroy. This suggests that an important if neglected consequence of Jacobitism in the 1715–45 period lay not so much in the fact that it prevented Highland involvement in the empire – an assertion already convincingly undermined[87] – but rather that it directed policy for the region into particularly distinctive and militaristic channels. Ironically, by providing the initial justification for independent companies, and, through them, later mass recruitment, Jacobitism laid the foundations for the future ghettoisation of the Highlands as an imperial-military reservoir.

86. G. Holmes and D. Szechi, *The Age of Oligarchy: Pre-industrial Britain, 1722–1783* (London, 1993), pp. 60–63, 66.
87. A.I. Macinnes, *Clanship, Commerce and the House of Stuart*, pp. 171–172.

CHAPTER TWO

Imperial Specialisation: the British-Highland Military, 1746–1815

The emergence of a pre-Culloden policy of Highland recruitment has tended to reinforce a somewhat deterministic view of the region's links with the British army in the seventy years following 1746. The continuities between clan society's 'strong military tradition' and the militarism inherent imperial service have been stressed. This convenient overlap, it has been argued, made an official policy of large-scale military recruitment manifestly appropriate for the region; accordingly, when faced with a series of global conflicts during the later eighteenth and early nineteenth centuries, British governments 'naturally' sought to utilise Highland society's apparently enthusiastic proclivity for war. The local management and success of this policy was, moreover, assured by the urgent need for attainted Jacobite families to rehabilitate themselves, regain forfeited properties and demonstrate their acceptance of Westminster's legitimacy and authority.[1]

There are, however, obvious flaws in these arguments. Areas like the Scottish and Welsh Borders, for instance, had similarly strong martial traditions, as did Irish Protestants, living as they did on something akin to a military frontier.[2] However, the recruiting relationship between these areas and the British army did not closely resemble that experienced by the Highlands. This suggests that greater account must be taken of how far levying in the region directly reflected or was relatively distinct from general British recruiting practice. Furthermore, only a minority of clans had been actively Jacobite, and, even then, tended to come from the less powerful kindreds. This raises doubts over whether Jacobite rehabilitation was a substantive factor behind the region's disproportionate level of recruitment. More crucially, the role of clanship has been assumed rather than analysed in detail. Clanship was in fact in severe decline from the 1750s, yet later levels of military levying actually surpassed those evident during the Jacobite

1. D.M. Henderson, *Highland Soldier: A Social Study of the Highland Regiments, 1820–1920* (Edinburgh, 1989), pp. 4 & 19; L. Colley, *Britons: Forging the Nation, 1707–1837* (London, 1992), pp. 131 & 295; J. Prebble, *Mutiny: Highland Regiments in Revolt, 1743–1804* (Harmondsworth, Middlesex, 1975), p. 93; B.P. Lenman, *Jacobite Clans of the Great Glen, 1650–1784* (London, 1984), pp. 204–5.
2. R.B. McDowell, *Ireland in the Age of Imperialism & Revolution, 1760–1801* (Oxford, 1991), p. 62.

era,[3] which suggests that clanship and the '45's influence upon central government and, indeed, later eighteenth-century Highland society in general, are in need of careful clarification. Precisely why the region's impressive military performance began to collapse in the early 1800s is another area in need of detailed examination. Typically, the failure of recruitment has been linked to the economic, social and estate policies of Highland landlords.[4] However, by ignoring the fact that Highland recruitment was also official Crown policy, such analysis has failed to investigate the extent to which the British state may have been responsible for ending the enlistment practices that had hitherto been so successful in the region.

The Crown's policy of Highland recruitment raises other, broader questions with respect to the region's perceived place within the empire as a whole. Given that such levying constituted the single most expensive and conspicuous central government concern in the north of Scotland, it inevitably played a major role in determining the precise relationship between Britain's metropolitan core and what was, by general consensus, a decidedly 'provincial' periphery. Indeed, the high-profile nature of the Highlands' military contribution had wider implications for Scotland as a whole. Despite suggestions that Scots involvement within the army induced both loyalty to Westminster and political centralism, it remains far from clear what precise effect unprecedented amounts of military and imperial patronage had upon Scotland's semi-autonomous political position within the United Kingdom.[5] After all, if managers like the third Duke of Argyll and Henry Dundas acquired, or were assigned, control of the distribution of military commissions, then their own peculiarly unofficial position as minister for Scotland may well have gained additional justification or acceptance. This raises the wider issue of whether the empire and the patronage it spawned, far from weakening the particularist features of Scottish political society, may in fact have served to renew or at least maintain some of its distinctive characteristics.

Military Patronage and the Management of Scotland, 1745–1810

Any attempt to trace the effects of military patronage upon Scotland's political culture must first highlight the negative repercussions of the last Jacobite uprising. Initially at least, the Austrian War of Succession and then

---

3. A.I. Macinnes, *Clanship, Commerce and the House of Stuart, 1603–1788* (East Linton, 1996), p. 217.
4. E. Richards, *A History of the Highland Clearances: Agrarian Change and the Evictions, 1746–1886*, vol. 1 (London, 1982), p. 150.
5. K.M. Brown, 'From Scottish Lords to British Officers: State Building, Elite Integration and the Army in the Seventeenth Century', in N. Macdougall (ed.), *Scotland and War, AD 79–1918* (Edinburgh, 1991), p. 152; L. Colley, *op. cit.*, pp. 120, 126–9 A. Murdoch, *'The People Above': Politics and Administration in Mid-Eighteenth Century Scotland* (Edinburgh, 1980), pp. 50, 132.

the '45 itself stimulated the deployment of Highlanders in British service and appeared to entrench Argathelian management of the resultant commissions.[6] However, the very nature of the uprising cast doubt upon the ability of the Campbells to maintain such dominance. Summarising the '45 as 'a Highland affair' may accurately reflect its geographic origins; what it fails to convey, however, is the backlash it caused against Scotland generally.[7] The uprising confirmed for most parliamentary politicians that the whole system of Scottish government was deeply flawed. Nor was this simply a matter of English prejudice; opponents of Argyll, in particular, suggested that the excessive favouritism, biased conduct and tyranny displayed by Scottish managers helped explain the excessively faction-ridden state of the country's politics which so weakened Britain as a whole. Indeed, Scottish appeals for the Anglicisation of their government and the imposition of impartial, direct Westminster control as a means of 'completing the Union' continued until the era of Henry Dundas.[8] This all had obvious implications for Scotland's distinctive system of political management. The intense hostility experienced by the third Duke of Argyll in the aftermath of the '45 most obviously reflected this change in circumstance: as representing Scotland's premier political interest he came in for particular attack, with the basis of his power being routinely condemned as all but covertly treasonous.[9]

Nor was Argyll himself unaware of the impact resurgent Jacobitism would have on his own position. On 19 August 1745, before the uprising gained serious momentum, he prophesied to Norman Macleod of Macleod that any trouble in the North would destroy his credibility, especially given the leniency he and other Scots judges had displayed after the '15:

> I wish it [Charles Edward Stuart's arrival] may not turn to the prejudice of us all by producing severities that the most moderate amongst us may not be able to prevent. What will they not say to us in England, who have all along endeavoured to give the English a better notion of the Highlanders than they had, and it will particularly fall upon me who

6. D. Warrand (ed.), *More Culloden Papers*, vol. 5 (Inverness, 1930), pp. 83–91, 111–119; P. Simpson, *The Independent Highland Companies, 1603–1760* (Edinburgh, 1996), pp. 127–8; A.I. Macinnes, *op. cit.*, pp. 168, 212.
7. M. Lynch, *Scotland: A New History* (London, 1992), p. 334.
8. S.R.O., Cunningham/Graham Muniments, GD 22/1/391; J.M. Simpson, 'Who Steered the Gravy Train, 1707–1766?', in N.T. Phillips and R. Mitchison (eds.), *Scotland in the Age of Improvement: Essays in Scottish History in the Eighteenth Century* (Edinburgh, 1996), p. 49; C. Kidd, 'North Britishness and the Nature of Eighteenth Century British Patriotisms', in *The Historical Journal*, vol. 39 (1996), pp. 364–5; D.J. Brown, 'Henry Dundas and the Government of Scotland' (University of Edinburgh Ph. D., 1989), p. 22.
9. H. Paton (ed.), H.M.C., *Polwarth Mss, 1725–80*, vol. 5 (London, 1961), pp. 203–5, 212; B.L., Newcastle Papers, Add Ms 32707, ff. 13, 87; G. Menary, *The Life and Letters of Duncan Forbes of Culloden* (London, 1936), pp. 258–9; A. Murdoch, *op. cit.*, p. 40.

have relieved all those who were in my power, from the distresses that the last affair brought upon them.[10]

As predicted, Scotland's overall political standing deteriorated as intense Scotophobia manifested itself in Westminster. In January 1746 Tweeddale resigned as Secretary of State; and it soon became apparent he would not be replaced. Secretary of the Treasury, Henry Pelham, while allowing Argyll's pre-eminence to survive, was determined to exert overall control and have it 'understood that there is no longer a sole minister for Scotland'.[11] Pelham's death in 1754 witnessed the emergence of his brother, the first Duke of Newcastle, at the head of a new ministry. Newcastle had voiced doubts previously over the very principle of a Scottish manager and appeared determined to control Scotland effectively; indeed, in the aftermath of the 1754 election he was even prepared for the possibility of Argyll's removal or retirement. Although conscious of the administration's desire to retain his influence for its own parliamentary purpose, Argyll did genuinely feel that Newcastle was determined to establish a 'new Scotch ministry' based upon the Treasury controlling and dispensing judicial, administrative and customs offices among competing and therefore dependent Scottish factions.[12]

This attempted curtailment of Argyll's position forms the backdrop to the Seven Years War that witnessed the re-emergence of mass Highland recruitment. Although viewed by many historians as a centralising, unifying force, Scots in general appeared to view imperial war in a more ambivalent light, and, above all, as a means of advantageously adjusting the Union between themselves and the English. Generally acknowledged as having a proportionally greater volume of disposable manpower, Scots saw war as perhaps the one area of public and imperial endeavour where England was relatively dependent upon Scotland. Conflict was thus invariably viewed in an extremely positive light by many Scots. Above all, it was seen, quite consciously, as the best means of obtaining patronage from a position of strength. The opinion of Simon Fraser of Lovat in 1735 is illustrative: 'dismal news of ye peace, and if it go on, adieu to poor Scotland . . . If it

10. For Argathelian apprehensions, see N.L.S., Fletcher of Saltoun Papers, Ms 16630, f. 112; D.C.M., 4/160.
11. A. Murdoch, *op. cit.*, pp. 35–37; J.M. Simpson, *op.cit.* p. 61; S.R.O., Seafield Muniments, GD 248/49/1/63; B.L., Newcastle Papers, Add Ms 32707, f. 87; Add Ms 32713, f. 283; Add Ms 32714, f. 436; Add Ms 32715, f. 68; B.L., Hardwicke Papers, Add Ms 35447, ff. 19, 27, 123; N.L.S., Fletcher of Saltoun Papers, Ms 16677, f. 119; H. Paton (ed.), *op. cit.*, vol. 5, pp. 188–192, 201–28, 236–67, 294–99.
12. R. Browning, *The Duke of Newcastle* (London, 1975), pp. 45–46; A. Murdoch, *op. cit.*, pp. 40–1, 51; B.L., Newcastle Papers, Add Ms 32687, ff. 131–135; Add Ms 32736, ff. 151, 332, 372, 448; Add Ms 32737, ff. 227, 483, 507; Add Ms 32854, f. 15; Add Ms 32857, f. 67; Add Ms 32995, ff. 63, 190, 193, 211, 383; Add Ms, 33049, ff. 285–90; B.A.M., Box 47/5/121; B.L., Hardwicke Papers, Add Ms 35448, ff. 120, 178, 224, 230, 234; N.L.S., Fletcher of Saltoun Papers, Ms 16517, ff. 44, 75; Ms 16677, f. 119.

is a solid peace they will not give a ten pence for us and we are still wise behind hand like true foolish Scotchmen'.[13] Any attempt to understand how Argyll may have felt about the prospects of war in 1756 should take note of this attitude, especially since the belief that England's military needs gave Scotland a political advantage dictated how Scots themselves then valued the Highlands. In 1756 a supporter of Newcastle expressed what may have formed the initial basis for the later Highlandisation of Scots culture in the nineteenth century. He explained that war drastically reconfigured Scottish attitudes towards the region, and that 'even those who wish not well to the Pretender, secretly wish well for the Highlands. They consider that they [Highlanders] are an awe upon England and make them [Scots] respectable there'.[14]

Even prior to the war, therefore, the Highlands' military potential was seen as a means of extracting concessions and political strength from the centre. The controversial conduct of the war certainly produced instabilities in national government that provided Argyll with various opportunities to entrench his position. Henry Fox, for instance, a relatively close associate, was promoted in the autumn of 1755 to Secretary of State for the Southern Department. Argyll adroitly used the reshuffle as an opportunity to improve his access to military posts. In addition, Newcastle increasingly appreciated Argyll's co-operation in shoring up government voting strength in the Commons and accordingly withdrew support from prominent anti-Argathelians like James Ogilvy, Lord Deskford.[15] The rapid sequence of ministries from late 1756 until June 1757 also worked generally, though by no means exclusively, in Argyll's favour. In March 1757, for instance, Fox sought to secure Argyll for his intended administration; a sure sign that Argyll's power was waxing under wartime conditions was Fox's willingness to recognise him as the 'independent' minister for Scotland. This was the antithesis of trends in Scottish political management during the preceding decade. As it was, Fox failed to develop wider support for his proposed administration: nevertheless, Argyll had come close to recovering the Scottish manager's official status. However, political events then moved against him, demonstrating the extent to which Scottish managers remained hostages to the vagaries of Westminster factionalism. By June 1757 Pitt and Newcastle had come together: both had reasons for removing Argyll from government involvement, and a list showing ten Scottish M.P.s as pro-Argyll suggests that his departure and its consequences for voting strength had been seriously

13. S.R.O., Seafield Muniments, GD 248/97/2/25, 52 & 82; GD 248/683.
14. B.L., Hardwicke Papers, Add Ms 35449, f. 2.
15. B.L., Holland House Papers, Add Ms 51429, f. 9; P.R.O., WO. 1/972, f. 39; B.L., Newcastle Papers, Add Ms 32854, f. 15; Add Ms 32857, f. 87; Add Ms 32859, ff. 237, 242, 323, 394–6, 425; Add Ms 32861, f. 417; Add Ms 33049, f. 295; B.A.M., Box 47/8/11, 19; B.L., Hardwicke Papers, Add Ms 35449, f. 29; N.L.S., Fletcher of Saltoun, Ms 16517, ff. 40, 80, 182, 209–11, 240; Ms 16518, ff. 7, 25; Ms 16690, f. 207.

considered. The vulnerability of 'Scottish ministers' probably explains why both Argyll and then Dundas remained content with their unofficial status, which distanced them from any formal administration and lessened the likelihood of their dismissal upon its fall.[16]

As it was, Argyll was not removed and, indeed, went on to consolidate his power until his death in 1761. War in general and military recruitment in particular played a central role in this reversal of fortune and expedited the Duke's recovery from his nadir in the immediate post-Culloden years. From the earliest period of Franco-British tensions in North America, Argyll had been aware that the deployment of Highlanders was being considered, and that this could work to his advantage. In September 1754, January 1755 and May 1756 proposals were discussed to raise several new Highland battalions, though both the King and Cumberland objected, opting instead to send regiments from Ireland to reinforce America.[17] Argathelian confidence that the international situation was tending to reinforce their domestic position was specifically boosted in 1755 when, in response to the annihilation of Lieutenant-General Edward Braddock's Ohio expedition, rumours circulated that Argyll's ally William Home, eighth Earl of Home, was to raise a battalion in Glasgow and that James Campbell of Inverawe was to be given a new Highland battalion.[18] However, the King and Cumberland still refused to countenance a Highland regiment, preferring, instead, to augment existing units and establish four battalions of Swiss and German Protestants.[19] In spite of this initial lack of new patronage Argyll clearly had reasons to be optimistic by late 1755. The fact that Highland troops had even been proposed was in itself significant. He knew that London's wish to avoid

16. P.W.J. Riley, *The English Ministers and Scotland, 1707–1727* (London, 1964), p. 292; J.C.D. Clark, *The Dynamics of Change: The Crisis of the 1750s and English Party Systems* (Cambridge, 1982), pp. 67, 99, 179–81, 192, 336–8, 419, 423–26; J.M. Simpson, *loc. cit.*, p. 62; B.L., Newcastle Papers, Add Ms 32997, ff. 148, 113; N.L.S., Yester Papers, Ms 7065, f. 10; M. Fry, *The Dundas Despotism* (Edinburgh, 1992), p. 105.
17. J.C.D. Clark, *op. cit.*, pp. 99–105; R. Browning, *op. cit.*, pp. 177–8; O.A. Sherrard, *Lord Chatham: Pitt and The Seven Years War* (London, 1955), p. 50; B.L., Newcastle Papers, Add Ms 32996, f. 3.
18. L. Namier and J. Brooke (eds.), *The History of Parliament: The House of Commons, 1754–1790*, vol. 3 (London, 1964), p. 88; N.L.S., Minto Papers, Ms 11005, ff. 34, 38; G.C.A., TD 132, Records of Mess'rs George Kippen, John Glasford & Co, TD 132/48; B.L., Newcastle Papers, Add Ms 32996, ff. 208, 218; N.L.S., Fletcher of Saltoun Papers, Ms 16690, ff. 207, 209; Ms 16517, f. 240; Ms 17505, f. 32.
19. R. Middleton, 'The Recruitment of the British Army, 1755–1762', in *Journal of the Society of Army Historical Research*, vol. 68 (1989), pp. 228–9; S. Ayling, *The Elder Pitt: Earl of Chatham* (London, 1976), p. 192; N.L.S., Fletcher of Saltoun Papers, Ms 16517, ff. 217, 222, 240; N.L.S., Minto Papers, Ms 11001, f. 16; B.L., Newcastle Papers, Add Ms 32861, f. 292; Add Ms 32862, f. 46; Add Ms 32859, f. 225; Add Ms 32996, ff. 3, 208, 218, 248, 257; B.L., Holland House Papers, Add Ms 51375, f. 127.

militarising the region was still strong, and that Newcastle and Philip Yorke, Lord Chancellor Hardwicke, were only too aware that any additional Highland battalions would undo much of their preferred strategy for limiting Argathelian power. That both were nevertheless prepared to sanction this option demonstrated to Argyll that he could be potentially indispensable to a government requiring additional troops: a prognosis confirmed when, on 1 January 1756, Campbell of Inverawe was promoted to major in the 42nd Highland Regiment while the fourth Earl of Loudon, the Duke's kinsman, obtained overall command of the British army in North America.[20]

Over and above this increased access to established avenues of military patronage, the prospect of new Highland regiments was strengthened by the course of the 'blue and grey water' debate on British foreign policy. Pitt and his allies were consistent promoters of a blue water policy that stressed the vigorous acquisition and defence of colonies rather than a heavy military commitment to the European continent. Austrian and Dutch subsidies as well as a perceived over-reliance on 15,000 Hanoverian and Hessian mercenaries were particular objections raised by Pitt. Continual criticism of non-domestic sources of manpower through the spring of 1756 ensured that he highlighted the Highlands as an alternative – a fact which doubtless explains why Argyll himself was decidedly hostile towards the use of German levies.[21]

Pitt's objective of reinforcing the American colonies with 8,000 men, when allied to his opposition to foreign troops, ensured that when he came to power in November 1756 he had little option but to look towards domestic manpower sources. The prospect of losing regiments from the Flanders theatre ensured that Cumberland suddenly reversed his hostility towards Highland levies and agreed on 4 January 1757 to two additional Highland battalions.[22] The resulting units, commanded by Archibald Montgomery, later eleventh Earl of Eglinton, and Simon Fraser, son of the executed Lord Lovat, have been remembered primarily for their pioneering role in the

20. L. Namier and J. Brooke (eds.), *op. cit.*, vol. 3, pp. 186–7; B.L., Newcastle Papers, Add Ms 32859, f. 394; Add Ms 32860, f. 78; Add Ms 32996, f. 355; N.L.S., Fletcher of Saltoun, Ms 16518, ff. 3, 15, 21, 32; Ms 16519, ff. 24, 107; Ms 16694, f. 216; Ms 16696, f. 22; D.H., Loudon Papers, A/972, f. 21.
21. J. Brewer, *The Sinews of Power: War, Money and the English State, 1688–1783* (London, 1989), pp. 169–70; J. Black, *Pitt the Elder* (Cambridge, 1992), pp. 76, 108; O.A. Sherrard, *Lord Chatham: A War Minister in the Making* (London, 1952), pp. 138–141; B.L., Newcastle Papers, Add Ms 32996, f. 281; Add Ms 32864, f. 488; B.L., Holland House Papers, Add Ms 51375, f. 47; Add Ms 51378, f. 164; N.L.S., Fletcher of Saltoun Papers, Ms 16518, ff. 32, 53 & 57; N.L.S., Mackenzie of Delvine Papers, Ms 1367, f. 28; N.L.S., Minto Papers, Ms 11001, f. 16; P.R.O., Catham Papers, P.R.O., 30/8/18, ff. 209–10.
22. E.M. Lloyd, 'The Raising of the Highland Regiments in 1757', in *English Historical Review*, vol. 17 (1902), pp. 466; P.C. Yorke (ed.), *The Life and Correspondence of Phillip Yorke, Lord Chancellor Hardwicke*, vol. 2 (Cambridge, 1913), p. 378; B.L., Newcastle Papers, Add Ms 32869, ff. 355, 367; Add Ms 32870, ff. 21, 25; Add Mss 32996, f. 281; N.L.S., Fletcher of Saltoun Papers, Ms 16694, ff. 110, 115, 213.

rehabilitation of Jacobite families. While that was admittedly important, this perspective nonetheless fails to convey the extent to which resumption of large-scale Highland recruitment significantly enhanced Argyll's position both within Scotland and in the rest of the United Kingdom. Although Pitt and Newcastle subsequently considered removing him in June 1757, Argyll's efficient management of recruitment protected him, and ensured, instead, that he obtained the distribution rights for all the additional companies added to the three Highland battalions in July. Indeed, the Duke and his allies subsequently appointed fourteen of the initial nineteen officers. By the end of the war over ten Highland regiments had been created, and though Argyll's control was never absolute, he commanded such a dominant position that even the anti-Argathelian Treasury interest in Scotland told prospective candidates to apply to him.[23] Such political power is difficult to quantify. Some figures do however reveal the scale of Argyll's control. In 1755, the Scottish Salt and Customs establishment totalled 501 places: nominees of the House of Argyll totalled forty-two. However, by 1761, out of a possible 401, the third Duke had either directly or indirectly appointed 158 military officers whose annual pay totalled £8,650. The Argathelians gained just over 8% of the Customs places: by contrast, their nominees accounted for almost 40% of commissions in the British-Highland military.[24]

Despite being part of Britain's centralised state apparatus, the extent to which Highland recruitment in this formative period was associated with Argyll is striking. Newcastle noted in 1757 that 'The Duke [Cumberland], I hear disapproves but submits – it is wholly the Duke of Argyll'. John Calcraft, a prominent regimental agent, commented that Montgomery and Fraser 'name their own officers in concert with the Duke of Argyll who is head of this undertaking'.[25] Such supervision clearly went beyond the 'advisory' role that Argyll, as Earl of Ilay, had developed with Sir Robert Walpole in the 1720s. When, for example, Lord Lindores requested a commission from the War Office in 1758, the Secretary of War, Lord Barrington, replied simply: 'The Duke of Argyll has fix't the dates, and I can make no alterations but by his Grace's desire'.[26] That a Secretary of War

23. J. Prebble, *op. cit.*, pp. 496–7; B.P. Lenman, *op. cit.*, pp. 192–3; P.R.O. Chatham Papers, P.R.O., 30/8/18, ff. 176–7; N.L.S., Fletcher of Saltoun Papers, Ms 16519, f. 140; Ms 16698, f. 50; Ms 16708, f. 201; Ms 16711, f. 188; Ms 16717, f. 51; Ms 17505, f. 151; Ms 17506, f. 127; D.H., Loudon Papers, A/993, f. 3: A/963, letter, Edinburgh, 22 August 1759, Capt. J. Sutherland-Loudon; A/966, letter, 9 March 1760, Lt. D. Calder-Loudon; P.R.O., W.O. 1/979, letters, 12 April & 17 July 1759, Lord John Murray & Argyll-Barrington.
24. S.R.O., R.H. 2/8/102; M.L., British Army List, 1740–1784; B.A.M., Box 47/11/84, 117; N.L.S., Fletcher of Saltoun Papers, Ms 16519, f. 27; Ms 16696, f. 22; Ms 16708, f. 201; Ms 16714, f. 81; Ms 16717, f. 51.
25. B.L., Newcastle Papers, Add Ms 32870, f. 72; Letter Book of John Calcraft, Add Ms 17493, ff. 24–6.
26. P.W.J. Riley, *op. cit.*, p. 286; P.R.O., W.O. 1/975, f. 543; W.O. 1/977, ff. 98, 159; W.O. 1/978, f. 71.

should defer to such an extent, and to a political figure who, a decade earlier, had seemed in London to stand in the way of Scottish accountability to Westminster, clearly shows how imperial patronage should not be automatically equated with British political centralism and control. That Argyll was able to engross such a substantial part of what amounted to an extremely lucrative branch of imperial patronage illustrates something of the metropolitan perceptions that helped shape the British-Highland military and influence its later development. Even prior to 1745, whilst officially no longer in government and facing a challenge for control from John Dalrymple, second Earl of Stair, as well as the Atholl family, Argyll nonetheless established primary if not exclusive rights over appointments to Highland units. This continued even when, after Culloden, he faced considerable hostility in other areas of Scottish administration. For example, he was automatically entrusted with supervising commissions for the Highland companies sent to India in 1748. Argathelian dominance in this area may have arisen in part from the high-profile military career of John Campbell, second Duke of Argyll. More fundamentally, however, the family's traditional supremacy in matters relating to government in the Highlands helped ensure that whatever state patronage was intended for the region could only bypass Argyll if an entirely new administrative approach was constructed at the metropolitan centre. In face of larger imperial concerns this was, to say the least, unlikely. The expectation that regiments would use local Highland networks to gain access to untapped sources of manpower gave the Argylls a further advantage in that their role as managers of the region was well understood in London and even, to an extent, conceded by political enemies in Scotland. From the start, therefore, the British-Highland military was characterised by the paradox of a substantial increase in state influence in the region being achieved through the traditional process of informal political management and reliance on local proprietary influence.[27]

When considering the possibility that the impact of imperial patronage was devolutionary as much as centralising, it is instructive to note that Argyll's management of military commissions can be compared in some respects with that of the Irish Lord Lieutenant. During the early 1750s Newcastle had used the military high command in Scotland as an additional support mechanism for Argyll's political enemies. Yet just as the Lord Lieutenant and not the Irish Commander-in-Chief controlled military com-

27. L. Leneman, *Living in Atholl – a Social History of the Estate, 1685–1785* (Edinburgh, 1986), p. 144; N.L.S., Culloden Papers, Ms 2968, f. 217; N.L.S., Yester Papers, Ms 7058, f. 28; D.C.M., 4/120 & 123; S.R.O., Grant of Monymusk, GD 345/1175/2/27–28x. Campbell's control of state patronage warns against seeking an early change in Argyll's role within the region. See E. Cregeen, 'The Changing Role of the House of Argyll in the Scottish Highlands', in N.T. Phillipson and R. Mitchison (eds.), *Scotland in the Age of Improvement: Essays in Scottish History in the Eighteenth Century* (Edinburgh, 1996), pp. 10 & 17.

missions in Ireland, so, in November 1759, Lord George Beauclerk, Commander-in-Chief in Scotland, objected to Argyll's failure to consult him over appointments. Furthermore, though he lacked the institutionalised patronage base of the Irish establishment, Argyll's supervision of Highland regimental commissions did, like the Lord Lieutenant's, routinely extend to include field officers and colonels. The ability of these two distinctive military establishments to ring-fence vacancies for their own nationals did, however, differ in two crucial respects. While in peacetime the Irish establishment provided a constant and reliable source of domestic patronage, this was undermined by any outbreak of war, which invariably witnessed regiments leaving Ireland and the jurisdiction of the Lord Lieutenant. By contrast, war was the primary means whereby the British-Highland military expanded – a crucially important counterpoise to the permanence of arrangements in Ireland. In addition, most Irish Lord Lieutenants, unlike Argyll, were burdened with numerous English political connections that forced them to grant commissions to non-Irish clients. The result was that while Irish regiments during the Seven Years War often had a substantial minority of English or non-Irish officers, Highland regiments were staffed almost completely by Scottish officers.[28]

That Argathelian control over such a large proportion of commissions was ceded on the grounds of the family's expertise in Highland affairs also goes some way towards explaining the pattern of British army recruitment in Scotland established during the Seven Years War, and which continuing until around 1800. Unable to justify his management of Lowland recruitment to anywhere near the same extent, Argyll found it was in his own political interest to promote specifically Highland regiments as opposed to 'Scottish' battalions. It was this political agenda, more than any fundamental ideological objection, which explains why in 1760 Argyll promoted Highland fencibles and not a national militia, and why the Scottish Borders did not experience anywhere near the same level of imperial militarisation as the Highlands during the Seven Years' War. The regions had, after all, many similarities: economy, climate and, above all, a proven historical record of quasi-military activity. Yet in March 1760 proposals forwarded by Loudon to Argyll for a regiment of 500 men from amongst 'the people of the Borders, formerly active and warlike', came to nothing. That the

28. J.W. Hayes, 'The Social and Professional Background of the Officers of the British Army, 1714–1763' (University of London, M.A. Thesis, 1956), p. 18; R.B. McDowell, *op. cit.*, p. 99; K.P. Ferguson, 'The Army in Ireland from the Restoration to the Act of Union' (Trinity College Dublin, Ph.D., 1980), pp. 64–7; A.J. Guy, 'The Irish Military Establishment, 1660–1776', in T. Bartlett & K. Jeffery (eds.), *A Military History of Ireland* (Cambridge, 1996), pp. 223–5; P.J. Marshall, 'A Nation defined by Empire, 1755–1776', in A. Grant and K. J. Stringer (eds.), *Uniting the Kingdom? The Making of British History* (London, 1995), p. 210; S.J. Connolly, 'Varieties of Britishness: Ireland, Scotland and Wales in the Hanoverian State', in A. Grant and K. J. Stringer (eds.), *op. cit.*, pp. 200–1.

regiment never materialised is not surprising, given that Argyll knew it could only benefit political enemies like the Marchmonts. More fundamentally, however, the Scottish Borders also lacked what the Highlands did not – clear and recent evidence of militarism in the form of the 1745 uprising. It was the combination of these specific political concerns and more generally perceived cultural distinctions that helps account in large part for the differing military experience of the Highlands from areas of Lowland Scotland.[29]

Control of commissions also ensured that the third Duke was able to utilise all sections of Highland elite society for recruiting purposes, including allies like Atholl or opponents such as the Campbells of Breadalbane, all of whom willingly or reluctantly ended up reinforcing his political prestige in London. Indeed, when the largely hostile Gordon interest obtained a regiment in late 1759 by appealing over his head to the King, they nonetheless felt obliged to nominally consult Argyll, who retained influence over the likes of Lord Adam Gordon by continuing to assist his military career.[30] This all served to reinforce his management of electoral contests: military patronage, for instance, was crucial in Sutherland during the 1761 election. Argyll brought about the removal of the incumbent M.P., George Mackay, through the influence of William Gordon, seventeenth Earl of Sutherland, whose support he ensured by obtaining for him the only other fencible regiment raised during the Seven Years War. Sutherland, and the case of Perthshire discussed below in Chapter 4, underline how Argyll's successes in the North were often inextricably linked to his management of the British-Highland military. More fundamentally, Argyll, but most especially Dundas, had the structure of the Highland electorate aiding their management strategies. Table 1 illustrates the extent to which the region's constituency was more militarised and concerned with army patronage than other Scottish voters and so, theoretically at least, more amenable to the influence of the Crown or its manager.[31]

29. J. Robertson, *The Scottish Enlightenment and the Militia Issue* (Edinburgh, 1985), pp. 106–8; B.P. Lenman, 'Militia, Fencible Men & Home Defence, 1660–1797', in N. Macdougall (ed.) *op. cit.*, pp. 187–9; B.L., Hardwicke Papers, Add Ms 35449, f. 221; D.H., Loudon Papers, A/993, ff. 8–9, 16.
30. P.R.O., Chatham Papers, 30/8/33, ff. 46–7; N.L.S., Fletcher of Saltoun Papers, Ms 16709, ff. 89, 253; Ms 16710, ff. 95, 120; Ms 16716, f. 131; B.A.M., Box 47/11/151, 155; S.R.O., Townshend Papers, RH. 4/98/1, letter, 9 November 1759; B.L., Newcastle Papers, Add Ms 33047, f. 285; S.R.O., Seafield Muniments, GD 248/49/2/7.
31. B.L., Newcastle Papers, Add Ms 32890, f. 434; Add Ms 32891, ff. 421; Add Ms 32995, ff. 383, 307; N.L.S., Mackenzie of Delvine Papers, Ms 1461, ff. 276–7; S.R.O., John Macgregor Collection, GD 50/180/47; R.M. Sunter, *Patronage and Politics in Scotland, 1707–1832* (Edinburgh, 1986), pp. 42–3, 135–140; O. Anderson, 'The Role of the Army in Parliamentary Management during the American War of Independence', in *Journal of the Society for Army Historical Research*, vol. 34 (1956), pp. 146–8.

Table 1. Military Officers, their Relations & the Scottish County Electorate, 1788[32]

County	Electorate	Military officers & %	Half-pay officers & %	Voters linked With military	Total & % of electorate & %
Lowland	1,548	120 (7.7)	44 (2.8)	61 (3.9)	225 (14.5)
Highland line	820	106 (12.9)	24 (2.9)	17 (2)	147 (17.9)
Highlands	294	60 (20.4)	10 (3.4)	6 (2)	76 (25.8)

It is also revealing that when contemporaries discussed Argyll's organisation of recruitment they invariably made an immediate link with his ever more secure status as manager of Scotland. Newcastle, of all people, referred in 1757 to 'the Old Governor of Scotland' mustering '2,000 of his Highland friends'. More pointedly, within three weeks of Pitt's decision to establish additional Highland regiments, General James St. Clair noted: 'I think the Duke of Argyll stands unrivalled as to Scotland': sentiments echoed in 1761 by Newcastle and a Perthshire voter who observed: 'It is universally allowed that the Duke of Argyll is more the minister for Scotland just now than ever he was in his life'.[33]

It speaks volumes for how far Argyll had won acceptance for his admittedly unofficial position as manager that, after his death, few objected in principle to the continuation of such a position. When George Grenville forced out James Stuart Mackenzie in 1765, for instance, he seemed prepared to accept John Campbell, Lord Lorne, in a somewhat similar capacity. Various Scots such as William Murray, first Earl of Mansfield, and, later, John Stuart, Lord Mountstuart, attempted throughout the 1760s and 1770s to establish themselves in such a role, but this did not occur, and Scottish business came under the control of the Northern Department to an unprecedented extent. There was, therefore, something of hiatus between the 'aristocratic' and 'faction'-based management of Argyll and the emergence of Henry Dundas as representing Scotland's socially dominant landed interest within the Union.[34] Nonetheless, those

---

32. C.E. Adam (ed.), *View of the Political State of Scotland in the Last Century* (Edinburgh, 1887). Lowland: Ayr, Berwick, Clackmannan, Dumfries, Fife, Haddington, Kinross, Kirkcudbright, Lanark, Linlithgow, Mid-lothian, Peebles, Roxburgh, Selkirk, Stirling and Wigton. Highland line: Aberdeen, Banff, Bute, Kincardine, Dunbarton, Elgin, Forfar, Nairn, Orkney, and Perth. Highland: Argyll, Caithness, Cromarty, Inverness, Ross, and Sutherland.
33. J.M. Simpson, *loc. cit.*, p. 68; B.L., Letter Book of John Calcraft, Add Ms 17493, f. 22; B.L., Newcastle Papers, Add Ms 32870, ff. 21, 25; N.L.S., Mackenzie of Delvine Papers, Ms 1461, f. 201; B.A.M., Box 47/13/27, 46.
34. N.L.S., Fletcher of Saltoun Papers, Ms 16728, f. 115; A. Murdoch, *op. cit.*, pp. 111–25; J. Dwyer and A. Murdoch, 'Paradigms and Politics: Manners, Morals and the Rise of Henry Dundas, 1770–1784' in J. Dwyer, R.A. Mason and A. Murdoch (eds.), *New Perspectives on the Politics and Culture of Early Modern Scotland* (Edinburgh, 1982), pp. 220, 230, 240–3.

who sought to establish themselves during this vacuum clearly understood how military patronage could reinforce and heighten their status. Mountstuart was noted in 1773 as ensuring that those who gained state employment under his auspices were fully aware of their obligations. Struck, no doubt, by the benefits his great uncle had experienced by promoting distinctively Scottish forms of recruitment, he also proved conspicuous in lobbying for a militia in 1775. Similarly, one of the first concrete signs of Dundas's rise to Scottish pre-eminence during the American war was the willingness of lairds such as Sir James Grant of Grant to present their recruiting proposals through him.[35]

When Dundas did eventually secure his position, it was under circumstances altogether different from those experienced by Argyll. The former never had to face the same level of Scotophobia or, until just before the time of his death, fundamental questioning of the desirability of a semi-autonomous manager. More crucially, the basis of Dundas's power was quite different: his status in Scotland was inextricably linked to his relationship with William Pitt the Younger and the various offices he held as President of the India Board of Control, Secretary of War or First Lord of the Admiralty. Dundas was Scottish manager largely, though not exclusively, through his status as a high-profile British minister; Argyll's power, by contrast, depended almost absolutely upon its Scottish sources.[36] However, Dundas's experience was similar in some fundamental respects to that of Argyll. Instability at national level, for instance, meant he could find himself a victim of changing circumstances, as in August 1783 when the Fox-North coalition dismissed him as Lord Advocate. Conversely, as it had done for Argyll in the mid-1750s, war produced a series of weak administrations in London during the period 1782–84 which Dundas manipulated to promote recognition of his primacy north of the Border – a manoeuvre he repeated in 1801 when Henry Addington's administration allowed him to maintain control in return for the use of Scottish M.P.s.[37]

Dundas's influence in other spheres of the British state and empire was such that he was never as reliant upon military patronage as Argyll had been; but, along with naval commissions it still represented the largest single sector of government employment he could offer Scots. Estimates for the period 1784–90, when opportunities in the forces were more limited than in later years, suggest that over one in four Scottish applications were for the armed forces. Furthermore, Dundas exhibited the same determination to build up his political support through such means. Given the figures in Table 1, it is not altogether surprising that one of the tactics planned by Dundas in 1786 to prevent any co-operation between the Scots opposition and independent

35. M. Fry, *op. cit.*, pp. 67–8; B.A.M., Box 54/4/146; S.R.O., Seafield Muniments, GD 248/56/4/24 & 32.
36. J. M. Simpson, *loc. cit.*, pp. 67–8; M. Fry, *op. cit.*, pp. 104, 129, 295; D.J. Brown, *loc. cit.*, p. 2.
37. M. Fry, *op. cit.*, pp. 83, 88–94, 242–3; D.J. Brown, *loc. cit.*, p. 44.

peers was to deny the latter commissions.[38] Dundas used his India House connections to initiate the battalions raised by his kinsman John Mackenzie, Lord Macleod, in 1777 and 1781; likewise, in 1787 his allies supervised appointments to the 74th Highland Regiment. Both units were part of Dundas's strategy to promote Macleod and Sir Archibald Campbell of Inverneil, who had either been or still were M.P.s in his interest.[39]

The substantial expansion of the armed forces after 1793 allowed Dundas to extend his use of military commissions for political purposes, most obviously in the case of Gordon and Sir James Grant of Grant, both of whom were pivotal in Dundas's attempt to balance the unstable electoral interests of the North-East. What is even more striking about the initial award of fencibles and regular regiments in 1793 is how many went to Highland magnates who were by no means allies of Dundas. Francis Humbertson-Mackenzie of Seaforth, Elizabeth, Countess of Sutherland and, most obviously, John, fourth Earl of Breadalbane, were Whig or, at best, independent peers. Awarding regiments was clearly an attempt to co-operate with or lull into neutrality those powerful landed interests that were still outwith Dundas's control: nationally, a rapprochement with the Portland Whigs was still over a year away. The Scottish manager was able to use military patronage as a lubricant for his own distinctive political agenda – in this case, to return all 45 Scottish M.P.s as pro-government, an unprecedented feat which would surely have demonstrated to London the utility of maintaining and encouraging a strong unofficial minister north of the Border.[40]

Yet a fuller understanding of the Scottish manager and his relationship with the political centre must also focus on what Scots thought of and expected from the arrangement, and not just on those methods used to ensure political loyalty. This 'bottom-up' agenda is best illustrated, ironically, by highlighting the period 1765–1784 when Scotland was without an undisputed manager. The result was administrative drift and a heightened level of electoral contests and expense, made worse by the refusal of English politicians like Lord North to fill the vacuum.[41] More specifically, in terms of military patronage, the absence of a manager during the American Revolutionary War witnessed inefficient distribution of regiments. In

38. M. Fry, *op. cit.*, p. 133; D.J. Brown, *loc. cit.*, pp. 89, 186–191.
39. N.L.S., Melville Papers, Ms 1070, f. 156; B.L., Liverpool Papers, Add Ms 38192, f. 15; G.C.A., Campbell of Succoth Papers, TD 219/10/117; M. Fry, *op. cit.*, pp. 84, 101.
40. J.E. Cookson, *The British Armed Nation, 1793–1815* (Oxford, 1997), pp. 133–35; N.L.S., Melville Papers, Ms 4, f. 164. For a sceptical though balanced assessment of how far military patronage could influence Scottish politics, see D.J. Brown, *loc. cit.*, p. 191.
41. M. Fry, *op. cit.*, pp. 33–4; D. J. Brown, 'Nothing but Strugalls and Corruption': The Commons' Elections for Scotland in 1774', in C. Jones (ed.), *The Scots and Parliament* (Edinburgh, 1996), p. 100; B.A.M., Box 54/4/109, 112, 117, 121, 136.

1778 this resulted in embarrassing and counter-productive competition between Alexander Gordon, fourth Duke of Gordon, and Colonel Gordon of Fyvie, and in the failure of those like Sir James Grant of Grant to obtain battalions. Even more worrying for government was that with no effective channel to ensure their defence concerns were addressed at the centre, many localities in 1780 took to forming, without official permission, the type of volunteer units which were to become so popular after 1794.[42]

A different type of problem, though springing from the same defect in Scottish administration, occurred in 1779 when it became clear that the unregulated creation of battalions had produced recruitment levels that threatened the economic interests of landlords. It is profoundly ironic, but hardly surprising given the family's close association with recruitment, that landlords turned to the politically inactive John Campbell, fifth Duke of Argyll. As a former Commander-in-chief in Scotland it was he who eventually persuaded the government to halt levying for a year. Nonetheless, the vacuum in management hampered lairds like Duncan Campbell of Glenure in their efforts to provide for their sons. Throughout the 1770s, and especially during the American war, Glenure was mortified by the fifth Duke of Argyll's refusal to lobby for commissions. Instead, Glenure approached the third Earl of Breadalbane and Lord Frederick Campbell in an attempt to extract patronage from the centre. Offended by this unwillingness or inability to award his political loyalty, Glenure, in a comment that warns against taking the deferential nature of the Scottish electorate at face value, noted: 'If I am disappointed in this, while all the world besides are getting steps, nay great strides for their sons, I cannot help thinking I have brought my hogs to a bad market'. Indeed, an indication of what they hoped to obtain from their political managers is that Scots very quickly came to think of Argyll as a figure who all but guaranteed their military careers. In 1762 an officer conceded he had 'suffered much by the death of the Duke of Argyll, met with more delays and entered into the army with less advantage'.[43]

Moreover, faced with substantial gentry pressure in their own areas of influence, magnates like Atholl, Breadalbane and Seaforth may well have come to appreciate a distinctively Scottish link to the centre that acknowledged their local importance and supported their recommendations. Ultimately, such a link tended, in the end, to reinforce their social status as channels of patronage. Both Argyll who, in 1747, sought to maintain the concept of a Scottish minister at a time when it was deeply unpopular, and, later, Dundas, understood that a crucial part of their job description involved

42. S.R.O., Gordon Castle Muniments, GD 44/43/195/1, 4, 39; GD 44/43/197/22; S.R.O., Seafield Muniments, GD 248/56/4/4, 10, 13; N.L.S., Melville Papers, Ms 3834, f. 7.
43. B.A.M., Box 54/4/173; T. Hayer (ed.), *An Eighteenth Century Secretary at War: the Papers of William, Viscount Barrington* (London, 1988), p. 301; S.R.O., Campbell of Barcaldine Papers, GD 170/1135/26; GD 170/3155; GD 170/1116/3–4; GD 170/146/10; N.L.S., Fletcher of Saltoun Papers, Ms 16725, f. 131.

the type of lobbying that Glenure and others sought. Indeed, for the manager to retain authority within Scotland entailed his ring-fencing for Scots whatever domestic patronage was available while simultaneously expanding their share of imperial employment. This explains why Dundas, just as Argyll had done previously, sought to secure and protect regiments for clients or those prominent enough to make such demands of him. He fought, for instance, to safeguard the 92nd Highlanders when threatened with disbandment in December 1796; similarly in 1809 he attempted to ensure the succession of Seaforth's son to the colonelcy of the family's erstwhile regiment, the 78th Highlanders.[44]

Military commissions arguably represented the single largest sector of imperial patronage affecting Scotland, and, for that reason, were absolutely crucial in determining how Scots saw managers like Argyll and Dundas. While most analysis of attitudes to political management north of the border has focused on the constitutional and intellectual objections of Scots, who saw in a separate manager a barrier between Scotland and a complete Union, it is clear that when concerned with reaping the benefits of military and imperial expansion outside the United Kingdom itself, they considered a recognisably Scottish minister beneficial, even vital. When such a figure did not exist, as during the 1770s, Scots gentry in particular found they lacked the political weight and, more importantly, discernible and effective channels through which to approach central government. It is possible to argue therefore that if the '45 came close to ending the principle of a Scottish manager, the unprecedented expansion of the empire ensured that many Scots felt compelled to both maintain and reinvent the office in one form or another.

The British-Highland Military and Perceptions of Clanship

That Highland regiments re-appeared within ten years of Culloden and went on to reinforce the 'semi-independent' Argathelian management system does not, however, mean that they were an inevitable or even probable government policy.[45] Indeed, the '45 threatened to end what had promised to be one of the few sectors of British patronage created after 1707 which was reserved largely for use north of the Border. Far from inspiring the belief that had developed since 1725 that Gaels ought to be concentrated within designated regiments, the uprising persuaded the British military elite that generating any focus for 'Highland interests' was to be avoided if at all possible. Thus,

44. H. Paton (ed.), *op. cit.*, vol. 5, pp. 262–3; M. Fry, *op. cit.*, p. 131; D.J. Brown, *loc. cit.*,. pp. 23, 91, 100; A.U.L., Gordon Military Papers, Ms 2284/17; S.R.O., Seaforth Muniments, GD 46/6/25/13; B.A.M., Box 45/4/70; N.L.S., Fletcher of Saltoun Papers, Ms 16690, f. 78; S.R.O., Gordon Castle Muniments, GD 44/47/15/2/43; S.R.O., Breadalbane Muniments, GD 112/52/601/13; N.L.S., Melville Papers, Ms 1054, f. 43.
45. A. Murdoch, *op. cit.*, pp. 124–5.

regiments anticipated in 1747 by the Hanoverian chiefs Kenneth Mackenzie of Seaforth and William Gordon, sixteenth Earl of Sutherland, failed to materialise, as did any hope that militias would be maintained locally to counter the banditry brought on as a result of the army's punitive policies.[46]

Yet complete demilitarisation was not as inevitable as the backlash against clanship might at first suggest. We should bear in mind regarding the Crown's *volte face* over the military use of Highlanders that the post-1746 strategy of de-militarising the clans never went so far as actually discouraging the recruitment of Gaels: indeed, the opposite was the case. Cumberland, for instance, advocated a cannon-fodder policy designed to prevent the region's ability to cause further trouble. Recruitment into the Scots-Dutch and Lord Loudon's Regiment was encouraged as one method; while battalions garrisoned in the region were ordered to enlist Jacobite prisoners or those found guilty under the Disarming Act.[47] Military service by Highlanders therefore came to be seen as acceptable only within an exclusively overseas, imperial context. During the '45 itself, it had been anticipated that an expedition to Cape Breton would mean the effective transportation of Highland companies into military exile. This idea was resurrected in 1748 when it was suggested that men from Lord Loudon's Regiment be settled in Nova Scotia, where their presence would counter that of the French Acadians.[48] Nor was the North American empire the only theatre of operations where it was felt Highlanders were best sent as cannon fodder. In 1748 six Highland companies were raised for an expedition to India. Lieutenant John Grant, son of Sir Archibald Grant of Monymusk, was ordered 'not to be scrupulous, even in listing common men who were engaged in the rebellion'.[49] It was in order to promote this use of Highlanders

---

46. B.P. Lenman, 'Scotland & Ireland 1742–1789', in J. Black (ed.), *British Politics and Society from Walpole to Pitt, 1742–1789* (London, 1990), pp. 86–87; I.H.M. Scobie, 'The Independent Companies of 1745–7', in *Journal of the Society of Army Historical Research*, vol. 20 (1941), p. 32; S.R.O., Mitchell Collection, RH. 2/5/12, p. 63; N.L.S., Mackenzie of Delvine Papers, Ms 1327, ff. 97, 135, 151, 162–3, 167; B.L., Hardwicke Papers, Add Ms 35450, ff. 171, 183, 189; B.L., Newcastle Papers, Add Ms 32715, f. 323; Ms 33049, f. 253.
47. H. Paton, (ed.), *op. cit.*, vol. 5 p. 262; B.L., Hardwicke Papers, Add Ms 35451, ff. 66, 74–5; Add Ms 35509, f. 309; N.L.S., Mackenzie of Delvine Papers, Ms 1367, f. 170; *The Glasgow Courant*, 11–18 August 1746; *The Caledonian Mercury*, 24 August 1747; *Scots Magazine*, vol. 8 (Edinburgh, 1746), p. 394.
48. *Scots Magazine*, vol. 8 (Edinburgh, 1746), pp. 137, 469; *Edinburgh Evening Courant*, 14 April 1746; N.L.S., Fletcher of Saltoun Papers, Ms 16630, f. 110; T.R. Clayton, 'The Duke of Newcastle, the Earl of Halifax and the American Origins of the Seven Years War', in *Historical Journal*, vol. 24 (1981), p. 574; B.L., Newcastle Papers, Add Ms 32713, ff. 283, 335; Add Ms 32714, f. 466; Add Ms 32717, ff. 23, 35; Lord J. Russell (ed.), *Correspondence of John, Fourth Duke of Bedford*, vol. 1 (London, 1842), pp. 563–64.
49. S.R.O., Grant of Seafield Muniments, GD 248/413, 'Journal of Lieutenant John Grant', p. 4; GD 248/49/1/17; S.R.O., Grant of Monymusk Papers, GD 345/1175/2/26–28x.

in attritional conflicts that William Wildman, Lord Barrington, made a speech which, ironically, has been misinterpreted as an example of how the army was an open and unprejudiced source of British patronage for Scots. Barrington was in fact commenting on proposals for limiting army service to a certain number of years; he opposed the measure, preferring, instead, to see enlistment for life. This, he argued, would prevent militarised Highlanders returning home. He then added: 'I am for having always in our army as many Scottish soldiers as possible . . . and of all Scottish soldiers I should choose to have and keep in our army as many Highlanders as possible'.[50]

It must stand as one of the most ironic aspects of the '45, therefore, that while it stimulated the demilitarisation of Highland society, it also intensified the large-scale recruitment of Gaels for Britain's imperial army. Yet this still does not explain why the Crown was prepared to deploy Highlanders within such distinctive, differentiated units. Here the question, or, to be more precise, the perception of clanship assumes a significance that belies the system's rapid decline in socio-economic terms. Indeed, while much attention has focused on the processes whereby Highland elites undermined and destroyed its foundations, it is equally important to realise that the perception of clanship proved more difficult to erase and that the British-Highland military was shaped in part by the existence of this discrepancy. Initially, the decay of the region's social framework was all but masked in London by the nature of post-Culloden Scottish politics. Opponents of Argyll such as Hugh Hume, third Earl of Marchmont, and James Ogilvy, Lord Findlater, for example, routinely employed rhetoric which emphasised the continuing influence of 'clannish' Highland interests. Given its synonymity with Jacobitism, such a charge was of course effective political mud slinging. Debate over Lord President Duncan Forbes of Culloden's successor in 1747 as well as the new Scottish sheriffs' conditions of tenure were all couched in these terms and had the effect of perpetuating impressions in London that the Highlands remained dominated and characterised by clanship.[51] Regardless of their inaccuracy, these assumptions ensured that when war commenced again in 1756 central government did not think to question the recruitment of Gaels in specific, customised Highland regiments. Nowhere was this belief that clanship was alive and well more apparent than in the reaction to the commissioning of Simon Fraser of Lovat. Lord Hardwicke noted simply that 'The event will certainly be the raising [of] the Jacobite clan Fraser under this young Lovat'.[52] While he disagreed absolutely that Fraser ought to be colonel, Hardwicke never doubted for a moment that Fraser could raise the men. It is ironic that within barely a decade of the battle that hastened its

50. D. Henderson, *op. cit.*, pp. 4–5; L. Colley, *op. cit.*, pp. 120 & 126.
51. H. Paton, (ed.), *op. cit.*, vol. 5, pp. 185–7, 205, 262; N.L.S., Mackenzie of Delvine Papers, Ms 1461, ff. 151 & 156; B.L., Hardwicke Papers, Add Ms 35448, ff. 5 & 30.
52. B.L., Newcastle Papers, Add Ms, 32870, f. 58; B.L., Hardwicke Papers, Add Ms 35447, f. 303.

real and ongoing demise, central government belief in clanship's continuing existence now lubricated Highland colonisation of the British fiscal-military state. The rapid establishment of Lovat and Montgomery's Regiments and, indeed, the Seven Years War in general, consolidated this metropolitan belief in clanship, generating further divergence between social realities within the region and impressions held at the political centre. Comments by Andrew Fletcher, Argyll's secretary, in March 1757 reveal how, from an English perspective, imperial recruitment confirmed old perceptions as much as generating any belief in the region's new British status: 'The extraordinary success with which the two Highland corps have been recruited gives great satisfaction to all concerned, some of the John Bulls cannot believe that such a body of men could be raised in so short a space'.[53] The tangible achievement of having mobilised over 2,000 men so quickly simply clouded the more complex reality that clanship was already a dying force within the region.

The distribution pattern of regiments during the American and French Revolutionary Wars underlines how governments continued to believe that clanship constituted an effective levying mechanism. The first new regular regiments raised in the United Kingdom during both conflicts were assigned to Highland proprietors – namely, Fraser of Lovat in 1775 and, in 1793, Mackenzie of Seaforth. A similar pattern characterised the initial seven fencible regiments of 1793, five of which were Highland.[54] In neither conflict were Lowland landlords favoured on anywhere near the same scale, especially in proportion to the populations they commanded. After the British defeat at Saratoga in mid-October 1777, for example, which transformed the military situation in America by hastening the likelihood of a Franco-American alliance, the army raised eleven new replacement regiments totalling 12,000 men. Six of these were officially recognised as Highland, while urban Scotland raised only two regiments. The distorting effect of the government's ongoing belief in clanship meant that while the essentially middle-ranking Macdonalds of Sleat were offered a regiment without having asked for one, two of Scotland's premier aristocratic families – Marchmont and Queensberry – were refused battalions in December 1777.[55] Furthermore, an acceptance that clanship's militarism was grounded in a strong sense of local association and kinship ensured successive London administrations were prepared to adopt specific forms of recruitment that catered to

53. N.L.S., Fletcher of Saltoun Papers, Ms 16519, f. 71.
54. B.L., Liverpool Papers, Add Ms 38342, f. 99; S.R.O., Kennedy of Dalquharran Papers, GD 27/6/34/1; *Scots Magazine*, vol. 60 (Edinburgh, 1793), p. 152; J.W. Fortescue, *A History of the British Army*, vol. 4 (London, 1902), p. 83.
55. E. Robson, 'The Raising of a Regiment in the American War of Independence', in *Journal of the Society of Army Historical Research*, vol. 27 (1949), pp. 107–9; *Parliamentary History*, vol. 19 (London, 1814), pp. 687–90; J.W. Fortescue (ed.), *The Correspondence of King George III*, vol. 3 (London, 1928), pp. 521 & 531.

and sought maximum results from these characteristics. Highland landlords therefore found it relatively easier than other elites within Britain and Ireland to obtain command of battalions, as opposed to smaller, less lucrative independent companies. The latter form of military unit carried only limited potential in terms of commissions and did not guarantee prolonged service, even for the period of any given conflict. Just how crucial perceptions of clanship could be in securing favourable conditions of state service can be seen from arguments used by Lord Barrington when, in 1778, he was asked in the Commons why regiments had been authorised for Scotland but largely refused to those Irish and Welsh gentry who had offered to raise men. Barrington pointed out that 'from old habits in Scotland, corps may be the best method in that part of the Kingdom, that does not in the least hold true for Ireland. Nobody in Ireland has any clan or following, the reasons given for raising Highlanders in *corps* does not in the least degree apply'.[56]

During the 1790s, however, social conditions in the Highlands finally ensured that a serious gulf emerged between the government's expectations and the region's capacity to supply men. Nowhere was this more apparent than in Henry Dundas's sponsorship of a scheme that amounted, in effect, to an official attempt to resurrect clanship as a viable military force. In support of the scheme it was argued that 'much good in place of mischief may on various occasions rise from such a connection'.[57] The idea was that 16,500 men would be raised under the auspices of their 'clan chiefs' and deployed within the United Kingdom or Ireland as an alternative to fencible regiments. Given its wholly unrealistic character and the negative landlord reaction to it, the scheme has failed to attract much scholarly attention. Yet despite its naive and uninformed nature, the 1797 scheme should not be instantly dismissed: it is in fact worthy of examination in several respects. First, by highlighting the government's ignorance of how Highland society had developed since 1746, it reveals how Westminster had constructed a regionally distinct recruiting policy upon a premise that was increasingly at odds with clanship's actual extinction on the ground. Second, by quickly rejecting the proposals, landlords were admitting openly for the first time that clanship no longer existed in a meaningful sense. The events of 1797 thus represented, from London's perspective, the first high-profile failure of the Highlands in terms of recruitment, bringing home forcefully the realisation that the area could no longer supply men on a scale that justified an especially adapted recruiting policy.[58]

This emphasis on clanship's recruiting potential, however misinformed,

---

56. *Parliamentary History*, vol. 19 (London, 1814), pp. 634, 686–7; J. Fortescue (ed.), *The Correspondence of King George III*, vol. 4, pp. 34–5.
57. S.R.O., Seaforth Muniments, GD 46/6/34 & 35.
58. *Sixth Report of the Royal Commission on Historical Manuscripts* (London, 1877), p. 620; S.R.O., Macpherson of Cluny, GD 80/938/3; B.A.M., Box 59/4/18, 98; N.L.S., Melville Papers, Ms 14838, f. 182; N.L.S. Melville Papers, Ms 6, f. 157; Ms 1048, f. 3; B.A.M., Bundle 353, manuscript on 1797 plan.

poses questions with respect to the army's relationship with the region. First, political rehabilitation of Jacobites has been assigned as one of the underlying reasons for heavy Highland recruitment in the Seven Years War and American conflict, in particular. This however presupposes that Highland gentry could not atone for previous misdemeanours unless serving in Highland regiments. In light of the fact that Scots-Dutch officers had been allowed to transfer into British army service from 1755, it could be argued that the Brigade provided an effective means of demonstrating loyalty even prior to the emergence of Lovat's battalion in 1757.[59] Albeit that Mackenzie of Cromartie and Fraser of Lovat did obtain regiments during the American Revolutionary War in order to advertise their loyalty the majority of Highland units actually went to families with little or no need to rehabilitate themselves. Indeed, in 1777 John Murray, fourth Lord Dunmore, who had been a page-in-waiting to Charles Edward Stuart, and therefore an ideal candidate for such rehabilitation, was refused a regiment despite offering to raise 4,000 men. Instead, the Crown requested assistance from those whom it considered to have retained the largest reserves of population and local clan influence – namely, Breadalbane, Gordon, Seaforth, Macdonald of Sleat, Sutherland, Atholl and Argyll – the majority of whom had been Hanoverian in 1745.[60] Ultimately, what clinched Highland regiments was the retention of what London perceived as 'clan' power, not a track record of political disaffection. Second, because governments framed their decisions in such terms, who obtained regiments was not always a matter of Highland landlords pressurising a reluctant political centre for patronage. Pressure also emanated out from the centre into the region. Administrations often in fact had very definite ideas on those best qualified to receive patronage, which resulted in certain proprietors facing implicit government pressure to raise men without having actually lobbied for a regiment. This was the case with the fourth Duke of Atholl, the third Earl of Breadalbane and Sir Alexander Macdonald of Sleat in 1778; and with Seaforth, Gordon, Sir John Sinclair and Cameron of Locheil in the mid-1790s.[61]

Although clanship dominated external, governmental and metropolitan perceptions of the region, that should not be taken to mean that the internal, Highland dynamic for involvement within the army was similarly based upon the survival of traditional clannish militarism. Table 2 shows the substantial, if intermittent, growth in the number of officers from Highland

59. B.P. Lenman, *Jacobite Clans of the Great Glen, 1650–1784*, pp. 206–9; N.L.S., Fletcher of Saltoun Papers, Ms 16693, f. 127; D.H., Loudon Papers, A/972, f. 6; A/966, letter, 11 December 1755.
60. J.W. Fortescue (ed.), *The Correspondence of King George III*, vol. 3, p. 515.
61. J. Prebble, *op. cit.*, pp. 20, 493–5; C.D.T.L., GD 221/5516/1; S.R.O., Macgregor Collection, GD 50/11/1/77; N.L.S., Mackenzie of Delvine Papers, Ms 1239, f. 264; S.R.O., Gordon Castle Muniments, GD 44/43/94/16; GD 44/47/13/2–3 J. Fortescue (ed.), *The Correspondence of King George III*, vol. 3, p. 516; H.M.C., *Laing Manuscripts*, vol. 2 (London, 1925), p. 657.

regiments, and reveals that the nature of the region's militarism had changed dramatically from the era of clanship and was now grounded on the reality of state and imperial service.

Table 2. Officers and Half-Pay Officers
of Highland Regiments, 1740–1784[62]

Year	Total army officers	Officers of Highland Regts	%	British Half-Pay	Highland Half-Pay	%
1740	2,080	27	1.2	–	–	–
1762	4,449	401	9	300*	26	8.6
1765	2,773	26	0.9	2,453	300	12.2
1770	2,326	28	1.2	2,164	256	11.8
1774	2,912	26	0.8	1,945	218	11.2
1780	4,765	444	9.3	1,491	145	9.7
1784	3,336	97	2.9	2,626	278	10.5

The exact interaction between this not inconsiderable 'military interest group' and clanship is in need of careful clarification. Anxious to develop or, in some cases, to resurrect their careers, this elite often proved vociferous and vocal in their appeals to the centre for employment. From 1768 to 1770, for example, and again from 1775 to 1779, Lord John Murray, Colonel of the 42nd Highland Regiment, lobbied hard for a second battalion. In order to justify his proposals Murray pointed to the existence of over 105 Highland half-pay officers – enough to staff three entire battalions. A similar situation developed at the commencement of the American Revolutionary War when officers in both Scotland and the colonies such as Captain Ranald Mac-Donnell of Keppoch, Alexander Robertson of Straloch and Lieutenant Daniel Shaw, all of whom had served in the conflict of 1756–63, presented offers of men.[63] Such lobbying inevitably served to remind the military establishment of the region's recruiting potential and explains why, in June 1775, Thomas Gage, Commander-in-Chief in North America, felt that his request for reinforcements in the shape of 5000 Highlanders was not unwarranted.[64] More specifically, either intentionally or otherwise, such

62. M.L., British Army Lists, 1740–1784. *The figure of 300 for 1762 does not include the Irish half-pay establishment, which in that year stood at approximately 100. Thereafter, Irish establishment is included. Figures only include Highland officers in officially designated Highland regiments and assume a roughly equal death rate amongst the officers.
63. J.R.L., Bagshawe Muniments, B. 5/1, pp. 100, 119, 141–49, 172, 184, 197, 265 & 275; S.R.O., Campbell of Barcaldine, GD 170/1140/2/1; P.R.O., C.O. 5/115, ff. 51 & 72; P.R.O., W.O. 1/993, letters 10 October 1775 & 30 January 1776; W.O. 1/996, letter 5 February 1776; W.O. 1/993, letter 21 February 1776; W.O. 1/995, f. 813; P.R.O., W.O. 1/995, f. 567; W.O. 1/997, letters 30 November 1777 and 5 January 1778; W.O. 1/993, letter 20 January 1776; S.R.O., Robertson of Straloch Papers, GD 1/90/8, 12a, 16.
64. J. Fortescue (ed.), *The Correspondence of King George III*, vol. 3, pp. 175–6

petitioning tended to confirm the outdated, clan-based thinking of government, which saw in such offers of regiments and men concrete proof of the region's continuing bellicosity. It was of course in the material and financial interests of such officers to emphasise and, if necessary, exaggerate the military capacity of the region: one obvious method was to appeal to the centre's preconceived ideas about clanship. For example, those lobbying for regiments often highlighted, without authorisation or clarification, the recruiting potential of larger landlords. Thus Lord Dunmore mentioned the estates of the Duke of Gordon and Macdonald lairds such as Lochgarry in his petition to the War Office. Likewise, in March 1777 and again in 1780, Lord John Murray told the King he could obtain men from Sir Robert Menzies and the estate of Macdonald of Clanranald: the tutors of the latter, in particular, were upset at this lack of consultation. Murray also informed the administration of manpower reserves on the Atholl and Gordon estates, which left London with the impression that those proprietors were willing and able to raise men. Consultation had, in fact, been minimal, and advisers to Atholl felt that Murray had taken advantage of pressure on elites to demonstrate and confirm their patriotic credentials.[65] In a sense the region's military elite now served much the same function as Scottish politics had performed during the period between Culloden and 1756; that is, both masked the decay of clanship. Thus, as a result of concerns over broader imperial issues, successive London governments failed to comprehend that much of what they understood as ongoing clannish militarism was in fact practical evidence of the Highlands' emergence as a region specialising in and to some extent now dependent upon imperial-military service.

There is little doubt that both Highland grandees and lesser gentry deliberately manipulated perceptions of clanship to obtain patronage and facilitate their entry into state employment. In November 1775, Simon Fraser of Lovat, defending his own 71st Highland Regiment, noted that the rapid creation of such units was possible only if they were staffed with chiefs-cum-officers such as Charles Cameron of Locheil or Norman Macleod of Dunvegan. In effect, Fraser was arguing that 'clan chiefs', through their command of military populations, were entitled to preferential state patronage. In 1778 Lord Macleod of Cromartie informed Lord North that it was vital that tenantry from the estates of the Chisholm and Macleod family be accessed by granting the rank of major to their lairds. Likewise, when, in the same year, Seaforth claimed that 4,000 men had been enlisted purely through his kin connections, he underlined the belief that disproportionate patronage for Highland elites was justified on the grounds that it provided a British tap into clannish localism. The often substantial material benefits derived from this attitude towards clanship are clearly evident in the case of Norman

65. J. Fortescue (ed.), *The Correspondence of King George III*, vol. 3, p. 515; B.A.M., Box 65/1/147, 161–2; Box 65/2/1–2; J.R.L., Bagshawe Muniments, B. 5/1. pp. 119 & 389.

Macleod. By repeatedly agreeing to higher commissions in return for men, the state ended up promoting Macleod to the rank of lieutenant-colonel by 1779, a mere four years after he first entered the army. The extent to which Highland lairds proved successful in trading their estate populations for state offices was sufficiently conspicuous to draw comment from King George III himself. After the 1778 mobilisations he remarked: 'I shall say nothing in regard to complaints that may arise from the English officers as to the great promotion among the Scotch occasioned by the new Highland levies'.[66] Similarly, in 1793, at a time when Frederick, Duke of York was determined to avoid granting any new regular regiments, clan rhetoric was again deployed to facilitate Mackenzie of Seaforth's acquisition of a battalion. Dundas related how he had finally won Pitt's agreement: 'my motives for proposing Seaforth as the Commandant were *first* that *his* being in that situation would be popular with the clan'. For local elites, therefore, it was crucial that the central authorities maintained a belief in clanship. Lord Alexander Macdonald of Sleat conceded that the ability of major landlords to acquire regiments was vital, given that 'young people in that part of the world have not the same occasional advantages of recommendation or the same means to acquire commissions as their southern neighbours enjoy'.[67] In effect, as Highland elites destroyed clanship's socio-economic basis within the region, it nonetheless remained in their interest to disguise the fact given that it had emerged as a means of obtaining preferential treatment from the state. This points to an alternative interpretation of clanship for the period between its demise as a form of social organisation and its later reinvention by Scotland's anglicised elite as a distinct, though non-threatening, form of cultural expression. Studies of the British state in the eighteenth century have revealed how its previously underestimated fiscal and military strength ensured the development of interest groups who lobbied and 'colonised' the state to obtain its protection or benefit. Clanship, even as it expired as a social reality, emerged in a new and crucial role as the Highlands' own distinctive and very effective lobbying mechanism.[68]

State Recruiting and the End of Proprietary Regiments, 1765–1815

The scale of the Highlands' contribution to the army shows how effectively the rhetoric of clanship secured military patronage for the region's elite. Table 2 reveals the militarisation of Highland society and the eventual, if intermittent, institutionalisation of the British-Highland military as part of

66. J. Almon (ed.), *The Parliamentary Register*, vol. 3 (London, 1776), pp. 206–7; S.R.O., Seafield Muniments, GD 248/52/2/67; N.L.S., Stuart-Stevenson Papers, Ms 8250, f. 26; J.R.L., Bagshawe Muniments, B. 5/1, p. 286; J. Fortescue (ed.), *Correspondence of King George III*, vol. 3, pp. 523–4; vol. 4, pp. 11–12.
67. S.R.O., Seaforth Muniments, GD 46/6/25/2, 4, 6, 8–9, 13.
68. J. Brewer, *The Sinews of Power: War, Money and the English State, 1688–1783* (London, 1989), pp. xvii, 22, 40, 104–105.

Imperial Specialisation

the standing army. One of the primary effects of the American Revolutionary War, therefore, was that it perpetuated conceptions of the region's militarism and helped determine recruiting policy when hostilities recommenced again in 1793. During that particular conflict thirty separate levies were raised under the denomination of Highland units. Recent estimates for the Revolutionary and Napoleonic period suggest that in spite of an increase from around 3,300 in 1790 to approximately 15,000 full- and half-pay British army officers by 1814, the ratio of Scots kept pace at around 25% of all those commissioned. Of course many regiments were Highland in name only, and attention has been quite correctly drawn to the substantial military contribution of Lowland and urban Scotland. Yet in seeking to redress an undoubted over-emphasis on the northern region's military capacity, it should be recognised that, in proportion to its own relatively small percentage of the country's total population, the Highlands was still in all likelihood the most intensely recruited part of Scotland at the turn of the century. Statistical information available to contemporaries (see Appendix 1) suggested that six out of Scotland's ten most heavily recruited parishes were Highland: this could only have reinforced impressions that the region remained a disproportionately important element within the national military structure.[69]

However, this does not mean that the British-Highland military was based on a secure, deep-rooted and unchanging relationship between the metropolitan authorities and Highland elites. Stagnation and a lack of new regiments were as apparent as conspicuous expansion. The periods between 1763–75 and 1783–93, in particular, pose questions as to the structure of the recruiting regime in the Highlands. Table 2 suggests that, rather than being continual, large-scale military recruiting was in fact episodic.

Given their crucial impact upon the region's development in this period, it is surprising how much organisational trends and, indeed, the structure of the British army in general, have been neglected by Scottish historians. Increasing Highland involvement in Britain's military machine took place against a backdrop of transition and evolution. The last half of the eighteenth century witnessed the army move away from reliance on *ancien régime* methods of recruitment, and increasingly experiment with various *ad hoc* forms of enlistment before, finally, the French and Napoleonic wars brought into existence a largely professionalised and centrally controlled army of unprecedented size.[70] The army's excessive use of Highland manpower was one such form of *ad hoc* experimentation and arose from peculiarities within the structure of Britain's military establishment. While the country's overall commitment to its armed forces matched and, indeed, surpassed that of most other European powers, Britain, for obvious reasons, put a degree of

---

69. J.E. Cookson, *The British Armed Nation, 1793–1815* (Oxford, 1997), pp. 126–9.
70. J.E. Cookson, *op.cit.*, pp. 16–19.

emphasis on naval strength that left the army with some unique problems in comparison to its continental counterparts. Unburdened with the naval priorities and constitutional niceties that curtailed the peacetime maintenance of British armies at their full, wartime strength, European standing armies tended, especially during periods of peace, to dwarf their British equivalent. Compared with Britain's 45,000-strong peacetime army after 1763, for example, Austria maintained a force of between 110,000 and 150,000 men.[71]

Starting from a much smaller base, Britain faced a problem in the initial, opening years of a conflict of bringing her army up to strength. Crucially, this problem of rapid mobilisation grew as Britain's international status changed. While her national interests were identified primarily with naval defence, secure trade routes, or the European balance of power, and allies such as the Austrians provided most of the necessary manpower, Britain's ability to create a large army was less of an immediate problem. However, once she began to acquire large swathes of territory in North America and India, the issue of maintaining a standing army became more and more pressing. The solution lay in developing alternative reservoirs of men that could be used to compensate the lack of initial strength. This explains Britain's reliance on the prefabricated armies of German mercenaries that were so prominent during the wars of 1756–63 and 1775–1783. Regiments from the Duchy of Wurttemberg and no fewer than 19,000 Hessians were deployed against the Americans in 1775–6. The Irish establishment of 12–15,000 men can be viewed in much the same light, and represented a more systematic British attempt at maintaining a flexible army of reserve over and above its own official, peacetime standing forces.[72]

However, both these avenues proved to have major limitations. Diplomatic isolation prevented Britain from acquiring the 20,000 Russian mercenaries she had intended using in 1775 to smother the American rebellion before it gained momentum. Although German troops were eventually deployed in some numbers, both Frederick of Prussia and the Holy Roman Emperor, Joseph II, limited British recruitment of men from their territories. Furthermore, the agreements which governed the use of such mercenaries tended to limit their flexibility; thus, as the war in America drew to a close it was discovered that, as a result of treaty stipulations, German troops could not be deployed in India where men were urgently required.[73] Likewise,

71. J. Brewer, *op.cit.*, pp. 31–42; P.G.M. Dickson, *Finance and Government under Maria Theresa, 1740–1780: Finance and Credit*, vol. 2 (Oxford, 1987), pp. 10–19.
72. P.H. Wilson, *War, State and Society in Würtemberg, 1677–1793* (Cambridge, 1995), pp. 75–6, 85, 238; C.W. Ingrao, *The Hessian Mercenary State: Ideas, Institutions, and Reform under Frederick II, 1760–1785* (Cambridge, 1987), pp. 2–3; K.P. Ferguson, The Army in Ireland from the Restoration to the Act of Union (Trinity College, Dublin Ph.D., 1980), pp. 60–2, 99–100.

Ireland, although undoubtedly an increasingly important sector of Britain's imperial-military establishment, was not without problems. In 1758 the Irish Commons petitioned against British over-recruitment in light of the damage being sustained by the country's linen and agricultural sectors. At the height of the American Revolutionary War, in order to ease political pressure from the Dublin Parliament for free trade with the empire, it was agreed to limit the extent to which regiments not on the Irish establishment could beat for recruits within Ireland. Conversely, a strategy of granting trade rights for additional military contributions was rejected by Dublin in 1785. Furthermore, attempts in 1778 to utilise Catholic manpower ran into severe and sustained opposition.[74] Above all, the Protestant interest were determined that the Irish establishment should be maintained in the role for which they believed it had been instituted. The 12,000 men bankrolled by the Irish Parliament were seen as a defence force that guaranteed Protestant security. This explains why Dublin was reluctant to allow battalions from its establishment to serve elsewhere within the empire. In 1763, 1765 and 1768 proposals for an augmentation from 12,000 to 15,000 men failed when London refused to give assurances that the additional troops would not leave Ireland in the event of an emergency elsewhere. Eventually, the Lord Lieutenant, George Townshend, fourth Viscount Townshend, managed to secure the increase; but Irish sensitivities to the loss of men for imperial purposes resurfaced in 1775 when Dublin, fearing the establishment of a dangerous precedent, refused to accept Hessian mercenaries as replacements for regiments sent to America. The 15,000-strong military establishment created in 1770 was certainly an impressive resource; yet only 4,000 were technically available for overseas service at any given time. Although the establishment increased during each conflict, a large proportion of its forces nevertheless remained in Ireland. Only 8,000 out of a total of 24,000 men were serving abroad in 1761: during the American Revolutionary War, despite considerable success at deploying troops in other theatres, over 8,500 men – 55% of the establishment – still remained in Ireland. Overall, the tendency for the Irish Parliament to link Britain's use of its regiments to concessions in other contentious areas of imperial policy, as well as the overriding priority given to internal defence, meant that military

73. H.M. Scott, *British Foreign Policy in the Age of the American Revolution* (Oxford, 1990), pp. 217–18, 266, n 64; J. Fortescue (ed.), *The Correspondence of King George III*, vol. 3, p. 407; W.B. Donne (ed.), *The Correspondence of King George III with Lord North from 1768–1783*, vol. 2 (London, 1867), pp. 99–100; P.R.O., Chatham Papers, P.R.O., 30/8/240, ff. 3–9 'Memorial regarding army, 1781–2'.
74. *Scots Magazine*, vol. 20 (Edinburgh, 1758), p. 40; P.R.O., W.O. 4/103, p. 408; P.R.O., W.O. 4/101, p. 396; W.O. 4/102, p. 8; S.R.O., Campbell of Barcaldine Papers, GD 170/1140/2/1; GD 170/1090/33, 36, 38, 42; GD 170/1380/2; GD 170/1067/11; R.K. Donovan, 'The Military Origins of the Roman Catholic Relief Programme of 1778', in *Historical Journal*, vol. 28 (1985), pp. 83–85, 94–5.

arrangements with Ireland by no means represented a wholly efficient or flexible army of reserve.[75]

It is against these structural weaknesses within Britain's military machine that the reliance on Highland troops must be seen. The cycles of sudden expansion and demobilisation shown in Table 2 as well as the distribution pattern of Highland regiments, appearing as they did at the commencement of particular conflicts, support the argument that the region had come to be envisaged as a kind of unofficial, *ad hoc* military reserve. In late 1756, once he had abandoned further British deployment of Hessian mercenaries, Pitt approved the new 77th and 78th Highland battalions. Similarly, in the first, crucial year of the American Revolutionary War the failure to secure enough foreign mercenaries, when coupled with Ireland's supply of only 3,243 additional men, meant the military felt obliged to turn to the Highlands or, more specifically, Fraser of Lovat who raised 2,000 men by April 1776. The region's utility was obvious in one other particular: once any given imperial crisis was over, be it in 1763 or 1783, Highland regiments, much like the German mercenaries, could be demobilised in large numbers (see Table 2), leaving their pensioned officer corp as the means of initiating any future recruiting drives. In one sense, the later eighteenth-century Highlands, unburdened with the problems of internal security that absorbed a relatively large proportion of Ireland's manpower, could be said to have been Britain's imperial-military reserve *par excellence*, all the more effective as a result of its inherent flexibility. Certainly, it is ironic that Highland regiments, so often seen as proof of Gaeldom's final integration into the United Kingdom, were in fact evidence that the region's population had come to be seen as the nearest domestic, British mainland equivalent of Irish infantry or German and Russian mercenaries.[76]

That the army's use of Highland landlords to supply men can be characterised to some extent as an expedient, emergency measure meant, however, that the long-term stability and future of the region's recruiting industry was never on a

---

75. *Caledonian Mercury*, 12 June 1775, p. 2; 6 Sept. 1775, p. 2; N.L.S., *Edinburgh Advertiser*, 8 Aug. 1775, p. 83; R.B. Macdowell, 'Colonial Nationalism and the Winning of Parliamentary Independence, 1760–82', in J.W. Moody & W.E. Vaughan (eds.), *A New History of Ireland: Eighteenth-Century Ireland, 1691–1800*, vol. 4 (Oxford, 1986), pp. 199–200, 204–7; J. O'Donovan, 'The Militia in Munster, 1715–78', in G. O'Brien (ed.), *Parliament, Politics and People: Essays in Eighteenth Century Irish History* (Dublin, 1989), pp. 40, 43; T. Beckett, 'The Augmentation of the Army in Ireland, 1767–69', in *English Historical Review*, vol. 96 (1981), pp. 541–2, 550 & 558; A.J. Guy, 'The Irish Military Establishment, 1660–1776', in T. Bartlett & K. Jeffery (eds.), *A Military History of Ireland* (Cambridge, 1996), p. 216.
76. P.R.O, SP 41/27, 'Recruits Raised in Ireland, 29 September 1774–29 September 1777'; W.B. Donne, (ed.), *The Correspondence of King George III with Lord North from 1768–83*, vol. 1 (London, 1867), pp. 274–6; J. Dalrymple, *Letters from Sir John Dalrymple to the Right Honourable Lord Viscount Barrington* (London, 1779), pp 2–4.

particularly secure footing. As the army developed its new professional ethos, such stopgap measures appeared inefficient, costly and undesirable. In this respect it is worth noting the role of the Hanoverian monarchs. Through their influence the Highlands came to be part of the military resources of an army high command steeped in German concepts of militarism. At one level this resulted in an infusion of ideas from the Continent which put particular stress on the suitability of those from mountainous areas for military service.[77] This undoubtedly helps explain the disproportionate emphasis put on the region's military capacity. Moreover, all three of the eighteenth-century monarchs, as well as Frederick, Duke of York, Commander-in-Chief during the 1790s, actively promoted the latest ideas on the development and organisation of armies arising from the fact that across western Europe nation-states had established increasingly firm control over their military machines. Crucially, this involved the promotion of certain forms of recruitment above others. The trend within the British army as elsewhere was the development of an extremely loyal and professionalised military officer class – paid for and maintained from state revenue. The whole process was somewhat inconsistently enforced, and often met with serious setbacks and difficulties – most notably whenever armies needed to expand rapidly under wartime conditions. Nonetheless, to encourage this new professionalism a coherent promotion structure was preferred amongst most military executives: by this means, loyalty and long service brought the prospect of regulated and imminent promotion.[78]

All of this had important implications for the Highlands. Emphasis was increasingly put on officers established within the army's ranks. The objective was to build up expertise in long-established regiments, with their officers and veterans recruiting new soldiers as the necessity arose. The alternative method to this form of recruitment lay in new battalions, which involved the use of local connections and interest to raise men. Referred to as 'proprietary recruiting' or 'recruiting for rank', this method was indicative of a lack of direct state authority in localities. Mobilised in the north of Scotland by the large landlords, and in the Lowlands and England by urban cooperatives, these new regiments invariably raised men quicker than older, established units. Figures from Britain's partial mobilisation of 1790 reveal the extent to which new units outperformed veteran regiments. In one month new independent companies raised 5,700 men, while older units brought in only 2,400. In the case of new levies this was accomplished by tapping

77. C. Duffy, *The Army of Frederick the Great* (London, 1974) p. 54; A. Allardyce, *Scotland and Scotsmen in the Eighteenth Century*, vol. 1 (Edinburgh, 1888), p. 335.
78. T. M. Barker, *Army, Aristocracy, Monarchy: Essays on War, Society, and Government in Austria, 1618–1780* (New York, 1982), pp. 129–44; C. Jones, 'The Military Revolution and the Professionalisation of the French army under the Ancien Regime', in M. Duffy (ed.), *The Military Revolution and the State* (London, 1980), pp. 37–45; J. Shy, *Towards Lexington: The Role of the British Army in the Coming of the American Revolution* (Princeton, 1965), pp. 364–69.

reservoirs of manpower that professional officers, through their lack of an immediate legal or economic lever, could not rival. However, this entailed the appointment of junior or new officers to higher rank in return for their quotas of men. Officers were thus appointed on the basis of their access to suitable manpower – which was what made this particular method so attractive to Highland elites – and not on the basis of their military record. Essentially, it was a form of military entrepreneurship in which the costs of recruiting were offset by increased access to state allowances and senior, more lucrative commissions. Significantly, it was this particular practice that proved the most appropriate and successful in the Highlands. Yet within the military high command such a system was seen as distorting the promotion structure and discouraging the established officer cadre.[79]

The particular recruiting tactic that gave rise to the Highland regiments, therefore, was far from being a preferable option and ran contrary to trends increasingly evident within most of the military machines of western Europe. Despite the best attempts of senior figures in the British-Highland military like Fraser of Lovat to assert otherwise, one major objection to new regiments was that they were a particularly expensive method of recruitment. In 1775, faced with accusations of favouritism upon receiving command of two new battalions, Lovat argued: 'This mode of raising men, would be a public saving of two fifths of the levy money; for the two battalions would not be more than £3 or 3 guineas a man, while that of the other regiments is £5 or 5 guineas a man'. In reality the opposite was the case, especially given that such regiments brought with them additional costs in the form of pay and pensions for their new officers. In 1790 it was calculated that recruits raised by older regiments cost 5 guineas while those acquired by new units, after adding the burden of additional commissions, cost anything from £10.9.9 to £12.15.11. Similar arithmetic applies to Highland regiments. In 1769, 3,000 additional men raised in Ireland by established regiments cost £36,000 – £12 a man; yet in 1775 Fraser's 2,000 men cost £47,000 – over £23 a man.[80]

New battalions, with Highland contingents featuring prominently amongst them, were thus unpopular on grounds of professional morale and financial prudence. In August 1775, King George III, a strong proponent of professionalism, noted regarding pressure to institute new regiments: 'I shall never agree to disobliging the whole army by giving them to every young man that pretends he can soon complete them'.[81] Such hostility makes

---

79. P.R.O., Chatham Papers, P.R.O., 30/8/242, ff. 123–25; A.N. Gilbert, 'Military Recruitment and Career Advancement in the Eighteenth Century', in *Journal of the Society of Army Historical Research*, vol. 57 (1979), pp. 39–40; P. Stigger, 'Recruiting for Rank in 1764, 1804 & 1857', in *Journal of the Society of Army Historical Research*, vol. 70 (1992), p. 239.
80. J. Almon (ed.), *The Parliamentary Register*, vol. 3, pp. 206–7; P.R.O., Chatham Papers, P.R.O., 30/8/242, ff. 123–25.
81. W.B. Donne (ed.), *The Correspondence of King George III with Lord North from 1768–1783*, vol. 1 (London, 1867), p. 265.

the King's acceptance of Fraser's new battalions all the more significant, and underlines how the metropolitan perception of clanship's distinct military potential led to tangible favouritism within official military policy. In mid-January 1778, when again faced with a shortage of recruits, the King reiterated his opposition to new levies, believing they destroyed the ability of veteran regiments to refill their ranks. However, in a telling qualification he added that this was particularly the case in England, suggesting he felt social conditions north of the border made resorting to new levies relatively more acceptable. The American Revolutionary War represented a period when the forces of professional and proprietorial recruiting were finely balanced. Despite an obvious preference amongst Britain's senior military for exclusively professional methods, the army as yet lacked the mechanisms of conscription or annual quotas from militia forces to maintain a steady, replenishing supply of men, and so was forced to rely to some extent on the economic and social power of local interests such as Highland landlords. Nonetheless, attempts were made to prevent excessive promotion simply as a result of an ability to recruit large numbers of men. In early 1778 the King was determined that Highland officers with only three years' experience would not be commissioned as majors, adding that a senior minister was 'very much mistaken when he thinks all officers recommended by the Gentlemen raising Scotch corps will be accepted'.[82]

Symptomatic of the Crown's determination to avoid, where possible, the irregular promotion of personnel simply as a consequence of their recruiting ability was the emphasis placed on returning half-pay officers to full-time service. These men were the commissioned personnel of regiments disbanded at the end of each of the major eighteenth-century conflicts, and who, as their designation suggests, had become entitled to an annual pension equivalent to half their pay. The cost of the British half-pay establishment which, by 1785, totalled £201,000 per annum, was one reason why policy was directed towards their re-entry into service; another was of course to ensure the use of as many experienced officers as possible. Provision for the resumption of their careers was, however, rather limited in one crucial respect: those choosing to return to a full-time career could only do so at the rank they had held when demobilised.[83] This rigid adherence to regularised promotion simply cast into greater relief the ability of entrepreneurial recruiters to bypass experienced officers, which only served to generate further hostility toward the principle of recruiting for rank. Although during the American Revolutionary War those undertaking to raise new regiments continued to nominate half-pay officers for re-entry into the army at a higher rank, attitudes had hardened by the commencement of war with France in

82. J. Fortescue (ed.), *The Correspondence of King George III*, vol. 4, pp. 12 & 18.
83. P.R.O., W.O. 123/113, p. 100; W.O. 123/115; A Bruce, *The Purchase System in the British Army* (London, 1980), pp. 22–6, 33–5; J. Shy, loc. cit., p. 79. For annual half-pay, see *Parliamentary History*, vols. 13–15 & 19 (London, 1813–4); *Journal of the House of Commons*, vols. 37–8 & 40 (London, 1803).

1793. Those obtaining new regiments found Frederick, Duke of York, and the army high command were determined that vacancies, especially field-officer commissions (the rank of major and above), should be given to experienced officers in preference to their own candidates. Whereas in the 1775–83 war the average of half-pay officers appointed to the 71st, 73rd 74th and 76th Highland Regiments was only one in fourteen, regulations relating to the professional background of prospective officers meant that, after 1793, the average in Highland units was proportionately much higher. In the case of the Breadalbane Fencibles half-pay personnel totalled over one in four of its entire officer corp by late 1794; while in the Grant Fencibles the ratio was over one officer in three.[84] This fundamentally undermined the process of entrepreneurial recruiting by removing any significant element of motivation. In 1779 Lord John Murray noted that 'Officers, or others who get a step by their commissions will give any money besides what is allowed [by government bounties] to secure it, which cannot be expected from officers from half pay returned to the same rank, or officers of a regiment who have no advantage by it'.[85] Seaforth was informed in 1793 that only men from the half-pay list could be made officers in his regiment – otherwise it would be considered something of a 'job'. Mackenzie was deeply unhappy with this rule, noting that there was now little incentive for his officers as they could only retain the rank they presently held. The same rules also applied in the case of Major Allan Cameron of Erracht, who was denied the rank of Lieutenant-Colonel.[86] Even more crucially, by limiting the ability of large landlords to initiate the military careers of their clients, such recruiting regulations had a seriously detrimental effect upon one of the main employment sectors for the region's lower gentry. Even where a single step in promotion was allowed, as with Lieutenant Patrick Macleod of Geanies, appointed Captain in the second battalion of the 78th Seaforth Highlanders in February 1794, the Crown's determination that recruiting for rank be made as efficient as possible resulted in conditions of service that were all but prohibitive. Expressing his objections to the fact that no bounty was to be given, Macleod's father reveals how the curtailment of entrepreneurial recruiting was seen by Highland gentry as especially unfortunate in that it denied them a traditional means of low-cost social advancement:

> To have this a Ross-shire regiment you would have not found it easy to name officers who could accept of commissions on your terms as I

84. *London Gazette*, 11 May 1776; 24 March 1778; 2–20 June 1778; Marchioness of Tullibardine, *A Military History of Perthshire* (Perth, 1908), pp. 151–66; S.R.O. Seafield Muniments, GD 248/464/Recruiting Lists.
85. S.R.O., Campbell of Barcaldine Papers, GD 170/391/1(b); P.R.O., W.O. 1/991, f. 304; W.O. 1/993, letter, 21 February 1776; W.O. 1/995, f. 829; W.O. 1/996, letter, 19 November 1776; W.O. 1/997, f. 6; W.O. 1/1002, letter, 2 January 1779.
86. S.R.O., Seaforth Muniments, GD 46/6/25/6; M. McLean, *The Raising of the 79th Highlanders* (Inverness, 1980), pp. 6–7.

interpret them; in England where men of great family and interest will sacrifice anything for rank, merely as a laddie to climb to the top of their profession, you can have little difficulty. But the case must differ widely with the younger son of a little Scots laird.[87]

The last two regular Scottish units of the French wars raised on the principle of men for rank were commissioned in 1804. They were both Highland levies in that they were 2nd battalions of the 78th and 79th Highland Regiments; yet they differed from the earlier proprietary units in that they were raised almost exclusively on professional principles, with the majority of their officers, ensigns excepted, coming from within the army. This marked the final victory of professionalisation, though recruiting for rank was resurrected later in the century.[88]

Although the methods of proprietary recruiting that found so much favour within the region had been increasingly attacked since the American Revolutionary War, if not before, the real reason why the system could not survive was simply the altogether unprecedented scale of the French Revolutionary and Napoleonic Wars. Recent studies have emphasised the fundamental changes this forced upon British recruiting strategy. By 1814, over a quarter of a million men were in the regular army, with another half million in the home defence and volunteer units. This level of recruitment not only exposed the limited population resources of the Highlands and quickly exhausted the landlords' economic and social levers of coercion, it also ensured that the unofficial, *ad hoc* status of the region as a flexible military reserve was rendered insignificant. In April 1809 six Highland regiments had their status altered in recognition that there were simply not enough Highlanders to fill them.[89] Equally destructive of the old regional recruiting order was the fact that the war forced governments to increasingly rationalise and then integrate the different regular and militia branches of its military machine. Given its earlier, disproportionate contribution, it is hardly surprising that this process commenced in Scotland when, in 1794, fencibles were asked to extend their service into Ireland to allow regular units to be deployed elsewhere. Those regiments, such as the first battalion of the Breadalbane, Grant and Sutherland Fencibles, that refused were subsequently disbanded in 1799. A similar fate befell the regular regiment raised at great cost by Sir James Grant in 1795, also the second battalion of the 78th Highlanders, and was only narrowly avoided by the 92nd Gordon Highlanders in 1796. Yet elite families in the region had grown accustomed to their regiments remaining inviolate until peace necessitated their disbandment. Considerable money and effort had after all gone into such units and landlords invariably anticipated their maintenance for a sufficient time to

87. S.R.O., Breadalbane Muniments, GD 112/52/606/10; S.R.O., Seaforth Muniments, GD 46/6/25/60.
88. P. Stigger, *op. cit.*, pp. 240–41; J.E. Cookson, *op. cit.*, p. 113.
89. L. Colley, *op. cit.*, p. 287; D.M. Henderson, *op. cit.*, p. 7, n. 34.

make the whole operation profitable and worthwhile. Seaforth mirrored the sentiments of proprietary recruiters in general when he noted to Dundas in 1809 that 'I felt the reg't *as my due* either considered from my zeal for the common good or from the great exertions I had *in that line*'.[90]

The policy of demobilising regiments that no longer fitted within an increasingly integrated recruiting system could not but offend landlords like Sir James Grant. Indeed, Highland elites were rapidly disabused of the notion that theirs was a favoured and secure position within the British military. For John, fourth Earl of Breadalbane, these developments represented a particular reverse. From as early as 1796 he had attempted to secure the position of fencible officers by obtaining pensions for such personnel (those who served in fencible levies did not receive half-pay). Subsequent demobilisation and the limited ability of John, fifth Duke of Argyll, to find alternative employment in India for officers from reduced Highland units caused further disquiet. The alienation of Breadalbane brought on by the disbandment of the fencibles is made clear from his reaction to the Crown's suggestion in 1799 that he raise a line regiment from amongst his recently discharged men. Breadalbane declared himself 'disgusted', adding with respect to the new offer: 'All this is very fine, but still it cannot remove the indignity offered us all ... I am so completely in the dumps at the late orders'.[91] Likewise, following disbandment of the various fencibles and, more crucially, volunteer forces in 1801–2, the reputation of Henry Addington's administration was noted by contemporaries as having suffered considerably in the Highlands. Instead of the multiplicity of home defence units that had emerged during the early 1790s, government moved instead towards a simplified local militia and line regiment system. Increasingly, the army came to be supplied by these militia regiments which first conscripted their men and then transferred them to regular regiments. In 1804 and 1807, legislation was passed which allowed set proportions of local militia to go annually into the army, while parishes were forced by a fining system to replace such men. In 1811 this was formalised by putting a set number of militiamen annually into the regular units. Crucially, the new element of annual quotas removed any need for recruits to be awarded with land, finally doing away with the primary element that had sustained the old recruiting formula in the Highlands.[92] The dismay that greeted the rationalising of Britain's military machine in the period from 1795 to the 1810s says something of what

90. J.E. Cookson, *op. cit.*, pp. 147–8; S.R.O., RH 2/4/222, pp. 65–6; S.R.O., Melville Castle Muniments, GD 51/1/846; N.L.S., Melville Papers, Ms 6, f. 139; Ms 1048, ff. 64, 96, 118, 189; Ms 1054, f. 43.
91. S.R.O., Seafield Muniments; GD 248/1545, p. 23; S.R.O., Campbell of Balliveolin Papers, GD 13/292–4.
92. J. Fortescue, *The County Lieutenancies and the Army, 1803–1804* (London 1909), pp. 4, 30, 145; N.L.S., Melville Papers, Ms 1048, ff. 120, 184; Ms 19578, f. 35; N.L.S., Sutherland Papers, Dep. 313/764/26; Dep. 313/754/8; S.R.O., Campbell of Balliveolin Papers, GD 13/339b, 380.

had motivated Highland elites since 1756 to involve themselves so disproportionately. It suggests, ultimately, that a considerable level of economic dependence underpinned their participation within the army.

Conclusion

In the seventy years following Culloden military recruitment emerged as the single most successful British government policy implemented in the Highlands. Parliamentary accounts in 1778 for the new Highland regiments brought into existence in that year give some indication of recruitment's financial scale and impact. Exclusive of the Black Watch, Highland regiments were costed at over £171,500 annually.[93] The emergence of such a distinctive and lucrative regional strategy revolved around a series of central government misconceptions on the one hand and on the other a desire within the Highlands for secure access to military patronage. However misplaced or misinformed in their assumptions, London governments continued to award regiments to Highland landlords on the understanding that clanship, with its well known military attributes, remained the primary method of social organisation in the region. That they continued to do so when prominent social indicators such as emigration actually pointed to the reality of clanship's extinction strongly suggests that the longer-term impact of the '45 on Britain's metropolitan centre has been seriously underestimated. As the last military uprising within the United Kingdom, the '45 had a seminal effect upon recruiting policy if only because it highlighted, in spectacular fashion, the region's military potential at a crucial time in Britain's military and imperial expansion. Indeed, when the Seven Years War produced unprecedented demands for men, the example of the '45 helped rationalise a strategy of Highland recruitment. Crucially, the 1756–63 war, usually seen in a Scottish context as removing the taint of disloyalty left by the events of 1745, actually reinforced traditional conceptions of the region in that, to contemporaries, clanship had again produced significant numbers of men. By forcing anxious Highland elites into an impressive recruiting performance, the '45 not only set the precedent for government policy during the American War of Independence and beyond, but also demonstrated that it was continuing to influence conditions in the Highlands long after its seemingly final end at Culloden.

A particular domestic effect of mass Highland recruitment was that it served to underpin the idea of a Scottish manager, albeit an unofficial one. The third Duke of Argyll's supervision of recruiting during 1756–61 not only justified his retention as premier political manager in a personal sense, but also demonstrated that the role of the Scottish minister could adapt and make itself relevant within a British political landscape constantly adjusting to the acquisition of a worldwide empire. Indeed, while political management in

93. J. Almon (ed.), *The Parliamentary Register*, vols. 3 & 8, pp. 206 & 177–78.

Ireland was buffeted by constitutional strain between Dublin and Westminster – not least because of British recruiting demands[94] – in Scotland political management was free of such tensions and was thus able to produce, in the form of Highland regiments, an effective, distinctive Scottish response to the centre's demand for military resources. Crucially, this meant that while the issue of military recruitment undermined British trust in autonomous arrangements in Ireland, it proved the value of them in Scotland. A caveat is necessary at this point, however. The survival of Argyll was by no means due to military recruitment alone: the adversarial nature of Westminister politics was a substantial factor, as was, above all, the relative insignificance of Scotland within that system. Furthermore, the Seven Years War distracted and diverted Newcastle and those seeking to impose more centralist policies upon Scotland. Similar preoccupations also allowed Dundas to survive the arrival of Addington's administration in 1801. That international conflict could have this effect upon Scotland's position in relation to the centre and, more specifically, that imperial patronage tended to buttress distinctive political arrangements north of the Border, call into question the orthodoxy that the British empire's eighteenth-century expansion inevitably served to generate a closer Scottish-English union.[95]

Underlying the argument that Highland recruitment was symptomatic of Scotland's ability to react in a distinctive manner to the empire is the fact that such levying took a very specific, entrepreneurial form. However, trends toward professional recruiting ensured that the specialised relationship between Highland landlords and British governments had a relatively short lifespan. Thus, despite its spectacular successes between 1756 and 1799, proprietary recruiting collapsed in a relatively short time between the mid-1790s and 1805. This suggests that the whole recruiting episode from 1745 to 1815 was not in fact based upon any real continuity from the days of clanship but was, rather, a specific niche economy generated by imperial expansion. Such an arrangement was to be quickly abandoned by government when the altered nature of war from 1793 signified it could no longer serve its purpose. Traditionally, the end of military recruiting within the region has been attributed almost exclusively to the commercialising policies of landlords. However, it is important to remember that any specialised economy is vulnerable to change; ironically, war itself, by altering so fundamentally in the French revolutionary period, was equally responsible for ensuring that the days of landlord recruiting in the Highlands would be short-lived.

94. L.M. Cullen, 'Scotland and Ireland, 1600–1800: Their Role in the Evolution of British Society', in R.A. Houston and I.D. Whyte (eds.), *Scottish Society, 1500–1800* (Cambridge, 1989), pp. 242–3.
95. L. Colley, *op. cit.*, pp. 129–32; P.J. Marshall, *loc. cit.*, p. 211.

CHAPTER THREE

The Annexed Estates: Improvement, Recruitment and Re-settlement, 1746–1784

The Board of Annexed Estates represented the most ambitious and high-profile agency of government intervention in the Highlands during the period from the mid-1750s until the end of the war in America, and provides a framework within which the local effects of recruitment can be studied. As an experiment in social engineering, annexation has been dismissed as limited in its impact and failing absolutely in its role as a pioneering mechanism for inculcating methods and ideologies of improvement into the region.[1] Criticism has centred upon its top-heavy administration, poor capital resources and overall inability to successfully translate ambitious plans for social and economic improvement from theory into practice. Beyond popularising planned villages in the Highlands and acting as a reward panel for military service, its reputation has been largely that of a conspicuously early example of a series of ineffective government interventions in the region.[2] Yet a major weakness in this appraisal is that it fails to address some of the broader implications arising from the fact that the Annexed Estates Board acted as both the premier improving agency for government while simultaneously recruiting then resettling military personnel. Loss of productive land and tenurial efficiency through the excessive maintenance and deployment of military manpower had, after all, been a charge that Whig and improvement theory had levelled explicitly against clanship. This suggests that an important dimension of the annexed estates experiment lies not so much in the failure of its stated objectives as in the fact that it represents the earliest post-Culloden example of the significant contradictions and tensions that existed between agrarian improvement, military recruitment and subsequent estate resettlement.

1. M. Lynch, *Scotland: A New History* (London, 1992), p. 363.
2. T.C. Smout, 'The Landowner and the Planned Village in Scotland, 1730–1830', in N.T. Phillipson and R. Mitchison (eds.), *Scotland in the Age of Improvement: Essays in Scottish History in the Eighteenth Century* (Edinburgh, 1996), pp. 79, 89–91; A.I. Macinnes, 'Scottish Gaeldom: The First Phase of Clearance', in T.M. Devine and R. Mitchison (eds.), *People and Society in Scotland, 1760–1830,* vol. 1 (Edinburgh, 1988) p. 74; A.M. Smith, *Jacobite Estates of the 'Forty-Five* (Edinburgh, 1982), pp. 229–31.

The Post-Culloden Highlands and Theories of Improvement

In attempting to understand how the Board's apparent priority of promoting Lowland-style progress in the region came to involve the very different and, at times, contradictory role of military recruitment and resettlement, it is worth noting that 'improvement' was in fact a contentious issue, and that what, exactly, it entailed was by no means clear. Certainly during the '45, and in the years immediately following Culloden, an unprecedented degree of unanimity had been evident amongst the Whig political nation north and south of the border over the need to fundamentally address and solve the 'Highland problem'. Not surprisingly, the last Jacobite campaign entrenched pre-existing Whig propaganda that equated clanship with perpetually non-industrious and disorderly behaviour.[3] Indeed, Whig political and intellectual elites believed that clanship was merely a mechanism for military mobilisation and, as such, was an unacceptable basis for securing material progress. In Argyll, as early as 1737, if not before, tacksmen were perceived to be the only secure possessors of land; this insecurity for the rest of the population produced a willingness amongst them to live under excessive and uncertain labour services, and led to a form of 'slavish dependency' inimical to the interests of the state.[4] It was also supposed that under this system poverty and the resulting conflict over limited resources like cattle produced a bellicose society that sought to defend its existing wealth rather than invest in efficient agriculture and commerce. Concepts of the Highlands in both the pre- and post- 1746 period, therefore, nearly always emphasised the military role of clanship and largely ignored its other complex social and economic priorities.[5]

These perceptions resulted in a belief that the economic and social progress of the Lowlands needed to be imitated within the Highlands for the sake of public order and security. It is therefore tempting so see the subsequent emergence of improvement policies in the region as an inevitable, rational and wholly consistent sequence of events. Thus, for example, the spate of legislation relating to ward tenure, disarming, heritable jurisdictions and the annexed estates could be viewed as part of a purposeful and coherent process.[6] But conflict, and not consensus, characterised the background to the Annexing Act of March 1752. The obvious failure of conciliatory policies after the '15 uprising ensured that many leading

---

3. R. Clyde, *From Rebel to Hero: The Image of the Highlander, 1745–1830* (East Linton, 1995), p. 3.
4. E.R. Cregeen, 'The Tacksmen and Their Successors: A Study in Tenurial Reorganisation in Mull, Morvern and Tiree in the Early Eighteenth Century', in *Scottish Studies*, vol. 13 (1969), pp. 101–118.
5. R.A. Dodgshon, *Land and Society in Early Scotland* (Oxford, 1981), pp. 281–283; A.J. Youngson, *After the 'Forty-Five: the Economic Impact on the Scottish Highlands* (Edinburgh, 1973), pp. 14–15.
6. A.M. Smith, *op. cit.* p. 21.

politicians were determined that Jacobite families would never again under any circumstances be allowed to regain their landed property. Indeed, annexation was on the political agenda even while the uprising continued. By 17 May 1746, a mere month after Culloden, Argyll and Andrew Fletcher, Lord Milton, discussed investing the Crown with the estates of certain Jacobite families. Likewise, the staunchly Hanoverian Donald Mackay, third Lord Reay, wrote to the Sutherland M.P. George Mackay suggesting complete and inalienable annexation of all rebel properties. By contrast, Lord President Duncan Forbes suggested breaking up such estates amongst politically reliable favourites.[7] By the middle of November 1746 Milton informed the first Duke of Newcastle that MacDonnell of Glengarry had offered to sell his estate for a reasonable price. Milton added that it was an invaluable opportunity to extend the presence of the Crown and alter the social and economic experience of a particularly disaffected Highland district. Uncertainty over policy direction was such that in October 1746 Argyll believed the estate of Appin would be sold to a Lowlander as opposed to becoming the property of the state. Similarly, as late as 1749, he retained some hope that he himself might gain private control of the estate of Stewart of Ardsheal.[8]

Not only was it unclear how, exactly, social and economic change was to be implemented on the ground, but the parliamentary campaign surrounding annexation witnessed the politicisation and deliberate manipulation of the issue of the region's improvement. During the passage of the bill, sustained opposition was evident from Cumberland and John Russell, fourth Duke of Bedford. The latter had recently resigned from government and wished to construct a serious parliamentary opposition to the Pelham incumbency in order to be invited back into the ministry upon advantageous terms. Bedford argued that to invest the Crown with Highland properties was an act of political chicanery designed merely to enhance the existing power of certain authoritarian Scottish magnates allied to the administration – namely, Argyll.[9] A whole series of politically motivated disputes over the executive board that was to manage the estates followed in the wake of the Annexation Act itself. Cumberland sought to destroy the project's credibility by sending a list of suspected Jacobites within Scottish government to his father. Pelham was forced to investigate these claims, which inevitably delayed the appoint-

7. H.M.C., *Laing Manuscripts*, vol. 2 (London, 1925), pp. 381–2; A.M. Smith, *op. cit.* p. 19; N.L.S., Fletcher of Saltoun Papers, Ms 16615, f. 112.
8. J.S. Shaw, *The Management of Scottish Society, 1707–1764* (Edinburgh, 1983), pp. 172–76; N.L.S., Fletcher of Saltoun Papers, Ms 16631, f. 5; Ms 16626, f. 137; Ms 16615, f. 151; B.L., Newcastle Papers, Add Ms 32712, f. 452; S.R.O., Campbell of Barcaldine Papers, GD 170/942/9.
9. *The Parliamentary History of England from the Earliest Period to the Year 1803*, vol. 13 (London, 1813), pp. 1240–41; A. Murdoch, *'The People Above': Politics and Administration in Mid-Eighteenth Century Scotland* (Edinburgh, 1980), pp. 37–9, 74–5.

ment of Commissioners.[10] Largely successful attempts were also made to ensure that those with political interests in the Highlands were excluded from any real power on the board. This policy was taken to a surprisingly high social level when James Murray, second Duke of Atholl, and John Campbell, third Earl of Breadalbane, were debarred from official involvement. The overall result of these delays and indifference was that Commissioners were not appointed until June 1755 – nine whole years after Culloden and a full three years after the Annexing Act itself.[11] This suggests that while a post-1745 consensus over the desirability of improvement in the Highlands existed up to a point, it should not be overstated. The fate of officially inspired initiatives show that, from the government's perspective at least, the dimensions and practicalities of improvement were by no means clearly defined or accepted, and, indeed, that the whole process ranked far down its list of priorities, even during a period of peace. It is also clear that the whole issue was often subordinated to the wider vagaries of Westminster factionalism. It may be unfair to accuse the Cumberland-Bedford interest of using the rhetoric of improvement without genuine regard, or indeed of not wishing to see real change in the region. Nonetheless, the fact that the legislation that gave rise to the annexed estates was itself subject to intermittent pressure was a significant foreshadowing of the later disruption suffered by the board's improvement agenda as a result of other prominent public policies, namely military recruitment and demobilisation.

While the disputes surrounding the annexed estates warn us against supposing that there was a pre-existing and wholly acceptable strategy of improvement ready to be implemented in the region immediately after Culloden, the delay was, ultimately, only a short-term phenomenon. But consistent policies for transforming the estates nevertheless continued to be subject to uncertainty, contradiction and re-interpretation, and there is a clear need to grasp some of the basic characteristics of improvement in order to understand why this was so. The central problem when discussing 'improvement' is that the word itself is deceptively simple. Usually, especially in relation to the post-Culloden Highlands, it is taken to mean a clear, coherent and definite set of recognisable estate policies such as rouping, shortened tacks, single-tenant farms and, inevitably, removal and eviction.[12] Improvement did indeed encompass the specifics of estate management; yet,

10. N.L.S., Fletcher of Saltoun Papers, Ms 16677, f. 133; Ms 17563, f. 8; B.L., Hardwicke Papers, Add Ms 35447, ff. 233, 309; B.L., Egerton Mss, Ms 3433, ff. 1–5.
11. N.L.S., Fletcher of Saltoun Papers, Ms 16677, f. 114; S.R.O., Campbell of Barcaldine Papers, GD 170/942/9; B.L., Hardwicke Papers, Add Ms 35450, f. 179; Add Ms 35448, ff. 51, 57, 162, 206, 210; A. Murdoch, *op. cit.*, pp. 74–75; A.M. Smith, 'State Aid to Industry – An Eighteenth Century Example', in T.M. Devine (ed.), *Lairds and Improvement in the Scotland of the Enlightenment* (Glasgow, 1978), p. 47.
12. A.I. Macinnes, *Clanship, Commerce and the House of Stuart, 1603–1788* (East Linton, 1996), p. 228.

for contemporaries, it also involved a whole series of different intellectual, social, economic, demographic and patriotic objectives that not only varied in relative importance under different conditions but were by no means completely consistent or even necessarily compatible with each other.

It was precisely these incompatibilities and ambiguities within improvement that framed and limited the efforts of the board and, indeed, those of private landlords. Initially, Commissioners attempted to follow the estate policies and orthodoxies of Lowland agrarian change. The salient features of agricultural improvement as formulated and increasingly practised in the Scottish Lowlands during the first half of the eighteenth century involved the issuing of leases to ensure security of tenure, better organised husbandry, restriction of subtenure, and single-tenant farms of sufficient size to allow for reliable production of market surpluses.[13] When, in June 1755, Commissioners finally met to implement their remit, they advocated a policy of issuing 'profitable leases to continue for a certain limited term in room of the dependent and precarious possessions which normally prevailed'. A limit of £20 was set on tacks, while subletting was strictly forbidden. Factors for the various estates, meanwhile, promoted and implemented policies of dividing off farms and increasing their average size to ensure agricultural and commercial viability.[14] The imposition of strict subtenancy laws, the creation of consolidated farm holdings, as well as plans for the development of villages at Ullapool, New Tarbat, Beauly, Inveruie in Knoydart, Kinloch Rannoch and Callander appeared to confirm the optimistic expectation that models of agrarian improvement could be imported directly into the region and that in time the Highlands would develop a market economy similar to that of the Lowlands. However, while these specific estate policies provided a practical framework within which to commence innovation, agrarian progress was never in fact a monolithic and highly defined process. When coupled to the social, demographic and patriotic dimensions of improvement, this lack of consensus ensured that change in the region remained a matter of considerable debate and subjective interpretation. Sir John Clerk of Penicuik claimed that the small size of agricultural possessions and insecurity of tenure underpinned Highland poverty, and that future managers of estates held by the Crown should not issue leases under a certain rent or length of time. Yet, in contrast, Sir Archibald Grant of Monymusk stated that holdings in Scotland averaged out at 221 acres, suggesting that they were in fact too large and ill-apportioned in terms of investment capacity. Interestingly, Grant's expertise was grounded in the North-East, where a tenurial pattern of smaller croft holdings emerged alongside more theoretically conventional

13. T.M. Devine, *The Transformation of Rural Scotland: Social Change and the Agrarian Economy, 1660–1815* (Manchester, 1994), pp. 22–29.
14. For the social implications of single-tenant farms, see A.M. Smith, *Jacobite Estates of the 'Forty-Five*, pp. 58–9, 65–7; S.R.O., F.E.P. E721/2, pp. 56 & 66, 119; F.E.P. E721/6 pp. 35, 38, 47; F.E.P. E769/79/55(2); N.L.S., Fletcher of Saltoun Papers, Ms 17589, f. 129.

single-tenant farms. This lack of agreement was vital in determining the emergence of distinctive solutions and patterns of development in the Highlands, all the more so given that, by contrast with the ambiguities within improvement, there was a relative consensus that change should not lead to social and demographic decline.[15]

Uncertainty, exemplified by the debate on farm size and consolidation, and which type of improvement was best suited to the region, was aggravated by the fact that agrarian reorganisation and rental increase formed only one part of the board's wider agenda. The actual objective of the Annexation Act was 'the promoting amongst them of Protestant religion, good government, industry and manufactures, and the principle of duty and loyalty to His Majesty'.[16] Notwithstanding his manifestly self-interested viewpoint, Simon Fraser of Lovat in 1774, while petitioning the Treasury for the return of his father's estate, suggested that these wider considerations had delayed, if not quite subverted, the agenda of improvement. Thus he noted of annexation: 'The object . . . was to secure the future loyalty of the inhabitants, at the same time that it was in contemplation to improve the country . . . [but] the improvement of the country was a secondary consideration which of itself alone would never have produced that Act'.[17] This emphasis on social control and population development was underlined in a comment by Sir Gilbert Elliot, M.P. for the county of Selkirk, and a noted improver appointed to the Commission. Elliot informed an associate in June 1755 that 'we have opened the Commission for the forfeited estates and flatter ourselves that under our protection a loyal, well policed colony will soon flourish'.[18] The lack of rhetoric about agrarian improvement was not evidence of its unimportance, far from it, but does serve as a reminder that the process of change on the estates was to embrace other considerations, not least an increase in population. Despite later association with eviction and depopulation, concepts of improvement in the eighteenth century actually attached crucial importance to nurturing a profitable and preferably numerous tenantry. It was this particular concern that served to modify and, at times, circumscribe the scale, intensity and direction of change in the region. Thus, while Commissioners initially implemented the population-shedding policies of consolidation and restriction of subtenure, it also became increasingly clear during the late 1750s that this would involve

15. J.M. Gray (ed.), *Sir John Clerk of Penicuik* (Edinburgh, 1892), p. 259; A. Grant, *A Dissertation on the Chief Obstacles to the Improvement of Land and Introducing Better Methods of Agriculture throughout Scotland* (Aberdeen, 1760), pp. 48–55, 58 & 80. For discussion of the absence of uniformity in improvement, see T.M. Devine, 'The Making of a farming Elite? Lowland Scotland, 1750–1850', in T.M. Devine (ed.), *Scottish Elites* (Edinburgh, 1994), pp. 62–7, 70–72.
16. *Statutes at Large from the Twentieth Year of the Reign of George II to the Thirtieth Year of King George II* (London, 1769), 25 Geo. 2 C. 41, p. 455.
17. S.R.O., F.E.P. E769/53/1.
18. N.L.S., Minto Papers, Ms 11009, f. 30.

large-scale eviction and depopulation.[19] By 1761 the board had come to realise that:

> There remains a considerable class of inhabitants namely cottars, tradesman, to whom the leases are no security, on the contrary, the tacksman or leasees by force of these leases might depopulate the Annexed Estates of the cottars and tradesmen unless there is provision made to the contrary in the leases now being granted.[20]

Subtenant eviction in the period from 1755 to 1760 was seen to conflict with the wider aim of social improvement and 'to be very inconsistent with the intention of the act of parliament'. In 1762 the board debated whether the number of subtenants removed since 1760 should be collated and, where possible, accommodated on specifically created holdings. Within seven years, therefore, the Commission had begun to reassess its own methods of improvement and the wider social consequences arising from agrarian change.[21] The substantial influence these concerns could have on the pattern of tenurial development is exemplified by the comments of Lieutenant-General Humphrey Bland, the army's Commander-in-Chief in Scotland. In December 1753 Bland wrote to Lord Chancellor Hardwicke giving his views on possible future policies for the Commission. He stated that in order to secure the loyalty and welfare of the region farms needed to be small, not exceeding £5 or £6 a year in rent, and leased only to the former subtenants of large tacksmen. Bland continued:

> Besides, should the farms be made larger, numbers of poor families who now live upon little farms of 50/- or £3 a year would be destitute of the means of subsisting as they can't become subtenants to the others which would of course depopulate the country.[22]

Bland's tenurial ideas demonstrate how a model of improvement in the Highlands had not yet taken shape. This was complicated still further when in May 1756, within a year of commencing their administration of the estates, Commissioners were faced with the outbreak of the Seven Years War and the substantial social upheaval and dislocation that came with any large-scale military conflict. Indeed, in seeking to understand the limited success of the Commission, it is worth remembering that in the 32-year existence of the annexed estates, Britain was at war for 14 – and initiated large-scale recruitment for 16 – exactly half its lifespan.

19. V. Wills, 'The Gentleman Farmer and the Annexed Estates: Agrarian Change in the Highlands in the Second Half of the Eighteenth Century', in T.M. Devine (ed.), *Lairds and Improvement in the Scotland of the Enlightenment* (Glasgow, 1978), p. 39.
20. N.L.S., Minto Papers, Ms 11015, f. 69; N.L.S., Fletcher of Saltoun Papers, Ms 17589, f. 126.
21. S.R.O., F.E.P. E769/91/2; F.E.P. E721/6, pp. 36–8, 215, 297.
22. B.L., Hardwicke Papers, Add Ms 35447, f. 53.

Recruitment and the Annexed Estates

The impact of the Seven Years War on the board's evolving improvement agenda was both considerable and complex. The implementation of a largely civilian series of measures was broadly undermined in two distinct ways. Cumberland, for strategic reasons, had eventually been prepared to sanction the large-scale use of Highland troops in late 1756; but this significant concession to what was viewed in London as Argyll's 'Highland interest' ensured that other government-funded initiatives in the region became far more vulnerable. Indeed, it required a systematic lobbying campaign by prominent Scots to secure the £69,910 needed to clear the debts on the property of Perth and thereby ensure the estates would be managed by the Crown in the long term. Furthermore, the emergence of large-scale Highland recruitment worked against the continuation of undiluted Lowland-style improvement policies insofar as it was felt such practices dislocated valuable populations and so 'did not obviously match the best interests of the realm'.[23]

It is at the estate level that the impact of war on improvement can be best illustrated. The annexed estate of Lovat in eastern Inverness-shire, for example, demonstrates how recruitment and improvement interacted on the ground. Ironically, the board's official brief of instilling loyalty into disaffected populations left it especially susceptible to demands that it assist the process of raising men for the army. This was particularly the case when on 4 January 1757 Simon Fraser, eldest son of the executed Lord Lovat, obtained a lieutenant-colonel's commission to raise a new battalion of Highlanders. This regiment has attracted much of the extravagant romanticism attached to such units; the lack of proprietorial coercion and the fact that fifteen of its commissioned officers were Frasers has given it the reputation of a post-Culloden clan levy.[24] Yet, as was to be the case with all other Highland regiments of the British army raised in the latter half of the century, Fraser's battalion was in fact the product of a regional co-operative effort. West Highland gentry as a whole, not just Frasers, were well represented. The MacDonnells of Glengarry and Macdonalds of Morar and Clanranald gained eight commissions, the Camerons five, and even the somewhat isolated MacNeill of Barra secured a captaincy. This broadening of recruitment geography had the effect of reducing excessive manpower loss in one particular locality, and, furthermore, was a highly successful levying mechanism. By March 1757 Fraser had raised over 1,100 men – an impressive performance that underlined the efficiency of the regional recruiting system then being perfected in the Highlands.[25] Given

---

23. A.M. Smith, *Jacobite Estates of the 'Forty-Five*, p. 43; A. Murdoch, *op. cit.*, pp. 74–76; J.S. Shaw, *op. cit.*, pp. 178–81.
24. J.S. Keltie, *A History of the Scottish Highlands, Highland Clans and Highland Regiments*, vol. 2 (Glasgow, 1875), p. 457.
25. J. Browne, *History of the Highlands and the Highland Clans*, vol. 3 (Glasgow, 1838), p. 248; N.L.S., Letter Book of Lord George Beauclerk, Ms 13497, p. 61.

that Lovat had taken men from well beyond the territory associated with his family, the idea of a clan levy hardly obtains. In order to compensate for his own lack of proprietary authority, however, Lovat requested in early February that 'the factors and other officers on the annexed estates may have directions from the commissioners for managing the said estates, for each of them to give their utmost aid and assistance to the military officers who shall be employed in raising the said troops'.[26] The process of recruitment was further expedited by the emergence of severe famine in the region and by the operation of an Impress Act. This legislation, implemented in the spring and winter of 1756, and again in 1757, was designed to facilitate the voluntary enlistment of men who might otherwise be targeted for conscription. This carrot-and-stick strategy proved highly successful across the Highlands as a whole and contributed significantly to the rapid creation of Fraser's battalion.[27] On 1 March 1757 Lovat informed the War Office that his personal interest had secured 582 men. The estate of Lovat, and the smaller Fraser properties surrounding it, yielded 306 men in three days, demonstrating that, despite the effort to spread the burden of recruitment, the property itself experienced a substantial drain of manpower – in 1755 the estate's male population had totalled 769. Although the traditional figure of 800 men raised personally by Fraser is a serious exaggeration, it is nevertheless clear that perhaps one man in four in the new battalion was from the erstwhile family lands or other, smaller Fraser estates.[28]

The intensity of this military activity on the ex-Lovat property explains why the estate is an early example of the inability of post-Culloden improvers to construct and institute a consistent and balanced land-use policy for the region encompassing both agriculturally feasible units and an employable level of tenantry. This was because land, rather than being considered wholly in terms of its economic value and improvement potential, partly maintained its role as the basis for military mobilisation. As a result, the latent strain between policies of establishing single-tenant farms and retaining large

26. S.R.O., F.E.P. E721/2, p. 11. On 7 February 1757 Simon Fraser personally visited the offices of the board in Edinburgh to stress the need for rapid recruitment. Subsequent reports by the board to the Treasury also emphasised the significant role played by factors in recruiting for the army; see S.R.O., F.E.P. E723/1, Reports dated 13 November 1758 and 7 January 1760.
27. A.H. Millar (ed.), *Scottish Forfeited Estate Papers, 1715–1745* (Edinburgh, 1909), p. 157; S.R.O., F.E.P. E769/91/3; E769/79/27(2); E723/1, p. 44; N.L.S., Fletcher of Saltoun Papers, Ms 17505, f. 185; Ms 17589, f. 40. The economic dynamic to recruiting was evident even when large-scale war was absent. See S.R.O., Seafield Muniments, GD 248/458/3/2. For the effect of the Recruiting Act in securing supposed 'volunteers', see N.L.S., Murray Erskine Papers, Ms 5079, f. 125; Ms 5080, f. 9; D.H., Loudon Papers, A/972, unnumbered letter dated Inverness, 12 April 1756, Captain Aeneas Mackintosh-Loudon; S.R.O., F.E.P. E769/79/28.
28. N.L.S., Minto Papers, Ms 11035, f. 13; N.L.S., Fletcher of Saltoun Papers, Ms 16519, f. 24; P.R.O., W.O. 1/974, f. 365.

reserves of population was significantly exacerbated. In order to increase his rate of enlistment, Fraser, on 7 February 1757, secured an assurance from the Commissioners in Edinburgh 'that the parents of such of the tenants sons as were fit for service, and would enter voluntarily, would be continued in their possessions, and that the young men upon returning home, when the service of their King and country was over, would meet with proper encouragement'.[29] Given that the core precepts of improvement in the region meant the demilitarisation of tenantry and the purely commercial use of land, such recruitment tactics represented a fundamental contradiction of the board's objectives. This manifested itself in several ways. Crucially, the development of single-tenant farms and efficient agriculture was disrupted through fluctuations in the managerial tenant group as they accepted military commissions. This drain of substantial tenants sprang from a belief that the army, as opposed to agriculture, offered an alternative means of securing income and livelihoods – an understandable reaction given the board's erosion of tacksman status through the restriction of subtenure and tightly controlled conditions of tack holding.[30] The lands of Lettoch, Groam, Mains of Lovat, Knocknairay, Milns of Kimoraick, Meikle Portclair, Barnyards, Moniack, Inchberry, Knockchoilim and Little Garth lost their tacksmen to the army – 10% of the estate's holdings. In terms of fulfilling the aims of the board, the loss of prominent tacksmen was significant. Endowed with relative expertise and capital, it was precisely this class of tenant that commanded the resources necessary to remove sub-tenantry and become single leaseholders upon consolidated farms.[31] Another important aspect of intense estate recruiting, particularly for single tenants, was the social origins of the vast majority of Highland recruits. Of 159 Highland soldiers resettled on the annexed estates after the war, 129 – or 81% were from the day labouring class (see Table 3).[32] In effect, therefore, the army disproportionately removed the region's reserves of relatively mobile labour, resulting in a scarcity of servants and an increase in wage levels. Traditional reliance on subtenantry, cottars or familial labour made the issue of hired help less of a problem for tacksmen and multiple-tenant farmers. Waged labour was largely, though by no means exclusively, the concern of single tenants. Thus, tenants on the farms of Dalttiack and Wester Borlum stated that such was the scarcity of labour 'on account of the war' that they had been forced to hire servants from beyond the estate at wage levels which threatened the profitability and viability of their holdings.[33]

The unsettled conditions affected all social groups, however. Despite the loss of relatively wealthy tacksmen, vacancies left by the process of recruit-

29. S.R.O., F.E.P. E769/91/163(1).
30. S.R.O., F.E.P. E769/91/20, 85, 93, 136 & 139.
31. S.R.O., F.E.P. E769/91/2, 11, 24,70, 80, 94, 203, 233; A. M. Smith, *Jacobite Estates of the 'Forty-Five*, p. 65.
32. S.R.O., F.E.P. E777/288/6, 20; E783/90/2; E787/28/1, 4–5.
33. S.R.O., F.E.P. E721/6, p.134; E769/79/44(1) 45(2) & 55(2–3); E769/91/121.

ment could in some instances complement the board's strategy of establishing single tenancies. Several farms, especially in Stratherrick, abandoned by tacksmen and settled by colonising tenants from areas such as Argyll or Strathspey, had the majority of their subtenantry removed. However, the lower social groups could also benefit from the turnover in leading tenantry. Erstwhile subtenants instituted improvements in order to obtain tacks from the board and entrench their position so that returning officers such as Lieutenants John and Simon Fraser, tacksmen of Knockchoilim and Fanblair respectively, found 'the Honourable Board intended to make the subtenants independent of the principal tacksman and not removable by him'. Likewise, subtenant families whose sons joined the army, as in Easter Bunchgavy and Fanblair, used the military as a social ladder to secure advancement in status from sub-to multiple-tenant.[34] The balance of benefit and loss sustained by the gentry and lower tenantry due to military levying should be treated with caution in view of the changing tenurial structures already appearing on the Annexed Estates. Recruitment did not so much prevent the development of single-tenant farms on Lovat as slow down their emergence and promote, instead, the creation of multiple-tenant farms. Comparison of rentals both before and after the Seven Years' War demonstrates that, in 1755, 59% of farms were held by leases to a single person (the majority being tacksmen). The disruption wrought by levying meant that while tacksman farms had decreased in number, the largest growth in farm-holding type had been in multiple-tenant, as opposed to single-tenant, farms. In 1755, multiple tenancies constituted 41% of all agricultural units, while by 1770 they constituted 50%.[35] More specifically, actual reversal of policy occurred as single-tenant farms such as Barnyards, Moniack and Relich became multiple-tenant farms. Above all, recruitment ensured the estate became increasingly dominated by conflicting social expectations and competing claims for land, which produced confusion and inconsistency in the management regime. Between 1757 and 1770 claims for settlement on holdings arising from recruitment and demobilisation were responsible for a turnover of tenantry upon one farm in four.[36] It is testimony to the intensity of the army's first post-Culloden recruiting drive in the region that the estate of Lovat was not alone in this respect. The barony of Coigach in Lochbroom, which formed the westerly section of the annexed estate of the Mackenzies of Cromartie, also experienced levying and resettlement of military personnel. Indeed, between 1756 and 1770 one farm in three – paying 36% of the estate rental

34. S.R.O., F.E.P. E769/79/34(2); E769/91/37(1), 70, 81(2), 89, 94, 103, 120, 203, 222, 235.
35. V. Wills, *Statistics of the Annexed Estates, 1755–56* (Edinburgh, 1973), pp. 14–27; S.R.O., F.E.P. E769/71; E769/72/3; E721/7, p. 74.
36. Figures for the number of farms affected by either recruitment or demands following demobilisation are drawn from the estate petitions for Lovat from 1756–1770 and from the board's minute books for the same period. See S.R.O., F.E.P. E721/2–11; E769/79/1–108; E769/91/1–323; E787/28/1.

– witnessed removal and changes in tenantry as a direct result of demobilised soldiers and officers receiving favourable terms of settlement. The level of tenurial insecurity engendered by events on both these estates could only have had a negative impact on the ability and willingness of tenants to invest in and improve their farms.[37]

The Annexed Estates and Military Demobilisation

The military's disruptive impact upon the implementation of Lowland-style improvement in the region continued well after recruitment ceased. By late 1762, with the completion of peace proposals between Britain, France and Spain, the emphasis switched naturally to the demobilisation of the country's wartime army and navy establishments. Mass reduction of the armed forces was traditionally viewed with considerable trepidation within society as a whole. Thousands of men lacking a trade or profession were released back into communities with little or no provision for their employment. The result was often vagrancy and a substantial crime wave as soldiers (sailors were widely perceived to have fewer problems finding employment) failed to readjust to civilian life.[38] However, several interrelated factors led to a diminution in the general hostility towards ex-members of the armed forces. Initial defeats in 1755–6 had been blamed on the relatively slow build-up of British military and naval forces, and raised the question of how Britain's society was to maintain a reserve of experienced men who could be rapidly mobilised in any future conflict. This concern was heightened in the post-1763 period by the fact that Britain's vastly enlarged empire in North America induced political and military apprehension amongst elites, as opposed to triumphalism or complacency. A resumption of hostilities was widely anticipated once France and Spain recovered from their financial exhaustion and sought to regain their commercial and territorial losses. More generally, contemporary economic theory stressed the need for strong armed forces to conquer and then defend national markets: a powerful navy, especially in British eyes, was inextricably linked to an effective merchant fleet and the commercial wealth that international trade secured. In this sense the settlement of sailors in particular, but military personnel in general, meant enhancing the material progress and improvement of the country, and so could be said to have represented an aim generally in line with the board's remit. Unlike the mass reductions of 1697, 1713, and to a lesser extent 1748, these social, imperial and military concerns ensured that the 1763 demobilisations were relatively well planned and much less arbitrary. The Scottish

37. Figures for Coigach are taken from the estate rentals, petitions and reports for 1756–1770. See S.R.O., F.E.P. E746/72/1–10; E746/75/1–74; E721/19; E746/113/1–86.
38. J. Innes, 'The Domestic Face of the Fiscal-Military State: Government and Society in Eighteenth-Century Britain', in L. Stone (ed.), *An Imperial State at War: Britain from 1689–1815* (London, 1994), pp. 108–116.

press carried articles highlighting the unemployment and subsequent emigration of trained soldiers and seamen arising from hasty, financially driven demobbing. Both official and private efforts were correspondingly made to ensure that demobilised soldiers and, in particular, sailors were securely and rationally resettled.[39] The altruism of these measures should not be overestimated, however. The aim was to ensure rapid re-enlistment when hostilities recommenced. In Parliament, legislation was passed which enabled and encouraged military personnel to adopt and practise certain trades. This was reflected in the individual actions of prominent improvers like James Ogilvy, Lord Deskford and later third Earl of Seafield, Sir Ludovick Grant of Grant and Sir Archibald Grant of Monymusk. In the spring of 1763 Deskford instituted a policy of resettling sailors and soldiers on his properties of Portsoy and Whitehalls in Banffshire; Sir Ludovick Grant also offered five acres to ex-military personnel on his Morayshire estates; while at Monymusk in Aberdeenshire twenty-nine Chelsea Pensioners were resettled on improvable muir.[40]

The Board of Annexed Estates was therefore only one particular agency, albeit the most public and high-profile, which sought to accommodate ex-military personnel in the North of Scotland. However, the Commission had already begun several years earlier to concern itself with devising and implementing policies that allowed for the simultaneous development of improved agriculture and the retention of a numerous population. This twin approach had to some extent been facilitated by the particularly acute pressures exerted by the war on the process of improvement. The region's prominent and celebrated role in supplying the army with men, for instance, made the removal and dispersal of superfluous subtenantry for purely commercial reasons appear a far more questionable policy. Indeed, subsequent labour shortages and high wages engendered a willingness on the part of the board to adopt tenurial models which attached as much importance to the retention of smaller tenantry and cottars as to the exclusive promotion of consolidated and improved agricultural holdings. War, as it was to do throughout the rest of the century, served to promote and entrench positive views of a heavily populated Highlands. Indeed, recruiting and population became increasingly linked within theoretical approaches to the region's development. In 1760 a memorandum circulated among Commissioners entitled *Hints Towards a Plan for Managing the Forfeited Estates* gave striking prominence to the military dimension. In a noticeable shift of emphasis, the duties of the board now appeared to be twofold. The first, as before, was to civilise the population; the second was 'the propagation of a

39. For the British reaction to unprecedented victory and imperial expansion, see L. Colley, *Britons: Forging the Nation, 1707–1837* (London, 1992), pp. 101–3. For the economic justification of military resettlement, see S.R.O., F.E.P. E723/2, 3 March 1763, 'Preamble to Report on sailor settlement scheme'.
40. *Scots Magazine*, vol. 25 (Edinburgh, 1763), pp. 175, 246–7, 257; S.R.O., Grant of Monymusk, GD 345/796/25.

hardy and industrious race, fit for serving the public in war'. In order to achieve this it was recommended that large Highland farms should be

> divided into small enclosures of one or two acres, and be perfectly dry. That these small enclosures be cropped with potatoes, turnip and sown-grass alternatively. And it ought to be a rule to cultivate them with the spade instead of the plough. In the next place, this method will afford work and bread to the men who at present are in great measure idle, and will consequently will render them hardy and fit to be soldiers.[41]

This emphasis on small, enclosed croft holdings closely reflected the suggestions of General Bland in 1753, and again indicates how improvement in the Highlands was not set immutably in one particular form but rather remained susceptible to re-interpretation as new pressures and influences came to bear upon the region. Given this fluidity, these new tenurial ideas were less a sharp divergence from Lowland practice than simply the adoption of arrangements designed to ensure the equally desirable objectives of successful agrarian improvement and military recruitment. With its strong military priorities, the memo of 1760 provided a practical model with which the board could respond to problems of population balance and wartime labour shortages. In October 1761 Lord Milton proposed removing, at a cost of £500, one eighth of all pre-existing large leases and creating a series of small individual holdings for day labourers and artisans. Entitled 'King's Cottagers', the scheme was accepted by the Treasury in March 1762. It was intended that this new class of tenant would pay rent directly to the Crown, and, in return, receive a few acres of enclosed land to be cultivated by spade, as opposed to the plough.[42] The significance of these developments should not be underestimated. In promoting forms of landholding that reduced the element of agriculture to ancillary levels and relying, instead, on the non-agrarian occupations of the tenant, the board was in fact creating a crofting-style system. This drift towards accommodating populations through tenurial innovation was given further impetus when in November 1762 Milton received a report from proprietors in Kincardineshire detailing the collapse of the local fishing industry. Wholesale impressment by the navy had drastically reduced the number of experienced crews and had led to a noticeable decline in commercially active boats. The increasingly high-profile issue of military demobilisation allowed the Commission in January 1763 to finally draw all these disparate concerns together and suggest a far more comprehensive strategy involving the settlement of large numbers of soldiers and sailors. Official approval for the plan was secured in March 1763,

41. N.L.S., Fletcher of Saltoun Papers, Ms 17506, f. 28; N.L.S., Minto Papers, Ms 11017, f. 13; Ms 11035, f. 53.
42. S.R.O., F.E.P. E721/6, pp. 127–8, 216, 265–6; N.L.S., Fletcher of Saltoun Papers, Ms 17589, f. 126.

ensuring that the apparatus of the annexed estates, from Commissioners to factors, became focused on settlement as much as on improvement.[43]

The proposals, which were significantly more ambitious than the King's Cottager scheme but identical in tenurial terms, involved placing 500 sailors on the annexed estates themselves and another 500 on private property – most noticeably, the lands of Lord Deskford, Kenneth Mackenzie of Seaforth and the town of Campbeltown. Expenditure was estimated at £6,610 – equivalent to almost 90% of the Commission's nominal annual income. Each married man was to be given three acres and a house rent-free for three years. In addition, sailors settled on the annexed estates were to receive a £2 bounty, while those located on private property were to receive £3. The accommodation of soldiers was on an altogether less ambitious scale, reflecting the belief that sailors were economically and militarily the more important of the two groups. Nevertheless, the intention was still to settle 500 men in varying concentrations upon the estates of Perth, Strowan, Monaltry in Highland Aberdeenshire, Barrisdale, Lovat and Cromarty. Expenditure was set at £3,000, with 300 married men to receive a house, three arable and six pastoral acres rent-free for three years, and a bounty of £3. The 200 unmarried men were to receive £1 per annum for three years, and if they married within a certain time were to obtain the same benefits as their wedded counterparts.[44] By authorising settlement in a series of small agricultural villages where, it was hoped, a manufacturing sector would emerge to serve the surrounding countryside, the Commission had adopted the latest thinking on the economic value of planned urban centres. However, the plantation of soldiers lacked the obvious commercial underpinning of fishing that rationalised the accommodation of sailors: instead, it relied on an even more explicitly military justification. The proposal was equated with the ancient Roman *colonia*, set up in order to pacify local populations and act as recruiting basins for imperial defence. Later, during the American Revolutionary War, the inhabitants of the small hamlets of Borelandbog and Strelitz, which had been created on the estate of Perth, were targeted for recruitment, as were men on the plantation established at New Tarbat.[45]

Despite appearing rational and well conceived, the scheme was in fact a

43. N.L.S., Fletcher of Saltoun Papers, Ms 17590, f. 63; S.R.O., F.E.P. E721/7; E723/2. For the impact of the Seven Years War on the Kincardineshire fishing fleet and across Scotland's main fishing areas in general, see D.J. Withrington and I. R. Grant (eds.), *The Statistical Account of Scotland*, vol. 14 (Wakefield, 1982), pp. 222–225; S.R.O., Board of Trustees for Manufactures and Fisheries, N.G. 1/1/113, pp. 79 & 148.
44. S.R.O., F.E.P. E723/2; E72/14, pp. 1–6.
45. T.C. Smout, 'The Landowner and the Planned Village in Scotland, 1730–1830', in N.T. Phillipson and R. Mitchison (eds.), *Scotland in the Age of Improvement: Essays in Scottish History in the Eighteenth Century* (Edinburgh, 1996), pp. 79, 89–90; N.L.S., Fletcher of Saltoun Papers, Ms 17564, f. 73; S.R.O., F.E.P. E777/188/70; E777/191/32 & 34; H.R.A., Minutes of the Commissioners of Supply, Cromarty: 1/3/2, meeting dated 20 January 1779.

complete failure as well as an undoubted financial disaster for the board. By May 1765 resettlement costs had run well over budget and amounted to £13,115 – a huge level of expenditure which, given the Commission's chronic problem of under-funding in other areas, was indicative of how far military concerns had displaced the agenda of civilian improvement. As early as 1764, 154 sailors had deserted their stations, forcing the board 'to inform your Majesty that it has not succeeded according to their wish and expectations'. Indeed, within three years the plan was effectively abandoned and factors were told 'to condescend more particularly to the other articles of improvement and manufactures' – an admission that the wider aims of the Commission had been neglected in favour of the military.[46]

Failure arose from a series of different though associated problems. A primary cause was the unrealistic speed with which the scheme had been implemented. The board was acutely aware that the Navy had been demobilising its crews since the autumn of 1762; many of these men, it was feared, were already employed on foreign ships or otherwise on the brink of emigration to find some new form of livelihood.[47] This brought a level of urgency to the settlement of sailors that was to prove detrimental in terms of planning. In a sense the whole idea was fundamentally compromised by the fact that, from the start, it catered to the process of demobilisation and not rational, economic criteria. Constraints on time forced the board to situate the new fishing settlements on sites such as New Tarbat, Ullapool and Inveruie that had already been earmarked for village development since 1755. Although suggestive of integration between settlement strategies and previous plans for urban expansion, such a correlation was in fact indicative of hasty planning and a failure to explore the differing geographical and market requirements of manufacturing villages and fishing stations. Certain obstacles facing the development of fishing were also ignored as a result. Access to wood for barrels and boats was not considered, putting additional pressure on costs. Failure to seriously address the basic problem of the overly bureaucratic, time-consuming and expensive salt laws was another example of the board's lack of long-term planning – especially with regard to isolated west-coast areas where the dearth of custom houses was a major barrier to sustained development.[48]

The question of personnel was another factor in the failure of the scheme. Perhaps understandably, it was taken for granted that naval seamen were experienced fishermen. The reality was often somewhat different, however. Lord Deskford found most of his discharged sailors 'have not the least skill in the business', as was the case with men who arrived at the property of

46. S.R.O., F.E.P. E723/2; E721/9. For early concern over the financial implications of the settlements, see N.L.S., Fletcher of Saltoun Papers, Ms 17590, f. 68.
47. S.R.O., F.E.P. E746/186/1.
48. V. Wills, *loc. cit.*, pp. 41–52; J. Dunlop, *The British Fisheries Society, 1786–1893* (Edinburgh, 1978), pp. 115–116; S.R.O., F.E.P. E721/7, p. 27.

Alexander Garden.[49] This problem also affected the settlement of soldiers. No economic criteria whatsoever were applied in selecting these colonists: indeed, access to land was determined almost exclusively by military considerations and by the decision to favour applications from battalions that had served overseas. This fatally undermined the board's aim of using military settlement as a form of internal colonisation. Indeed, it speaks volumes for the contempt in which Highland society was held by economic theorists that, even prior to the Seven Years War, retired soldiers – not normally considered paragons of economic or moral virtue – were nevertheless viewed as a means whereby 'civilised' lifestyles and behaviour could be imported directly into the region. Both the sailor and soldier schemes officially adopted this strategy and stressed how ex-military colonists would graft new work practices and manufacturing skills onto local populations. However, Highland officers, especially from the 88th and 89th battalions of Colonel John Campbell and Robert Murray-Keith, were at the forefront in exploiting the policy of favouring experienced soldiers, and recommended the majority of their men on the basis of military service.[50]

Table 3. Origin and Social Profile of Military Personnel, Annexed Estates, 1763–4[51]

Colony	Total Soldiers	Total from Highlands	Local to shire in which settled	Total of labourers
Strelitz	62	12 (19.3)	21 (33.8)	21 (33.8)
Borelandbog & Benniebeg	42	4 (9.5)	11 (26.1)	19 (45.2)
Rannoch	23	21 (91.3)	17 (73.9)	19 (82.6)
Lovat & Cromarty	139	122 (87.7)	97 (69.7)	109 (78.4)

Table 3 reveals that the settlement of soldiers on the annexed estates was little more than an exercise in military demobilisation, and in no real sense involved the successful introduction of non-Highland personnel or skills. Apart from those settled on the estate of Perth, already the most Lowland and improved in character, the vast majority of soldiers were Highlanders and

49. A.M. Smith, *Jacobite Estates of the 'Forty-Five*, p. 157; N.L.S., Fletcher of Saltoun Papers, Ms 17590, f. 68; S.R.O., F.E.P. E730/29/1; E723/2; E727/50/4(1); E727/50/9.
50. J. Innes, *loc. cit.*, p. 116; A.M. Smith, *op. cit.*, pp. 31 & 58; Anon, *Political Observations Occasioned by the State of Agriculture in the North of Scotland* (n.p., 1756), p. 18; S.R.O., F.E.P. E727/14, pp. 6–8; E727/48/1(2).
51. S.R.O., F.E.P. E777/288/6,20; E783/90/2; E787/28/1, 4–5. The Highlands are taken to mean the counties of Caithness, Sutherland, Ross, Cromarty, Inverness and Argyll. In Rannoch, 18- or 78%- of the colonists were in fact from Perthshire, but are listed as Highlanders since they were born in the 'Highland' and Gaelic speaking parishes of Blair Atholl, Fortingale, Logierait, Kenmore, Killin and Dull.

thus part of the perceived problem which internal colonisation was supposed to address. Crucially, the bulk of them were agricultural day labourers and had few or no manufacturing skills, which reduced the aim of stimulating industrial development to a matter of wishful thinking. Internal colonisation by sailors also proved illusory. In June 1763 in Lewis, Doctor John Mackenzie, adviser to Mackenzie of Seaforth, informed the board that 'a good number of sailors and soldiers natives here, returning upon the reduction, are willing to settle as fishers'. Seaforth later agreed to settle 33 sailors from the overcrowded station at New Tarbat: however, only half of those sent over to Lewis came from outwith the Highlands.[52]

The priority given to military qualifications at the expense of ability to improve was compounded by the board's decision to encourage settlement outwith the annexed estates themselves. Large numbers of demobilised sailors preferred the prospect of settling on the properties of Lord Deskford, Francis Garden and Robert Farquhar of Seathraw, which were situated on the north-east coast and already exhibited relatively improved agriculture and fishing. The immediate result was a failure to wholly concentrate effort and investment in relatively underdeveloped north-western areas. Similarly, in Campbeltown, there was little demand or potential use for the 24 sailors sent there by the Commissioners. Local men pressed by the Navy during the war had already returned home and recommenced their fishing activities. Indeed, Peter Stewart, Provost of Campbeltown, complained that the arrival of large numbers of men under the aegis of the board had resulted in a surplus of labour and a collapse in wages which had impaired the town's own attempts at a post-war reconstruction of its fishing industry.[53]

The Annexed Estates and Crofting

Comprehensive failure can too easily disguise the fact that the efforts of the Annexed Estates Commission nevertheless had crucial long-term consequences for the Highlands. In order to implement the directives of the settlement scheme, estate factors had been required to find at least 1,500 arable acres and 3,000 grazing acres. This in itself represented an estate management challenge of some magnitude. Furthermore, estates like Lovat and Coigach witnessed substantial upheaval as half-pay officers added to the disruption created by efforts to recruit and then settle ordinary soldiers. On the estates of Lovat and Cromarty the factor, Captain John Forbes of New, stated that to construct the military settlements would require the appropriation of particular sites 'where the present tenants may be hurt by grounds taken off them'. In other areas such as Strowan and Monaltry the accommodation of soldiers led to the removal of subtenantry and erosion of traditional farm size and

52. S.R.O., F.E.P. E727/50/17, 21, 37; E727/14; E732/15/1.
53. N.L.S., Fletcher of Saltoun Papers, Ms 17590, f. 68; S.R.O., F.E.P. E721/8, p. 32; E727/50/3, 4(1), 5–7, 22(1).

arable holdings.[54] The overall importance of military demobilisation in a Highland estate context, therefore, lay in the fact that it generated an unusually intense period of acute pressure on landed resources. This ensured that crofting was further entrenched as a logical response to the competing settlement demands of single tenants capable of improvement and large amounts of smaller tenantry, either removed to make way for favoured single tenants, or with legitimate claims through involvement in the military. Amid the welter of these conflicting expectations the creation of small individual croft holdings appeared to solve several problems simultaneously. They retained the labour required by single tenants while also encouraging populations to shift over into industrial or artisan occupations by denying them enough land to survive on through purely agricultural activity. Ironically, the primary effect of these early crofts on the annexed estates was actually to encourage the Commissioners to create consolidated single-tenant farms by allowing for the break-up of existing multiple tenancies and the clearing of their redundant populations onto excessively divided holdings. On Strowan, for example, the settlement of Lieutenant Archibald Campbell, which entailed the removal of three small tenants, was authorised on the understanding that it would encourage one amongst their number who, though an excellent weaver, 'neglects his trade striving with a poor farm which is likely to get the better of him'.[55] A similar outcome resulted from Lieutenant Archibald MacDonnell's request for the farms of Carnochroy and Achaglean on the estate of Barrisdale. The board ordered the farms' poorer subtenants to be removed to the coast and given crofts upon the same conditions as those accommodated under the King's Cottager scheme.[56] These were significant developments: had the Commission limited themselves to creating such holdings for soldiers only, then crofting tenure would have been restricted to a few numerically insignificant examples. However, once it became a recognised solution to the problem of dislocated subtenant populations, its implementation across the region became far more likely and more widespread. Thus the crucial impact of returning military personnel upon any Highland estate lay less in their actual settlement than in the domino effect they created amongst the main body of the population. This was precisely what occurred on the estates of Lovat and Coigach. On the former, over the period 1762–1770, fifteen half-pay officers put pressure on the authorities to be accommodated on certain farms or to utilise more fully the possessions they already held. In order to justify their applications, officers, in an astute and quite deliberate way, emphasised their enhanced ability to improve as well as the positive example generated by prominent local men instituting progressive farming methods and work practices. Captain Hugh Fraser noted how his 'first education was in the farming way before he went to

54. S.R.O., F.E.P. E727/14, p. 9–11, meeting dated 20 February 1764; E721/7, p, 59; E773/32/2(10).
55. S.R.O., F.E.P. E721/7, pp. 162 & 166.
56. S.R.O., F.E.P. E721/7, p. 156; E721/8, p. 125.

the army, and by his being quartered in different villages in England, Scotland and Ireland, he had occasion to observe the different methods of farming practised in those parts'.[57] It remained clear, however, that the settlement of such half-pay officers meant the removal of smaller tenantry. As early as February 1762, Lieutenant James Fraser requested the farm of Glenconvinth and the eviction of 'several tenants who are not able to improve'.[58] Later, when discussing the resettlement of small tenants removed from a farm in Stratherrick as part of a final attempt to stabilise arrangements on the estate, Forbes summarised the impact of such demands upon tenurial patterns. He observed: 'I do not see any place so proper as Bunchgavy because the tenants there have but small possessions, and can more easily be accommodated in shorts [sic] and pendicles, than men of more substance who possess larger farms'.[59]

Coigach, likewise, saw the arrival of five half-pay officers and a corresponding use of crofting to settle those removed as a result. As with other aspects of the annexed estates, the contemporaneous settlement of demobilised sailors provided local managers with a model of how to proceed. In April 1763 a report on the suitability of establishing fishing at Lochbroom was submitted to the board. It stressed that while cod and herring were plentiful, 'the fishers cannot subsist in this desert country by sales of fresh fish in their neighbourhood'. It was clear, the report argued, that a certain amount of acreage to 'support' the fishermen was necessary, though 'trade must be their only object because there is but little cultivated ground'. As a result of these recommendations the fishermen settled at Coigach received a maximum of two acres.[60] Another memorandum by the factor in July 1764 illustrates the rapid adoption of these distinctive tenurial arrangements for more general estate management. It advocated settling as fishermen 90 families whose individual annual rents totalled a maximum of 30 shillings. Although this proposal proved too radical and expensive to implement comprehensively, ongoing pressure exerted by half-pay officers ensured that smaller tenantry from the farms of Auchiltibuie, Riddroch, Ullapool and North Langwell were either dispossessed entirely or lost substantial amounts of arable and particularly pastoral land. Ensuing congestion, division and piecemeal crofting on the farms of Corrie, Bibiscally, Rive and Dornie were given further momentum in the early 1770s when the factor argued that the poverty of smaller tenantry meant that radically reduced holdings were the only effective means of settlement. Moreover, the use of crofting at the fishing complex at Isle Martin was advocated for the small tenants of South

57. S.R.O., F.E.P., E721/7, pp. 156 & 289; E769/91/1–323. For a similar tactic by ordinary soldiers manipulating the programme of improvement, see S.R.O., F.E.P. E721/7, p. 68.
58. S.R.O., F.E.P. E769/91/54. For a similar scenario on the farm of Dunballoch, see S.R.O., F.E.P., E721/8, p. 35.
59. S.R.O., F.E.P. E769/91/149, 154(1–2), 190(1–2), 221(2).
60. A.M. Smith, *Jacobite Estates of the 'Forty-Five*, p. 162; S.R.O., F.E.P. E721/19; E746/75/1–74; E746/79/1–10; E746/1–114; E746/186/1.

Langwell, whose loss of grazing to Lieutenant Simon Mackenzie had made their traditional arable holdings untenable.[61]

Crucially, the emergence of crofting was not limited to estates like Coigach and Barrisdale managed directly by the Commission. Co-operation with other proprietors in attempting to establish new industries, most especially fishing, sparked a debate on the pivotal relationship between landholding and full-time specialisation in one particular economic activity. It was quickly recognised that the amount of land given to colonists would determine their progress and success as fishermen or artisans. Peter Stewart in Campbeltown, who urged the board to promote fishing in underdeveloped areas such as Skye and Lewis, recommended that traditional agricultural practices and landholding systems be abandoned. He added that activities such as summer transhumance to sheilings ought to be prevented so that communities could focus more consistently on full-time fishing. His advice was mirrored by Alexander Garden who, in March 1763, argued that if colonists were awarded more than three acres, it would 'probably induce them to become farmers rather than fishers'.[62] The idea that reduced landholding could ensure a genuine commitment to commercial endeavour formed a central and defining characteristic of the crofting system. The Commissioners in turn applied pressure on those private landlords settling ex-military personnel to adopt the strategy of limiting land-holding. This ensured the dissemination of crofting-style tenure beyond districts controlled by the board itself. In mid-August 1763 John Campbell, third Earl of Breadalbane, petitioned the Commission for support in settling some 30 soldiers who had returned to his estate in Netherlorne. The poorer sort, he hoped, could be settled on the coast, supplied with boats and tackle by the Commission, while he built houses and kailyards to be leased at a reduced rent. The board agreed to the proposal, but demanded the Earl ensure that resettled soldiers secure a livelihood by fishing alone. The case of the Netherlorne soldiers contains some important implications for the origins of crofting. Lorne was, by Highland standards, a reasonably well-developed area commercially. The Bonawe furnace and Easdale slateworks, as well as some pre-existing though limited developments in fishing, meant that large sections of the local population already relied on relatively small amounts of land – providing Breadalbane with a useful pre-existing tenurial model for more generalised implementation.[63] Given crofting's nineteenth-century

61. S.R.O., F.E.P. E721/19, pp. 20, 22, 24, 34; E746/113/44, 57, 60, 84–6; E746/75/5; E 746/175/22.
62. S.R.O., F.E.P. E727/50/37; E727/14.
63. S.R.O., F.E.P. E728/44(1); E727/14, petition dated 15 August 1763; S.R.O., Court of Sessions Productions C.S. 96/3108, 'Log Book of Campbeltown Registered Vessel, *The Peggy*', pp. 31–32, 66. I am grateful to Prof. A.I. Macinnes for his suggestion that the relatively advanced industrial sites of Bonawe and Easdale in all probability provided an additional local model of reduced agricultural holdings.

reputation as the most obvious symptom of industrial underdevelopment in the Highlands, it is ironic that extractive industry may well have provided a local model for the croft holdings Breadalbane constructed for his soldiers.

Nor was Lorne the only area that witnessed the implementation of crofting ideas. In Lewis Dr John Mackenzie informed the board that Seaforth had authorised the use of at least £150 for the development of fishing settlements. Especially anxious to encourage commercial expansion upon the west coast, the Commission donated an additional £300 in November 1763. Again, the emphasis was not on efficient agriculture but on settlement patterns that supported and complemented industrial or commercial activity. On 17 November Mackenzie informed the Commissioners that he had commenced settling ex-soldiers and sailors on what amounted, in effect, to the first planned crofting settlement in the Outer Hebrides, at Holm in the Point district of Lewis. He concluded by arguing 'that giving acres of land to the fishers is inexpedient as it would divert them from their proper business and that a kail yard and a potato croft is sufficient'.[64] It remains difficult to quantify the long-term consequences of these events, but it seems clear that the high-profile innovations of the settlement scheme gifted to Seaforth a theoretical model that he then applied to the more general management of his estate. In 1765, only two years after developments at Holm, Seaforth began the process of farm division on the west coast of Lewis and in the Park district in order to benefit more fully from kelp production and fishing. While holdings generally retained their essentially agricultural character until the 1790s, Seaforth's willingness to experiment with new tenurial structures in the mid-1760s should be seen in the context of his recent co-operative venture with the annexed estates.[65]

Conclusion

Any attempt to evaluate the Board of Annexed Estates' performance as an agency of improvement should recognise that it was never a free agent, and that as an official state institution it was inextricably linked to the increasingly powerful influence of the military in the Highlands. Recruiting activity, evident upon all the estates managed by the Commission, produced insecurities in both the tenurial structure and the influential land management class of the tacksman. This contrasts markedly with orthodox improvement theory which stressed how progress could only be achieved within the protective framework of secure and stable tenurial arrangements. The impact of recruitment on the Lovat estate demonstrates that the drive to achieve agriculturally feasible, rational and profitable single-tenant farms was com-

64. S.R.O., F.E.P. E727/14; E721/7; E746/186/1; N.L.S., Fletcher of Saltoun Papers, Ms 17589, f. 143.
65. S.R.O., Gillanders of Highfield Papers, GD 427/33 & 150. For the creation of small lots in the early 1770s, see GD 427/206/17.

promised by promises to maintain the sub-tenant families of soldiers. Moreover, the military reductions of 1763 reinforced confusion over policies relating to farm structure and size. Yet, paradoxically, the acute pressure exerted by demobilisation also forced a series of tenurial innovations that finally addressed the growing problem of social dislocation brought on by non-subletting leases.

The Board of Annexed Estates has gained a reputation for promoting planned villages and more generalised 'progress' in the Highlands. But the actual performance of the Commission demonstrates how the specific aim of Lowland-style agrarian improvement in the Highlands was rapidly undermined. By pursuing the sailor and soldier resettlement plan the board was promoting the development of the historically important crofting system. Furthermore, by encouraging such settlement outside the annexed estates, as in the Isle of Lewis and on the Lorne properties of the Breadalbane family, the board ensured that these early crofting arrangements survived its own relatively short life, and provided a practical model that was to have a profound impact upon the region as a whole. The role of the board in the period from 1756 to 1763 also calls into question the evolutionary nature of the crofting system: if anything, it had a purposeful and planned beginning. The development of crofting tenure as early as 1763 also contradicts current assumptions about the timing of its emergence. While there has been an acknowledgement that 'similar models' existed in the 1760s, they have been dismissed as strictly 'ephemeral' in nature. Instead, the crofting system is seen as emerging in Argyll in the last decade of eighteenth century and in the first years of the nineteenth. It appears, however, that this interpretation fails, at least chronologically.[66]

It is clear that the era of government intervention in the mid- to late eighteenth century was characterised primarily by the belief that tenurial and land practices in the region ought to be geared to population retention, as well as efficient agriculture, especially when such populations had a clear military usefulness. This calls into question the assumption that the state did not, as was the case on the continent, seek to influence or modify the process of improvement in order to avoid excessive social dislocation and disruption. This may well have been true of the Lowlands, but that particular area lacked the high-profile military utility of the Highlands and did not arouse the same level of state concern. The deliberate modification of subtenant removal and the emphasis on settlement apparent on the annexed estates had more in common with a continental model of social engineering than with the situation in the Scottish Lowlands, where similar social concerns were

66. S.R.O., Breadalbane Muniments, GD 112/9/3/3/14. Netherlorne rentals of the 1780s reveal the continued presence of soldiers settled on £3 plots: A.I. Macinnes, 'Scottish Gaeldom: The First Phase of Clearance', pp. 83–85; J.B. Caird, 'The Creation of Crofts and New Settlement Patterns in the Highlands and Islands of Scotland', in *Scottish Geographical Magazine*, vol. 103 (1987), pp. 67–79.

alleviated by a generally buoyant and more diverse economy.[67] This marks a noticeably early and significant difference between the two regions in terms of approaches to improvement. It also suggests that the Board of Annexed Estates' true significance lies in the fact that the state and its military concerns were responsible, to a degree not previously recognised, for providing an initial example that led to a later, more generalised regional slide into excessive subdivision and crofting.

67. T.M. Devine, 'Social responses to Agrarian "Improvement": the Highland and Lowland Clearances in Scotland', in R.A. Houston & I.D. Whyte (eds.), *Scottish Society, 1500–1800* (Cambridge, 1989), p. 151; J. Innes, *loc. cit.*, p 119.

CHAPTER FOUR

The Campbells of Breadalbane: Recruitment and Highland Estate Management, 1745–1802

Although the state-sponsored Annexed Estates Commission pioneered tenurial models that sought to accommodate the differing and often conflicting demands and expectations of military levying and improved estate management, it was private, individual landlords, as the main agents of recruitment in the region who more fully developed and implemented its ideas. The episodic distribution of land as a reward for military service made for a confusion in Highland estate management that was all but absent in Lowland Scotland. Recruitment, therefore, needs to be taken into account when considering the ability or inability of Highland landlords to implement improvement. In the Lowlands, fundamental agricultural change from the early 1760s has been summarised as 'a revolution from above, with landlord power a principal influence'. By contrast, Highland proprietors, while endowed with the same legal, social and economic power – if not more – have been judged as failing to effect similar improvement compared with their Lowland counterparts.[1] Examination of the Lorne, Glenorchy and Lochtayside estates of the Campbells of Breadalbane enables us to judge whether large-scale recruiting activity limited, hampered or altered the options open to Highland landlords in the management of their properties. Charting recruitment through all its phases, from its political origins down to its impact upon the various tenurial groups upon Highland estates not only addresses the issue of landlord and tenant relations but also highlights intertenantry links, curiously neglected as an aspect of social conditions in the

1. T.M. Devine, *The Transformation of Rural Scotland: Social Change and the Agrarian Economy, 1660–1815* (Edinburgh, 1994), p. 165; T.C. Smout, 'Scottish Landowners and Economic Growth, 1650–1850', in *Scottish Journal of Political Economy*, vol. 11 (1964), pp. 218, 228–230; R.H. Campbell, 'The Scottish Improvers and the Course of Agrarian Change in the Eighteenth Century', in L.M. Cullen & T.C. Smout (eds.), *Comparative Aspects of Scottish and Irish Social History, 1600–1900* (Edinburgh, 1977), pp. 205–12; A.I. Macinnes, 'Scottish Gaeldom: The First Phase of Clearance', in T.M. Devine & R. Mitchison (eds.), *People and Society in Scotland, 1760–1830*, vol. 1 (Edinburgh, 1988), p. 80; T.M. Devine, 'Social Responses to Agrarian 'Improvement': The Highland & Lowland Clearances in Scotland', in R.A. Houston & I.D. Whyte (eds.), *Scottish Society, 1500–1800* (Cambridge, 1989), pp. 151 & 158.

region. Moreover, such a case study not only provides information on western coastal areas closely associated with later eighteenth-century recruiting, but also on more southern and eastern inland areas.[2]

The Political Origins of Estate Recruitment: the Argyll and Sutherland Fencibles of 1759

The political backdrop to recruitment on the Breadalbane estates during the mid- and later decades of the eighteenth century was one of hostility between its proprietors and the ducal House of Argyll.[3] In June 1759 Lord Chancellor Hardwicke notified John Campbell, third Earl of Breadalbane, that his estates in Highland Perthshire and Argyll had been highlighted as a suitable source of recruits.[4] Hardwicke inquired how many men he could spare, adding that the government had already consulted the Duke of Argyll over the levy, which was to be modelled loosely on the Argyll militia of 1746. The Lord Chancellor's initial and subsequent requests as well as the political infighting over what eventually became the fencible regiments of Argyll and Sutherland reveal several crucial aspects of British army recruitment in the region. First, its centralised and highly politicised nature: Argyll, who was also expected to contribute men, was perceived as the natural manager while Breadalbane was seen as something of a natural counterpoise to Argathelian dominance. Second, it demonstrates that initiative and pressure often came from government and not, as has been suggested in the past, from proprietors themselves.[5] The fact that Argyll and Breadalbane had raised men in 1746 was important. Previous recruiting performances provided central government with a precedent and a benchmark against which it could measure both its own demands and the response of proprietors. The '45 continued therefore to overshadow government policy for the region. However, such requests contradicted the government's own demilitarising policy, and indicate that Westminster continued to act on the assumption that the Highlands had not developed from its militarised condition of the 1740s.

In his reply Breadalbane argued that maintaining the large numbers of men necessary for estate recruiting was incompatible with the process of improvement. As a result, he was not in a position to offer a substantial number of recruits; he added pointedly that this was because he had implemented

---

2. S.D.M., Carpenter, 'Patterns of Recruitment of the Highland Regiments of the British Army, 1756–1815' (University of St. Andrews, M.Litt. Thesis, 1977), pp. 87–88. See also M. Clough & E. Richards, *Cromartie: Highland Life, 1650–1914* (Aberdeen, 1989), p. 38.
3. B.L., Hardwicke Papers, Add Ms, 35450, ff. 179, 204, 207, 214, 237, 241, 244; B.L., Newcastle Papers, Add Ms 32727, f. 13; B.A.M., Box 47/5/121 & 133; Box 54/4/127.
4. B.L., Hardwicke Papers, Add Ms, 35450, f. 261.
5. J. Prebble, *Mutiny: Highland Regiments in Revolt, 1743–1804* (Harmondsworth, Middlesex, 1975), pp. 95, 97, 101.

estate policies which government itself had earlier promoted and encouraged.[6] Given their mutual antipathy, it is ironic that both Argyll and Breadalbane were in a similar situation. They were in fact hostages to their earlier high-profile military backing for the Hanoverian state in 1745: a state which now, paradoxically, sought the very military capability that as commercial landlords both had commenced eroding through improvement. It is also testimony to the pressure exerted by government that Highland landlords like Argyll and Breadalbane were reacting initially to events outside their control. Argyll's managerial position did eventually enable him to protect his own interests by manipulating his political opponents. He envisaged, for example, Breadalbane's tenantry as a resource that could limit excessive recruitment upon his own estate. Despite obvious apprehension, however, neither landlord refused to raise men. Proprietors by no means regretted or disliked the displays of patriotism which recruiting entailed; indeed, Scottish elites during the Seven Years War attracted attention for the conspicuous nature of their commitment and loyalty. But landlords were fully aware of recruitment's detrimental side-effects and usually attempted to control the process in their own localities to ensure some form of damage limitation.

Having been asked to supervise recruitment in Argyll and Highland Perthshire, there is little doubt that the Duke of Argyll implemented a self-interested political agenda. In July 1759 he wrote to Barrington requesting commissions and nominating field officers. Simultaneously, Breadalbane became aware that he had been deprived of patronage with respect to senior posts. He informed Hardwicke that Argyll obviously did not wish to see him gain additional political interest in Argyllshire and had sought to deny him influence with the proposed regiment.[7] Fearing that his political opponents would dominate the whole process, Breadalbane offered, instead, to raise 500 men from his own Perthshire estate. He argued this would involve conceding one years rent – a total of £2,162 – in return for which he expected complete control of all commissions as a form of indemnity. Breadalbane calculated that twenty officers' posts would be worth £2,309.[8] Several characteristics of Highland recruiting during the rest of the century can be illustrated by these developments. First, in order to retain political credibility the Earl had been forced, against his better economic judgement, to offer a substantial number of men. This necessity aside, however, the value of lost rent relative to commissions demonstrates that he had not abandoned attempts to utilise his estate as a profitable concern. Military entrepreneurship, whether forced on Highland landlords through political pressure or not, still represented estate commercialism – if in an alternative form. Despite

6. B.L., Hardwicke Papers, Add Ms, 35450, ff. 262–285.
7. P.R.O., W.O. 1979, unnumbered letters dated 17 & 30 July 1759; B.L., Hardwicke Papers, Add Ms 35450, ff. 266, 268 & 270.
8. B.L., Hardwicke Papers, Add Ms 35450, ff. 270, 272–74; S.R.O., Breadalbane Muniments, GD 112/15/359/3.

Breadalbane's assertions that recruiting was incompatible with improvement, his own calculations illustrate that in terms of profit and, above all, valuable political prestige, military levying represented an entirely rational estate strategy.

The Earl's determination to benefit financially from recruiting nonetheless masked the fact that he remained vulnerable to government pressure. Although gentry like John Stewart of Invernahyle and Duncan Campbell of Glenure made it clear they would raise men for his proposed battalion, Breadalbane's offer was declined. Gentry in his interest consequently refused to raise men for what they perceived as Argyll's 'private corps'.[9] Ironically, by August 1759 the Highland county with the best reputation for conspicuous loyalty to the British state was exhibiting a distinct reluctance to contribute to the army. As a result, government applied even greater pressure on Breadalbane. Hardwicke wrote:

> I presume that if your lordship should sit still and not exert yourself to furnish any men to this regiment [Argyll's] that will be misrepresented here, and there are persons in another camp at court who I suspect would take that up. The neglect would be called a backwardness to serve the government in this exigency; and some impartial persons might be drawn to say 'Tis from ... a *personal disobligation*, but that is not reason not to exert to serve the King and his government'. There is nothing more difficult than to set such things right at court.[10]

This was, in essence, an instruction to Breadalbane from the Lord Chancellor to raise men or face political oblivion. The complex amalgam of state expectation and coercion shows that, far from representing a remnant of clanship's military ethos, regiment raising in the post-Culloden era was in fact symptomatic of the chiefs' desire for cultural, social and political acceptance and assimilation.[11] Paradoxically, this left erstwhile chiefs susceptible to demands that they conform to obsolete perceptions of clanship still held at the political centre which, in fact, clashed with 'modern' notions of improvement increasingly held in what was the supposed Highland periphery. The issue of recruitment, therefore, contradicts earlier models of British imperialism which stress a 'progressive' metropolitan core and a relatively 'backward' and provincial Highlands: indeed, the relationship between landlords and government in this instance shows precisely the opposite.[12]

---

9. B.A.M., Box 47/11/94; S.R.O., Campbell of Stonefield Papers, GD 14/145–6; S.R.O., Campbell of Barcaldine Muniments, GD 170/1061/10; GD 170/1061/17/1; B.L., Hardwicke Papers, Add Ms 35450, f. 281.
10. B.L., Hardwicke Papers, Add Ms 35450, f. 277.
11. D.M. Henderson, *Highland Soldier: A Social Study of the Highland Regiments, 1820–1920* (Edinburgh, 1989), p. 20.
12. N.C. Landsman, 'The Provinces and the Empire: Scotland, the American Colonies and the Development of British Provincial Identity', in L. Stone (ed.), *An Imperial State at War: Britain from 1689 to 1815* (London, 1994), p. 260.

Faced with little real choice, the Earl agreed to Argyll's proposal that he supply 200 men. Argyll's ally, James Murray, second Duke of Atholl, likewise received little or no consultation until matters had been finalised. In August 1759 Milton wrote: 'The Duke of Argyll bids me to acquaint your Grace of the government's resolve to send a regiment of Highlanders to Germany, and that it would be very acceptable to His Majesty if your Grace could raise two companies of 100 men each'.[13] This was an entirely different proposal from what Atholl had originally envisaged. However, given the need for patriotic display, especially from Highland elites, both Breadalbane and Atholl had in effect been presented with a *fait accompli*. Argyll's managerial control ensured that opponents like Breadalbane completed the recruiting process while he gained most of the political rewards. As a result, leading families increasingly recognised that it was not enough merely to contribute men; the best option was in fact to raise an entire regiment. A report of 1760 to Atholl concluded:

> They are talking of raising three more regiments and though you should not have one raised by way of a battalion in Atholl, you may lay your account, there will be recruiting there if there are men amongst you to be got . . . but what weighs most with me is it would be a fine puff for your Grace to raise a battalion at this period and though you have had great merit all along in raising companies in different corp, that is less known above, than if you had the nomination of a battalion that will be known by your name.[14]

The political pressure to oversee the recruitment of battalions was clearly intense. Many proprietors felt compelled to raise their own levies and derive maximum benefit from a process that was likely to occur on their property regardless. Failure to obtain management of an entire battalion entailed the loss of estate men for no real political or material gain. The 1760 report to Atholl noted that in three years his estate had lost 700–1,000 men. This represented a huge material loss to the Atholl family: quite literally, these men were conceived of in terms of a lost harvest.

Contributing in no small measure to this pressure was the fact that military commissions could decisively influence the political balance of power in the counties. Argyll's unrivalled access to military patronage, for instance, has already been noted with respect to the victory of his candidate in Sutherland during the 1761 election. A similar situation also undermined Breadalbane's electoral performance in Perthshire. The county's M.P. during the late 1750s was Lord John Murray, half-brother to Atholl and colonel of the 42nd

13. B.L., Hardwicke Papers, Add Ms 35450, f. 281; B.L., Newcastle Papers, 33047, f. 285; B.A.M., Box 47/11/115. Breadalbane and Atholl did at least get the benefit of commissions for prominent tacksmen and creditors. J.M. Bulloch, *Territorial Soldiering in the North East of Scotland during 1759–1814* (Aberdeen, 1914), p. 25; S.R.O., John Macgregor Collection, GD 50/26/31/1.
14. D.H., Loudon Papers, A/993, ff. 7–8; B.A.M., Box 47/12/3.

Highland Regiment. Both Argyll and Atholl supported his opponent, John Murray of Strowan, who, in turn, was opposed by Breadalbane. By February 1761 it was clear that electors were not prepared to oppose Argyll for fear of jeopardising their relationship with government and their hopes of future promotion. Indeed, it was widely accepted that Argyll's interest would ensure that 'some of the voters who have civil employments and several who are in the military, may be induced by that means to give him their promises'. Table 1 demonstrates that the Highland electorate contained a relatively high level of military personnel, and it was therefore hardly surprising that officers like Major Robert Campbell of Finab, normally in Breadalbane's interest, nevertheless backed Argyll's candidate. After his election defeat the Earl openly conceded that 'if he [Argyll] had not made use of the influence his public station gave him, Mr Murray would not have been chose for Perthshire'.[15]

Recruitment and Estate Management, 1745–1783

Government, electoral, social and peer pressure explains why certain estates, especially those of politically active elites and their clients, experienced significant levels of recruitment.[16] Levying was conspicuous upon the Breadalbane estates during every conflict from the 1745 uprising until the French Revolutionary War. Land in exchange for military service, moreover, continued alongside the use of bounties as a mechanism whereby men were procured locally, which, in turn, linked recruitment firmly to the tenurial condition and overall development of the estate.

During the early stages of the 1745 campaign John Campbell, Lord Glenorchy and future third Earl of Breadalbane, came under severe political and military pressure from both sides to raise men. In August 1745 Sir John Cope, Commander-in-chief in Scotland, requested that Glenorchy raise his father's Lochtayside tenantry and join the Earl of Loudon's 54th Highland Regiment. The following month the Jacobite high command ordered Lochtayside and Glenlochay men to enlist in their service at a rate of one recruit per merkland – a total of 310 men. Eventually, in late 1745, when the third Duke of Argyll commenced raising the Argyllshire militia, the Breadalbane family mustered four companies from its estates in that particular county – in all a total of 400 men.[17] The threat of estate devastation by the Jacobite army

---

15. L. Namier & J. Brooke (eds.), *The House of Commons, 1754–90*, vol. 3 (London, 1964), pp. 186–7. Despite Lord Chancellor Hardwicke's opposition to Murray of Strowan several voters conceded that Argyll's local power was an equal consideration. B.A.M., Box 47/12/71, 116, 118; Box 47/13/27, 46, 52, 90; B.L., Hardwicke Papers, Add Ms 35449, ff. 243, 272; Add Ms 35450, ff. 305 & 309.
16. Pressure to recruit was invariably passed onto smaller, laird families by their noble patrons. See B.A.M., Box 47/11/119,123,128 & 141; Box 47/12/5; S.R.O., Campbell of Barcaldine Papers, GD 170/1061/18/1.
17. B.L., Hardwicke Papers, Add Ms 35450, ff. 40 & 63, 72; S.R.O., Breadalbane Muniments, GD 112/9/49; GD112/16/1/5; GD 112/11/7/1/15(1–2).

did however prevent mobilisation of Lochtayside manpower for the Crown. This situation was compounded by the attitude of Breadalbane's tenantry. Their hostility towards armed service on either side suggests that Highland communities had little or no enthusiasm for military activity which left lands and farms unprotected and which produced difficulties within their own local, agrarian economies. There was widespread concern that farming would be undermined by indiscriminate or intensive levying. Glenorchy himself highlighted how districts of Lochaber were lying waste due to excessive Jacobite recruitment and a consequent lack of agricultural labour. A similar situation, compounded by subsequent destruction in the aftermath of Culloden, ensured that arable land in Stratherrick and Glenmoriston lay unused for periods stretching from five to fifteen years. Fear of crop loss through delayed harvesting and the devastation of unprotected farms not only account for the reluctance of many areas to mobilise, but also help explain the desertion levels evident amongst Highland contingents on both sides.[18] Breadalbane tenantry were certainly not prepared to enlist unless enough men were left to guarantee normal agricultural activity. Manpower drain on the Duke of Argyll's property and that of Sir James Macdonald of Sleat did reduce rent payments and productivity; while on Breadalbane's Argyllshire estate tenant loss to the militia meant that a substantial number of managerial personnel were missing through the autumn, winter and spring of 1745–6. The Earl was forced to write off his rent for that particular year. In 1757 Glenorchy and Netherlorne rentals totalled £1,549; even allowing for increases over the intervening decade, it is clear that mobilisation in 1745 entailed significant financial loss, emphasising how recruiting which utilised tenant manpower could often be incompatible with efficient agriculture and profitable estate management.[19]

Similar problems arose during the Seven Years War. Breadalbane contributed around 300 men to the Black Watch and the regiments of Murray-Keith and Argyll, having calculated this number could be spared without ruining productivity. Manpower demands, especially those arising from the Argyll Fencible Regiment, resulted in the re-adoption of recruiting methods used during the Spanish War of Succession which determined liability for men on the basis of estimated or real rent. In November 1759 Argyll heritors agreed that every £10 of real rent made them liable for one recruit. Duncan Campbell of Glenure was thus expected to find seven men for his rental of £77.17.4 in Lismore and Appin; similarly, Breadalbane's overall Argyll rental produced a quota of 155 men. Given that bounties on the open market were three to five guineas above the amount provided by government, recruitment necessarily involved granting land or, alternatively, expenditure of £22–£37 for Glenure

18. B.L., Hardwicke Papers, Add Ms, 35450, ff. 51–2, 65; N.L.S., Saltoun Papers, Ms 16604, f. 65; S.R.O., F.E.P., E769/43/9(1); E769/91/91(1).
19. B.L., Hardwicke Papers, Add Ms, 35450, f. 266; G.U.B.R.C., J.A. & J.L. Campbell & Lamond, W.S., UGD 37/2/1, pp. 43 & 51; S.R.O., Breadalbane Muniments, GD 112/14/12/7/7.

and £488–£813 for Breadalbane. Without the use of land as a substitute for monetary bounties, levying would have cost 28–48% and 31–52% of Glenure and Breadalbane's respective rents. Land as a recruiting mechanism was thus underpinned by clear financial logic. Moreover, by this method the pressure to find men or, alternatively, the finance to purchase recruits, could be exerted downwards onto tenantry. In Glenorchy, tacksmen were held responsible for quotas; while in Kintyre failure to provide recruits meant tenantry, already suffering labour shortages, were obliged to pay £5 for substitutes. Recruitment under these conditions amounted to a second rental demand and constituted a serious additional drain on the relatively underdeveloped capital reserves of Highland tenantry.[20]

The cost and disruption arising from levying witnessed the development of quite deliberate recruiting strategies. The early years of the 1756–63 conflict saw Breadalbane use recruitment as a social purgative. He encouraged or forced men from certain social backgrounds into the army, adding: 'I have carefully glean'd this country of useless mouths who fed upon the industrious, by getting them to engage in the army or navy'.[21] Clearly, he intended that, where at all possible, recruitment would assist and complement the development of a more dependable tenantry, as well as the general process of improvement. A military census of Breadalbane's Argyll lands in 1759 reveals the social agenda within estate recruitment. Involving 51 farms, mostly in Glenorchy and Lorne, the census showed a male population of 265: 42 men were marked for service – 15.8% of available numbers. In all, recruiting affected exactly 50% of the farms listed.

Table 4. Social and Tenurial Origins of
Glenorchy and Netherlorne Recruits, 1759[22]

Tenurial group	Total & %	Total Recruits & %	Social profile of unmarried men	Revised total of recruits & %
Tenants*	116 (43.7)	2 (4.7)	17 (51.5)	19 (45.2)
Married men & Cottars	44 (16.6)	7 (16.6)	3 (9)	10 (23.8)
Unmarried men	105 (39.6)	33 (78.5)	13 (39.3)	13 (30.9)
	265	42	33	42

20. B.L., Hardwicke Papers, Add Ms 35450, f. 268; S.R.O., Campbell of Barcaldine Papers, GD 170/1061/10, 18(1); GD 170/1534; S.R.O., Campbell of Breadalbane Muniments, GD 112/39/226/1; GD 112/15/359/3; GD 112/9/48; S.R.O., John Macgregor Collection, GD 50/17/2; N.L.S., Fletcher of Saltoun Papers, Ms 16709, f. 49; Ms 16714, ff. 8 & 32.
21. B.L., Hardwicke Papers, Add Ms 35450, ff. 262 & 281; A.H. Miller (ed.), *Scottish Forfeited Estates Papers, 1715–1745* (Edinburgh, 1909), p. 301.
22. S.R.O., John Macgregor Collection, GD 50/17/1–6.* Not only denotes those holding directly from Breadalbane himself, but also the subtenants of large tacksmen like Campbell of Achalader or Glenure.

Table 4 illustrates quite clearly that the third Earl chose to focus on landless, unmarried social groups and those least involved in the estate's tenurial structure. In practical economic terms this was eminently sensible. Their removal was the least damaging with regard to lost agricultural expertise and proven rent-paying ability. These particular concerns explain the dearth of tenants within the numbers of recruits. Young, non-tenant personnel provided the best hope of continuing to extract commercial profits from the estate while simultaneously generating additional profits from military commissions and income. Given the preponderance of unmarried recruits, their social origins are important. The revised set of figures, which add the background of these men, illustrate a crucial point concerning recruitment in the Highlands during the 1756–1815 period. The level of recruits from a tenant background closely reflects their presence within the estate structure. The majority of such recruits were in fact representatives – often sons or brothers. Their involvement in the levy was the result of their relations seeking another farm or simply defending their own farm possession. These families contributed the minimal number of men required to affirm and entrench their status as tenants. By contrast, analysis of the cottar class reveals that they contributed over and above their representation within the estate. The reasons for this were primarily socio-economic. Such people were not responsible for large holdings, steelbow commitments, or investments like house and byre building. Albeit that these unmarried men and cottars were certainly related through kinship to the tenantry, it remained the case that landlords deliberately practised a policy of selective enlistment that ensured recruits did not reflect the established tenurial hierarchy or incumbent rent-paying families.

While an obvious strategy for minimising economic and financial disruption in the short term, in the longer term this policy meant that those involved in the estate's tenurial arrangements faced competitive pressure from personnel who had previously lacked land and social status. Moreover, efforts to protect tenant personnel did not by any means take priority over the completion of levying: as a result, failure to contribute sons could involve the removal of those with otherwise impressive records of rent payment and capital investment in their farms. Alternatively, on Lochtayside, tenant holdings were divided for the benefit of soldiers and their families with arable lands of a half-plough being given in certain cases to favoured personnel. This suggests that established tenantry were losing land as a result of recruitment. In direct contrast to the dispossession of well-stocked tenantry, recruitment also necessitated the creation of crofts in Netherlorne in 1763 in light of the inability of returning soldiers to finance and stock a standard farm tenancy.[23] The creation of such holdings was a legacy of the

---

23. S.R.O., John Macgregor Collection, GD 50/11/1/25; S.R.O., Breadalbane Muniments, GD 112/11/4/1/62; GD 112/11/3/4/1 & 2; GD 112/11/3/3/4; A.H. Miller (ed.), *op. cit.*, p. 301.

policy whereby cottars and landless labourers were specifically targeted for enlistment. Estate recruitment could thus clash profoundly with agrarian improvement in two distinct ways. The removal of tenant personnel went against theories that stressed the need to encourage those able to bring capital resources to bear upon the development of land. Conversely, the planting of under-capitalised individuals on reduced holdings rendered agricultural surpluses increasingly unlikely. Recruiting, in summary, could involve the removal of elements of the established tenantry and their replacement with non-tenant personnel who obtained possession through largely non-commercial criteria.

In 1778 Alexander Campbell, third son of Archibald Campbell of Achalader, gained a captaincy in the 74th Highland Regiment commanded by Lieutenant-Colonel John Campbell of Barbreck. Achalader was factor on Breadalbane's Perthshire estate and so was in an ideal position to furnish assistance to his son. The scheme 'planned out by him for levying the men was that certain tenants within the estate behoved to furnish one or more as required'.[24] Pressure was also applied to subtenants and crofters and the response of these lower social orders meant that, as in the late 1750s and early 1760s, tenants who did not furnish men were dispossessed of their holdings and reduced in social status. Crucially, however, such removals did not entail outright eviction from the estate but rather involved resettlement upon less desirable holdings. The result was an increase in subdivision and a series of bitter, internecine recriminations between the affected families that lasted for over a decade.[25] The increase in reduced holdings did not arise simply from punitive removals, however. On the farm of Ceilvellich in Glenquaich six crofts and two cottars were imposed by Achalader upon the tenants, with over half those settled having been involved in recruitment. Besides this crofting policy, it was also normal practice for those who had complied with the demand for men to have new tenant holdings created for them. However, the increased number of tenancies meant that townships like Baillemore, officially multiple-tenant farms, were in reality embryonic crofting communities, appearing gradually through piecemeal division.[26]

The recruitment of Alexander Campbell's company of a hundred men affected at least 26 farms – 10% of Breadalbane's Perthshire estate. Farms either had more crofters added, entirely new crofts created, or their tenant profile otherwise altered in some way. More importantly, crofts tended to emerge on farms already possessed by three or more tenants; it was thus upon already crowded multiple-tenant farms that crofting was concentrated. As

24. S.R.O., Breadalbane Muniments, GD 112/11/1/6/4; GD 112/11/3/1/18, 30; GD 112/11/1/4/62(2); GD 112/11/1/4/100; GD 112/11/3/1/18; P.R.O., W.O. 25/3200; M.M. McArthur (ed.), *Survey of Lochtayside, 1769* (Edinburgh, 1936), xv.
25. S.R.O., Breadalbane Muniments, GD 112/11/1/4/89; GD 112/11/1/4/59; GD 112/9/62.
26. S.R.O., Breadalbane Muniments, GD 112/11/1/4/42; GD 112/11/4/2/34(1–4).

well as Baillemore, the farms of Blarmore, Bliarliargan and Klytirie were partially crofted. These were already amongst the largest multiple tenancies on the estate, and had 27 tenants and three crofters between them. This strategy was in all likelihood an attempt to reduce dislocation by intensively settling a selective number of farms. Thus, while the impact of recruitment was by no means universal over the entire estate, several large farms were effectively reduced to crofting townships in this period.[27]

Loss of tenant land through recruitment was also evident in Argyll. In 1782 the tenants of Gualachullian in Glenorchy lost control of their croft to a soldier. Inveriananmor, likewise, was 'now let to Peter Sinclair, subtenant from Lower Fernoch, father to Sinclair, a fencible soldier'.[28] In the summer of 1783 the Argyllshire factor, John Campbell of Lochend, was ordered to inquire into the farms under his jurisdiction, and, in particular, to address the issue of developing richer, more substantial tenants. Clearly, as in the 1750s, it was intended that recruiting should not prevent or excessively disrupt the development of improved holdings. However, pressure for land exerted on the tenurial structure helped divert implementation of this particular estate strategy which, by June 1783, had moved away from a policy of farm enlargement towards one which placed equal emphasis on population settlement. Commercial and rental concerns were, admittedly, alleviated by structuring certain farms in large single tenancies for the exploitation of the cattle market. However, it was also suggested that any farms 'that are found proper for raising corns, be divided as much as may be'. The factor's final report in September 1783 stressed a policy of division amongst more able tenants, creating separate, individual single tenancies.[29] However, newly planned farms on the Island of Luing lost arable land as one or two crofts were divided off each one; indeed, 20% of the Island of Seil's arable land had been crofted by as early as 1785. Ex-soldiers featured prominently in the demand for these vacancies. This pressure on croft holdings was paralleled by a similar process whereby wealthier soldiers sought out tenant possessions.[30] In response, Campbell of Lochend targeted the Glenorchy farm of Stronmilchan near Dalmally and 'proposed [it] be divided into crofts for the accommodation of soldiers and others'. It was anticipated there would be thirty to forty claims for land. An important point to note, however, is that not all these demands arose necessarily from soldiers. As in Perthshire, a

27. The figures for Perthshire farms affected by recruitment from 1775–1785 are drawn from estate petitions. See S.R.O., Breadalbane Muniments, GD 112/11/1/2–6; GD 112/11/2/5; GD 112/9/62; GD 112/16/4/1/3; M.M. McArthur (ed.), *op. cit.*, pp. 203–207.
28. S.R.O., Breadalbane Muniments, GD 112/9/3/4/4.
29. S.R.O., Breadalbane Muniments, 'Robert Robertson's Report on Netherlorne, 1796', R.H.P. 972/5; GD 112/14/12/7/8; GD 112/12/1/2/14–15.
30. S.R.O., Breadalbane Muniments, 'Robert Robertson's Report on Netherlorne, 1796', R.H.P. 972/5; S.R.O., GD 112/14/13/4/29; GD 112/9/3/3/14; GD 112/10/2/1/35–36x; GD 112/16/4/1; GD 112/16/4/1.

domino effect was created by civilian tenantry being removed from their farms to make way for favoured military personnel. It was the acute pressure created by these displaced families, as opposed to soldiers or their dependants seeking settlement, that more often than not stimulated the development of crofting. Thus the farm of Ballavicar on the Island of Seil was broken up into fourteen crofts to provide land for soldiers as well as tenants dispossessed by Lochend's plan; while Coiash in Glenorchy was set out for twenty cottars incapable of stocking a croft.[31]

Estate petitions reveal that 20% of farms across Glenorchy and Netherlorne experienced the effects of recruitment for the American Revolutionary War. Seventy-six crofts were created by the 1783 report, whose author, significantly, was Campbell of Lochend: he had been the factor responsible under the auspices of the Board of the Annexed Estates for settling soldiers on crofts in 1763. This had obviously influenced his thinking when faced with similar pressures in 1783. These developments contradict the argument that crofting emerged in the 1790s and point, instead, to its genesis thirty years earlier.[32] Furthermore, while piecemeal overcrowding, as opposed to systematic crofting, characterised developments on Lochtayside, and with only three farms broken up completely in Argyllshire, subdivision was nonetheless a conscious policy generated in part by soldiers' land claims and, more importantly, the tenantry they displaced. This suggests that the emergence of crofting as part of the transformation of multiple-tenant farms into single-tenant farms should be seen as much less a matter of gradual stages of development.[33] The impact of military recruitment should not be exaggerated, however. Population growth, for example, put pressure on arable holdings. More specifically, the famine of 1782-3 was a significant dynamic that entailed both a loss in capital reserves and increased downward social mobility. Nevertheless, the role played by ex-soldiers was of crucial importance as a catalyst that ensured a few, select farms were converted comprehensively and rapidly to crofting tenure.[34]

The Breadalbane Fencibles, 1793–5

Many of the same pressures and responses generated by recruitment during the 1775–1783 war were to become apparent again during the French

---

31. S.R.O., Breadalbane Muniments, GD 112/9/3/4/1–15; GD 112/3/3/14; GD 112/16/4/1/2; J.R. Western, 'The Recruitment of the Land Forces in Great Britain, 1793–99' (Edinburgh University, Ph.D. Thesis, 1953), p. 107.
32. S.R.O., Breadalbane Muniments, 'Robert Robertson's Report on Netherlorne, 1796', R.H.P. 972/5; GD 112/14/12/7/9; GD 112/11/1/4/1–94; GD 112/11/1/6; GD 112/41/74/254/3; J.B. Caird, 'The Creation of Crofts and new Settlement Patterns in the Highlands and Islands of Scotland', in *Scottish Geographical Magazine*, vol. 103 (1987), pp. 67–9.
33. A.I. Macinnes, 'Scottish Gaeldom: The First Phase of Clearance', pp. 83–84.
34. S.R.O., Breadalbane Muniments, GD 112/11/2/5/19.

Revolutionary War. There was, however, on this occasion one crucial difference from these earlier recruiting drives: John Campbell, fourth Earl of Breadalbane, obtained command of an entire regiment which ensured his particularly strong and self-interested commitment to military levying. In February 1793, after negotiations with Henry Dundas, he received the Crown's authorisation to raise two battalions of 500 men each – subsequently increased in March to 1,000 men each. Recruiting proceeded rapidly and, in late April, the Earl informed the War Office that both his units were at full strength.[35] The apparent ease with which he had completed his objective was, however, undermined by shifting government demands brought on by the changing direction of the war. The years from 1793 until the beginning of 1795 represented a period when Britain was generally on the military offensive in Europe. As a result, unprecedented numbers of line regiments were in the process of formation, making recruits significantly more expensive and difficult to procure. Allied to this was the fact that, while the government considered fencible regiments useful up to a point, it also felt that they diverted much-needed manpower from the line regiments that bore the brunt of the offensive. The result was pressure on landlords to raise new fencible battalions for service in Ireland, thus allowing line troops to be redeployed on the continent or elsewhere. In October 1794 these new fencible battalions, as well as line regiments, received permission to recruit from existing units like Breadalbane's which had refused to extend their service beyond Scotland. In the event over 600 men volunteered from the Earl's regiment. The government sought to further rationalise available manpower by reducing the Earl's battalions back to 500 men each. The aim was to transfer the surplus men into a new, third battalion liable for duty in Ireland. In order to benefit from his own men, and to atone for the mutiny of his first battalion, the Earl agreed to these proposals in December 1794. This meant, however, returning to a national recruiting market made profoundly inauspicious by two years of intensive levying.[36]

These changes in public policy prolonged Breadalbane's recruitment drive which lasted, albeit with periods of relative inactivity, from March 1793 until the spring of 1795. Escalating government demands and two years intermittent recruitment in a highly competitive market ensured that the Earl utilised manpower from both his Perthshire and Argyll estates. His initial

35. J.E. Cookson, *The British Armed Nation, 1793–1815* (Oxford, 1997), pp. 131 & 134; *Scots Magazine*, vol. 55 (Edinburgh, 1793), p. 153; N.L.S., Melville Papers, Ms 4, ff. 103, 124, 164, 179 S.R.O., Breadalbane Muniments, GD 112/52/22; GD 112/52/23/4 & 9; GD 112/52/23/4; GD 112/11/4/3/50; GD 112/52/23/22.
36. J. Western, *op. cit.*, pp. 5–7, 10–11; J. Prebble, *op. cit.*, pp. 325–7; S.R.O., Campbell of Balliveolin Papers, GD 13/220, 227a; S.R.O., Melville Castle Muniments, GD 51/6/77/1–4, 7; N.L.S., Melville Papers, Ms 6, ff. 139, 207; S.R.O., John Macgregor Collection, GD 50/18/18; S.R.O., Breadalbane Muniments, GD 112/52/23/4, 9, 14, 16; GD 112/52/41/5, 12–13; GD 112/52/102/2, 4, 6; GD 112/52/12/5, 12–13; P.R.O., W.O. 1/617, f. 29.

effort in March 1793 involved securing men in Perthshire for his first battalion before moving into Argyll and levying for his second battalion. He re-initiated recruitment in early 1794 and again, in the first two months of 1795, to augment his third battalion.[37] The actual mechanics of estate recruitment were deceptively simple. Immediately upon authorisation of his regiment the Earl instructed his Perthshire and Argyllshire ground officers to order all those capable of service to repair either to Taymouth, Killin or Dalmally. This prospect produced an atmosphere of apprehension, as well as population mobility, as young men departed the estate in order to avoid enlistment. There was initial confusion over what, exactly, the Earl would require from his tenantry, and various rumours circulated that crofters beneath a certain size-holding and families without sons would be exempt. Initially at least, efforts were indeed made to avoid breadwinners and only sons in an attempt to avert local poverty. However, young, physically underdeveloped men were catalogued and told that if the Earl required additional recruits he would return for a certain number. Expectations were also raised by the belief that, regardless of social status, only those inhabitants whose sons worked locally would be expected to contribute and that purchasing 'hired' or 'substitute' men would not be required. However, those such as the tenants of Ardeonaig district, who had seven of their thirty sons in the Lowlands, were advised to bring them back home as Breadalbane intended asking for sons, brothers, brothers-in-law and other 'near relations'.[38]

In order to actually implement recruitment the Earl ordered censuses of available and, more importantly, suitable manpower. Generally, ground officers noted the name, farm, social status and number of suitable personnel in each district, and who, precisely, could or had contributed in respect of sons, relations or hired recruits. Given the emphasis placed on the development of commercial landlordism in the region, it is not surprising that detailed estate surveys have usually been associated with commercial improvement and estate re-organisation.[39] Yet some of the most detailed estate reports, especially of a social and demographic nature, were obtained for the purposes of recruitment as opposed to improvement. Recruiting lists from 1793 underline the considerable population resources at the fourth Earl's disposal: the Argyll estate held 1,726 men, while the Perthshire lands, lying in

37. W.A. Gilles, *In Famed Breadalbane* (Perth, 1938), pp. 201–4; S.R.O., Breadalbane Muniments, GD 112/52/23/4, 9–21; GD 112/74/70/7; GD 112/11/3/2/68–69 & 85; GD 112/11/2/5/41; GD 112/11/5/1/90(1–2); GD 112/11/5/2/25; S.R.O., Campbell of Balliveolin Papers, GD 13/221a.
38. S.R.O., Breadalbane Muniments, GD 112/11/1/4/59; GD 112/11/2/5/7, 20, 30–31, 41, 65; GD 112/11/3/2/1, 7 & 107; GD 112/11/3/3/32(1), 98; GD 112/11/3/4/59; GD 112/11/4/1/62; GD 112/11/4/3/12 & 13; GD 112/11/5/1/57 & 83; GD 112/11/7/1/20; GD 112/525/23; S.R.O., John Macgregor Collection, GD 50/11/1/70.
39. A.I. Macinnes, *Clanship, Commerce and the House of Stuart, 1603–1788* (East Linton, 1966), p. 221.

the south-eastern zone of the Highlands generally characterised by low or static population growth, nonetheless contained 1,198 male tenants, crofters, cottars and villagers.[40]

The scale of recruitment on Breadalbane's lands, as with many other Highland estates during this period, has been seriously exaggerated to the extent of suggesting that all three battalions were drawn from the Earl's own tenantry.[41] The argument that landlords raised their regiments almost exclusively from their own estates is simply not supported by the evidence. A profile of the first battalion of Sir James Grant's fencible regiment, also raised in 1793, shows that 437 – nearly two thirds – of its 703 soldiers were Highland by birth. However, only 194 – just over one man in four – came from the Moray and Inverness-shire parishes on Sir James's property. Analysis of Breadalbane's second battalion reveals an even lower proportion of estate recruits. Only 41% of the 1,104 men were Highland, while recruits from parishes dominated by the Earl's estate numbered only 139–12.5% of the battalion.[42] These figures do not mean that estate recruitment was a negligible phenomenon, however; indeed, its scale and impact upon Breadalbane's property was striking. Between 1793 and 1795, 453 men were raised directly from within the estate population or as a consequence of their monetary resources (see Tables 7 and 8). The Perthshire estate was responsible for 368, the Argyll lands for 85, although this latter figure is almost certainly an under-estimate. Despite the fact that later eighteenth-century Highland history is dominated by the break-up of militarised clanship, it is worth noting that the overall 1790s recruitment level was greater than the number raised in 1745–6. More importantly, recruitment's impact on tenure can be seriously underestimated if enlistment figures are contrasted crudely with the large numbers of available men. In reality, even a limited number of recruits – the 85 men from Argyll, for instance, constituted only one man in twenty – could nonetheless involve a relatively high number of farm holdings. Recruitment affected 63% of the entire farm structure within Perthshire; and 42% in Argyll. This meant that, at a conservative estimate, even a property as large as Breadalbane's experienced levels of recruitment approaching three farms out of every five. This alone suggests that the

40. The Perthshire total of 1,198 does not represent all males, merely those in some way connected to the rental. Likewise, however, these numbers overestimate the reserves of men Breadalbane could choose from. For example, of the 296 males from his Kilninver lands in Argyll, 67, or 23%, were under 10. The number of males either too old or young may have, at a conservative estimate, amounted to over 30%, or 518 of the 1,726 men on the Argyll estate. S.R.O., Breadalbane Muniments, GD 112/16/13/8/10; GD 112/16/5/1/5–6x; GD 112/16/7/3/23; GD 112/52/524/1–2, 4–5; GD 112/52/522; GD 112/52/525/23; GD 112/52/527/12, 14; GD 112/52/539/14, 42; GD 112/52/588/7–8; GD 112/594/13.
41. J. Prebble, op. cit., p. 320.
42. S.R.O., Seafield Muniments, GD 248/464; S.R.O., Breadalbane Muniments, GD 112/52/544. See also J.E. Cookson, op. cit., p. 129.

fourth Earl exercised his proprietary power over estate populations effectively and systematically.[43]

Given the apparent similarity in methods of military mobilisation in the era of clanship, such activity, especially by a conspicuous improving landlord like the fourth Earl, could be deemed wholly inconsistent at best and at worst indicative of ongoing commercial under-development. Temporary reductions in rent and the cancellation of proposed augmentations in Argyll on account of levying lend support to such a view.[44] Yet it is precisely in a commercial and market context that Highland estate recruiting is best understood. As with other fencible colonels, the government allowed Breadalbane three guineas per recruit. Due to various market conditions, including alternative avenues of employment in the Highlands, the strength of the Lowland economy and the purchasing power of the army, the real cost of recruits was substantially higher. However, if a man cost the Earl £15 in the open market, government still only forwarded three guineas, leaving the rest to be made up from private funds. Conversely, if Breadalbane gained a free recruit, he was still entitled to three guineas. By offering his tenantry proxy bounties in the form of land the landlord increased his chances of gaining free or relatively cheap recruits while simultaneously reducing the need to compete in the inflationary national recruiting market. In this context estate levying made perfect economic sense and was an entirely rational strategy, born of and adapted to contemporary conditions.

Table 5 illustrates that 159 men were purchased as substitute recruits and presented to the Earl by tenants or other social classes in lieu of their own service. Assertions that Highlanders lacked experience in commercial transactions fail to take account of the often protracted and detailed bargains which tenantry concluded with these recruits and which they then repeated with their landlords over the precise value of their substitutes. For instance, some soldiers presented to the regiment did not require a monetary bounty, but their families expected the Earl would supply them with meal on a regular basis. In other instances Breadalbane negotiated various cash deals with his tenantry that involved his supplying the standard government bounty, which they would then match or at least add to, thus allowing for larger, more realistic sums to attract men. Thus, in February 1795, as the Earl sought to

43. The figure of 453 men does not represent the total level of recruitment on the Perthshire or Argyll estates. Given the relatively poor state of Argyll petitions, that total is in all likelihood a conservative figure. S.R.O., Breadalbane Muniments, GD 112/52/524/1–4; GD 112/52/522; GD 112/13/8/8x; GD 112/16/7/3/27; GD 112/9/62; GD 112/11/2/5/1–94; GD 112/11/3/1/1–31; GD 112/11/3/2/1–111; GD 112/11/3/3/1–94; GD 112/11/3/4/1–77; GD 112/11/4/1/1–78; GD 112/11/4/2/1–76; GD 112/11/4/3/1–70; GD 112/11/5/1/1–102; GD 112/11/5/2/1–115; GD 112/11/7/1/1–59; GD 112/11/2/1–61; GD 112/11/7/3/1–35; GD 112/11/7/4/1–52.
44. S.R.O., John Macgregor Collection, GD 50/13/56. For marginal rental increase in Argyll over the period from 1788–97, see S.R.O., Breadalbane Muniments, GD 112/9/3/3/14, 17, 20, 26, 28.

complete his third battalion, his Glenorchy tenantry offered an additional bounty to prospective Highland recruits. In order to arrive at a realistic market bounty that did not entail crippling expenditure by their landlord, the estate population had agreed, in essence, to supply the necessary, additional credit.[45]

Table 5. Percentage of Hired or Family Recruits, Perthshire Estate, 1795[46]

Social Group	Hired Recruits & %	Family Recruits & %	Volunteers & %
Tacksman	8 (80)	2 (20)	–
Single Tenant	4.5 (47.3)	4 (42.1)	1 (10.5)
Multiple Tenant	99.5 (53.3)	83 (44.5)	4 (2.1)
Crofter	37 (35.2)	59 (56.1)	9 (8.5)
Cottar	9 (20.9)	21 (48.8)	13 (30.2)
Villager	1 (7.1)	7 (50)	6 (42.8)
	159	176	33

Agreements between tenantry and landlord reveal that the number of recruits with conditions attached, as opposed to completely free, totalled 50%. If taken as illustrative of conditions generally, this means that Breadalbane gained approximately 79 free men: a profit of £248 on government bounties. Yet the true market price of substitute men suggests that these partial savings were not the prime benefit.

Table 6. Relative Cost of Rent and Hired Recruits, Breadalbane Estate, 1793–5[47]

Farm	Status of Buyer	Annual Rent	Cost of Recruit	Recruit as % of Rent
Rouckvie	Tenant	£1.14.3	£9.0.0.	525
West Tombreck	Tenant	£3.4.6	£3.3.0.	97.6
West Tombreck	Tenant	£3.4.6	£8.0.0	248
Croftvellich	Tenant	£5.11.3	£8.0.0	143.8
Tomchrocher	Tenant	£3.14.9.	£3.0.0.	80.2
West Turrerich	Tenant	£3.10.1	£12.12.0.	359.5
Achnafaundich*	Tenant	£10.10.0	£19.8.0	184.7

45. T.M. Devine, 'Social Responses of Agrarian "Improvement": the Highlands and Lowland Clearances in Scotland', pp. 159–160; J.M. Bulloch, *op. cit.* p. 143. S.R.O., Breadalbane Muniments, GD 112/52/522; GD 112/525/23; GD 112/52/524/4; GD 112/11/4/3/9; S.R.O., Campbell of Ballaveolin Papers, GD 13/221a.
46. 'Volunteers' were those who represented themselves, as opposed to joining on behalf of their fathers, brothers etc. S.R.O., Breadalbane Muniments, GD 112/525/23 & GD 112/11/3-7 (Estate Petitions).
47. S.R.O., Breadalbane Muniments, GD 112/11/3-7 (Estate Petitions). *An Argyllshire farm with its rent dating from 1788.

Table 6 illustrates the cost paid locally in Perthshire for hired recruits. On average, men on the open market cost tenantry £8.18.1. Thus, by recruiting from his estate and gaining 368 free recruits, or, as was more usual, at the standard government bounty, Breadalbane saved at a conservative estimate £2,365 – equivalent to half his entire Argyllshire rents.[48]

The crucial role played by tenantry in shielding their landlord from the expensive recruiting market constitutes an underestimated but nevertheless vital use of large estate populations, even in areas like Lochtayside and Netherlorne where economic factors like kelping, which promoted demographic growth, were largely or completely missing. One other point needs to be emphasised. The economic rationale and imperative underpinning recruitment from domestic resources meant that commercial self-interest, as opposed to traditional notions of clan obligation, ensured that landlords like Breadalbane fulfilled promises regarding grants of land.[49] While the old ethos of land as a reward for service doubtless acted as a mutually recognised framework that helped initiate and expedite the enlistment process, events on the Breadalbane estate confirm that the later eighteenth-century recruiting relationship was very different from its clan predecessor, and was perceived by landlords to be grounded on a cash nexus.[50] Ultimately, its rationale centred upon issues of capital and profit; the raising of men was as much a matter of commercial development as black cattle farms, and as modern an estate practice as sheep farming.

Yet however effective it was at procuring relatively cheap recruits, estate recruitment unquestionably had some negative side-effects. Table 6, for instance, demonstrates that the cost of substitutes represented a significant drain on tenant resources – often over two years' rent. The financial implications did not end with the expense of bounties, however. The availability and cost of labour were also affected. Even prior to 1793 there is evidence that recruiting reduced the labour supply. In 1780–81, at the height of the American Revolutionary War, estate authorities attempted to ensure a cheap and reliable workforce by strict enforcement of longer servant contracts which favoured the employer while labour was in short supply and therefore expensive. Attempts to combat such shortages also affected the social status of women. In 1795 a female crofter was removed from the Lochtayside farm of Kilytrie and given a cottar possession on the assumption that women with smallholdings would enter the day-labour market to

48. Calculations are based on the fact that 79 free recruits represented a saving of both the government bounty and the average market price. This equals £703. The other 289 recruits purchased or provided from kin sources by his tenantry usually cost the Earl, at most, the government bounty of 3 guineas. Nevertheless, this still shielded him from the true market price – £8.18.1. Thus, for every recruit given in by his tenantry Breadalbane saved at least £5.15.1. At 289 this totals £1,662. The two together total £2,365.
49. S.R.O., Campbell of Ballaveolin Papers, GD 13/292.
50. E. Richards, *A History of the Highland Clearances: Agrarian Change and the Evictions, 1746–1886*, vol. 1. (London, 1982), pp. 147, 150–1.

supplement their income. A similar objective lay behind the Argyll factor's suggestion in 1797 that all widowed female tenants with no male family to manage their farms be removed and reduced in social status.[51] Such labour problems were usually a short-term phenomenon, however. More significant difficulties arose from the strain and pressure brought to bear upon the estate as a direct result of recruitment. The underlying reasons for this disruptive impact are shown in Tables 7 and 8, both of which contrast tenure on the Perthshire and Argyll estates with the social background of local recruits.

Table 7. Structure of Perthshire Estate,
1793 and Social Origin of Recruits, 1793–5[52]

Farm Type	Total & % of Estate Farms	Total Farm possessors & %	Total Recruits & %
Tacksman	26 (9.9)	26 (2.3)	10 (2.7)
Single Tenant	34 (13)	34 (3)	9.5 (2.5)
Multiple Tenant	162 (62)	578 (51.9)	186.5 (50.6)
Crofts	29 (11)	312 (28)	105 (28.5)
Villager	7 (2.6)	122 (10.9)	14 (3.8)
Cottar	3 (1.1)	41 (3.6)	43 (11.6)
	261	1,113	368

Care is obviously needed when attempting analysis of an estate's tenurial profile. Rentals tend as a source to hide almost as much as they reveal. What Tables 7 and 8 actually illustrate are those who paid rent directly to the proprietor and who were recognised as holding an official possession. The number of crofters and cottars is therefore masked, as is the intricate social hierarchy beneath the rent-paying tenantry. Rentals fail to register, for example, the existence of two distinct types of crofter: those who held directly from the Earl; and a second type who received land from the tenantry, paid rent only to them and were of little immediate concern to the proprietor. Thus, while tenant numbers can be taken as accurate, the number of crofters and cottars are invariably under-estimated on official rentals.[53]

51. S.R.O., Breadalbane Muniments, GD 112/11/2/5/9(1), 32, 75, 87; GD 112/11/3/1/7, 30, 31; GD 112/11/3/2/1,68, 107; GD 112/11/3/3/8, 31, 39; GD 112/11/5/1/80; GD 112/11/5/2/66, 81. For the 1780s see GD 112/11/1/4/45. For the 1790s see GD 112/13/8/8x; GD 112/16/4/2/39.
52. S.R.O., Breadalbane Muniments, GD 112/525/23 & GD 112/11/3–7 (Estate Petitions). The term 'villager' represents artisans settled in agricultural hamlets like Stron-Fernan, Wester-Portbane and Aberfeldy. See GD 112/9/62; GD 112/11/1/3/12/2; GD 112/11/2/1/1; GD 112/11/1/6/7.
53. For the problematic nature of rentals as source material, see R.A. Dodgshon, *Land and Society in Early Scotland* (Oxford, 1981), pp. 279–80; S.R.O., Breadalbane Muniments, GD 112/11/2/5/57; GD 112/11/3/2/2; GD 112/11/3/2/26; GD 112/11/3/4/34; GD 112/11/4/2/52. After a period of promotion during the late 1770s and early 1780s, Breadalbane avoided the expansion of official croft holdings. In 1786 he refused three crofters, then subletting from tenants, permission to rent their possessions directly. See GD 112/16/4/1/4; GD 112/11/1/4/26, 54; GD 112/11/2/5/44; GD 112/11/3/1/9/1; GD 112/11/7/2/65.

Table 8. Structure of Argyll Estate, 1788 and Social Origins of Recruits, 1793–5[54]

Farm Type	Total & % of Estate	Total farm possessors & %	Total recruits & %
Tacksman	27 (23.6)	27 (9.5)	2 (2.3)
Single Tenant	18 (15.7)	18 (6.3)	1 (1.1)
Multiple Tenant	36 (31.5)	126 (44.6)	29 (34.1)
Subtenant	4 (3.5)	7 (2.4)	17 (20)
Croft	27 (23.6)	80 (28.3)	21 (24.7)
Cottar	2 (1.7)	24 (8.5)	15 (17.6)
Total	114	282	85

Particular care is required in areas where subtenure was still prevalent. The total of seven on the Argyll estate, for example, only represents the number of subtenants on farms out of tack in that particular year. Yet most, if not all tacksmen, and even some multiple tenants, would have had some subtenants upon their farms. In light of the estate documentation's masking effect it is not at all surprising that Argyll subtenantry and, indeed, the cottar class in general upon both properties, made a relatively larger impact in terms of recruitment than their presence on rentals might at first suggest.

Both Tables 7 and 8 show the distinctive social pattern to estate recruitment highlighted earlier in Table 4. As in 1759, tenantry tended to recruit roughly in proportion to their presence on the estate, while crofters and the cottar class, in particular, contributed a proportionally higher number of recruits than their social superiors. For example, it required on average three or four tenants to supply one recruit; however, the ratio of cottar to recruit was usually only 2:1 or 1:1 at most. The result of this discrepancy was intense social strain between tenantry and the lower tenurial orders as relatively higher numbers of the latter pursued claims for land, often, though by no means exclusively, at the expense of the former. One particular feature of the levying process exerted this pressure on tenant possessions. Table 5 demonstrates that it was the relatively rich tenant classes who tended to rely on substitute recruit. In certain respects this made commercial sense. More used to dealing with market conditions and in greater need of familial labour to help manage their farms, tenantry had a greater incentive to deploy their capital resources in this way. Conversely, crofters and cottars, lacking similar commitments to agricultural holdings, tended to draw on their own kin resources in relatively larger numbers, which also had the obvious value of keeping recruiting costs down. However, while a tenant family may have felt their holding was guaranteed by their presentation of a recruit, the Earl made it clear that he owed a greater obligation to those who supplied men from their own families and at a cheap rate. This distinction in the value of recruits

---

54. S.R.O., Breadalbane Muniments, GD 112/9/3/3/14; GD 112/11/3–7 (Estate Petitions).

was in all likelihood made by Breadalbane in an effort to prevent his richer tenantry from excessive expenditure that would then reduce their ability to stock and improve their farms. Tenants who recruited in Glasgow or Edinburgh were told that the Earl did not approve; while the mother of a local boy who had 'publicly rouped himself' for £15 was informed that the Earl felt 'the mother of an Irish recruit in these circumstances is equally entitled to notice'.[55] Lower social groups accordingly played upon the tenantry's tendency to buy recruits. In an extremely aggressive petition three crofters and one cottar from Crannich and Carwhin targeted the entire tenantry of the district, giving detailed information on their failure to supply sons. Out of a total of 47 tenants, only five had done so. Another eight had given in sons between them, which meant only four additional recruits, while a total of seven tenants had purchased men from elsewhere. Conversely, the petitioners, who stressed their own contribution from kin sources, were all promised possessions by the Earl.[56]

Although insecurity of tenure has been highlighted as characteristic of farm holding under clanship, British army recruiting ironically stimulated precisely the type of uncertainty that had supposedly been replaced with more 'improved' estate management. In March 1795 the Perthshire factor noted how he was being swamped with petitions asking for land and the transfer of tenancies, adding: 'the business [has] become more and more complicated' and 'the itch for exchanging has become epidemical'.[57] Likewise, in his 1796 report on Netherlorne, Robert Robertson noted the distress suffered by Argyll tenantry as a result of frequent removals, adding: 'some of them merely to make room for people that had no title to land. My Lord Breadalbane might in part be the cause of this confusion'.[58] As demand for land became ever more intense, so those who had spent money and time on the enhancement of their possessions as opposed to recruitment found themselves peculiarly vulnerable. The increased productivity and value of their holdings invariably attracted the attention of those anticipating settlement as a result of their positive response to the Earl's request for men. In sixteen cases where possessors tried to keep their holdings from aggressive targeting by such people, or have smaller holdings returned to them to allow

55. S.R.O., Breadalbane Muniments, GD 112/11/4/3/50; GD 112/13/8/8x.
56. S.R.O., Breadalbane Muniments, GD 112/74/255/1; GD 112/11/2/5/5, 35, 42; GD 112/11/3/4/55; GD 112/11/4/3/1; GD 112/13/8/8x. For instances of hired recruits being seen as unlikely to bring much favour, see GD 112/11/2/5/5 & 35; GD 112/11/4/3/10(1–3).
57. A.J. Youngson, *After the 'Forty-Five: The Economic Impact on the Scottish Highlands* (Edinburgh, 1973), p. 14; S.R.O., Breadalbane Muniments, GD 112/74/70/5 & 17. For further information on Breadalbane estate petitioning, see M.E. Vance, 'Emigration & Scottish Society: The Background of Three Government Assisted Emigrations to Upper Canada, 1815–1821' (University of Guelph Ph.D., 1990), pp. 83–86.
58. S.R.O., Breadalbane Muniments, GD 112/11/7/1/3; 'Robert Robertson's Report on Netherlorne, 1796', R.H.P. 972/5.

for further improvement, only three succeeded. Even model tenants who had spent large sums on improvements were nevertheless removed in order to satisfy the demand for places; this was the case with Alexander Thomson in East Tullocheann who had spent £13 on various aspects of his holding. Not surprisingly, Thomson remarked bitterly that it was 'a new transaction contrary to any that took place in the country'.[59] Similar removals occurred in Argyll: indeed, despite Breadalbane's preference for tenants of substance on the farm of Oban on the Island of Seil, the entire tenantry were removed for 'others who had claims for service in the fencibles'. Likewise, Duachy in Netherlorne had 'two substantial decent tenants who were deprived to accommodate Sergeant Hugh MacCrown, they are greatly hampered having t'wixt them but one sixth of the farm'.[60] Such a poor record of keeping tenants upon the possessions in which they had invested was a serious breach of improvement theory and estate management practice.

The primary effect of estate levying was therefore a period of intense competition for land. Petitions demonstrate clearly that recruitment was seen by some as an opportunity to gain social advancement at the expense of others. Tacksmen like Lieutenant John Campbell of Ardtettle in Glenorchy discovered that subtenants would not enlist under his auspices, but, instead, presented their own requests for removal from under the control of superior tenants in order to hold directly from the Earl. Others used their compliance to request a return to tenancies from which they had been removed previously, in order to reverse their family's decline in social status. Indeed, it is ironic to note that a number of families, evicted during the American Revolutionary War for failing to recruit, deliberately supplied men in 1793–4 in an effort to remove those who had earlier taken over their tenancies as a reward for supplying men.[61] Given the scale and intensity of the competition sparked by recruitment, it is surprising that it has not been remarked upon previously as an important aspect of social change in the region. Between 1793 and 1795 there were at least 104 petitions with respect to the Perthshire estate by tenants, crofters, and cottars asking for the holding of another incumbent. This affected over one farm in four and involved the livelihoods of hundreds of people. Although they formed just over half the number of individual holdings on the estate, requests for land held by single or multiple tenants represented 66.3% of this total. Crofters and cottars made up a disproportionate 46.3% of these requests for tenant possessions. Conversely, tenant requests for repossession of crofter and cottar land back into their own, larger holdings made up only 10.5% of these demands, with the rest consisting mainly of tenants or crofters asking for a

59. S.R.O., Breadalbane Muniments, GD 112/11/3/2/22; GD 112/11/3/4/3, 7, 10, 44, 66; GD 112/11/4/1/32, 38; GD 112/11/4/2/5, 51, 91; GD 112/11/4/3/12; GD 112/115/1/16; GD 112/11/5/2/20, 55; GD 112/11/7/1/34; GD 112/7/2/12.
60. S.R.O., Breadalbane Muniments, GD 112/11/7/3/1, 15.
61. S.R.O., Breadalbane Muniments, GD 112/74/69/21; GD 112/11/4/2/65; GD 112/11/7/1/15(1–2), 90 (1–2); GD 112/11/3/1/18, 28; GD 112/11/3/2/22, 111; GD 112/11/3/3/80; GD 112/11/3/4/46.

direct exchange with others of a similar social status. Recruiting thus produced two distinct types of pressure: lateral pressure, whereby removal involved turnover in personnel but no change in social status. More importantly, however, it also resulted in upward pressure on tenants as opposed to downward movement against the possessions of crofters and cottars: in effect, the generally better recruiting performance of the lower orders was transferred into a proportionally greater pressure on tenant holdings.[62] The significant scale of this petitioning suggests that our understanding of later eighteenth-century recruiting in the region needs to be revised to include an acknowledgement that the evictions which routinely followed in its wake were often driven by the social expectations and ambitions of estate populations, as well as by the coercive power of Highland landlords determined to punish non-compliance.[63]

Estate Management and Resettlement

The fact that tenurially insecure social groups had improved their claims on land meant that the Breadalbane estate was dominated by issues of reorganisation and settlement during the period from 1795 to 1802. Indeed, land promises that had expedited recruitment in the short term posed significant estate management problems in the medium to longer term. In February 1795 the Earl announced that those who had contributed would now be considered for possessions. In order to prevent disruption through piecemeal, uncoordinated settlement he had previously stalled applications for land by issuing deliberately ambiguous promises of accommodation. Generalised assurances, it was agreed, made the process of accommodating personnel in suitable possessions considerably easier and rational. In reply to a specific request, Breadalbane noted that he was 'surprised the petitioner can represent any *promise* being made to him beyond that of a general nature, on the contrary he avoided at the time he raised his regiment to involve himself in particular promises'.[64]

The exact nature of recruiting promises made by Breadalbane remains unclear and was certainly a matter of intense controversy at the time. What is not in doubt is that gentry such as David Campbell of Glenlyon, Captain Colin Campbell of Carwhin and Archibald Campbell of Easdale, as well as Breadalbane himself, promised landholdings in one form or another. In late December 1794 John Kennedy, factor on the Perthshire estate, admitted that 'some have your Lordship's general promise in writing to provide them in an

62. Figures drawn from estate petitions. S.R.O., Breadalbane Muniments, GD 112/11/3–7 as well as 1793 and 1796 rentals and removal lists; GD 112/9/62 & 64, GD 112/13/8/8x.
63. J. Hunter, *The Making of the Crofting Community*, (Edinburgh, 1976) p. 24.
64. S.R.O., Breadalbane Muniments, GD 112/74/70/7; GD 112/14/12/7/17; GD 112/11/2/5/5, 14; GD 112/11/3/2/65; GD 112/11/3/4/10; GD 112/3/4/40, 46; GD112/11/4/2/76; GD 112/11/4/3/74; GD 112/11/7/1/6.

opening *when it occurs* on account of their having presented a recruit'.[65] Yet it was equally the case that tenantry petitioned on the basis that they had been given specific and well-defined promises. Some, for example, claimed they had received assurances of possession for life; others claimed they had been promised settlement in particular areas such as the Island of Seil, or, indeed, upon certain farms such as Achnamaddy on Lochowside, Bochoil in Glenorchy and Carie on Lochtayside. Certainly, in 1799, Campbell of Easdale, while denying the legitimacy of other claims, conceded that in the case of John Clark from Ardnahua in Netherlorne 'I do believe he was told, that when the regiment was disbanded, he would if he wished for it, get a possession at Ardnahua where his father was originally a ten't'.[66] While the Earl attached considerable importance to the settlement of those who had complied, his ability to honour requests was in some cases undermined by the fact that those who were threatened with dispossession supplied a man to fend off eviction. Nonetheless, it also appears from estate reports that the authorities were less than entirely forthright, and did not attempt to clearly dispel the high expectations of tenantry with respect to permanent settlement on their own particular, preferred farms.

Breadalbane sought to counter such pressures by conceding benefits other than land. The supply of meal to aged parents or families was one obvious alternative. Duncan Mackercher, crofter on the farm of Tommachrocher on Lochtayside, gained no extra land but was appeased by the weekly supply of two pecks of meal to his family while his service in the regiment lasted. In other cases it was agreed that the estate would pay for the ploughing of certain holdings; while in Easdale the Earl guaranteed work at the slate quarries which helped secure families with small, subdivided holdings. Yet even these alternative policies were not always enough. The high expectations of recruits made it difficult to contain the pressure for settlement and often led to sustained petitioning by soldiers determined to obtain land in one form or another. Gilbert Livingston from Seil refused an offer of two bolls per annum for his cottar family and insisted, instead, that he had been promised a croft in his home district; eventually, he was awarded such a holding in Netherlorne.[67]

65. S.R.O., Breadalbane Muniments, GD 112/74/69/21; GD 112/11/4/2/37; GD 112/11/2/5/5, 14, 30; GD 112/11/3/2/3, 7, 48, 50, 72; GD 112/11/3/3/15; GD 112/11/3/4/42, 46.

66. Other Lochtayside farms which tenantry believed had been specifically promised to them included: Craggan of Ardeonaig, Edramuckie, Ardvoil, Inverinnan, West Turrerich, Keppranich and Lower Tullochuill. S.R.O., Breadalbane Muniments, GD 112/12/1/5/18–19; GD 112/16/4/2/12; GD 112/11/2/5/3, 5, 14, 30–31, 36, 53, 62, 77; GD 112/11/3/1/24; GD 112/11/3/2/7, 20, 48, 50; GD 112/11/3/3/8, 15, 47, 62; GD 112/11/3/4/25, 42, 46, 47(1); GD 112/11/4/1/40, 59; GD 112/11/4/2/11; GD 112/11/4/3/1, 21, 70; GD 112/11/5/1/90 (1–2); GD 112/11/5/2/6, 10; GD 112/11/7/1/3, 15; GD 112/11/7/3/27; GD 112/11/7/4/26.

67. S.R.O., Breadalbane Muniments, GD 112/11/2/5/65; GD 112/11/4/1/60; GD 112/11/3/3/30; GD 112/11/7/1/3/4; GD 112/11/2/5/27; GD 112/11/3/1/7; GD 112/11/7/1/3/4–5.

The problem of regulating settlement was exacerbated by Breadalbane's continued introduction of sheep walks. In 1795, tenants in Callechan and Tullichglass on the south side of Lochtay lost their sheiling lands. Without sufficient grazing, Callechan could not be sustained in its traditional *baille* (joint tenant) form and was broken up into small lots in order to resettle numbers of its tenantry and other individuals with a claim on the Earl. This helped fulfil the demand for land and for higher rents from sheep. It is profoundly ironic that recruitment indirectly promoted the development of sheep walks upon the Perthshire estate. As demand for accommodation from the lower social orders intensified, so arable and infield became increasingly subdivided. Greater numbers of landholders meant established souming levels for black cattle became increasingly untenable, which, in turn, resulted in grazing being removed for sheep and the arable areas of townships being turned over to intensive cultivation.[68]

It was against this background of heightened expectation amongst sections of the estate population and ongoing development of commercial pastoralism that Breadalbane and his senior advisers began, in late 1794 and early 1795, to address the problem of estate reorganisation. Subsequent reports from both Argyll and Perthshire confirm how recruitment served to entrench and give greater weight to the issue of population within the wider context of estate management. In November 1794 Campbell of Lochend's memorial on Netherlorne revealed how the estate regime tended to vacillate between concern over farm size and feasibility and the creation of new holdings for the accommodation of population. It revealed that the plan formulated in 1783 had not been implemented fully, and that the preferred strategy of single-tenant farms had not been entirely successful or even possible. Despite a certain number of crofts having been created to alleviate pressure on arable holdings, farms still retained too many tenants on each division. Uncertainty and ambiguity over how best to deal with the issue of population was likewise evident in Perthshire. Given the prevalence of settlement demands, it was not entirely surprising that Breadalbane mooted the idea of curtailing the growth of large sheep farms. Lochend, however, argued that the opposite was the case, and added: 'I have always contended that the number of people on your estate of Breadalbane was well as in this country [Netherlorne] was a barr [sic] to improvements and a loss to the proprietor'.[69]

Despite the emergence of a certain measure of agreement about the anti-improvement consequences of over-population, the need to fulfil promises of land forced the estate to implement measures which actually involved accommodating the very same tenantry who were increasingly viewed so

68. S.R.O., Breadalbane Muniments, GD 112/11/4/1/21–22, 23, 73; GD 112/11/4/2/20–21; GD 112/11/4/3/40; GD 112/11/5/1/54 (1–3); GD 112/11/7/1/38.
69. S.R.O., Breadalbane Muniments, GD 112/12/1/5/18, 48–50x.

unfavourably. In 1796 and 1797, the fourth Earl ordered further reports on the condition of his Argyll and Perthshire properties. The surveyor, Robert Robertson, conducted an intensive inquiry, and was subsequently ordered to divide the land around Lochtay into lots to create individual farms with fifteen-year leases. The operation illustrates clearly the tenurial consequences generated by recruitment. Rather than prioritising an agenda of agrarian improvement and favouring personnel with stock and capital, Breadalbane categorised, in a particular order, those who were to be given farms. The first to be settled were those who had served in the fencibles and who had the ability to stock possessions. Second were the industrious tenants who were also able farmers; while those who had not recruited, regardless of ability, were to be removed.[70]

That tenantry who had supplied recruits could take precedence over industrious, able farmers demonstrates how the process of estate levying to some extent constrained landlords and diverted them from commercial management strategies. From February to August 1797 Robertson, in accordance with the Earl's instructions, divided land along Lochtayside in such a manner that 'to answer the abilities of the people, the lots of some larger and some smaller [farms] were made *so small*, as in their uncultivated state barely to be sufficient for the sustenance of tenants having little or no other employment than as farmers'.[71] Farms of a size that all but necessitated a separate occupation beyond agriculture equate closely to the classic definition of crofting and underline how over-population, although clearly recognised as a problem, was nonetheless being actively encouraged. In Argyll, a similar situation had developed. By 1796 Robertson had compiled a detailed report that again exhibited the indecision and tension within estate planning. Breadalbane, for instance, had expressed disquiet at the removal of land from farms in order that crofting policies could be implemented, and asked whether they ought to be returned to the tenantry concerned. Yet further division, as opposed to remedial consolidation of holdings, appeared inevitable as Lochend noted that only additional crofting could alleviate land claims. As late as 1803 the Argyll factor conceded that 'in admitting tenants into small possessions . . . I would be injurious to your Lordship's interest to increase the population on the estate unnecessarily', but added that exceptions included those who had claims 'in consideration of services by themselves or by near relations in the army'.[72] Robertson summarised that in order to avoid future inconsistent management, which swung from consolidation policies towards the retention of population, crofting needed to be institutionalised 'to provide decaying tenants or any other people that Lord Breadalbane

---

70. S.R.O., Breadalbane Muniments, GD 112/14/12/1/2; GD 112/16/3/5/3; GD 112/16/4/2/17; GD 112/11/7/1/42(1–18).
71. S.R.O., Breadalbane Muniments, GD 112/12/1/2.
72. S.R.O., Breadalbane Muniments, GD 112/41/5, p. 44.

thinks himself obliged to provide for, and perhaps if necessity requires it to place two people in one croft'.[73]

It is no coincidence that crofting re-emerged strongly in the mid- to late 1790s. As in 1763 and 1783–4, this was precisely when pressure on land produced by recruitment was at its strongest. Yet while it is tempting to see recruitment simply in terms of preventing the imposition of full-blown orthodox improvement, and although there is little doubt that surveyors like Robertson viewed excessive division as unhelpful and unproductive, it is important to realise that crofting did not in fact adversely affect estate profitability. Robertson himself conceded that land laid out in small lots paid more rent per acre than land held by multiple or single tenants. Crofts in Netherlorne, already acknowledged as rented in higher proportion to tenant land, were, nevertheless, augmented in 1797 at a rate that ranged from 10% to almost 30% higher than other holdings.[74] Crucially, therefore, the relative profitability of crofting complemented the broadly economic rationale behind recruiting. Just as taking recruits from the estate exhibited awareness of market conditions outside the region, so there is also evidence that Breadalbane sought to integrate recruitment and the tenurial adjustments required by it into a wider commercial strategy. Within the various estate reports on the future of sheep and tenantry on Lochtayside commissioned by Breadalbane in the mid-1790s was a tract entitled 'Observations on Highland Estate Management'. Written by Sir John Murray-Macgregor of Landrick, a prominent beneficiary of lucrative state service in the East Indies, it stated that Highland landlords needed to adapt conventional improvement policies to social and economic realities in the North of Scotland. The paper continued: 'It is from richness in the number of men and a moderate revenue in money that the Highland chieftains and proprietors ought to look for wealth and importance'. It was of course extremely naive to believe that landlords would forego an increase in their rents or abandon the economic mores of their time, which stressed the idea of property as primarily an economic and commercial resource. Yet this pro-population strategy was made realistic and, importantly, financially acceptable by what Macgregor saw as 'advantages far beyond easy and overcharged rents, from the various public offices, civil and military to which their ability to support the state would give themselves and their relatives the fairest and strongest pretensions'.[75]

73. S.R.O., Breadalbane Muniments, 'Robert Robertson's Report on Netherlorne, 1796', R.H.P. 972/5; GD 112/12/7/22. Lochend gave this policy practical expression by arguing that the farm of Oban on the Island of Seil could afford to lose an additional amount of land in order to make out two crofts which could settle four soldiers. S.R.O., Breadalbane Muniments, GD 112/12/1/5/48; GD 112/11/7/1/3.
74. S.R.O., Breadalbane Muniments, GD 112/12/7/22, 23x; GD 112/4/2/39; GD 112/9/3/3/35.
75. S.R.O., Breadalbane Muniments, GD 112/16/3/5/4. For all their apparent obsolescence, similar sentiments were evident in Argyll in 1800. See GD 112/41/5, p. 35.

Recruiting was thus set firmly within a context where Highland property performed the same function as Lowland estates in that it still provided revenue to the landlord. However, profit did not from being organised exclusively in terms of market orientated agriculture, but rather from the estate's demographic productivity allied to a still substantial commercial rental. The development of strategies that emphasised population retention for state service was not only symptomatic of the region's increasingly specialised imperial economy, but indeed meant that Highland landlords, to a far greater extent than the rest of their Scottish counterparts, saw government employment and state intervention as an inherently attractive prospect. This distinctive, regional concept of political economy not only recognised but, indeed, was perhaps overly dependent upon the interventionist tendencies of the fiscal-military state. Such thinking was exemplified in a letter written by the fourth Earl in February 1803, when the Peace of Amiens had allowed the state to withdraw its military patronage and scale down its commitment to population retention:

> The more I have considered it, the more I am convinced that without the aid of government improvement in these districts cannot be carried on a general system, or to any great extent . . . unless the patriotic patronage and interference of the government of the country is extended to them. The great population, the small size of the farms, and the prejudice of the people all seem to combine as insurmountable bars to any innovation. By enlarging the farms I might have increased my revenue considerably, but my object was to retain the people.[76]

Clearly, Breadalbane had chosen to implement Murray-Macgregor's vision of property management rather than the orthodox practices of Lowland agrarian improvement. In so doing he demonstrated that recruitment and state service had emerged as profoundly influential factors in the overall nature of the estate's development.

Conclusion

Examination of the Breadalbane estate in the last half of the eighteenth century suggests that socio-economic issues and the particular practices of Highland landlordism must be balanced by study of the political aspirations of landlords and the extent of central government pressure upon proprietors to recruit. It is also clear that the relationship between tenantry and landlord did not operate in a vacuum, or, indeed, was characterised simply by downward pressure of elites upon their populations. Tension between the tenantry and the landless orders was obviously a crucial aspect of eighteenth-century Highland life. Indeed, inter-tenantry friction was an active dynamic in shaping the development of new tenurial structures like crofting. Military

76. S.R.O., Breadalbane and Gavin of Langton Papers, RH. 4/196.

recruitment's social importance lay in the fact that it was a catalyst that exacerbated this tension while simultaneously disturbing the already fragile balance between estate groups. It raised the expectations of the largely landless cottar and tenurially vulnerable subtenant groups while severely disrupting the process of improvement through the episodic removal of uncooperative tenants. Above all, by inducing periods of acute pressure on land it forced the adoption and institutionalisation of subdivision as opposed to the theoretically preferable single-tenant farms. However, recruiting should not be viewed as evidence of the landlords' failure to improve. It was more an alternative strategy whereby the primary aim of improvement – increased revenue – was achieved through the systematic exploitation of tenantry as a military resource and an ongoing, parallel reliance on the land's commercial profitability.[77] If improvement was all about maximising an estate's inherent resources, then to late eighteenth-century Highland landlords recruiting was merely diversification and a different means towards a similar end.

77. T.M. Devine, 'Social Responses of Agrarian "Improvement": the Highlands and Lowland Clearances in Scotland', pp. 160–61.

CHAPTER FIVE

Military Recruiting and the Highland Estate Economy, 1756–1815

Events on the lands of the Breadalbane family emphasise how any proper understanding of the nature and consequences of Highland recruitment must examine its impact at estate level. In a predominantly rural and agrarian society, with little or no specialised commercial or manufacturing sectors, it was the landed estate that provided the immediate framework and point of reference for the majority of the population, as well as the context for most socio-economic activity. Analysis of the development of Highland estates between 1763 and 1815 has for obvious reasons focused on the rise of commercial landlordism. The new attitude of proprietors witnessed the implementation of land-use strategies requiring the internal relocation of populations in order that estate resources could be more profitably exploited. This change entailed the rapid break-up of the tacksman and joint-tenant system and its replacement across some parts of the region with large single-tenant farms. In kelping areas a different structure emerged, with small excessively subdivided croft holdings representing the new tenurial form.[1] The practice of deploying estate populations as a recruiting resource for the British army, however, would seem to contradict this picture of revolutionary change. There is certainly enough evidence for the direct use of land in return for enlistment to lend some support to the argument that military recruitment constituted a form of continuity from the days of militarised clanship: that while there was the element of profit within recruiting, it ultimately disguised what amounted to the non-commercial use of estate resources.[2]

Although the argument that recruitment is evidence of vestigial clanship is not altogether unhelpful, it has resulted in a rather superficial treatment of the subject. Over-concentration on the decline in Highland militarism, for example, has turned out to be a somewhat circular line of investigation leading back to an emphasis on how the forces of commercialism undermined the basis of both clanship and recruitment. From this perspective later eighteenth-century military employment was based almost exclusively upon

1. M. Gray, *The Highland Economy, 1750–1850* (Edinburgh, 1957), pp. 58–63.
2. E. Richards, *A History of the Highland Clearances: Agrarian Change and the Evictions, 1746–1886*, vol. 1 (London, 1982), pp. 147, 149–50; T.M. Devine, 'Social Responses to Agrarian "Improvement": the Highland and Lowland Clearances in Scotland', in R.A. Houston & I.D. Whyte (eds.), *Scottish Society, 1500–1800* (Cambridge, 1989), p. 160.

obsolete clannish practices, and its demise a certainty with the coming of socio-economic change.[3] The one major weak point in this argument is that compared with 1745 there were by 1805 far larger numbers of Highland males involved in military service of one sort or another. The 11,336 Highlanders in the volunteer establishment alone, for instance, represented almost the same number as the Jacobite clansmen mobilised in 1715, the largest of the military uprisings that punctuated the first half of the eighteenth century.[4] This suggests that pitting military recruitment against commercial change is a rather crude method of analysis. Instead, recruiting needs to be viewed as something born of its own time, and greater attention should be paid to the contemporary motivation of proprietors, tacksmen, joint tenantry, and crofter and cottar groups. Indeed, in order to balance existing analysis respecting the decline in Highland militarism, it is necessary to examine why the military economy expanded in spite of clanship's decay, and how it affected the nature, scope and scale of estate change during the period from the 1760s until 1815.

Motive and Incentive: Highland Landlords and the British 'Fiscal-Military State'

The reasons why landlords recruited have already in one respect been well documented. The military deployment of their populations, above all during the Seven Years' War, has been seen as instrumental in rehabilitating Jacobite families. However, while undoubtedly a vital concern in 1756–7 for all Highland landlords, including many Whigs, rehabilitation was less of an issue by the time of the American Revolutionary War. Only for those such as Charles Cameron of Locheil, Kenneth Mackenzie of Cromartie and a few other minor lairds did this agenda have any real relevance, and they constituted but a small part of the total involved in recruiting.[5] Above all, arguments about the need for political rehabilitation hardly explain the example of the Argyll or Sutherland families – the most consistent recruiters of Highland manpower – or indeed the motivation of Highland landlords in general during the apogee of recruitment in the 1790s.

The financial attractiveness of the British state rather than any direct need

3. J. Prebble, *Mutiny: Highland Regiments in Revolt, 1743–1804* (Harmondsworth, Middlesex, 1975), pp. 263–66, 275, 362–63; E. Richards, *op. cit.*, pp. 151–52; R. Clyde, *From Rebel to Hero: The Image of the Highlander, 1745–1830* (East Linton, 1995), pp. 159, 162–3.
4. Marquis of Cambridge, 'The Volunteer Army of Great Britain, 1806', in *Journal of the Society of Army Historical Research*, vol. 13 (1931), pp. 114–72; A.I. Macinnes, *Clanship, Commerce and the House of Stuart, 1603–1788* (East Linton, 1996), p. 163.
5. B.P. Lenman, *Jacobite Clans of the Great Glen, 1650–1784* (London, 1984), pp. 186–202; L. Colley, *Britons: Forging the Nation, 1707–1837* (London, 1992), p. 140.

to atone for the events of 1746 offers an alternative, contemporaneous explanation for landlord involvement in the military. Recent historiography has completely altered our understanding of the nature of the state in eighteenth-century Britain. Far from being weak, under-governed and non-absolutist, certain key features of the United Kingdom's administration made it in some respects as much, if not more of, an absolutist state as either France or Prussia. Britain in fact developed as a 'fiscal-military state', exhibiting financial efficiency through the uncontested authority of the Crown in parliament. The vast sums of money raised by government were overwhelmingly aimed at military spending, with 75–85% not uncommon in this period. This allowed Britain to develop a military machine that, despite its smaller size in real terms, actually represented a proportionally higher level of mobilisation than that of France. The strength of this military complex lay above all in its money supply: British finance retained a level of creditor confidence that was the envy of western Europe. The fiscal-military state therefore became an immensely attractive financial proposition, with impressive reserves of revenue. The direct result was its 'colonisation' by certain elements within Britain who sought material advantage from their involvement within the echelons of the civilian or military appendages of government.[6]

The North of Scotland thus lay within the orbit of the richest administration in western Europe; and regiment raising, rather than representing some outdated preference for clannish militarism, should be seen as the region's primary method of 'colonising' and gaining access to the British fiscal state's material resources. In this particular sense Highland proprietors differed little from the monied interest in the City of London or any other of the lobbying groups who aimed to derive financial benefits from the state.[7] To establish and maintain strong links and patronage opportunities with this fiscal-military government constituted the central, over-riding reason why Highland landlords raised regiments. This was the motivation for recruiting noted by the second Duke of Atholl in 1760, Sir Alexander Macdonald of Sleat in 1777, and the Earls of Seaforth and Breadalbane in 1793. In the case of the latter his supporters felt that raising a regiment 'may be very right, and create a union between the Earl and the present administration'. Similar sentiments were echoed by An-

6. R.V. Jackson, 'Government Expenditure and British Economic Growth in the Eighteenth Century: Some Problems of Measurement', in *Economic History Review*, vol. 43 (1990), pp. 219–20; L. Colley, *op. cit.*, pp. 283–319; J. Brewer, *The Sinews of Power: War, Money and the English State, 1688–1783* (London, 1989), pp. 4–6, 27–40, 114–116, 121–122, 187–191 and 201; J. Brewer, 'The Eighteenth-Century British State: Contexts and Issues', in L Stone (ed.), *An Imperial State at War: Britain from 1689 to 1815* (London, 1994), pp. 57–8.
7. P. Harding & P. Mandler, 'From "Fiscal-Military" State to Laissez-Faire State, 1760–1850', in *Journal of British Studies*, vol. 32 (1993), p. 68; A.G. Olson, *Making the Empire Work: London and the American Interest Groups* (Harvard, 1992), pp. 134–136.

drew Macpherson of Benchar, a Badenoch tacksman, when, in 1778, he heard that Alexander Gordon, fourth Duke of Gordon, was to raise a battalion of fencibles:

> I know how deeply his Grace's honour is engaged for his battalion, and that as it is his first essay for support of government in the military line, they will have an attentive eye upon the progress and will be apt to judge of his future ability by the success attending this particular instance . . . The more his consequence is established with the administration he will have it more in his power to do for his dependants.[8]

Recruitment can thus be seen as very much a political act intended to establish a landlord's credit and favour at the metropolitan centre. This, incidentally, warns against supposing that Highland landlords in the post-Culloden era abandoned politics and concentrated simply upon the improvement of their estates.[9] The idea that politics and estate improvement existed in two different, incompatible spheres of activity is not altogether helpful. Instead, politics in the Highlands, with recruitment as a pre-eminent example, should be viewed as having evolved into the means whereby revenue normally obtained through private, commercial estate improvement was supplemented by state employment and income. This reliance on state monies was especially important in the Highlands because landed estates were not always able to guarantee regular, assured levels of revenue. This may appear a rather doubtful argument given that, by the 1790s, Highland estate rentals were probably rising faster than anywhere else in the United Kingdom. Nevertheless, one of the most persistent complaints regarding estate management during the era of first-phase clearance was the lack of regular, dependable rents. The replacement of tacksmen by small joint tenantry, for example, left landlords deeply apprehensive that their income from rents would become increasingly inconsistent and unreliable. Dogged by a lack of capital reserves, small tenantry were undoubtedly prisoners to the vagaries of bad crops and poor cattle prices. This problem of sustaining rent payments often dominated approaches to estate management, as James Macgregor, factor in Strathspey, conceded in 1778 to Sir James Grant: 'I own I am not for Lord Kaimes' plan of giving leases upon an improved estate, it may answer very well in the Merse or Lothians but not in my humble opinion

---

8. J.E. Cookson, *The British Armed Nation, 1793–1815* (Oxford, 1997), p. 132; B.A.M, Box 47/12/10; C.D.T.L., GD 221/5516/1; G.U.L., Campbell of Inverneil Papers, Journal, September 1792-February 1793, p. 267; N.L.S., Melville Papers, Ms 5, f. 1; J. Fortescue (ed.), *The Correspondence of George III*, vol. 3 (London, 1928), p. 531; S.R.O., Gordon Castle Muniments, GD 44/47/5/1/35.
9. E. Cregeen (ed.), *Argyll Estate Instructions: Mull, Morvern and Tiree, 1771–1805* (Edinburgh, 1964), ix–x; J. Dwyer & A. Murdoch, 'Paradigms and Politics: Manners, Morals and the Rise of Henry Dundas, 1770–1784', in J. Dwyer, R. A. Mason & A. Murdoch (eds.), *New Perspectives on the Politics and Culture of Early Modern Scotland* (Edinburgh, 1982), pp. 216–18.

on a Highland estate'.[10] Arrears on the Reay estate in Sutherland from 1798 to 1810 demonstrate the important point that just as rental income increased, so did the inability of many Highland tenants to pay. In 1798 arrears stood at 6.2% of the rent; by 1802 they totalled almost 12%; and by 1810 they had reached over 15%. This represents the flip side of the successful landlord drive to raise rentals. Such arrears were evidence that proprietors simply could not be sure how much, precisely, they would obtain from their tenants in any given year. In 1778 real rents paid to Norman Macleod of Dunvegan totalled £3,757; a year later the estate received only £3,071 – almost a 20% difference. One of the main reasons for such erratic payments was an over-reliance on droving. This was recognised by Macleod's trustees when in response to the dramatic rise in arrears in 1779 they insisted that only half the rent be paid in drovers' bills. Similar concerns in Sutherland prompted repeated attempts in the 1770s to put the tenantry 'on a more certain footing in the credit they give of their cattle'.[11]

In Lewis, the failure of droving credit in 1779 also resulted in exceptionally high levels of rent arrears. The problems of the cattle trade, however, were replaced latterly on the west coast by those of kelping. It was this industry, in particular, which put west Highland rentals upon a steep upward curve, providing many estate proprietors with an apparent opportunity to forego the search for additional sources of income. However, in 1794 the factor in Lewis highlighted the downside of this growing financial reliance on kelp. Although encouraging unprecedented rent augmentations, the industry also increased and, indeed, exacerbated arrears. In return for its future manufacture tenants had got into the habit of receiving meal on credit but were then failing to produce the corresponding level of kelp. Even more worrying was the fluctuating nature of overall production. Table 9 demonstrates the manufacture and income derived from kelp on Lewis between 1794 and 1799. The figures demonstrate clearly that while income increased dramatically, there were also large and unpredictable swings between total annual profits. In April 1798 it was calculated that Lewis would produce 331 tons; yet, as the table shows, production came to only 294 tons – a difference of 38 tons, worth a total of £633. Projections respecting Lewis kelp profits in 1808 stood at £11,000 per annum, but it was calculated they would fall to £6,000 in 1810. All these accounts show that while the connection between rapid

10. E.R. Cregeen, 'The Tacksmen and their Successors: A Study of Tenurial Reorganisation in Mull, Morvern and Tiree in the Early Eighteenth Century', in *Scottish Studies*, vol. 13 (1969), pp. 109–10; T.M. Devine, *Clanship to Crofters' War: The Social Transformation of the Scottish Highlands* (Manchester 1994), p. 32; N.L.S., Mackenzie of Delvine, Ms 1327, f. 127; S.R.O., Seafield Muniments, GD 248/227/2/31; D.C.M., 4/114.
11. S.R.O., Maclaine of Lochbuie Papers, GD 174/1319/1; S.R.O., John Macgregor Collection, GD 50/26/6; D.C.M., 3/68/4, 3/104/18; N.L.S., Mackenzie of Delvine Papers, Ms 1485, f. 271; N.L.S., Sutherland Papers, Dep. 313/3326; Dep. 313/1096; Dep. 313/1112/7.

rental increase and kelping is certainly justified, it must be balanced by the recognition that such profits were also unreliable, if not alarmingly erratic.[12]

Table 9. Lewis Kelp Production, 1794–99[13]

Year	Kelp harvest in tons	Kelping profits	% + or −
1794	232	£1,104	–
1795	357	£1,588	+43.8%
1796	185, 14 cwt	£1,400	−11.8%
1797	185, 3 cwt	£1,667	+19%
1798	293, 9 cwt	£2,452	+47%
1799	196, 7 cwt	£1,766	−27.9%

While the kelp industry was undoubtedly the single most important economic development in the North-West, the volatile nature of both its production and price was something that landlords had necessarily to take account of and cater for. There were problems also with the other new economic activity of sheep farming; initially, these arose from a lack of expertise and suitable tenants. In the mid-1770s and 1780s, for instance, neither Campbell of Glenure nor Maclaine of Lochbuie could find tenants capable of stocking farms with the number of sheep that guaranteed high payments of rent. Although this problem diminished as the industry established itself throughout the region, landlords continued to exhibit a degree of hesitancy, not least in light of the fact that the American Revolutionary War bankrupted a large number of sheep farmers in Argyll. Similarly, the harsh winter of 1782–3 saw sheep flocks suffer an equal rate of loss to cattle herds. As late as 1803 some elites believed that sheep prices would only remain high until the trade, which involved a few large capitalised tenants, had taken over most Highland estates. Then, it was feared, sheep farmers would combine against landlords who, with no other income, would be forced to reduce rents.[14]

The subsequent development of sheep farming was of course radically different, but the initial insecurities are testimony to the genuine apprehension felt by debt-ridden Highland elites at the prospect of fluctuating or unreliable incomes. That said, indebtedness was nothing new: owing substantial sums of money had been a common enough feature of Highland elite financial affairs ever since the seventeenth century. The new element within the debt structure was that with non-clan sources of borrowing such

12. S.R.O., Gillanders of Highfield Papers, GD 427/217/24; S.R.O., Seaforth Muniments, GD 46/17/3, letter 1 March 1794; GD 46/17/356–60; GD 46/17/16, 'Accounts, 1808–1810'; GD 46/17/15; GD 46/17/14/630.
13. S.R.O., Seaforth Muniments, GD 46/17/3.
14. S.R.O., Campbell of Barcaldine Papers, GD 170/1643/17/1; S.R.O., Maclaine of Lochbuie Papers, GD 174/1329/28; N.L.S., Sutherland Papers, Dep. 313/979/4, p. 20; D.J. Withrington and I.R. Grant (eds.), *The Old Statistical Account*, vol. 8 (Wakefield, 1983), p. 99; S.R.O., Melville Castle Muniments, GD 51/52/5.

as credit banking now increasingly available, foreclosure was far more likely. The crucial point was not the total level of debt 'but the balance between debt and income'. In order to service annual interest repayments finance needed to be 'a combination of stable or increasing income'. It was this balancing of debt with, above all, *reliable* earnings that explains why many Highland elites felt state revenue was an especially sensible option. Thus, when in 1775 John Murray, fourth Duke of Atholl, highlighted 'the contingencies which are likely to happen to Highland estates', he immediately went on to note that his grandfather had depended upon '£3,000 a year from government'.[15]

Recruitment and the military employment it guaranteed can thus be seen as an economic strategy born of the landlords' search for additional, relatively secure income. On 26 October 1793 a letter to Francis Humberston-Mackenzie, Earl of Seaforth, who had recently completed his new regiment, highlighted this. It noted that: 'this would be a proper time for you asking something for yourself and your family in consideration of your ready support'.[16] Given the condition of his finances, there was good reason for Seaforth to request assistance from the state. In 1795 the family debt stood at £90,994; by 1800 it had reached £108,000. By contrast, income from his Lewis, Lochalsh, Glensheal and Kintail estates, which constituted the bulk of his Scottish property, totalled only £9,049 in 1795. His debt problem was compounded severely by the fact that the French Revolutionary War, as had previously been the case during the Seven Years War and American conflict, drained available credit into lucrative government stocks and shares. Cheap borrowing had traditionally provided the answer to Scotland's lack of capital, but war meant that landlords like Seaforth tended to find their civilian avenues of credit income severely disrupted, which, in turn, confirmed the wisdom of seeking military employment.[17] As it was, the benefits arising from his involvement in the military were quickly made clear when, in February 1794, an adviser who had earlier discussed the sale of Lewis to alleviate debts now argued: 'I am strongly impressed with the hope that your

15. A.I. Macinnes, 'The Impact of the Civil Wars and Interregnum: Political Disruption and Social Change within Scottish Gaeldom', in R. Mitchison and P. Roebuck (eds.), *Economy and Society in Scotland and Ireland, 1500–1939* (Edinburgh, 1988), pp. 61–64, 67; T.M. Devine, 'The Emergence of the New Elite in the Western Highlands and Islands, 1800–60', in T.M. Devine (ed.), *Improvement and Enlightenment* (Edinburgh, 1989), pp. 117–18; N.L.S., Mackenzie of Delvine Papers, Ms 1407, ff. 143, 146.
16. S.R.O., Seaforth Muniments, GD 46/17/3, letter 26 October 1793.
17. J. Anderson, *The Interest of Great Britain with Regard to her American Colonies Considered* (London, 1782), p 104; S.R.O., Gordon Castle Muniments, GD 44/200/32; N.L.S., Mackenizie of Delvine Papers, Ms 1314, f. 114; S.R.O., Maclaine of Lochbuie Papers, GD 174/1410/125–7; S.R.O., Seaforth Muniments, GD 46/17/4, f. 265; GD 46/17/14/850; GD 46/4/14 and 13; GD 46/46/17/3, 'Accounts of Lewis Kelp'; GD 46/17/15, letters 26 April, 17 September, 27 October and 7 November 1795.

military career will dissolve all necessity of parting with the Lewis, whole or in part'.[18]

Quantifying the revenue derived by elites from recruitment is difficult in light of the indirect clothing allowances and off reckonings allowed to senior officers. The immediate reason for Seaforth agreeing to levy men in 1793 had been to acquire the rank of lieutenant-colonel: thereafter, it was understood he would sell his commission to his brother-in-law, Major Alexander Mackenzie of Belmaduthie, producing a profit of £3,500 – equivalent to 87% of an entire annual Lewis rent. Yet it was within a wider credit context that real, immediate benefits accrued to the Earl. In October 1795 he ensured army bills of £5,000 were sent to Humphrey Donaldson & Co. who, being aware that his regimental off reckonings were imminent, had earlier advanced that amount to him.[19] Alongside rising kelping rents, therefore, Seaforth, through his military activity, now had good connections with large financing companies: in essence, he had used his state employment to facilitate his private banking. This reinforcement of cash flow was one of the primary financial aspects underpinning the disproportionate involvement of Highland landlords within the British military. In October 1793, at a time when the outbreak of war had seriously destabilised the money markets, Murdoch Maclaine of Lochbuie used his position as quartermaster to the Argyll Fencibles to deposit military revenue in a bank used by himself and his local creditors, thus alleviating solvency problems.[20] Nor should the dramatic upturn in rentals produced by kelp and sheep profits disguise the substantial income derived directly from army wages and other imperial offices associated with military rank. In 1800, for example, as a direct result of the family's impressive recruiting record, Seaforth received the governorship of Barbados. In all, his salary and regimental profits totalled £2,300 – equivalent to the rents of his entire Glensheal and Kintail estates. Even by 1808 his governor's pension was still worth £2,000 – exactly one third of his entire landed rental and, moreover, equal to 18% of his by now enormous kelping income.[21]

Seaforth was by no means alone in seeing the financial opportunities offered by state service. In 1801 Sir James Grant calculated that his brother's regiment was worth £1,400 – equivalent to one fifth of the family's Strathspey rental.[22] Norman Macleod of Dunvegan's career represents one of the most successful instances of Highland elite 'colonisation' of the fiscal-military state. By 1773 his rental was £3,918; the

18. S.R.O., Seaforth Muniments, GD 46/17/15, letter 7 November 1795.
19. S.R.O., Seaforth Muniments, GD 46/17/3, letter 15 October 1795; GD 46/6/25/ 5–6, 9, 78.
20. S.R.O., Maclaine of Lochbuie, GD 174/1410/131.
21. S.R.O., Seaforth Muniments, GD 46/20/4/1/13; GD 46/17/16, 'Accounts 1808 & 1810'; GD 46/17/19/274, 356–60.
22. S.R.O., Seafield Muniments, GD 248/3410/10/3; GD 248/2901.

family debt, however, totalled almost £41,000. In May 1775, as events in America pointed towards an inevitable expansion in the British army, Macleod contacted his kinsman, Simon Fraser of Lovat, and subsequently obtained a captaincy in the latter's new regiment. The systematic use of his estate population in recruiting for rank ensured Macleod's rapid promotion to major in 1778 and lieutenant-colonel in 1780. Upon obtaining the major's commission, his estate trustees noted that his wages and off reckonings meant his entire rental could now be diverted into debt reduction. Macleod was eventually ordered to India and amassed during the 1780s the substantial sum of £100,000 which secured his estate from the prospect of bankruptcy.[23] The differing reactions of creditors in 1777 to the similar financial problems faced by Macleod and John Macdonald of Clanranald, then just a minor, clearly demonstrate the significance of obtaining secure and regular state income. Despite access to a far larger kelping income, and burdened with £10,000 less debt, tutors for the Clanranald estate found creditors were not prepared to show the kind of latitude being offered to Macleod. Indeed Clanranald's lawyer noted that 'It is hard to see them so clamorous when Macleod's affairs tho' in a worse condition brings no dispatch on the managers . . . they should consider how peaceable the creditors on Macleod's estate are'.[24]

Military income's real importance thus lay in providing an element of reliability that served to counter the erratic character of other, often more profitable areas of estate revenue. This also explains why lesser gentry and lairds were equally if not more reliant on military earnings when compared with prominent landlords like Seaforth and Grant. Archibald Maclaine of Lochbuie, for instance, was told in 1779 to set his estate in long leases and obtain a commission, to which his advisers added 'a company you might live genteelly upon, without other aid'. The pay of an army captain was £182 – over twice the amount of his highest rented farm and equal to almost one fifth of his entire rental. Similar concerns motivated Captain Colin Campbell of Glenfalloch. Through his connections with the fourth Earl, Glenfalloch gained a commission in the Breadalbane Fencibles. In 1794 his rental was £482; by February of the same year, however, his debts totalled £1,384. His pay as captain, meanwhile, equalled 37.8% of his landed income. Just how attractive military service appeared to lairds like Glenfalloch can be seen from the fact that his aim of obtaining a major's commission in the fencibles would provide him with assured income equivalent to 56.6% of his entire rental. Not surprisingly, the importance of this state revenue to Glenfalloch was

23. D.C.M., 3/104/2, 15, 19–20, 33; N.L.S., Mackenzie of Delvine Papers, Ms 1171, f. 337; H.M.C., *Laing Manuscript*, vol. 2 (London, 1925), pp. 481–483; E. Richards, *op. cit.*, p. 149.
24. S.R.O., Methven Collection, GD 1/8/17, pp. 30–34; GD 1/8/18, letter 1 May 1777.

such that he dreaded the prospect of peace and subsequent fencible disbandment.[25]

Deliberation amongst advisers to Elizabeth, Countess of Sutherland, underlines how the fiscal-military state and the empire were linked in a highly distinctive way to socio-economic conditions in the Highlands. A memorial in the mid-1780s reveals how elites saw recruitment as akin to one of the region's other specialised imperial economies, fulfilling a niche role that Lowland areas were less readily able to do as a result of their own highly developed commercial and manufacturing economies. Its ability to supply important military manpower, it was felt, meant the Highlands could then obtain favourable access to state support and assistance. Specifically relating to Sutherland, it was added that:

> No county in the empire can scarce boast of such universal attachment to government and loyalty to the Hanoverian family. It is admitted that in point of attachment and loyalty, the County of Argyll and the noble family of that name by holding in general the highest offices in the state and patronage always attending such offices, have been able to render the name Campbell at this day it is thought, the most numerous and wealthy in the empire.[26]

Here, again, is evidence that a feature of the Highland elite's overall response to inclusion within the empire was a preference for especially close links with central government's lucrative military machine, a strategy seen as a form of patriotic partnership. This explains why recruiting continued during a period of profound change and in spite of the extinction of clanship as a form of social organisation in the Highlands.

Military Recruiting and the Highland Estate

The determination of landlords to colonise the British army entailed a significant level of dependence upon their estate populations to supply the necessary number of men. However, the scale and impact of recruitment in the region during the period from the 1750s until 1815 has been masked by the traumatic nature of other socio-economic events during the era of first-phase clearance. Appendices 1 and 5 illustrate that military levying was a conspicuous activity across the whole region; indeed, Table 10 shows that in many districts it routinely removed 15%–25% of the male population.

---

25. S.R.O., Maclaine of Lochbuie Papers, GD 174/1319/3; GD 174/789/16; S.R.O., John Macgregor Collection, GD 50/26/6; GD 50/26/30/7 & 13.
26. N.L.S., Sutherland Papers, Dep. 313/979/4, pp. 9, 21–26.

Table 10. Impact of Recruiting upon Manpower and Farm Structure, 1778–1799[27]

Year	Estate	N° of Farms	Farms Affected	%	Man-power	Recruited	%
1778	Atholl	112	46	41	454	88	19.3
1778	Lochaber	37	33	89.1	284	75	26.4
1778	Strathavon	74	35	47.2	306	45	14.7
1795	Lochbuie	29	23	79.3	361	50	13.8
1799	N. Uist	43	22	51	1,313	83	6.3

Nor was this the case only in underdeveloped north-western areas or on the large estates of premier landlords. Although his estate was situated in the eastern zone of the region, an area already experiencing relatively improved agriculture and high levels of population decrease, Sir James Grant nonetheless recruited over 140 men from Strathspey in 1793. On the Mull lands of Murdoch Maclaine of Lochbuie, 50 men – one man in seven – were enlisted in the Dunbartonshire Fencibles during the period 1794–5. On the small estate of Aberarder in Inverness-shire a list from 1792 reveals that the laird was prepared to recruit 11 out of a total of only 19 suitable men; similarly, a 1776 census of Strowan and Lochgarry suggests that 28 out of a total of 68 men were selected for recruitment.[28] These enlistment levels do not usually compare with the most committed of the Jacobite clans, such as the Stewarts of Appin and Macdonalds of Glencoe, who mobilised 57% and 66% of their available manpower respectively in 1745–6. Yet in some instances post-Culloden recruitment was directly comparable with that achieved by the Hanoverian clans. The involvement of Lewis manpower in the '45, for example, had been restricted to one independent company of 100 men; however, in five weeks during the spring of 1793 Seaforth recruited no fewer than 220 men from his Lewis estate. Likewise, while 38% of Macleod of Macleod's 575 men in Waternish and Duirinish enlisted in 1745, along with one third of the Earl of Sutherland's 2,337 men, a similar level of one man in three from Kildonan entered the Sutherland Fencible Regiment raised in 1779 (see Appendix 1).[29]

Although levels of mobilisation in the post-1745 period were without doubt substantial and in some instances reminiscent of the levying power of

---

27. B.A.M., Military Census 1778; S.R.O., Gordon Castle Muniments, GD 44/47/7/4; GD 44/25/2/56; S.R.O., Maclaine of Lochbuie Muniments, GD 174/916, 923; C.D.T.L., GD 221/4388.
28. S.R.O., Seafield Muniments, GD 248/464; GD 248/190/3/21; S.R.O., Gordon Castle Muniments, GD 44/25/2/56; S.R.O., Maclaine of Lochbuie Papers, GD 174/927; S.R.O., Fraser-Macintosh Collection, GD 128/37/12; S.R.O., F.E.P., E788/9/1–2.
29. N.L.S., Fletcher of Saltoun Papers, Ms 17522, ff. 61–4, 66–7; S.R.O., Gillanders of Highfield Papers, GD 427/307/4; D.C.M., 4/252; S.R.O., D. Murray-Rose Papers, GD 1/400/4/2. In Assynt, in 1745, recruitment involved 29% of available men: N.L.S., Sutherland Papers, Dep. 313/3248–9.

clanship, it would be wrong to think, as some have been apt to do, that Highland regiments in the British army were little more than 'clan regiments'. Largely romantic assertions have been made to this effect regarding regiments such as the 78th Highlanders raised by Simon Fraser of Lovat in 1757 and the 93rd Sutherland Highlanders raised in 1799–1800 by Elizabeth, Countess of Sutherland.[30] Such analogies are in fact a lot less helpful than might at first seem the case. Precisely because the motives behind later eighteenth-century Highland recruiting were invariably entrepreneurial and commercial, methods used to levy local recruits differed significantly from the period of militarised clanship, and were in fact tailored to avoid excessive damage to estate profitability. Landlords were keenly aware that any benefits obtained through involvement in the army would be quickly cancelled if other wealth-generating sectors of the local economy were damaged as a result of over-recruitment. Sir James Grant mirrored the sentiments of many proprietors, especially those not directly involved in recruiting, when he noted that: 'If the country is to be drained not only in time of war but by every other method in time of peace, how is the ground to be laboured, manufactures to be carried on or the poor farmer to live?' Kelping, weaving and, indeed, aspects of agrarian improvement like ditching, enclosing and village development were extremely labour-intensive, and all the evidence suggests that landlords took this into account when faced with the prospect of taking men from their estates.[31] One obvious symptom of this was that, unless it was in their own immediate financial self-interest to recruit quickly for a regiment in which they were personally involved, Highland landlords usually discouraged enlistment upon their estates and protected their populations from the unwanted attentions of recruiting parties. This attitude was evident across the region from Sutherland to Argyll and, indeed, was an everyday feature of estate management during the period 1745–1815. Of course this concern to preserve economically valuable manpower was motivated in part by the realisation that if they failed to guard their populations, landlords faced losing manpower which they themselves might require as recruits at a later date.[32] As noted earlier, the second Duke of

30. J.S. Keltie, A History of the Scottish Highlands, Highland Clans and Highland Regiments, vol. 2 (Edinburgh, 1875), pp. 453–7; D.M. Henderson, Highland Soldier: A Social Study of the Highland Regiments, 1820–1920 (Edinburgh, 1989), p. 5.
31. A.J. Youngson, After the Forty-Five: the Economic Impact on the Scottish Highlands (Edinburgh, 1973), pp. 72–3, 82–4, 136–7; A.I. Macinnes, 'Scottish Gaeldom: The First Phase of Clearance', in T.M. Devine and R. Mitchison (eds.), People and Society in Scotland, 1760–1830, vol. 1 (Edinburgh, 1988), p. 79; S.R.O., Seafield Muniments, GD 248/266/2/88.
32. S.R.O., Seafield Muniments, GD 248/56/4/12–13; GD 248/683/2/64; GD 248/226/2/84; GD 248/227/2/57; S.R.O., Campbell of Barcaldine Papers, GD 170/1666/6; GD 170/1355/9; GD 170/1354/59; GD 170/1090/3; S.R.O., John Macgregor Collection, GD 50/180/33, 66–67; N.L.S., Mackenzie of Delvine Papers, Ms 1284, f. 109; Ms 1461, f. 199; Ms 1487, f. 133; N.L.S., Sutherland Papers, Dep. 313/1113/2; Dep. 313/1114/22–3, 31 & 33.

Atholl had experienced substantial losses of estate manpower in 1760; this was the dilemma faced by the fourth Duke of Gordon when fourteen local lairds and tacksmen from Badenoch and Lochaber obtained commissions in the Highland regiments ordered at the end of 1777. By the second week of January 1778, Gordon's estate advisers calculated he had lost perhaps 10% of his available manpower, at which point the Duke ordered his tacksmen to protect their subtenantry and take legal action against those suspected of using violence to obtain men.[33] The property of Archibald Maclaine of Lochbuie faced similar problems, though as a small local proprietor it was difficult for the Mull laird to oppose the recruiting demands of the fifth Duke of Argyll's Western Fencibles. By 1779 it was understood that fifty men from the estate had already joined the army, meaning that at a conservative estimate Lochbuie had lost 52% of those considered suitable for recruitment.[34] Attempts by landlords to screen manpower for their own purposes can be seen in much the same light as the draconian estate regulations which increasingly prevented or restricted tenant use of supplies of wood, or, on the west coast, of seaware. Simply put, they all represented an effort to protect what landlords saw as a valuable commercial resource and cash crop.

Ironically, the desire to limit manpower loss explains why landlords were anxious to have their proposals to raise men accepted quickly. In October 1775 Simon Fraser, the archetypal Highland recruiter, offered and received command of the first new Highland regiment of the American Revolutionary War. This event can be too easily related to the restoration of the Lovat estate a year earlier in 1774. Fraser was doubtless extremely grateful to Westminster for returning the family lands; but another, more immediately pragmatic concern was evident in 1775 – namely the commercial welfare of his newly returned property. Contemporaries noted that by getting his offer in early and gaining access to undepleted population reserves across the whole region, Lovat avoided the necessity of relying excessively on his own tenantry in eastern Inverness-shire and Morar. Thus, rather incongruously, the best method of raising a battalion while avoiding disruption to the estate economy was to volunteer a regiment quickly and hope that government obliged before others were able to make inroads into whatever manpower resources were available.[35]

The need to adapt recruiting for the sake of other sectors of the economy not only affected when landlords chose to levy men, it also determined the type of men selected for recruitment. Here the stark contrast between the social profile of clan regiments and Highland regiments of the British army is instructive. The undoubted militarism inherent within Highland clanship ensured that military levies of that era were able to draw on all sections

33. S.R.O., Gordon Castle Muniments, GD 44/25/7/15; GD 44/43/94/16; GD 44/43/195/15, 44; GD 44/43/197/33; GD 44/47/6/63; GD 44/47/2/15 & 37.
34. S.R.O., Maclaine of Lochbuie Papers, GD 174/1316/1; GD 174/1307/3; GD 174/1440/3; GD 174/1329/3.
35. B.A.M., Box 65/2/36.

of the community. Thus, chiefs or their nearest relations acted as commanding officers; tacksmen, the senior tenants of the clan, acted as captains, lieutenants and ensigns; while the main body of soldiery comprised the tenantry and lower social orders. A list of clan recruits from the Grant lands of Urquhart on Loch Ness from 1715 shows the full spread of senior tenants, joint tenants and their sons. Similarly, a 1702 list of the Duke of Atholl's fighting men in Blair Atholl and Glen Tilt reflects the intricate social pyramid of senior tenant (6.3% of all men), tenant (69.5%) and landless servants and cottars (24.2%). Clan regiments constituted the military mobilisation of entire male communities.[36] It is against this picture of proportional involvement by all or most social groups that the recruiting practices adopted for supplying the British army must be contrasted. When a landowner fell back upon his own populations, it made commercial sense to use the least profitable. This ensured that the enlistment of tenants was avoided where possible, while those with little active involvement in the rent-paying sector of the estate were especially targeted. This strategy has already been discussed with respect to the Breadalbane estate, and was mirrored in Lewis in 1778 where it was noted that 'a list will be made out of such as is able to serve and that can be spared without material *loss*'. In Sutherland in 1759, as the seventeenth Earl constructed his fencible regiment, the policy of choosing non-tenant individuals was also practised. All eligible males were told to rendezvous at a certain parish location where non-tenant personnel were chosen as a priority. Only then were 'those that remain who are tenants told that if the Earl cannot otherwise complete his regiment they will afterwards be called upon'.[37] This recruiting strategy is evident from the occupation profile of Highland soldiers. Table 3 shows that a large majority of soldiers settled upon the annexed estates in 1763 were agricultural labourers. Likewise, in McLean of Coll's company for the Breadalbane Fencibles, 54 of the 62 men belonged to the labouring class.[38] Table 11 confirms this pattern, and suggests that recruitment relied heavily upon cottars and agricultural day labourers.

Table 11. Social Origins of Recruits
from Atholl and North Uist Estates, 1778–1799[39]

Estate	Tenants as % of estate groups	Tenant Recruits & %	Cottars/Serv't % of estate groups	Cottar & Serv't recruits & %
Atholl	350 (77)	46 (52.2)	104 (22.9)	42 (47.7)
North Uist	393 (75.8)	22 (53.6)	125 (24.1)	19 (46.3)

36. S.R.O., Seafield Muniments, GD 248/46/7; B.A.M., Box 44/III/c.
37. S.R.O., Gillanders of Highfield Papers, GD 427/304/4; N.L.S., Mackenzie of Delvine Papers, Ms 1483, f. 277.
38. S.R.O., Maclaine of Lochbuie Papers, GD 174/2221/3; S.R.O., Breadalbane Muniments, GD 112/52/539/17.
39. B.A.M., Military census Atholl estate 1778; C.D.T.L., GD 221/4388.

Unlike earlier clan regiments, therefore, recruitment for Highland regiments in the British army was socially specific, with the result that their rank and file contained a disproportionately high number of the very lowest social orders who possessed little or no actual land within their own communities.

That landlords sought out those they considered the least productive again underlines how recruitment must be seen as an essentially modern economic activity, quite unlike earlier clan mobilisations which were considered 'backward', given their tendency to indiscriminately levy the tenants responsible for estate rents. Highland tenantry were deployed by improving landlords, essentially, as a cash or commercial crop. The main factor expediting proprietary reliance on estate manpower was the rapid increase in army bounties. Official bounty levels in 1757 were £3: by the American Revolutionary war Highland recruits were costing an average of 5 guineas, though some officers were prepared to pay as much as £12–£20. By 1794, even in the supposedly underdeveloped north-west, bounties had reached £21–£30.[40] By taking men from their own farms, landlords protected themselves from this inflation in bounty prices. In return for continued possession of their farms tenants were expected to supply recruits, be it in the form of an immediate family member who cost nothing, or a purchased man who had his bounty money paid by the tenant as opposed to the landlord. There is evidence that this exchange policy was prevalent across the entire region.[41] In Strathavon and Lochaber during the recruitment of the fourth Duke of Gordon's Northern Fencibles in 1778, it was decided that tacksmen would be responsible for the bounty money of local men. Smaller tenantry followed suit and presented soldiers free as a form of grassum. It was even suggested that recruits ought to be supplied in proportion to the amount of land held. Thus William Gordon of Achorachan in Glenlivet who held thirty-six oxgates was highlighted as being responsible for four men. This suggests the estate authorities envisaged a quota of a man per nine oxgates. Rentals show Glenlivet and Strathavon had a total of 494 oxgates, giving a rough levy of 55 men. From recruiting lists it is certain that the area supplied 42 men to the Northern Fencibles and 17 to other Highland regiments – giving a total of 59 men, remarkably similar to the ratio suggested by estate managers.[42] Similarly, in Lochalsh, tenantry were informed in 1793 that in order to reduce expenses Seaforth

40. S.R.O., Boyle of Shewalton Papers, GD 1/481/14–15; S.R.O., Campbell of Barcaldine Papers, GD 170/391/1(b); GD 170/1051/2; GD 170/1620/2; S.R.O., Maclaine of Lochbuie, GD 174/1424/2; S.R.O., Seaforth Muniments, GD 46/17/3, letter 27 March 1793; GD 46/17/14/539; GD 46/224/21.
41. S.R.O., Campbell of Barcaldine Papers, GD 170/1643/20; GD 170/1090/38; S.R.O., Gordon Castle Muniments, GD 44/47/9/16; GD 44/47/4/46.
42. S.R.O., Gordon Castle Muniments, GD 44/43/205/11; GD 44/47/2/85(1); GD 44/47/9/26 & 76. For rentals, see GD 44/23/6. For list of Strathavon and Glenlivet men, see GD 44/47/7/16(1); GD 44/43/336.

expected his estate recruits to cost no more than the official bounty: the result was that in some cases the Earl saved as much as £18 per recruit.[43]

The provision of land in return for military service within Highland society is a well-known aspect of Scottish history. Yet because it has been seen as an essentially feudal transaction, the economic rationale behind this arrangement as practised in the decades after Culloden has tended to escape attention. Such tactics in fact allowed landlords to avoid competition in the highly inflated recruiting market. In August 1779, having been given a second battalion for the 42nd Black Watch Regiment, Lord John Murray asked Major Norman Macleod of Macleod if he would take the lieutenant-colonel's commission. As already noted, the Skye laird represented a prominent example of how Highland elites colonised Britain's military machine. What becomes immediately obvious from an examination of his career is just how crucial the recruitment of his tenantry was in assisting this process. Having been appointed to a captaincy in 1775, the reputation of his estate for retaining large reserves of population resulted in his being offered a major's commission in Colonel Kenneth Mackenzie's (Lord Macleod) 73rd battalion in 1778. Likewise, in 1779, Lord John Murray explained that he had not originally considered the Skye laird for the lieutenant-colonelcy, but that his first candidate lacked the manpower to raise his quota of 70–80 men. Therefore, in just over four years Macleod rose from having no commission within the army to effectively commanding a regiment. The crucial point was that he did not purchase a single commission and relied, instead, upon paying his men in land or money which ensured that, on average, his recruits were two-thirds cheaper than those obtained by others recruiting on the open market. Table 19 shows that by using his tenantry to recruit for rank Macleod saved himself £3,500 – equivalent to 114% of his entire annual rental. Given his indebtedness, such a saving demonstrates the element of commercialism that underlay an activity which has been seen as little more than a remnant of traditional clan militarism.[44]

But it went deeper than that. As any given conflict continued, bounties got more expensive as men became harder to find. This meant that the longer a war lasted, the more valuable estate populations became. The result was that landlords tended to return to their estates each time they recruited for a new rank.

In 1778 the entire estate of the Seaforth family experienced intensive recruiting for the 78th Highland Regiment. However, in early 1780 Seaforth's brother received command of the 100th Regiment and the Earl

43. D.J. Withrington & I.R. Grant (eds.), *op. cit.*, vol. 17 (Wakefield, 1981), p. 548 n; S.R.O., Gillanders of Highfield Papers, GD 427/208/4; GD 427/304/1.
44. J.R.L., Bagshawe Muniments, B. 5/1, p. 286; N.L.S., Stuart-Stevenson Papers, Ms 8250, f. 26; S.R.O., Campbell of Barcaldine Papers, GD 170/1090/41; S.R.O., Boyle of Shewalton Papers, GD 1/481/13–14; D.C.M., 2/485/46, 47(1); 3/68/240, 307(1), 340; 3/70/47.

informed his Lewis factor that the estate '. . . must have men and many boys that two years ago we thought unfit for service [and] will now be stout fellows, at any rate you must strain every nerve as we are 100 short'. A list of prize money for 23 Lewis men enlisted in the 100th Regiment shows that 16 of the island's 93 farms had men drawn into the army, illustrating that even a secondary recruiting drive could affect almost one farm in five.[45]

The tactics of Seaforth and Macleod illustrate two crucial points. First, estate levying was never a singular event: in simple terms, the crop of men was harvested regularly as lairds recruited for consistently higher commissions. Second, as the case of Macleod demonstrates, men taken directly from estates were significantly cheaper than those acquired by non-proprietary means. The demarcation between methods is important: where recruiting took a non-estate form, bounties in the Highlands were as expensive as elsewhere. Only where there was a direct connection with the landlord, and where the strategy of land as a proxy bounty was implemented, could lower levels of recruiting costs be achieved. This can be illustrated by the actions of Murdoch Maclaine of Lochbuie in 1794. His estate in Mull had already experienced recruitment on account of the Argyll Fencibles raised in the previous year. A list of suitable men drawn up in 1793 reveals that Maclaine had a total of 361 men of military age, of whom 65 were deemed suitable for recruitment. In July 1794 he made an offer to his tenantry which constitutes the best surviving example of how estate recruiting actually operated. Maclaine stated he would not give his men any bounty, though the government had set aside five guineas for this purpose. Instead, he offered to reduce his rent by thirty shillings on any possession held by the family of recruits for a space of five years. Thus, Maclaine pointed out, his bounty would total £7.10.0–£2.5.0 more than the government allowed. As a result he recruited 50, or one in seven, of his own men, which allowed him to retain £262.10.0 worth of government allowances – equivalent to a fifth of his entire rental. However, the real savings came from the fact that such tactics reduced the extent to which Lochbuie was forced to enter the highly competitive recruiting market at a time when men recruited in Glasgow cost £21 each. This meant that the laird's savings on recruiting outlay came to £1,050 – over three quarters of his rental income.[46]

The recruiting terms offered by Lochbuie raise some interesting questions regarding the wider issue of land in return for military service. During the later nineteenth century a considerable amount of controversy surrounded this particular question. Campaigners sympathetic to the Highlander believed that the eviction policies of Highland landlords were nothing less than an outright betrayal of promises to keep recruits and their descendants on their farms.

45. S.R.O., Gillanders of Highfield Papers, GD 427/305/5(2), 11; S.R.O., Seaforth Muniments, GD 46/17/11.
46. B. Seton, 'Recruiting in Scotland, 1793–94', in *Journal of the Society of Army Historical Research.*, vol. 11 (1932), p. 41; S.R.O., Maclaine of Lochbuie, GD 174/916, 923, 927, 935; GD 174/2127; GD 174/1484/23, 28, 30, 33.

However, estate records show that proprietors often arrived at very specific, limited terms of time as a reward for supplying recruits. Thus, in the case of Lochbuie, any family who recruited gained their possession for a period of five years only. On the most infamous estate, that of Sutherland, the stipulations were made quite clear and were obviously understood by the tenantry because they specifically mention them in their petitions. Any family whose son had been in the third Sutherland Fencibles gained a lease of five years; meanwhile, those who had sons join the 93rd Regiment obtained a seven-year lease. These stipulations explain why large-scale eviction did not commence in Sutherland until 1807, seven years after the 93rd Regiment was raised. Likewise, on Macdonald of Sleat's estate very specific terms of accommodation were made out respecting recruits. Those who joined the Fencible Regiment of the Isles in 1799, but did not extend their service to Ireland, gained three years of possession; those who extended their service got five years.[47] This evidence clearly suggests that the nineteenth-century depiction of landlords as betraying those they had recruited is a distortion of the strictly limited obligations they agreed to, and in many cases honoured. Equally, however, there is evidence in estate records to show landlords quite consciously broke promises to retain the families of recruits. In 1778 Lord Macdonald raised the 76th Highland Regiment for service in America. He gave categorical, written orders, dated to the period when he recruited, for the retention of recruits and their families for life on the possessions they then held. Only a failure to pay rent was to deprive such persons of their holdings. These promises are particularly significant because they were not recalled later, when either memory or bitter experience was likely to cloud the issue; instead, they were a concrete set of promises in writing. They gave assurances of 'preference always to the lands which he [the soldier] now possesses'. Nonetheless, Macdonald failed to keep this promise; and while he never evicted such people from the estate, he did remove them from the farms explicitly promised to them, leading directly to intense alienation and, in some cases, to embittered emigration. Ultimately, it would seem that the whole issue of broken recruiting promises was simultaneously both a distortion of events and a folk grievance with a concrete basis in fact.[48]

Recruitment and the Highland Estate Economy

The extent of recruitment in the region clearly suggests that the Highlands were as much a militarising as a commercialising society. Landlords who

47. For discussion on the complexities of recruiting promises, see E. Richards, *A History of the Highland Clearances: Agrarian Change and the Evictions, 1746–1886*, vol. 1, pp. 150–54; S.R.O., Maclaine of Lochbuie Papers, GD 174/2127; N.L.S., Sutherland Papers, Dep. 313/985/6, 31; Dep. 313/1115/59a, 62; Dep. 313/1118/12; C.D.T.L, GD 221/5522/1.
48. C.D.T.L., GD 221/5522/1; GD 221/4389/1; GD 221/4433/1; GD 221/694/4; GD 221/4250/17, 44–3, 53.

sought additional state income to secure their own financial affairs felt that military employment similarly provided tenantry with the means of paying at least part of their rental obligations. Indeed, the high profile and contentious nature of wealth-generating activities such as kelping and sheep farming have meant that the role of military income as a crucial financial prop within the Highlands has to some extent been underestimated. Just how important such earnings were within an estate context is evident from the impact of half-pay officers. They proved, for instance, to be prominent bidders on the restored lands of the Locheil family in 1788. Likewise, the Napier report states that they formed a significant proportion of elite tenantry in the Western Isles by the early 1800s. Smaller tenants in Strathspey conceded during the 1770s that such officers furnished much higher rents than they could manage. The Old Statistical Account for the parishes of Kilmuir in Skye and Kingussie and Laggan in Badenoch drew attention to the ability of this class to pay substantial levels of rent: in 1772 five pensioned officers paid £363.14.5– or 64% of the Duke of Gordon's Laggan rental.[49] Table 12 demonstrates the financial strength of these annuitants and suggests they were an indigenous middle-tenant elite between the large capitalised sheep farmers and the mass of smaller joint tenants.

Table 12. Half-Pay Officers on Highland Estates, 1768–1804[50]

Date	Estate	Rent	N° of Officers	Rent paid by officers & %
1768	Lochaber (Gordon)	£639	1	£111 (17%)
1770	Coigach (Annexed Est)	£363	5	£85 (23%)
1773	Urquhart (Grant)	£1,007	2	£135 (13%)
1785	Badenoch (Gordon)	£1,440	6	£337 (23%)
1789	Macleod of Dunvegan	£2,697	6	£315 (12%)
1800	Lochaber (Gordon)	£2,939	3	£721 (25%)
1800	Strathspey (Grant)	£5,836	12	£357 (6%)
1804	Badenoch (Gordon)	£4,270	6	£643 (15%)

One area where such officers were especially prominent was on Skye. In the aftermath of the American Revolutionary War at least one colonel, a major, eight captains and three lieutenants rented farms on the island. This meant that at a conservative estimate military officers brought £1,213 of assured income into the area in the mid- to late 1780s. To put this amount of

49. C.F. Mackintosh, *Antiquarian Notes* (Inverness, 1897), p. 210; British Parliamentary Papers, 1884, XXXII, *Report of H.M.'s Commissioners of Inquiry into the Condition of the Crofters and Cottars in the Highlands and Islands of Scotland*, p. 495; D.J. Withrington and I.R. Grant (eds.), *op. cit.* vol. 20, p. 170; vol. 18, pp. 201 & 224; S.R.O., Seafield Muniments, GD 248/458/3/19; S.R.O., Gordon Castle Muniments, GD 44/27/4/18.
50. S.R.O., Gordon Castle Muniments, GD 44/51/743/8 & 31; GD 44/51/732/30 & 37; S.R.O., Seafield Muniments, GD 248/1035; GD 248/2900; S.R.O., F.E.P. E746/72/7; D.C.M. 2/485/56.

money in context: in 1799 it would have totalled 21.8% of Macdonald's entire Skye rental.[51]

Table 13. Military Officers and the Sutherland Estate, 1802[52]

Parish	Rent	% paid by military officers	Highest rented farm in parish held by officers
Golspie	£336.11.9	5.5%	4th
Clyne	£354.11.9	24.2%	2nd & 4th
Loth	£352.1.9	8.3%	2nd
Kildonan	£259.18.9	4.8%	–
Farr	£790.9.11	54.6%	1st & 3rd
Lairg	£214.7.2	40.5%	1st & 2nd
Dornoch	£742.0.0	1.78%	–
Assynt	£1,332.18.2	21%	2nd & 3rd

Furthermore, even on very large properties, officers often held a disproportionate level of the highest rented holdings. Table 13 shows that as late as 1802 a significant number of the Sutherland estate's most expensive farms were held by half-pay personnel, and that, overall, they were responsible for approximately 20% of the rent. More fundamentally, a military pension answered the rental demands of the landlord in a very specific way. Its reliable nature was undoubtedly its single most attractive feature, with the result that the Duke of Gordon allowed officers like Captain John Macpherson of Bellachroan to run up arrears in the knowledge that 'he will be good money at some time or another'. Proprietors also valued such tenants for their ability to improve, enclose and hold large reserves of cattle. It was rental concerns such as these that explain why military officers were encouraged to settle in Sutherland, Urquhart, Strathspey and North Uist.[53] Doubtless, the practical benefits such personnel brought to estate economies also helped convince landlords that their strategy of actively seeking state revenue was justified and provided concrete material assistance for the region's overall development and prosperity.

Army earnings also helped the financial position of lesser tenantry; indeed, they constituted one of the few positive reasons, as opposed to landlord coercion and the threat of eviction, why Gaels enlisted in such numbers. One

51. J. Mackenzie-Semple, 'Bygone Recruiting in Skye', in *Journal of the Society of Army Historical Research*, vol. 18 (1939), p. 52; J. Macinnes, *Brave Sons of Skye* (Edinburgh, 1899), pp. 7–171; F.J. Grant (ed.), *Commissariat Records of the Isles: Register of Testaments* (Edinburgh, 1902), p. 8; C.D.T.L., RH 2/8/24, p. 103.
52. N.L.S., Sutherland Papers, Dep. 313/2124.
53. S.R.O., Seafield Muniments, GD 248/537/3/16; GD 248/458/3/20; GD 248/347/1/76; GD 248/508/2/8; S.R.O., Gordon Castle Muniments, GD 44/27/11/110; GD 44/27/11/114; GD 44/27/12/5; N.L.S., Fletcher of Saltoun Papers, Ms 16728, f. 202; C.D.L.T., GD 221/868/2.

obvious example of this is the substantial growth in the number of Highlanders receiving Chelsea pensions. The extent to which Britain's military apparatus had been colonised by Scots is immediately apparent from the fact that Scotland had the highest density of Chelsea Pensioners within the British islands, and, in all likelihood, within the empire (see Appendix 2). Moreover, Highland counties accounted for four out of the ten Scottish counties containing the most pensioners, showing again that many areas in the region were heavily dependent upon state earnings. Table 14, showing the birthplace of pensioners from Highland regiments, serves to underline the substantial increase in the number of Gaels in the army during the last half of the eighteenth century.

Table 14. Chelsea Pensioners from
Highland Counties and Battalions, 1740–1800[54]

County	1740s	1750s	1760s	1770s	1780s	1790s	County Total
Argyll	3	18	93	26	98	35	273
Inverness	8	41	263	44	271	141	768
Ross & Cromarty	4	12	92	15	143	89	355
Sutherland	–	2	50	16	76	48	192
Caithness	2	3	49	6	54	37	151
Decade Totals	17	76	547	107	642	350	1,739

Though a key indicator of Gaeldom's specialised participation in British imperialism, this large, if intermittent, expansion in the number of Gaels receiving army pensions would not have been particularly important had it not been that a significant number chose to return to their own localities once discharged. During the post-1815 demobilisations, for example, 81 pensioners from Sutherland were released from the 93rd Highlanders. With an army pension of a shilling a day, this represented a potential flow of wealth into the county of £1,478 per annum. That many did indeed repair back to their homes can be found in evidence to the Napier Commission, which noted that in the 1830s there were over 40 pensioners in the parish of Assynt alone.[55] Appendix 2 shows that 634 pensioners (with a total income of £4,818) resided in the Highlands in 1770 – a number corresponding closely to the figures in Table 14, which again suggests a high rate of return. Table 15 confirms this pattern and shows that a large percentage of the demobilised soldiers who reappeared in their own communities did so with a state

54. Figures refer to the soldier's place of birth, not actual place of residence: also, only to those discharged with a pension for long service as opposed to one received for injury. P.R.O., W.O. 120/5, 7, 14–18.
55. S.R.O., RH2/8/99; British Parliamentary Papers, 1884, XXXV, *Report of H.M.'s Commissioners into the Condition of the Crofters and Cottars in the Highlands and Islands of Scotland*, p. 1740.

pension that enabled them to make a significant contribution towards the payment of rent demands.

Table 15. Chelsea Pensioners & Highland Estates, 1764[56]

Island	Returned Soldiers	Chelsea Pensioners	% Ch. Pen. of ret. sold'	Rent	Pensions as % of rent.
Lewis	34	18	52.9	£1,200	11.4
Harris	14	8	57.1	£544	11.9
Tiree	12	6	50	£773	5.8
Canna	3	3	100	£88.17.0	25.6

This high return rate was due at least in part to the preferential treatment pensioners anticipated from proprietors. For much the same reasons that half-pay officers were deemed desirable tenants, so the pensioner's regular income increased his chances of obtaining land. Sir James Grant, for example, encouraged their settlement and assisted local soldiers in their efforts to be put on the Chelsea list, as did the estate authorities on Jura.[57] A similar willingness to accommodate pensioners was evident upon the estate of Macdonald of Sleat. In 1800 a pensioner mentioned that lands to the value of his income had been promised to him. In December 1807 two pensioners, Donald Macleod and Donald Macdonald, presented a petition to Lord Macdonald that reveals the motive of social advancement behind the involvement of many Gaels in the army. They asked for the farms of either Glasvein or Brogaig in Kilmuir, and offered a rental increase of 28.5% and 38% on each farm, bringing the rent for each possession to £42. Astutely aware of the problem of fluctuating rents, they stated that each of their pensions would act as caution for the other. The attractiveness of such pensioners to the landlord can be illustrated by the fact that of the rents on the 126 separate tenant possessions in the parish of Strath in 1801, the standard military pension would have paid 115 of them with cash to spare. This means that within the ranks of the small tenantry those with military income constituted something of an elite. Furthermore, an important consequence of such state funding was that pensioners were considered ideal for the new crofting townships being created on Macdonald's estate inasmuch as their settlement provided concrete evidence that subdivided holdings were

56. M.M. Mackay (ed.), *The Rev. Dr. J. Walker's Report on the Hebrides, 1764 and 1771* (Edinburgh, 1980), pp. 39–225. Walker gives Harris a rental of £857. This, however, is a large over-estimate. See R.C. Macleod, *The Book of Dunvegan*, vol. 2 (Aberdeen, 1939), p. 96. Regarding Tiree, it was noted that 'most' of the returning men were pensioners. In order not to over-emphasise the impact of military money, and in the absence of an exact figure from Walker, just half the returning men are listed as pensioners.
57. S.R.O. Seafield Muniments, GD 248/227/1/82; GD 248/244/4/64; GD 248/509/1/66; GD 248/371/4/27–8; GD 248/684/2; GD 248/1540, pp. 55 & 118; S.R.O., Campbell of Jura Papers, GD 64/1/287.

feasible if sustained by external, non-agricultural sources of income, be it pensions, kelping, fishing or seasonal migration.[58]

The influence of military earnings extended, however, beyond those with an official Chelsea pension. Such income was vital, for instance, in enabling recruits to lower the arrears of their families at home. As early as 1759 Skye men serving in Montgomery's Highlanders in America were remitting substantial sums to their kin in Trotternish. Similar transactions were evident on Macleod of Macleod's estate during the 1770s and on Maclaine of Lochbuie's lands during the 1790s.[59]

Table 16. Military Earnings Relative to Rent, Lochbuie Estate, Mull, 1795–1796[60]

Farm	Rent	Military Income	% of Rent
Balmeanaich	£6	£1.10.0	25
Corrinahenaich	£30	£2.0.0	6.6
Glenbyre	£27	£6.11.0	24.2
Kinlochspelve	£3	£0.10.0	16.6
Finishish	£30	£10.5.0	34.1
Moy	£55	£1.10.0	2.7
Cameron	£35	£8.17.0	25.2
Scobull	£13.10.0	£1.3.8	8.6
Cillmor	£10	£2.2.0	21

Table 16 lists military income sent home by fencible soldiers to their kin on the estate of Lochbuie. It demonstrates that while such earnings were not necessarily large, they nonetheless represented a significant percentage of the rents for individual families. Where only the total farm rent is known, as opposed to the specific rent for the soldier's family, the percentage paid by military income is low. However, where individual rents can be verified, then the corresponding percentage of payment is as high as a quarter to one third.

This application of military revenue to the financial needs of Highland populations explains the relative popularity of the volunteer system in the region. For example, in stark contrast to their attempts to minimise the use of their tenantry in line regiments, landlords actively encouraged tenants to join the volunteers. Maclaine of Lochbuie argued that his own tenants were to be enrolled to ensure that the benefits of such income would accrue more closely to his own property. Such thinking was evident elsewhere across the High-

58. C.D.T.L., GD 221/3922; GD 221/4250/8, 41; GD 221/4257/8; GD 221/4390/11.
59. G.U.B.R.C., J.A. & J.L. Campbell & Lamond, W.S., UGD 37/2/2, pp. 129, 145–6; D.C.M., 3/70/47; S.R.O., Maclaine of Lochbuie Papers, GD 174/916; GD 174/1484/18.
60. S.R.O., Maclaine of Lochbuie Papers, GD 174/1506/1; GD 174/935; GD 174/2262; N.L.S., Minutes of Tutors of Maclaine of Lochbuie, Ms 20758.

lands. In Lewis, by January 1795, the pay of volunteers was being used to offset the increased price of meal. At Achnashine in Ross-shire in February 1800, a half-pay ensign, Alexander Mackenzie, stated that to get a company of volunteers 'would be beneficial to the place in general'. Meanwhile, in North Uist the formation of a company of 80 men in July 1803 provided income equivalent to approximately 15% of the island's rental.[61]

Table 17. Volunteer Pay Relative to Rent in the West Highlands and Islands, 1795–1802[62]

Estate	Total Rent	[Year]	Volunteer Earnings	%
Harris	£895	[1800]	£653	72.9
Skye/Macdonald/Macleod	£8,663	[1795]	£2,086	24.0
Glenelg	£1,277	[1795]	£736	57.7
Assynt	£1,332	[1802]	£624	46.8

Table 17 reveals the surprisingly high percentage of rents that could be met through part-time local military employment. In Sutherland, the volunteers consisted of 1,190 men, six officers at the rank of major and above, 14 captains and 28 lieutenants. In all, the entire annual pay for this establishment in 1803–4 came to £9,618. As had been the case with the fencible soldiers at Lochbuie, volunteers also deployed income for the payment of local debts. In 1804 the tenants of the farms of Kintomey and Swordly in the parish of Farr had £10.18.10 remitted to them: this constituted 19.5% of their rent. Militia men from the same area sent back £80 which was equivalent to 10% of the parish rental. The Countess of Sutherland stressed the importance of such military income when, in July 1805, she noted that the increases in her estate rental had been due in large part to the money brought in by such local units, as well as the incoming pay of soldiers in the wider regular army.[63] Clearly, military employment and the various forms of state income it generated were crucial in sustaining the overall economic position of the region's small tenantry.

61. S.R.O., Maclaine of Lochbuie Papers, GD 174/1506/letter 19 November 1797; S.R.O., Seaforth Muniments, GD 46/17/15/9; GD 46/17/14/484; C.D.T.L., GD 221/816/1; RH 2/8/24, 131; British Parliamentary Papers, 1841, *First Report from the Select Committee on Emigration (Scotland)*, p. 67.
62. S.R.O., Seafield Muniments, GD 248/1529, Inverness-shire Lord Lieutenancy Letter Book, 1798–1800, pp. 3, 42–5, 440–1; R. Brown, *Strictures and Remarks on the Earl of Selkirk's Observations on the Present State of the Highlands* (Edinburgh, 1806), pp. 45–6; C.D.T.L., RH 2/8/24, p. 103; D.C.M., 2/485/59; R.J. Adam (ed.), *Sutherland Estate Management, 1802–1816*, vols. 1–2 (Edinburgh, 1972); N.L.S., Sutherland Papers, Dep. 313/3285/9.
63. N.L.S. Sutherland Papers, Dep. 313/3282; Dep. 313/746/13; Dep. 313/987/31 & 33.

Tenant Attitudes and Estate Management Responses

The intensive nature of recruitment, its reliance upon the lower social orders, and the widespread dependence of many estate economies upon military income ensured that the enlistment process profoundly influenced tenurial arrangements, settlement strategies and patterns of social development in the Highlands. One tenant group affected by recruitment, though in a distinctly negative way, was the tacksman class. First impressions might suggest that military levying constituted a method whereby the middle clan elite could offset the erosion of their previously favoured tenurial position. It was certainly the case that the officer corp of regular and, in particular, fencible regiments relied upon large numbers of tacksmen and their sons; and the prominent estate role of half-pay officers discussed previously reveals the considerable advantages for those clan gentry who secured access to an army career. It has thus been argued that by maintaining the social standing and traditional military function of their class, one of recruitment's primary social effects lay in assisting the survival of the *Fir-Tacsa* to a degree that would not otherwise have been the case had estate enlisting ceased to be a feature of Highland landlordism after 1745.[64] The reasoning is obvious: tacksmen were the military linchpin of the clan, and their status as officers of the chiefs' military levies has been the role most consistently assigned to them by social commentators.[65] Increasingly, however, modern commentary has attempted to move beyond the stereotyping of eighteenth-century improving literature and define the broader responsibilities of the tacksman class. Studies have highlighted the non-militarised, social and organisational aspects of clanship: within this context tacksmen appear more as farmers and managers of agricultural resources, supplying security of tenure, seed, credit facilities and agrarian technology to a large body of subtenantry.[66] What has emerged in place of the traditional emphasis on their military role is a picture of the elite tenantry as developers of capital reserves and as the region's primary entrepreneurial class. Allied to this change in emphasis is a better understanding of the nature of farming in parts of the Highlands. Detailed analysis of land use and farming strategies has shown the crucial importance of large reserves of labour in overcoming technological under

---

64. N.L.S., Mackenzie of Delvine Papers, Ms 1483, f. 270; S.M.D. Carpenter, Patterns of Recruitment for the Highland Regiments of the British Army (St. Andrews University M. Litt. Thesis, 1977), p. 52; M.I. Adams, 'The Highland Emigration of 1770', in *Scottish Historical Review*, vol. 16 (1919), p. 290.
65. M. Gray, *op. cit.*, pp. 13–14; A.J. Youngson, *op. cit.*, pp. 12–14.
66. A. Mckerral, 'The Tacksman and his Holdings in the South West Highlands', in *Scottish Historical Review*, vol. 26 (1947), pp. 11–21; E.R. Cregeen, 'The Tacksmen and their Successors', pp. 95–100; R.A. Dodgshon, *Land and Society in Early Scotland* (Oxford 1981), p. 281; R.A. Dodgshon, ' "Pretense of Blude" and "Place of thair duelling": The nature of Scottish Clans, 1500–1745' in R.A. Houston, & I.D. Whyte, (eds.) *op. cit.*, pp. 170–176.

development and the rearing of crops in districts dominated by marginal, barely arable land.[67]

This warns against supposing that tacksmen moved naturally into an army career in the decades following Culloden. Instead, it is important to understand how their development as a commercialising class was affected by the recruiting process. The labour-intensive nature of the agrarian economy meant that tacksmen who retained possession of large farms were invariably hostile to any activity, be it seasonal migration or recruitment, which soaked up manpower and increased the cost of hiring and maintaining farm servants. In contrast to their reputation as clanship's military lieutenants, the need to adapt to new socio-economic and commercial conditions meant that throughout the 1756–1815 period tacksmen were unenthusiastic recruiters. In 1771 Macleod of Dunvegan's senior tenants failed to co-operate with a recruiting drive in Skye. In Urquhart in 1776 it was conceded that 'the gentlemen are not hearty in the matter'. A year earlier in Badenoch it was reported that tacksmen had remained strictly neutral, neither helping nor hindering recruitment: a charge also laid against the Duke of Gordon's and Earl of Seaforth's leading tenants in 1778.[68] Although failure on the part of tacksmen to aggressively promote recruitment was born largely of their economic self-interest, the result was that pre-existing landlord hostility towards them was entrenched and exacerbated. The most obvious example of this was on the estate of Sutherland during the recruitment of the 93rd Highland Regiment in 1799–1800. The estate authorities were angered by the inaction of large tackholders and their failure to promote enlistment. It was certainly the case that a review of tenure commenced in September 1799, just as tacksmen received a threatening letter which questioned their role in

> the unexpected and unaccountable delays and difficulties by which the recruiting has hitherto been obstructed . . . I have now in part executed, in part directed such measures as to enable the Countess to judge accurately of the merits and demerits of her own immediate tenants.[69]

This contradicts the argument that the tackmen's economic and social status was preserved by military levying. Elite tenant hostility towards excessive manpower loss was reinforced by the fact that the only sure method of securing cheap and reliable labour under such circumstances was to accommodate and rely upon large numbers of subtenants and cottars.

67. R.A. Dodgshon, 'Strategies of Farming in the Western Highlands and Islands of Scotland prior to Crofting and the Clearances', in *Economic History Review*, vol. 46 (1993), pp. 688–691, 700; M.M. Mackay (ed.), *op. cit.*, pp. 172, 160, 203–224; A.I. Macinnes, *Clanship, Commerce & the House of Stuart, 1603–1788*, p. 18.
68. D.C.M., 4/113; S.R.O., Seafield Muniments, GD 248/52/2/126; S.R.O., Gordon Castle Muniments, GD 44/47/2/75(2); GD 44/47/4/36; S.R.O., Gillanders of Highfield Papers, GD 427/304/1 & 2.
69. R.J. Adam (ed.), *op. cit.*, vol. 1, xxvi; vol. 2, p. 9.

However, this entailed land-use practices that guaranteed servants as opposed to efficient cattle production or profit margins, and was therefore a method that tacksmen sought to minimise where possible.[70] It was such concerns that ultimately dictated the negative attitude of leading tenants towards recruitment. In the Old Statistical Account military levying was directly equated with wage increase in the parishes of Edderachylis, Tiree, Stornoway and Urquhart and Glenmoriston. In the latter parish recruitment saw day wages advance from 8–9d to one shilling. This 33% jump was mirrored in Stornoway where it was noted that 'by reason of the multitudes levied for the army and navy, the great number of subtenants and the many hands wanted for the fishing boats, labourers and farm servants are become very scarce'. In June 1793, just as recruiting swept the island, George Gillanders of Highfield, the factor, conceded that labour for road-building simply could not be obtained and that wages had reached 9d per day. Recruiting thus helped produce, at the very least, a 12.5% increase in labour costs.[71] These effects on labour availability and wage levels were also evident elsewhere. By January 1760, just as the first Sutherland Fencible Regiment was completed, a local tacksman, James Mackay, complained of a dearth of day labourers. In Islay, in 1764, it was noted that 'the wages of a labourer are 6d and even 8d a day. This article was never so high till of late, occasioned by the great number of men sent into the war'.[72] This situation was also evident during the period of the American Revolutionary War. In April 1778 tacksmen and tenants in Badenoch came under severe pressure from the Duke of Gordon to supply men despite 'the condition in which we are already reduced for want of servants and labourers'. By November the estate of Mackintosh of Balnespick, which had witnessed intensive recruitment for Gordon's regiment, saw land fall out of production, while in Strathavon, tacksmen complained that the crops of subtenants who had subsequently become soldiers were still in the ground, and that to harvest them under prevailing circumstances would entail crippling expense.[73]

The effect of military activity on wages and how it determined the actions of tacksmen can be clearly seen from an earlier incident in Badenoch. In May

70. For regulations in Strathspey relating to the prevention of seasonal migration, see S.R.O., Seafield Muniments, GD 248/27/4; GD 248/251/7/9; J. Macdonald, *A General View of the Agriculture of the Hebrides or Western Isles of Scotland* (Edinburgh, 1811), p. 495; V. Morgan, 'Agricultural Wage Rates in Late Eighteenth Century Scotland', in *Economic History Review*, vol. 24 (1970), pp. 185, 199; D.J. Withrington and I.R. Grant (eds.), *op. cit.*, vol. 17, pp., 66 & 405, 495.
71. D.J. Withrington and I.R. Grant (eds.), *op. cit.*, vol. 17, pp. 268–69; vol. 20, pp. 28–29 & 204; S.R.O., Seafield Muniments, GD 46/17/3, letters 16 May and 17 June 1793.
72. N.L.S., Sutherland Papers, Dep. 313/1090/7; M.M. Mackay (ed.), *op. cit.*, p. 99.
73. S.R.O., Gordon Castle Muniments, GD 44/43/202/21; GD 44/43/210/22; GD 44/43/195/46; GD 44/47/2/75 (2–3); GD 44/47/5/1/33 & 52; GD 44/47/6/5(1); GD 44/43/204/26; GD 44/47/4/8.

1761, the Trustees for the Improvement of the Manufactures and Fisheries wrote to the Duchess of Gordon noting that her tackholders had spread the rumour that anyone spinning yarn was liable for transportation to the colonies. It was added: 'The trustees are sorry to find that the present scarcity of servants disposes the tenants and lower kind of gentry to discourage these improvements by various means'. Earlier, in January, they had noted 'the opposition the spinning meets with from the gentlemen farmers in the said Highland countries, who being difficulted [sic] by the scarcity of servants occasioned by the great number taken out of the country to the army, complain that the spinning makes their servants still scarcer and heightens their wages'.[74]

Had estate levying simply increased the costs faced by larger tenants, then the consequences might not have been particularly far-reaching. However, recruiting was ultimately a corrosive influence upon relations between the subtenantry and tacksmen. Inter-tenantry strain had of course already emerged as a prominent feature of Highland society as a result of strategies initiated by the tacksmen which, although aimed at increasing farm profits and answering rent demands, nonetheless represented a major assault on the traditional lifestyle of the smaller tenantry. Significantly, recruitment served to exacerbate these pre-existing tensions. The stricter imposition of labour dues and harsher conditions of subtenure in order to compensate for the reduction of available labour resulted in subtenant families attempting to remove themselves from under the tacksmen's control.[75] One obvious and effective way to accomplish this was to supply the landlord with recruits in order to obtain the right to hold lands directly from him. Thus, recruitment was extremely detrimental to the tacksmen's standing in that it provided an increasingly alienated lower tenantry with a mechanism for social advancement. One of the earliest examples comes from Sutherland during the Seven Years War. The estate authorities had already begun to question the expediency of setting farms in large tacks. However, in 1761 the factor, Dugald Gilchrist, pointed out that 'the most substantial of the tenants will look on it as a hard step to be put under a tacksman and more especially such of them who gave their sons into the Earl's regiment, as they were promised to be continued in their possessions'.[76] Recruiting in this case acted as the dynamic whereby theoretical reassessment of the tacksman's place in society was transformed into concrete policy. Thus when the Sutherland Fencible Regiment was demobilised in 1763, the Earl offered to settle ex-soldiers on 20 acres of improvable muir with advantageous terms of rent and, significantly, the assurance that no labour dues were to be performed. The result was one of the largest initiatives in new tenurial arrangements attempted on

74. S.R.O., Trustees for the Manufactures and Fisheries, N.G. 1/3/8, p. 35; N.G. 1/1/16, p. 16.
75. S.R.O., Gordon Castle Muniments, GD 44/47/9/12; GD 44/47/2/75(2).
76. N.L.S., Mackenzie of Delvine Papers, Ms 1484, f. 15.

the estate in the 1760s, and a major expansion in the number of small joint tenantry.[77]

This scenario was also evident across the Inverness-shire estates of the Gordon family. In 1778, for example, Alexander Macpherson, tacksman of Corrieconnallie, Achachar and Drumfour in Lochaber, attempted to remove his subtenants in order to better utilise his grazing resources. In response, the subtenants supplied men for the Duke's fencible regiment to ensure they would be kept on the farm. Added to this was the fact that, as a tacksman, Macpherson had already been forced to contribute his own quota of men. His three recruits had negotiated expensive conditions. This involved his supplying each of their parents with three guineas for every year the men were in the regiment. Second, their families were to get half a merk land from him on the same conditions that he, as a tacksman, held from the Duke.[78] This last stipulation is significant in that it illustrates the important process whereby the internal distinctions evident in the *baile*, or joint tenant farm, could be eroded by recruiting. For the tacksman in this specific case it entailed a 6% increase in the cost of his rent, on top of which he lost effective control over one sixth of his farm. Even more damaging for tacksmen in general was the fact that recruitment imbued the lower orders with a growing sense of confidence. The subtenants of Inchree in Lochaber, for example, deliberately targeted the farms of Auchaneich and Borhogie, then held by a prominent local tacksman, and asked how many recruits would be required to ensure they would gain possession of the holdings. Similar attempts, which involved securing independent possession from tacksmen, were evident on the farms of Blarichirn, also in Lochaber, Delanach, Crubinmore, Presmucherach, and Breachachie in Badenoch. The scale of social expectation released by recruitment is evident from the fact that the Duke's efforts to complete his Northern Fencibles in 1778 witnessed attempts by subtenantry to remove themselves from tacksman control which eventually involved nearly one farm in five on the Lochaber estate.[79]

That military service provided secure income for many families, and an effective means whereby lesser tenantry extricated themselves from beneath the authority of leading tenants, suggests that recruitment must not be seen merely as one prominent example of Highland landlordism's coercive treatment of a victimised people who were incapable of formulating any positive response. This is certainly not to deny proprietary coercion, or, indeed, the very real personal distress brought upon individual families by the enlistment of their immediate kin under conditions tantamount to conscription.[80] The case of small tenantry in Sutherland reveals the often intimidatory nature of

77. N.L.S., Sutherland Papers, Dep. 313/3263/11; N.L.S., Mackenzie of Delvine Papers, Ms 1487, f. 112.
78. S.R.O., Gordon Castle Muniments, GD 44/25/7/42.
79. S.R.O., Gordon Castle Muniments, GD 44/27/4/22; GD 44/47/5/9/5, 12; GD 44/27/12/38, 44; GD 44/47/9/7; GD 44/27/12/5.
80. D.J. Withrington and I.R. Grant (eds.), *op. cit.*, vol. 20, p. 204.

recruitment in the region. When levying commenced in 1799 for what was to become the 93rd Sutherland Regiment, tenantry in the heights of Kildonan and in Strathnaver combined in an attempt to prevent any men from being taken. Faced with no single examples to evict, it was hoped that the threat of landlord retribution would be nullified. In a powerful demonstration of the inherently weak economic position of estate populations, the factor casually brought up the subject of sheep farming at a meeting with those refusing to supply men. Unsurprisingly, the tenants suddenly appeared to find the prospect of service in the army a rather more attractive option. Yet, while commentaries have dwelt at some length on the brutal nature of recruiting in the region, they rarely credit populations with any ability to respond in a resourceful or effective way, an omission made all the more inexplicable in light of obvious sympathy for those involved.[81]

At first glance another similar example to that of Sutherland is the 1795 declaration by Maclaine of Lochbuie's tenants promising to remove as a result of their refusal to give men to the laird. While immediately suggestive of landlord coercion, closer inspection reveals how tenantry sought to retain some initiative in face of the legal, social and economic rights of the proprietor. The declaration was signed by 71 men, which amounted to a large majority of the tenant expertise on Lochbuie's estate: to have removed them all in one body would have entailed the immediate collapse of the laird's rental. The result was that even as late as 1804 many of the tenants in question were still on the farms from which they had supposedly been evicted.[82] In essence, the laird's bluff had been called. Albeit this was unusual, and hardly the common experience of Highland tenantry in this period, it reveals an effort, however limited, on the part of populations to produce pragmatic responses to the reality of military levying. Indeed, it is something of a distortion merely to highlight the landlord's undoubted bullying tactics without then taking stock of the fact that, for sections of the population, recruitment was seen as a means of defending their existing status, or, alternatively, as a vehicle of social mobility. This attitude is evident in the observation of Lieutenant-Colonel Norman Macleod of Dunvegan in early 1780: 'To procure the men it is absolutely necessary that I converse with, bestow favours on, and arrange the affairs of the fathers and connections of my recruits'. Mirroring his neighbour's statement, Lord Alexander Macdonald of Sleat noted to the Earl of Seaforth in 1795 regarding his own recruiting experience during the American Revolutionary War: 'There are a thousand stipulations upon such an occasion about 'lands when they shall return' and an interim accommodation for their fathers or mothers'.[83]

This suggests a degree of negotiation, compromise and interaction that is

81. R.J. Adam (ed.), *op. cit.*, vol. 1, xxv-vii; J. Prebble, *op. cit.*, pp. 104–5, 115.
82. S.R.O., Maclaine of Lochbuie, GD 174/926; N.L.S., Minutes of Tutors of Maclaine of Lochbuie, Ms 20758.
83. J.R.L., Bagshawe Muniments, B. 5/1. p. 364; S.R.O., Seaforth Muniments, GD 46/6/25/13.

rarely recognised during this period. Landlords adjusted their estate management strategies in order to accommodate tenantry who had contributed men. An example of this was the role played by recruitment in slowing the introduction of large-scale sheep farming into central Inverness-shire and Wester Ross in the period between the 1770s and 1800.[84] The increase in the commercial value of tenantry brought on by the prospect of new Highland regiments in late 1777 prevented the imposition of sheep farming on the Lochaber estates of Cameron of Glen Nevis and the fourth Duke of Gordon. Logically, commercial pastoralism could have emerged strongly in that area in the mid-1770s. The failure of cattle prices earlier in the decade had revealed the precarious nature of the existing rental structure, and by July 1776 Argyllshire sheep farmers had assessed the suitability of farms in the Badenoch and Lochaber lordships. Seven farms were specifically highlighted as suitable for sheep walks, and the prospect of a considerable augmentation was made clear to the Duke. However, anticipating recruitment, Gordon nevertheless decided in November 1777 not to set farms to Lowland tenants. Likewise, the following month Cameron of Glen Nevis and Martin of Letterfinlay were noted as being extremely reluctant to set their farms under sheep as they were aware this would entail the loss of their populations. Instead, Glen Nevis became a prominent recruiter for Gordon and was awarded the farm of Achtrichtan to accommodate some of his dependants. By early January 1778 Gordon himself had become involved in recruiting. By the end of the war those like Angus MacDonnell on the Lochaber farm of Inch who had contributed recruits began to request leases and the secure settlement of their families. Simultaneously, in 1782 the factor highlighted Inch as a suitable farm that could fetch a rent of £64 under sheep. However, a rental of 1784 shows that Gordon fulfilled his recruiting obligations and let the farm to MacDonnell for £60. Furthermore, the large augmentations in rent anticipated with the arrival of sheep did not materialise and, instead, Gordon's Lochaber lands were set for a rent of £1,338 – an increase of only £126.[85]

Recruitment's ability to retard the spread of sheep farming was also apparent on the Glensheal, Kintail and Lochalsh estates of the Earl of Seaforth in the mid-1790s. Indeed, the extent of concessions obtained by the tenantry became a major complicating factor when attempts were made from 1794 onwards to sell Glensheal. Seven-year leases and what was recognised as a low rental made a sale difficult to complete. While the rent stood at £1,299 per annum, potential purchasers were informed that the property could bring in an income of £1,800. A legal agent for Seaforth

---

84. S.R.O., RH 2/4/87, f. 151; T.M. Devine, 'Landlordism and Highland Emigration', in T.M. Devine (ed.), *Scottish Emigration and Scottish Society* (Edinburgh, 1992), p. 89.
85. S.R.O., Gordon Castle Muniments, GD 44/27/11/114; GD 44/193/20; GD 44/25/2/28; GD 44/25/7/25, 30, 35 & 42; GD 44/47/3/1/2; GD 44/27/4/23; GD 44/47/12/27.

explained this shortfall in potential and actual rents to an interested party in 1798: 'In making the last set, his Lordship was obliged to submit to some loss in consideration of the alacrity with which his people had enlisted in his regiment then newly raised'. A year later, as the estate again failed to find a buyer, Seaforth's lawyer explained his sale strategy to the Earl: 'I confirmed my assertion by appealing to your situation as a chieftain and as having raised two regiments of the line just before the last set, the influence of which I knew having been one of the conditions for granting leases'.[86] Although the estate's potential income of £1,800 may have been inflated to attract interest, these figures suggest that tenantry in Glensheal may well have managed to prevent rental increases of approximately 27%. Only in 1801, when the leases given at the time of recruiting expired, was the estate eventually sold – and even then at 10% less than the asking price of £42,000. Furthermore, the largely positive response of tenantry in Kintail and Glensheal to recruiting for the 78th Highland Regiment had elicited a promise from Seaforth that when the leases granted in 1794 expired in 1801, local tenant families would be preferred over strangers if they offered appropriate rents. This undoubtedly constituted a major concession to the tenantry. Thus, when in 1800 a Lieutenant Macdonald from Lochaber asked for a sheep farm in Glensheal, and informed Seaforth's advisers that under sheep the estate rental would double, Mackenzie of Fairburn informed Seaforth: 'In the first place, however, as I before proposed, I would call on the present tenants for their proposals'. Similarly, when Seaforth attempted in 1801 to create substantial single-tenant farms, as in Inversheal, he found this was extremely difficult to accomplish in the light of promises of accommodation. The situation was summarised by an adviser to Seaforth:

> It would have been certainly more advantageous for the farms to have been let each to a single tenant, but this would have left twenty-one totally unprovided. We found ourselves tied up by an express promise given at the former set to give the tenants a preference to strangers.[87]

Recruiting, as it had done almost twenty-five years earlier in Lochaber, prevented the wholesale imposition of large-scale sheep farming in Kintail and Glensheal during the 1790s. This suggests that Highlanders joined the regiment of their landlords to restore or protect the established tenurial structure and, indeed, whole way of life in the region. This is evident in the petition of the 72 men from Ranald MacDonnell of Glengarry's estate who, having become soldiers, asked in October 1794:

> That we may know where to be take ourselves, indeed, we expect to enjoy those possessions which our ancestors so long enjoyed, though

86. S.R.O., Seaforth Muniments, GD 46/17/11, letter 17 December 1798; GD 46/17/14/279.
87. S.R.O., Seaforth Muniments, GD 46/17/14/591; GD 46/17/19/23, 60, 77–188, 435.

now in the hands of strangers, as we do not wish that you should lose by way of us, we shall give as high a rent as any of your Lowland shepherds ever gave and we shall all become bound for anyone whose circumstances may afford you room to mistrust.[88]

However, it must not be assumed that the only motivation for Highland soldiers was a determination to conserve the existing social structure. This would suggest that recruits had little or no initiative or social ambition, and to some extent pigeonholes Highland soldiery as mere victims, and rigidly conservative ones at that. Analysis of what motivated many Highland soldiers must bear in mind their social origins. Table 11 shows how a desire on the part of landlords to maximise the profitability of their populations resulted in a policy of targeting the lowest social orders on their properties. From the figures it appears that the cottar and servant classes were likely to constitute a significant percentage of the personnel who actually enlisted in proprietary levies. This meant that recruiting and estate strategies as practised in the period from 1756 to 1815 gave legitimate claims for accommodation to those who, under normal social and commercial conditions, would not have held any or much land. This is an important point because it has a direct bearing on the nature and consequences of recruiting promises. Table 18 shows the type of land promises listed in the records of the Macdonald of Sleat family and the Maclaines of Lochbuie. It strongly suggests that the defence of farm holdings already held by themselves or their families was not the primary motivation for Highland soldiery. Instead, recruitment sparked a substantial social push from below, with the landless or lowest tenurial groups never constituting less than one fifth of all requests for land – indeed, in North Uist they approach 50%. Equally interesting is the fact that the number of requests for a transfer from an existing farm to that of another family was just as likely as an attempt to defend existing holdings.

Table 18. Type of Land Promise to Highland Soldiers, 1790s.[89]

Estate	Land for landless/cottar family and %	More land on same holding and %	Land for current possessor but on other farm and %	To maintain same holding and %
North Uist	19 (46.3)	10 (24.3)	12 (29.2)	
Skye	20 (29.3)	17 (25.3)	18 (26.8)	12 (17.9)
Lochbuie	6 (20)	12 (40)	6 (20)	6 (20)

What recruiting gave scope to, therefore, was the obviously considerable social expectations and ambitions of Highland tenantry and populations. Above all, it expedited the rise of largely landless populations into tenurial

88. S.R.O., Seafield Muniments, GD 248/683/63; S.R.O., Melville Castle Muniments, GD 51/1/844/3.
89. C.D.T.L., GD 221/4388; GD 221/4250–5, 'Estate Petitions'; S.R.O., Maclaine of Lochbuie Muniments, GD 174/916.

possessions, often, ironically, at the direct expense of incumbent families. This differs radically from the idea that recruitment from the Highlanders' perspective was all about preserving the old-established order and way of life.

The impact of returning soldiery tends to confirm this interpretation of Highland recruitment. In the early 1770s tenants emigrating from Mackay of Bighouse's estate in Strath Halladale explained: 'the rents were raised as soldiers returned upon the peace with a little money and offered higher rents and larger fines or grassums'.[90] Events between 1801 and 1803 on the Skye property of Macdonald of Sleat mirror what had occurred earlier in Sutherland. As was apparent in other areas such as the Breadalbane estate which had experienced intensive recruitment, the whole of the 1802 set was dominated by the resettlement of those who had given men to the Fencible Regiment of the Isles. Involvement in recruitment became as much, if not more, of a factor determining access to land as the ability to improve or stock tenancies. Macdonald's commissioners insisted that although no poor or inappropriate people were to be settled, this regulation was not to apply to those who had been promised possessions. This meant that as pressure for places increased, so the holdings of established tenants came under critical review. In Letterfour and Drumfearn in the parish of Sleat, tenantry lost part of their farms with the result that some who had spent money improving chose to emigrate. Likewise, in Peinmore in the parish of Kilmuir, as well as in Sollitot, standard-tenant holdings of a halfpenny rating were divided instead into third pennies as recruits and their families were accommodated.[91]

One easily overlooked feature of recruitment helps explain why the often small amounts of land requested by demobilised soldiers nevertheless resulted in such dislocation. The figures in Table 10 demonstrate that even where the overall levels of manpower affected by recruitment were low, the percentage of farms involved was relatively high. To obtain between 15–25% of available manpower routinely entailed taking recruits from half to three quarters of all farm holdings. Even in North Uist, where only one man in sixteen was recruited in 1799, this nonetheless affected over half the estate's entire farm structure. This meant that promises made during recruitment brought an element of complexity into estate management at odds with the actual number of men taken. With so few farms not in some way connected to a soldier, the task of organising places became far more convoluted. On Macdonald's estate this induced a series of removals and flittings in 1802–3 that materially contributed to an upturn in emigration from the area, and which were hardly conducive to the sense of security necessary for fostering improvement. The problem of honouring such promises can be illustrated by the exasperated sentiments of Lord Macdo-

---

90. P.R.O., T. 47/12, f. 29.
91. C.D.T.L., GD 221/4389/3; GD 221/4180/13; GD 221/4250/1, 54; GD 221/671/1; GD 221/726; GD 221/4251/38; GD 221/778.

nald's factor with regard to the farms of Cammuscross and Scullumas, both of which had soldiers' families on them and, yet, were simultaneously earmarked for the settlement of another recruit. He noted:

> Who is there to be removed to accommodate him and if that town is to be [given] out in acres how are those who gave recruits to Lord Macdonald and who have lands in Cammuscross to be accommodated? I now beg leave to ask a question. Does it occur to the Commissioners [of Lord Macdonald] that there will be many complaints from the people of Scullumas who have given sons if they are not accommodated with lands equal to what they lost?[92]

Estate petitions for the period 1800–1803 back up this picture of complex resettlement problems. From these and the estate rentals it appears that of the 179 farms on Macdonald's Skye estate, at least 63 had the profile of all or part of their tenantry determined by involvement in the army – over one farm in three. Again, it was noticed at the time that recruitment initiated pressure from below as ex-recruits of formerly low social status targeted the particular farms they hoped to obtain. In March 1801, the actions of Norman Macdonald, son of a tenant in Kilmuir, were summarised as follows: 'Norman the son has never held any land, he would not be able to take such a quantity but that he is still a sergeant to Captain Martin's company of volunteers and his pay there would come near to £30'. Likewise, by April 1803, after the demobilisation of the fencible regiments, it was noted: 'The young men in the country who have no lands are purchasing the cattle of those emigrants thinking they will have a claim for lands afterwards, among them are some of the late soldiers in the Regiment of the Isles, some who volunteered and others who did not'.[93]

Loss of tenant land to those who had recruited was also evident across the entire estate of Glengarry. In the 1790s the laird planted families and dependants of recruits on existing farms, often to the extent of five or seven croft holdings to one possession. Naturally, this piecemeal subdivision discouraged the incumbent tenantry and again underlines the extent to which estate levying disrupted traditional tenurial hierarchies. As in Skye, the social ambition of the less tenurially secure was also evident. Glengarry himself noted of one recruit: 'While Cameron, the subtenant on Inverguseran, was only a subtenant, his ambition led him naturally to be obliging and it was by such conduct alone he could cherish the hope of such success as afterwards attended him on being received as a tenant'.[94]

The substantial increase in land claims brought on by recruiting resulted in an increase in subdivision and the generation of crofting. On the Duke of Argyll's estate on the Ross of Mull in 1806 soldiers and their families made

92. C.D.T.L., GD 221/671/1.
93. C.D.T.L., GD 221/671/3; GD 221/771/2.
94. C.F. Mackintosh, *op. cit.*, pp. 142–143.

up over one in four of the 64 families pressing for accommodation; the result was that approval was given for the 'dividing and diminishing [of] some of the large farms'.[95] Indeed, given the lower social origins of many recruits, a policy of giving reduced holdings was entirely rational. Another factor that pushed the authorities in the direction of crofting was the large numbers of farms affected by recruiting promises. By crofting several, specific townships, the problem of honouring land promises across the entire estate was circumvented. In 1800 Cammuscross in Sleat and Iridgill in Uig were divided for this purpose: those who gave in sons as well as those removed from tenant possessions to oblige recruits were given preference. Likewise, in February 1802 it was confirmed that those with recruiting claims were to be accommodated on small lots in order to limit damage to the rest of the estate. It was not merely on Macdonald's lands that military promises stimulated the division of tenancies. The farms of Ballimartin and Ballephail on Tiree, for example, were crofted in 1801 in order to fulfil promises. Significantly, the need for additional landed possessions in this case meant that the fifth Duke of Argyll's preferred policy of retaining the four mail land unit as the minimum measurement of tenant holdings was done away with in 1803.[96]

In North Uist, crofting was explicitly linked to recruiting promises. This was in large part due to the fact that fulfilling such obligations was at odds with the process of estate improvement. In April 1801 the Uist factor proposed the large fertile farm of Houghary 'For the purpose of collecting into that farm as many as it may accommodate of the persons who held land under promises from Lord Macdonald'. A month later this tactic was adopted in light of the fact that 'The commissioners do not expect that the whole of the persons who had promises of lands from Lord Macdonald on account of the recruiting service can be accommodated in one farm, but it is desirable to collect them as much as possible in order to prevent the improvement of a variety of farms from being impeded by the dispersion of these people over the estate'.[97]

The managerial problems and supposedly detrimental impact upon improvement engendered by recruiting promises explains why by the end of the first decade of the nineteenth century the distinctly Highland trade in land for men was effectively at an end. The incompatibility of recruiting and effective commercial estate management had been understood as early as the 1770s. In January 1778 a senior adviser to the Duke of Gordon noted: 'I think the Duke will take no concern in raising men. I am very glad it is so, they would not be raised without being very hurtful to his interest'. The belief that material benefits gained from military employment were being increasingly outweighed by the loss of productive land to recruits was summarised in

95. S.R.O., Campbell of Dunstaffnage Papers, GD 202/97.
96. C.D.T.L., GD 221/705; GD 221/730/2; E. Cregeen (ed.), *Argyll Estate Instructions*, pp. 54–55.
97. C.D.T.L., GD 221/4180/4–5.

1793 by a tacksman from the Urquhart estate of Sir James Grant of Grant. He noted regarding the tenantry: 'The Urquhart people make very nice in expectation of advantageous conditions from you . . . which might be injurious to your interest in a future sale of your lands, to bring you under obligations which might be extremely inconvenient and disagreeable'.[98] This scenario became reality on the estate of Sutherland in 1803 when soldiers kept demanding certain rent stipulations or reductions. Indeed, the factor noted that 'Lord Gower will think he is never to be done of claims on account of soldiers'.[99] As a result of such thinking the estate had earlier in November 1802 forbidden any future use of land promises to obtain men for the army – a decision which, in effect, marked the end of the recruiting order as it had existed in the Highlands since the early 1740s.

Conclusion

Although military recruitment in the 1756–1815 period is reminiscent of militarised clanship, it was in fact grounded in an up-to-date appreciation by Highland landlords of the potentially lucrative benefits of colonising the British fiscal-military state. In contrast to the motives behind landlord involvement, however, the incentive and impact of recruiting upon the middle and lower orders is undoubtedly more complex. In the case of tacksmen, recruiting competed with their new position as the necessarily profit-conscious managers of the agricultural sector. It forced them onto the defensive by removing the normal economic criteria whereby those who held land on Highland estates were chosen. Conversely, as a result of a deliberate targeting policy the lower orders found recruiting gave expression to their tenurial ambitions. As such, one of recruitment's most important social effects lay in the fact that it undermined the hierarchical structure of Highland farms and expedited the emergence of crofting.

Indeed, the impact of recruiting promises upon the tenurial structure in areas like Skye poses some intriguing questions regarding the genesis of the crofting system. The lower social orders' demands for accommodation, as articulated through recruiting promises, suggest that, as in Breadalbane, the emergence of subdivided holdings often involved a substantial element of social expectation. This suggests that crofting should not be seen purely in terms of an estate management response to kelp profits, imposed from above by landlords onto an uncooperative, backward and passive population. Rather, its emergence appears to have been a far more ambiguous process, involving not just poor landlord-tenant relations but also intense inter-tenantry strain and, most ironically of all, the eviction of sections of the

---

98. S.R.O., Gordon Castle Muniments, GD 44/43/196/45; GD 44/198/21–22. For examples from Sutherland and Lochbuie, see N.L.S., Sutherland Papers, Dep. 313/1093/17; S.R.O., Maclaine of Lochbuie Papers, GD 174/1521. For Grant, see S.R.O., Seafield Muniments, GD 248/683/63.
99. N.L.S., Sutherland Papers, Dep. 313/1118/5; Dep. 313/1117/41.

community by other, upwardly mobile groups such as returning ex-soldiers. In summary, recruiting should be interpreted as one of the most influential factors in the decline of the old tenurial order in the Highlands; and rather than stressing its uncommercialised, apparently clannish nature, we should recognise that its real significance lies in its role as an agent of change.

CHAPTER SIX

The Military and Highland Emigration, 1763–1815

While recruitment clearly had a multifaceted and crucial impact at the local level, its influence was also evident within attitudes towards emigration, perhaps one of the most high-profile socio-economic processes shaping the region's overall development. Approaches to this particular subject have traditionally divided into two general, though distinct, strands of thought. One stresses the large and impersonal forces of severe demographic change and displacement brought on by the shift from a subsistence economy to a more specialised regional economy, dominated locally by commercial landlords and structurally by the needs of the wider and stronger British economy. Within this context landlords and their policies have been viewed as merely exacerbating factors in a wider process of economic integration.[1] While conceding the reality of demographic strain and economic subservience, other arguments point to the importance of landlords in actively influencing conditions in the region. Far from being neutral elements in the emergence of Highland emigration, proprietors consciously removed populations in order to complete a definite set of estate management and revenue strategies. Likewise, for much the same financial reasons they were equally capable of retaining population through various policies of farm division and crofting – all of which made the landlord class a deeply influential factor in the development of demographic imbalance and subsequent emigration from the region.[2]

However, in seeking to clarify the exact role of landlordism, the wider imperial context of Highland emigration can appear as little more than an adjunct or secondary issue. Given that eighteenth-century British government was executed by the landed class and in the interests of the landed class, it is understandable that the state has been seen as faithfully supporting Highland

1. E. Richards, *A History of the Highland Clearances: Emigration, Protest, Reasons*, vol. 2 (London, 1985), pp. 223, 499–500; M.W. Flinn, 'Malthus, Emigration and Potatoes in the Scottish North West, 1770–1870', in L.M. Cullen & T.M. Devine (eds.), *Comparative Aspects of Scottish and Irish Economic and Social History 1600–1900* (Edinburgh, 1977), pp. 54–60; M. Gray, *The Highland Economy, 1750–1850* (Edinburgh, 1957), p. 58.
2. A.I. Macinnes, 'Scottish Gaeldom: The First Phase of Clearance', in T.M. Devine & R. Mitchison (eds.), *People and Society in Scotland, 1760–1830*, vol. 1 (Edinburgh, 1988), pp. 79, 86; T.M. Devine, 'Landlordism and Highland Emigration' in T.M. Devine (ed.), *Scottish Emigration and Scottish Society* (Edinburgh, 1992), pp. 84–5, 100.

landlords in their attempts to prevent emigration. Largely as a result of the region's military capacity the British state undoubtedly maintained a considerable interest in the issue of Highland emigration, and intervened on several occasions in a manner that suggests its agenda was little different from that of the region's proprietors. Yet this state dimension formed an important element in attitudes to emigration, if only because the issue of military manpower was vital in providing Highland landlords with additional intellectual arguments for maintaining their opposition to population loss. Indeed, by emphasising the military nature of their tenantry, landlords were able to link their private concerns to the wider national interest and solicit strong support from central government.

But the notion that the state was little more than a prop for the landlord interest can be taken too far. Care is needed, for instance, in defining the differing sectors of the British state. Albeit the very nature of their relationship meant that provincial and metropolitan governments were in broad agreement over the direction of policy, and that the former did not openly defy the latter, that should not be taken to mean that each did not have its own particular sense of priorities. The relationship and links between the core of the empire and its North American provinces both before and after 1775 warn against the assumption that because London wished to prevent Highland emigration, colonial administrations and elites then fell slavishly into line.[3] More obviously, government policy, especially recruitment, did not and could not fall into line with the objective of preventing population loss. Indeed, due recognition needs to be given to the depopulating effects of military service and the role played by imperial settlement policies at the end of the Seven Years War and American Revolutionary War. Not only did these officially sponsored schemes prevent the return to Scotland of large numbers of military personnel, but, most importantly, they created a series of settlements which stimulated 'chain emigration' by acting as initial foci for much larger numbers of civilian emigrants.

The Tacksman and Military Emigration

The period after the end of the Seven Years War in 1763 witnessed a quickening in the processes whereby Highland estates were increasingly switched onto a commercialised and market-orientated footing. Traditional social hierarchies and functions were either broken or severely strained, resulting in heightened population mobility within both elite and non-elite tenant groups. Prominent amongst the various tenant orders adjusting to these socio-economic changes were the tacksmen. As the primary rent payers on most Highland estates, they were at the forefront of the region's reaction to change. Their traditionally high status, both social and economic, began to

3. J.M. Bumsted, *The People's Clearance: Highland Emigration to British North America, 1770–1815* (Edinburgh, 1982), xii–xiii.

be undermined in several crucial respects. First, there was the issue of rental increase: from 1754–74 rents on the Perthshire estate of the Breadalbane family rose from £2,118 to £4,599; at the other extreme of the Highlands, in Lewis, rents jumped from £936 to £2,535 in the period 1754–80. Furthermore, such increases proved to be merely a prelude to much sharper rises in the 1790–1815 period.[4] Yet rent augmentation was but one aspect of a more generalised assault on the tacksmen's status. In Argyll, in particular, critical scrutiny of their economic role had been evident prior to Culloden, and had extended subsequently into other areas of the region in the years preceding the Seven Years War. By 1750 plans to curtail the tenurial supremacy of tacksmen had been mooted for the Duke of Gordon's estate in Badenoch. Even in somewhat isolated Sutherland it was being argued by 1754 that rent was '. . . better secured by this method [small tenants] than by giving the whole to a tacksman, and it brings in a more immediate gain to the family'. The resultant imposition of such policies led to the dismantling of large tacks in Assynt from as early as 1763.[5] Across the region, wadsetters and substantial tenantry found that in order to access the difference between official and subtenant rent levels, landlords had determined upon fundamentally altering the tenurial structure of their estates. Wadsetters, for instance, found that cattle profits and the development of local credit banking provided landlords with the means of redeeming loans and regaining access to land that had increased dramatically in value since the original wadsett agreement. Similar commercial attitudes were brought to bear upon tacksmen. In 1771 John Grant of Tullochgrubin on the Grant estate in Strathspey noted this process in action, relating the decline of three prominent tacksman families, and added that 'there is a terrible revolution in this country'.[6] Although changes were to an extent tempered, as in Assynt, Strathspey and elsewhere, by landlord fears that the loss of elite tenants would threaten their rentals, the upward movement in cattle prices ultimately helped sustain the impetus for reorganisation.[7]

4. S.R.O., Breadalbane Muniments, GD 112/9/49, 53; S.R.O., Gillanders of Highfield, GD 427/49; N.L.S., Sutherland Papers, Acc 10225/Joass/10/7/Sett of Lewis; M. Gray, *op. cit.*, pp. 146–47; T.M. Devine, *Clanship to Crofters' War: The Social Transformation of the Scottish Highlands* (Manchester, 1994), pp. 32–3; M. McLean, *The People of Glengarry: Highlanders in Transition, 1745–1820* (London, 1991), pp. 72–3.
5. A. McKerral, 'The Tacksman and his Holding in the South West Highlands', in *Scottish Historical Review*, vol. 26 (1947), pp. 22–3; E.R. Cregeen, 'The Tacksmen & Their Successors: A Study of Tenurial Reorganisation in Mull, Morvern & Tiree in the Early Eighteenth Century', in *Scottish Studies*, vol. 13 (1969), pp. 95–134; S.R.O., Gordon Castle Muniments, GD 44/28/34/28; N.L.S., Mackenzie of Delvine Papers, Ms 1149, f. 154; Ms 1483, ff. 108, 135.
6. S.R.O., Seafield Muniments, GD 248/49/2/16–17x; GD 248/508/2/30.
7. N.L.S., Mackenzie of Delvine Papers, Ms 1319, ff. 19, 39; Ms 1483, f. 9; Ms 1484, f. 15; S.R.O., Seafield Muniments, GD 248/52/3/107; S.R.O., Gordon Castle Muniments, GD 44/43/287/51.

Ironically, the threat to the tacksmen was increased not simply through their inability or unwillingness to pay increased levels of rent, but also as a direct result of the strategies they adopted in order to answer the landlords' financial expectations. Many leading tenants embarked on what has been usefully described as 'a recrudescence of feudal demands', using their traditional powers of township and labour management to put unprecedented pressure on subtenants to improve production. Above all, tacksmen sought to rationalise and improve the cattle economy, which entailed a reduction in arable farming and a stricter use of pasture. Thus it was that during the late 1760s and early 1770s, attempts to reorganise their farms by Lewis, Kintail, Strathpsey, Badenoch and Sutherland tacksmen produced complaints of 'oppression' from their subtenantry.[8] The result, therefore, of efforts on the part of elite tenants to adjust to changing economic realities was a rapid deterioration in their relationship with the small tenantry. Even more so than their immediate superiors, this latter social group lacked relative capital reserves and often simply refused to take farms or countenance a sustained loss of their limited resources. 'Tacksman oppression' thus became a common, almost standard reason given by middle tenantry for choosing to emigrate. Such tenants undoubtedly provided the majority of emigrants. A 1774 rental of Macleod's Glenelg estate reveals that although almost half the farms had lost elements of their tenantry, only two tacksman families had departed, with the rest of the emigrants consisting of joint tenants with an average rent of only £5.9.0. Although attention has focused on the extent to which tacksmen themselves constructed and led emigrant parties in this period, the fact that a majority of those leaving consisted of multiple and joint tenantry tended to confirm pre-existing prejudices against the tacksman class, who were then rather conveniently held responsible by proprietary elites for rackrenting those subordinate to them.[9]

Emigration itself thus ensured a more radical imposition of anti-tacksman policies. In 1771 Sir Alexander Macdonald of Sleat attempted to minimise population loss by promising to break up large tacks in order to accommodate smaller tenantry, then preparing to emigrate in large numbers. This

8. E. Richards, *A History of the Highland Clearances: Agrarian Change and the Evictions, 1746–1886*, vol. 1. (London, 1982), pp. 144–46; S.R.O., Gillanders of Highfield Papers, GD 427/208/4; GD 427/209/25; S.R.O., Seafield Muniments, GD 248/508/1/77; S.R.O., Gordon Castle Muniments, GD 44/28/34/58; GD 44/27/10/14, 24, 131; N.L.S., Mackenzie of Delvine Papers, Ms 1485, f. 97; N.L.S., Sutherland Papers, Dep. 313/1104/ letter 8 July 1773; Dep. 313/1107/letter 7 June 1774.

9. M.I. Adam, 'The Highland Emigration of 1770', in *Scottish Historical Review*, vol. 16 (1919), pp. 281–4; M. McLean, *op. cit.*, pp. 4–5, 79; T.M. Devine, 'Landlordism and Highland Emigration', pp. 92–93; D.C.M., 2/105/1 S.R.O., Gillanders of Highfield Papers, GD 427/207/9–10; GD 427/11/7; B.A.M., Box 45/4/4, 45; N.L.S., Mackenzie of Delvine Papers, Ms 1487, f. 130; S.R.O., Gordon Castle Muniments, GD 44/25/7/42; P.R.O., T. 47/12, f. 29.

trend was if anything even more pronounced in Sutherland. After having promised to prevent oppression by leading tenants in July 1769 the tutors of the infant Countess had their prejudices confirmed when, in 1772, the subtenants of Kildonan tacksmen, as well as those of Robert Gray in Assynt and Lieutenant Robert Gordon of Achness in Farr, formed the bulk of emigrants from the estate. Anxious to prevent any major recurrence, and angered by the encouragement of emigration by many senior tackholders, the Assynt estate created a new set of leases that aimed to ensure the preferential settlement of joint tenantry. The successful conclusion of these arrangements prompted the factor, Captain James Sutherland, to note that he had 'no apprehensions of emigration from that country . . . now that their leases are out the poorer sort of people are much pleased that they are to have no tacksmen over them, and no wonder, for they have been squeezed to their last shilling by some'.[10]

It is against this general malaise and sense of increasing uncertainty within the ranks of Highland tenantry in general, and within the relatively elite wadsetter and tacksman class, in particular, that the opportunities offered by the army need to be seen. That members of the region's substantial tenantry should turn to the military as an alternative to an increasingly hostile estate environment is not altogether surprising, given that many were half-pay officers with previous military experience. Tables 12 and 13 showed that half-pay officers, though usually a minority on estates, were often responsible for a disproportionately high percentage of any given rental. This was equally true of wadsetters: indeed, in 1765 military personnel made up one in four wadsetters upon the Sutherland estate.[11] Faced with increasing erosion of their social status, half-pay military officers holding farms in the region adopted their own particular response by migrating back into the army. The relative ease with which they could resume their military careers serves as caution against assumptions that official policy always operated to support the immediate interests of the landlords. Indeed, the financial mechanics of how these annuitant officers returned to service reveals just how apposite an army career was to conditions in the region. Half-pay personnel were encouraged to exchange with another officer of the same rank wishing to leave the army. The transaction was completed by paying up the difference in the value of a half-pay pension and the regulated price of a full commission, both shown in Table 19. In light of the disproportionately high number of officers from Highland regiments within the British half-pay (see Table 2), this exchange policy was of particular significance to the North

---

10. I. Adams and M. Somerville, *Cargoes of Despair and Hope: Scottish Emigration to North America, 1603–1803* (Edinburgh, 1993), p. 93; D.C.M., 4/113 & 114; D.C.M., 2/488/21/1; D.C.M., 3/104/15; R.J. Adam (ed.), *John Home's Survey of Assynt* (Edinburgh, 1960), xxx–xxxv; N.L.S., Sutherland Papers, Dep. 313/1102/4; Dep. 313/1107, letters 7 January, 22 February and 14 July 1774; Dep. 313/725, meetings of Tutors, 17 February 1772 and 11 March 1773.
11. N.L.S., Sutherland Papers, Dep. 313/2119.

of Scotland. It was especially appropriate in a Highland context insofar as it cut dramatically the cost of returning to full-time military service, so providing a financially straitened elite with a relatively cheap alternative to further social and financial losses in civilian life. Indeed, half-pay was, in a sense, a form of free credit from the Crown amounting to approximately half the official purchase price of an army commission.[12]

Table 19. Half Pay and Exchange Rates, 1766[13]

Rank	Annual half-pay	Full value of half-pay	Regulated cost of commission	Difference
Lieut.-Colonel	£155.2.6	£1,551.5.0	£3,500	£1,948.15.0.
Major	£136.17.6	£1,368.15.0	£2,600	£1,231.5.0.
Captain	£91.5.0.	£821.5.0	£1,500	£678.15.0
Lieutenant	£42.11.8	£383.5.0	£550	£166.15.0
Ensign	£33.9.2	£301.2.6	£400	£98.17.6

Assisted therefore by official exchange policy, the period between 1763 and 1775 was characterised by a distinct re-militarisation of the Highland tacksman-officer class. In 1770, for instance, during one of Britain's routine war scares, a total of 60 half-pay officers were re-commissioned by the army – a relatively high proportion of one in nine were officers from Highland battalions. In 1772 Lieutenant George Mackenzie in Gairloch attempted to resume service in the 42nd Highland Regiment at his old rank. When he finally succeeded in 1773, he was nevertheless disappointed, as his commission had been demoted to that of ensign. That he was prepared to accept such a situation is less indicative of military zeal then of conditions in Wester Ross in the immediate aftermath of the temporary collapse in the cattle trade.[14] Events on Sir James Grant of Grant's Strathspey lands give a rough indication of how important the military had become to elite tenants as a source of material security. A 1773 rental lists 28 families of sufficient social status to be officially associated with particular districts or farms, i.e. Grant of Lurg, Delrachnie and so on. In the decade 1768–78 the regular army or East India Company military provided employment for members of eight of these tacksmen families – over one in four.[15] Similar tactics were evident in Lochbuie in Mull; while in 1771 Captain William Mackintosh of Crathiemor

---

12. S.R.O., John Macgregor Collection, GD 50/26/10/8; J.R.L., Bagshawe Muniments, B. 5/1, p. 38; *Edinburgh Advertiser*, 21 February 1775, p. 113; *Scots Magazine*, vol. 34 (Edinburgh, 1772) p. 54; P.R.O., W.O. 1/997, letter 5 January 1778.
13. P.R.O., W.O. 123/115.
14. *Scots Magazine*, vol. 32 (Edinburgh, 1770), p. 686; P.R.O., W.O. 1/996, letters, 15 January, 1 November 1776.
15. S.R.O., Seafield Muniments, GD 248/50/1/22; GD 248/50/2/65; GD 248/201/2/1/16; GD 248/227/2/85; GD 248/50/3/1; GD 248/52/2/97; GD 248/462/20; GD 248/1540, pp. 101–2.

in Badenoch 'turned his ploughshare into a sword', adding: 'It was against my inclination that I recommenced farming . . . it was to gratify my parents . . . but my father was sensible that my former profession was more agreeable'.[16]

The Campbells of Glenure and Barcaldine constitute a prime example of how middling Highland families migrated into the British military in response to socio-economic change. Though proprietors in their own right, the Glenure-Barcaldine family also held a number of farms from the Campbells of Argyll and Breadalbane, and the problems faced by them were typical of those experienced by tacksmen generally. In 1754 they rented seven large farms on the Breadalbane estate for a total of £56: by 1775, a mere two farms cost £52. As well as driving up rents, the third Earl removed John Campbell of Barcaldine, the elder half-brother of Duncan Campbell of Glenure, from certain farms in the Braes of Glenorchy and Benderloch.[17] More importantly, by the early 1770s Barcaldine's financial affairs made the sale of his estate all but inevitable. Rather than see it pass out of the family's control, Glenure raised the necessary £24,000 in order to secure the estate. Faced with an ongoing curtailment of their position within the local agrarian economy, the effective bankruptcy of the senior line, and crippling financial debts, the Glenure family embarked upon a systematic policy of obtaining military employment.[18] In December 1770 Major Allan Campbell, Glenure's brother, returned to full-time military service in the 36th Regiment. This reduced any income drain on the financially straitened John; moreover, in a positive sense it also allowed Allan to facilitate entry of younger kin into the army – a role he subsequently played for his nephew Colin. Likewise, in 1773 Lieutenant-Colonel Alexander Campbell, another brother, solicited the fifth Duke of Argyll for the colonelcy of the 57th Regiment so that he could then live exclusively upon army revenue. His earlier return to full rank neatly illustrates the practical benefits of the half-pay exchange system for financially encumbered families. By virtue of his pensioned status Alexander had avoided any need to pay the full, market-inflated commission price for a lieutenant-colonelcy, then reckoned at £5,000: instead, he paid only the regulated £1,948 – a saving equivalent to 20% of the Barcaldine family debt of £15,000.[19]

16. S.R.O., Maclaine of Lochbuie Papers, GD 174/1307/3; GD 174/1329/3; S.R.O, Gordon Castle Muniments, GD 44/10/69x & 170x.
17. S.R.O., Campbell of Barcaldine, GD 170/1135/22; GD 170/1139/2, 4, 21; GD 170/419/2; GD 170/420/1/32; GD 170/1135/22; S.R.O., Breadalbane Muniments, GD 112/9/49.
18. B.A.M., Box 54/5/162; *Caledonian Mercury*, 25 January 1775, p. 2; *Edinburgh Advertiser*, 24 January 1775; S.R.O. Campbell of Barcaldine Papers, GD 170/1643/16, 17/1.
19. D. Stewart, *Sketches of the Character, Manners and Present State of the Highlanders of Scotland*, vol. 2 (Edinburgh, 1822), appendix 3; *Scots Magazine*, vol. 32 (Edinburgh, 1770), p. 399; B.A.M., Box 45/4/73; Box 54/4/127, 173, 204; S.R.O., Campbell of Barcaldine Papers, GD 170/1067/4; GD 170/1090/21/1; GD 170/1090/34; GD 170/1666/7, 8/1; GD 170/1643/20; GD 170/3155, 3461.

The search for alternative avenues of employment also dictated the family's actions in the political arena. The Glenure family were traditional supporters of the Breadalbane interest and had benefited accordingly by being leased certain farms on the Earl's estate. In an effort to retain their support the third Earl agreed in the early 1770s to the continuation of Duncan's brother, Major Mungo Campbell, on his Lochaweside farm. Yet, when in 1774 the Glenure and Barcaldine family voted *en masse* for an anti-Breadalbane candidate in the county of Perth election, it was in order to secure the interest of the fifth Duke of Argyll. The defection of Glenure surprised local observers but was, in fact, evidence of his determination to gain access to military employment. As the fifth Duke was still considered the leading interest in obtaining commissions for Highland gentry, voting for his candidate was a symbol of the growing preference in the Glenure family for military service over the increasingly precarious prospect of remaining as tacksmen to the third Earl of Breadalbane. As a result, Mungo and the family were deprived of more farms over and above losses already induced by Breadalbane's estate management reforms. Glenure's reaction was to further consolidate the family policy of military service by spending £800 on ensigncies for his sons James and Colin; this familial militarisation was all but completed in August 1775 when Hugh, Glenure's youngest son, was appointed an ensign in the 35th regiment.[20]

The career of Glenure's eldest son, Patrick, highlights the direct link between local estate conditions and military service. A half-pay lieutenant since 1763, he obtained a lease on the farm of Glenduror upon the forfeited estate of Ardsheil in Appin. However, the slump in cattle prices in the early 1770s witnessed Glenure apply on behalf of his son to both Breadalbane and Argyll for their interest in getting Patrick back into the army. Neither, however, managed to persuade the War Office to provide for him, largely because the majority of preferments in this period fell under the jurisdiction of the Irish Lord Lieutenant – a scenario which, incidentally, must have persuaded many Scots of the need for a roughly equivalent political figure in Scotland. Glenure's subsequent voting power in the 1774 election did, however, put him in a relatively strong position. In June of that year Breadalbane failed to obtain a commission for Patrick, while later negotiations over a lease for a Glenorchy farm broke down as a result of commercial considerations.[21] The Earl's reluctance to settle Patrick on his estate explains

---

20. N.L.S., Mackenzie of Delvine, Ms. 1407, f. 18; B.A.M., Box 54/4/173, 198; Box 65/1/196; S.R.O., Campbell of Barcaldine Papers, GD 170/1078/1/1; GD 170/1135/22; GD 170/1138/8; GD 170/1354/32; GD 170/1666/5; GD 170/1379/6/1; GD 170/1139/6; P.R.O., W.O. 1/991, f. 76.
21. T. Hayter (ed.), *An Eighteenth-Century Secretary at War: The Papers of William Viscount Barrington* (London, 1988), p. 301; R.A. Roberts (ed.), *Calendar of Home Office Papers, 1770–72* (London, 1881), pp. 3 & 207; S.R.O., Campbell of Barcaldine Papers, GD 170/1643/6; GD 170/1140/2/1; GD 170/1135/26; GD 170/1078/1/2; GD 170 1139/6, 13; GD 170/1176/6.

why Glenure then committed himself to Argyll's interest. On 2 July 1774 the Duke was asked to assign Patrick a farm, or to try again and get him full military pay. When the latter proved impossible to obtain, agreement was finalised with respect to the farms of Glencripesdale and Beaich in Morvern, as well as several farms in the Duart peninsula of Mull for the grazing of 'flying stock'. The geographic spread of these farms clearly points to a substantial investment on the part of Patrick in the Argyll droving trade, a decision that appeared to bear fruit in the form of substantial profits within the first year.[22]

Despite Patrick's entrepreneurial success in civilian life, the military remained an attractive alternative. Just how attractive became clear in November 1775 when, after only six months as a tacksman in Morvern, Patrick returned to full-time service in Simon Fraser's 71st Highland Regiment at the higher rank of captain. Recruiting for rank undoubtedly provided substantial benefits: in all, the Glenure family saved £1,116 – the price of returning to full commissioned status (£166) and the purchase price of a company (£950) – see Table 19. These figures underline the cogent economic rationale behind the army option: in more immediate terms the savings represented 92% of the annual interest on the loan Glenure had obtained to secure the Barcaldine estate.[23] Once back in the army, Patrick progressively lost any interest in maintaining his droving concerns, despite high wartime profits. Finally, in early 1778, faced with disputes over rent levels in Glencripsdale, Patrick sold his cattle stocks for £700 in order to purchase a major's commission.[24] Once back in the army, Patrick noted the underlying socio-economic conditions which had prompted him to abandon his farms:

> The footing of Highland farmers is such that a man that has no property has only a toleration to stay in his master's will or at best for a term under 20 years . . . I will be very unfit to become a Morvern tenant and very imprudent in me it would be to change my way of life upon so slender a footing as the tack of a farm for the term of 10 or 12 years . . . all the perquisites etc. makes a field officer's situation in this country a very envious one. God knows I think it a line of life far more respectable and I am sure profitable one than being a Morvern drover or tenant.[25]

22. B.A.M. 54/5/193; S.R.O., Campbell of Barcaldine Papers, GD 170/1140/3; GD 170/1146/9; GD 170/1682/1; GD 170/391/1(a) & (c).
23. N.L.S., *Caledonian Mercury*, 12 June 1775, p. 2; S.R.O., Campbell of Barcaldine Papers, GD 170/1062/47–8; GD 170/1643/22; GD 170/391/1 (b); S.G. Checkland, *Scottish Banking: A History, 1695–1973* (Glasgow, 1975), p. 47.
24. S.R.O., Campbell of Barcaldine Papers, GD 170/1151/6; GD 170/1151/4; GD 170/1062/48; GD 170/1354/50; GD 170/1135/32; GD 170/1176/10/1; GD 170/1176/12/2; E. Cregeen, (ed.), *Argyll Estate Instructions: Mull, Morvern and Tiree, 1771–1805* (Edinburgh, 1964), pp. 112, 116.
25. I. Adams and M. Somerville, *op. cit.* p. 152.

Patterns evident within the British half-pay establishment strongly support the argument that conditions in the region led to an unusually high degree of re-militarisation. Table 2 shows that by 1774 Highland officers constituted a lesser percentage of the half-pay establishment because they were exchanging at a higher rate back into the army. Indeed, while the half-pay as a whole declined at a rate approaching one officer in five in the period between 1763 and 1775, the rate of decline amongst officers from Highland regiments approached one officer in three. Table 2, however, represents the entire half-pay establishment and includes officers from the wars of the Spanish and Austrian Successions. By 1765 these older men, who had already been given the chance to re-enter service during the Seven Years War, numbered 374. It is probable that in the post-1763 period they would not have been involved in the drift back into army service but were, rather, fully retired personnel. Instead, it was only those officers who had been demobilised in 1763 who were likely to exchange back onto full pay. Table 20 illustrates this more focused group. By highlighting those most likely to return to military service during the 1763–1775 period, the pattern of re-militarisation by Highland officers is even more marked.

Table 20. British and Highland Half-Pay Officers Reduced in 1763[26]

Year	British half-pay	% decrease	Highland half-pay	% decrease
1765	2,079	–	274	–
1770	1,896	8.8	236	13.8
1774	1,735	8.4	201	14.8

In the four years prior to the American War of Independence, officers from Highland backgrounds were almost twice as likely to return to full-time military service as those from areas outside the region. Furthermore, once the war increased opportunities within the army this pattern continued: between 1774 and 1780 the national half-pay establishment declined by 23% while the Highland equivalent fell by 33%. These patterns confirm that many officers holding farms in the region saw their involvement within a competitive agrarian economy as mere stopgaps between opportunities within the British military. Given the pressure experienced by families such as the Campbells of Glenure under the commercial regimes of landlords like Breadalbane, the move towards military service was an extremely rational form of economic restructuring. Although there have been suggestions that the participation of tacksmen within proprietary regiments helped slow down their disappearance as a tenurial and social group from the region,[27]

26. Annual Army Lists, 1740–1784.
27. S.D.M. Carpenter, Patterns of Recruitment of the Highland Regiments of the British Army, 1756–1815 (St. Andrews University M. Litt Thesis, 1977), pp. 52, 90–122; D.M. Henderson, *Highland Soldier: A Social Study of the Highland Regiments, 1820–1920* (Edinburgh, 1989), p. 17; M.I. Adams, *loc. cit.*, p. 290.

it is clear that military service was linked to the increasing economic discomfiture of the old clan elite, and that for many their involvement in the army was a practical alternative to, or parallel form of, emigration.

Highland Military Emigration and the North American Empire, 1763–1815

The drift of the tacksman-officer class back into the army demonstrates the often migratory effects of military policy upon the region's elite tenantry. No such effect appeared, however, to follow from broader colonial policy, given that successive governments were 'on the whole inclined to support Scottish and especially Highland hostility to the loss of its population'.[28] The end of the Seven Years War undoubtedly brought with it an increasing reassessment of the wisdom of allowing substantial levels of immigration into Britain's North American colonies. The sheer scale of the new empire in America left Britain with a series of major demographic, financial and military problems. From as early as 1760 it was calculated that the newly acquired territories would take over 100 years to colonise and require the immigration of at least 50 million people. Even on a more realistic scale, population loss to the enlarged empire would weaken the mother country considerably, prevent domestic commercial and economic expansion and lead, eventually, through demographic over-extension to Britain replicating Spain's fall from imperial primacy. Progressive population expansion in the colonies would also generate an immediate frontier problem requiring huge monetary and military resources, and, in the longer term, lead to the emergence of North America as the commercial and, therefore, political centre of the empire. How Scots responded to this debate was largely conditioned by their own peculiar concerns and links with North America. Those involved in Scotland's own internal development, such as Henry Home, Lord Kames, believed that inland provinces of agricultural colonists, as opposed to coastal colonies of trade, would be of little practical benefit. In addition, heavy population loss would undermine Scotland's ability to sustain the 'patriotic' processes of agrarian improvement and commercial development that now formed such a vital part of the country's sense of itself.

However, Scottish perceptions of the Atlantic empire must not be associated exclusively or automatically with issues of entrepreneurial trade and commercial development. Highland links with the colonies, for instance, were not primarily commercial but were rather determined by North America's role as an emigrant destination, or, from the elite's perspective, as a major source of state patronage through the army's expansion as an imperial garrison. Crucially, therefore, the American colonies were valued in Scotland for different reasons, depending on a particular regional perspective. A significant sector of this Scottish opinion was made up by the large number of military

---

28. J.M. Bumsted, *op. cit.*, xiii–xiv.

The Military and Highland Emigration, 1763–1815

officers who had served in America. Steeped in the problematic and contentious relationship between the British military and provincial authorities, Scots officers, from commanders-in-chief like John, fourth Earl of Loudon, to naval doctors like Roderick Mackenzie, were not only at the forefront of the deterioration in Anglo-colonial relations but were among the first to express a belief that the colonies were so determined upon independence that conflict was inevitable at some point in the not so distant future.[29]

Much of this general unease and apprehension regarding North America gained growing acceptance in the years following 1763. To compound matters, emigration levels increased to such an extent that, by 1775, 10% of the colonies' population had arrived there since 1760. It is generally accepted that the American Revolutionary War went on to confirm these British prejudices against the concept of an empire of colonisation. The result was that the anti-emigration stance that had emerged by the mid-1770s continued to be enforced with respect to the remainder of British North America until the 1810s. In several respects this appeared to be an easy strategy to enforce. The loss of the old empire broke trans-Atlantic connections and links built up during the eighteenth century. The remaining British possessions, though an obvious destination for emigrants after 1783, were, it has been argued, swamped with vast numbers of American loyalists and in no fit state to encourage or accept any further immigrants, especially if they happened to be relatively poverty-stricken Scottish Highlanders. The result was that Highland emigration ran at only around one third of the level evident previously, and did not recover any real momentum again until the early 1800s.[30] That said, London was still anxious enough to order its provincial governors to desist from practices that stimulated population loss from the British islands. In 1773 Lieutenant Governor Thomas Debrisay of St John's Isle (later Prince Edward Island) was told not to encourage emigration by circulating details in the Irish and Scottish press regarding the large reserves of land available in the colony. Likewise, the Lieutenant Governors of Cape Breton in 1786 and St John's Isle in 1781 as well as the Governor of Nova Scotia in 1784 were informed that encouraging emigrants from Britain or, indeed, America was to be avoided. In

---

29. N.C. Landsman, 'The Legacy of the British Union for the North American Colonies: Provincial Elites and the Problem of Imperial Union', in J. Robertson (ed.), *A Union for Empire: Political Thought and the British Union of 1707* (Cambridge, 1995), pp. 298–9; P.J. Marshall, 'A Nation defined by Empire, 1755–1776', in A. Grant and K.J. Stringer (eds.), *Uniting the Kingdom? The Making of British History* (London, 1995), p. 211; S.R.O., Grant of Monymusk Papers, GD 345/868; B.L. Hardwicke Papers, Add Ms 35910, ff. 18–30; N.L.S., Minto Papers, Ms 11002, f. 64; Ms 11014, f. 81; Ms 11015, f. 82; Ms 11017, ff. 26–27; N.L.S., Mackenzie of Delvine Papers, Ms 1140, ff. 206–207; Ms 1314, f. 51.
30. M. Fry, *The Dundas Despotism* (Edinburgh, 1992), p. 128; M. McLean, *op. cit.*, pp. 118–90; J.M. Bumsted, *op. cit.*, pp. 70–1; J. Anderson, *The Interest of Great Britain with Regard to her American Colonies Considered* (London, 1782), pp. 48–9, 56, 97; P.R.O., C.O. 42/94, ff. 4–6.

July 1792 Dundas reiterated to Governor John Graves Simcoe of the newly created province of Upper Canada his concerns over any rapid increase in British North America's population. He argued that colonial government needed above all to be stable in order that provinces could develop as useful societies: immigrants, however, held differing religious and political sympathies which, if they were introduced quickly and in large numbers produced internal strains that made government both difficult and expensive.[31] The most significant consequences for Scotland of this determination to retain population were the banning of emigration in 1775 and the Passenger Act of 1803, the latter, in particular, being designed to stem the loss of Highlanders. Similarly, in 1786, Dundas again attempted to obtain an outright ban on emigration. Such a policy, in peacetime at least, was not acceptable to senior cabinet members like Pitt, who opposed the measure. Given that in the years preceding the American Revolutionary War the Highlands alone provided nearly one in five of all British emigrants, it is hardly surprising that a Scottish official like Dundas was even more determined than his English counterparts to prevent the loss of population. Overall, although somewhat prone to exaggeration (by 1792, for example, some Highland elites had developed decidedly ambivalent attitudes with respect to population), the extent of British, and more especially Scottish, elite opposition to emigration is unmistakable.[32]

What is far less clear, however, is the extent to which colonial policy corresponded in practice with the objective of retaining populations within the Highlands. Indeed, several factors, both direct and indirect, served either to undermine or contradict attempts to prevent the movement of British subjects within the empire. Though obviously limited in their ability or inclination to run contrary to orders from Britain, it is nevertheless clear that both before and after the American Revolutionary War provincial officials did not share the same degree of enthusiasm for a policy which entailed the deliberate restriction of their own authority and prestige. George Johnstone, governor of West Florida, had been a keen proponent of the colony's population growth, and his family were conspicuous in opposing the curtailment of land grants introduced in 1773–4. The reality was that governors felt their position was best served by increasing population so that both revenue and the number of government offices under their control grew in proportion. Thus in December 1783 Governor John Parr of Nova Scotia noted that the arrival of an estimated 30,000 loyalists made both his province and himself 'more honourable'. The separation of New Brunswick

31. S.R.O., Gordon Castle Muniments, GD 44/27/11/42; P.R.O., S.P. 54/46, ff. 89b & 91; P.R.O., C.O. 217/56, ff. 212, 226; C.O. 217/103, ff. 74–5; C.O. 226/5, ff. 35, 52 & 74; C.O. 226/7, ff. 120 & 134; C.O. 42/316, f. 122; C.O. 42/16. f. 77.
32. B. Bailyn, *Voyagers to the West: Emigration from Britain to America on the Eve of the Revolution* (London, 1987), pp. 29–30, 32, 48, 50–56; T.M. Devine, 'Landlordism and Highland Emigration', p. 87; *Caledonian Mercury*, 1 March 1786 and 5 April 1792.

from Nova Scotia in 1784, as well as the establishment of lieutenant-governorships in St John's Isle and Cape Breton in response to the administrative challenge posed by the settlement of former soldiers and loyalists, ushered in a period of intense rivalry on the part of the new provincial governments as they sought to justify their existence through increasing their populations. Thus the lieutenant-governor of Cape Breton noted that the provincial establishment in 'Nova Scotia is jealous and don't wish with thorough sincerity the success of this government least its growing importance and value should rise it to the first rank . . . I am compelled to view these and other proceedings with more a painful concern because they appear as if they are calculated to . . . discourage industrious and useful settlers from emigrating to this island'.[33] The opinion of Governor Simcoe was an unusually explicit example of what was generally a more subtle, implicit provincial disagreement with metropolitan thinking. In 1792, in direct contradiction to Dundas, Simcoe argued:

> Emigrations of hardy, industrious and virtuous men maybe reasonably expected from the Northern parts of Great Britain . . . It is <u>indispensably necessary</u> that a <u>capital</u> should be established . . . and that as soon as possible, almost instantaneously, a great body of emigrants should be collected in its vicinity, so as to become the very transcript and image of the British people . . . In regard to population at large, with all due deference, I humbly submit that without taking place to any great extent, this country will not be able to pay its own expenses . . . I conceive it would be for the interest of Great Britain that the population of Upper Canada should be not only progressive and regular, but immediate and rapid.[34]

Care must be taken, therefore, to distinguish between the imperial core's hostility towards an empire of colonisation and an understandable desire on the part of Britain's remaining North American provinces to expand and develop. These fault lines between metropolitan policy and provincial expectations were crucial in ensuring that emigrants arriving in Nova Scotia or Quebec did not experience any real hostility or obstruction from the local authorities. Furthermore, wider issues of imperial demography encouraged colonial authorities to accept and settle emigrant parties on vacant Crown land. The radically altered international context after 1783 forced London to concede that if emigration from Britain itself could not be prevented legally, then it was infinitely preferable that British subjects contribute strength to the empire, as opposed to the United States. Such concerns meant that in late 1791 the governor of Nova Scotia fed and provided general assistance to 650

33. B. Bailyn, *op. cit.*, p. 57; S.R.O., Townshend Papers, RH 4/56/11–12; P.R.O., C.O. 226/8, ff. 61–2; C.O. 217/56, f. 126; C.O. 217/60, f. 146; C.O. 217/104, ff. 57, 139–144, 159–62.
34. P.R.O., C.O. 42/94, ff. 4–6, 98; C.O. 42/316, f. 163; C.O. 42/317, ff. 108–111.

West Highland emigrants at Pictou in an unsuccessful effort to prevent the continuation of their journey south to North Carolina. His actions gained official approval in the hope that it would induce Scottish immigrants 'to give their preference to Canada' – a policy that continued until the 1800s when, in response to renewed emigration from the Highlands, permission was given in 1803 for the recruitment of a Canadian fencible regiment with the express aim of steering populations clear of America by offering free land to its soldiers and their dependants. The regiment's popularity – it eventually involved over 2,100 people – underlines how Gaels continued to perceive military service as an especially appropriate method of emigration well into the nineteenth century. However, landlord opposition and a series of minor mutinies brought about by the government's failure to provide passage money for the soldiers' extended families ensured that the scheme was quickly abandoned. Nonetheless, that such a levy was even sanctioned only two months after the Passenger Act is clear evidence that, rather than lose populations to a foreign country, British governments were prepared to construct military policies that sought to direct emigrant flow rather than stem it outright. The continuing importance of imperial security in producing this crucial shift in the government's stance on emigration is evident in the fact that in January 1813 the War Office seemed willing to approve plans by Thomas Douglas, fifth Earl of Selkirk, to raise a new fencible regiment for service in Canada, then being seriously threatened by the outbreak of war between Britain and the United States. Eventually, however, the idea was dropped, not as a result of any objection in principle to the emigration of Highlanders, but rather because the state refused to pay travel costs for the immediate families of recruits.[35]

Albeit that socio-economic conditions in the colonies, as well as post-1783 concerns over America's demographic strength, helped subvert Britain's anti-emigration policy indirectly, one of the most high-profile and important factors operating directly against the domestic retention of population was the government's own strategy of settling military personnel and their dependants in the colonies under exceptionally favourable conditions. During the period 1763–75 the thrust of British military policy in North America had been the maintenance of a large officer corp and a readily available pool of men who could be relied upon to control newly won areas and augment the regular army garrison in the event of renewed war. The result was that in 1763 military personnel were awarded grants of land without the usual quit rent payments. The same thinking underlay the much larger settlement of ex-

35. P.R.O., C.O. 42/82, ff. 15–19; C.O. 42/317, f. 169; C.O. 43/10, f. 93; S.R.O., Seafield Muniments, GD 248/1530, pp. 104–6; GD 248/1532, p. 37; GD 248/1534, pp. 286, 323; S.R.O., Loch Muniments, GD 268/216/17; M. McLean, *op. cit.*, p. 149; M.E. Vance, Emigration and Scottish Society: The Background to Three Government Assisted Emigration to Upper Canada, 1815–1821 (University of Guelph, Ph.D., 1990), p. 15; H.M.C. *Laing Manuscripts*, vol. 2 (London, 1925), pp. 730–2, 740–3.

military and loyalist personnel at the end of the American Revolutionary War. Although some colonial administrators feared that domiciling committed loyalists on the frontier with the United States would result in a permanent state of unofficial hostilities, it was eventually felt that the remainder of British North America required a barrier of population that would act, effectively, as a defence mechanism. It was decided that Quakers and other religious groups not inclined to take up arms were not suitable. Instead, in late 1783, General Frederick Haldimand, commander-in-chief in Quebec, argued that 'it seems good policy that the frontiers be settled by a people professing different religions, speaking different languages and accustomed to other laws and government from those of our restless and enterprising neighbours of New England'. Although the reference is specifically to French Canadians, such thinking clearly suggests that the value of Gaelic-speaking Highlanders as an imperial-frontier people was probably never less in doubt than in the decades following Britain's defeat in America.[36]

The Highland landlords' agenda of population retention was thus undermined to some extent by wider concerns for imperial security. Nowhere was this more evident than in the fact that by guaranteeing land to soldiers who fought in America the army was to all intent and purposes inviting Highlanders to emigrate directly under its auspices. Indeed, Scots in general had been mooted as ideal military-frontier settlers since at least the era of the Union. The departure of Highlanders for Georgia in 1735 as soldier-settlers on the Anglo-Spanish frontier, as well as rumours in 1748 that Lord Loudon's Regiment was to be sent as part of a military colonisation scheme to Nova Scotia, meant that military service in the colonies was strongly equated with emigration even prior to the Seven Years War. If not so before, then without doubt the Seven Years War furnished Highlanders with cogent proof of how the army could be utilised as a mechanism of emigration.[37] Contemporaries commenting on the underlying causes of population movement during the early 1770s believed that a factor consciously motivating Highland soldiery during the 1756–63 war had been the prospect of obtaining settlement on cheap and secure land. The precedent of 1763

36. J.L. Bullion, 'Securing the Peace: Lord Bute, the Plan for the Army, and the Origins of the American Revolution', in K.W. Schweizer (ed.), *Lord Bute: Essays in Re-interpretation* (Leicester, 1988), pp. 19–20; E. Richards, 'Scotland and the Uses of the Atlantic Empire', in B. Bailyn and P.D. Morgan (eds.), *Strangers within the Realm: Cultural Margins of the First British Empire* (London, 1991), p. 95; P.R.O., C.O. 42/24, ff. 107–111; C.O. 42/11, f. 42; C.O. 42/16, ff. 46 & 145, 309.
37. B.L., Egerton Mss, Ms 929, ff. 92–3; W.R. Brock, *Scotus Americanus* (Edinburgh, 1982), p. 79; A.W. Parker, *Scottish Highlanders in Colonial Georgia: the Recruitment, Emigration and Settlement at Darien, 1735–1748* (Athens, Georgia, 1997), pp. 48–51; J. Innes, 'The Domestic Face of the Fiscal-Military State: Government and Society in Eighteenth-century Britain', in L. Stone (ed.), *An Imperial State at War: Britain from 1689–1815* (London, 1994), p. 116; P.J. Marshall, *op. cit.*, p. 210; B.A.M., Box 65/2/2; P.R.O., W.O. 1/973, f. 955.

certainly influenced how Gaels perceived military service when conflict was renewed in 1775; indeed, some Highlanders viewed the coming of hostilities in a positive light. When queried in September 1775 regarding their decision to voluntarily enter a war zone, Gaels on the point of emigrating answered that the war brought with it the definite prospect of military service, and thus relatively easy access to land. Nor was this distinctively Highland response to the developing imperial crisis in any way misguided or naive. Although land grants had been increasingly restricted in the two years prior to the outbreak of war, exceptions had been made for officers, non-commissioned officers and private men from the forces. This trend simply intensified under wartime conditions. In April 1775 colonial officials in New York and North Carolina adopted a land settlement policy for Highland families on the basis of immediate or future military service. Likewise, in June of the same year Lieutenant-Colonel Allan McLean, son of the Mull laird of Torloisk, received permission to raise a Highland regiment of emigrants. Not only did McLean obtain settlement rights prior to any actual service, he did so on such favourable terms (200 instead of 100 acres per soldier) as to make the agreement extremely difficult for provincial governments to fulfil upon demobilisation in 1783.[38]

Changes in conditions of service for the regular regiments during this period further enhanced the attractiveness of the army as a free ticket across the Atlantic. In order to allay fears of an unconstitutional expansion in the military, Parliament was assured in 1775 that regiments such as Fraser of Lovat's two battalions were destined for service in America only, and that upon conclusion of hostilities their disbandment was guaranteed. These conditions meant that anyone entering the regiment did so in the knowledge that they would serve merely for the duration of the war in America – the one theatre of British military operations conspicuously associated with land grants. The experience of Major Duncan Macpherson of Cluny whilst recruiting for Fraser's regiment in early 1776 underlines the link between military service and emigration in that it was personnel already planning to migrate into the Lowlands who eventually formed the majority of his men.[39] Comments by Mackenzie of Seaforth's factor reveal the often sophisticated understanding amongst even the most isolated Highland tenantry of both the opportunities that military service offered them, and of some of the problems

38. M. McLean, *op. cit.*, pp. 100–102, 108; J. M. Bumsted, *op. cit.*, p. 23; W. Thom, *Informations Concerning the Province of North Carolina, Addressed to the Emigrants from the Highlands and Western Isles of Scotland* (Glasgow, 1773), p. 10; J. Fortescue (ed.), *The Correspondence of King George III*, vol. 3 (London, 1928), pp. 175–6, 197; I. Adams & M. Somerville, *op. cit.*, pp. 90, 145; P.R.O., C.O. 42/12, f. 164; C.O. 217/56, ff. 26–7, 111–12.

39. J. Almon (ed.), *Parliamentary Register*, vol. 3 (London, 1776), pp. 208–209; S.R.O., Campbell of Barcaldine Papers, GD 170/1666/7; S.R.O., Methven Collection, GD 1/8/18, letter 1 May 1777; S.R.O., Gordon Castle Muniments, GD 44/25/6/41; GD 44/47/2/75 (2); GD 44/27/12/5.

surrounding British land settlement policies within the thirteen colonies. In January 1778 he reported that rumours of General John Burgoyne's defeat at Saratoga had significantly lessened the enthusiasm of Seaforth's Kintail tenantry for military service. The reality that the war against the Americans was now likely to be a long and bloody affair undoubtedly explained part of this reaction. Yet the significance of Saratoga from the perspective of Highland tenants was that such a defeat, for the first time, cast doubt on Britain's ability to retain authority over the lands that so attracted people in Kintail. The defeat called into question the future viability and legality of any land claim held as a result of army service to the Crown. That Seaforth's tenantry had envisaged their involvement in the military with precisely this objective in mind is evident from the fact that the factor had earlier noted of the regiment's possible destination: 'I suppose that many of the Lewis lads would rather go to America than anywhere else'.[40]

While a lack of economic opportunities, commercial underdevelopment and intense levels of landlord coercion undoubtedly formed the primary dynamics behind excessive Highland involvement within the military, there were clearly other elements influencing the expectations of the recruits themselves. What little testimony is evident from the rank-and-file soldiery suggests that military service was quite consciously envisaged as a means of social and material advancement. In 1782 a Mull soldier in Nova Scotia informed his family that relatives formerly in the 42nd and 74th Highland Regiments had settled in New York State and had begun to do well for themselves. Exactly the same sentiments were expressed by a piper from Glenorchy in Fraser of Lovat's 71st Highland Regiment. In 1778 he confidently noted to his relatives in Argyll that 'I am as well as ever I was in my life, my pay is as good as one shilling and six pence per day and I hope my fortune within two years will be as good that I will have 200 acres of free ground of my own in this country . . . if it hade not been for this war this is the best country in the world'.[41]

Indeed, for a population imbued with an essentially peasant mentality which attached ultimate importance to the land, colonial military service as practised by Britain in the last half of the eighteenth century must have seemed almost tailor-made: a cheap, state-subsidised form of emigration. Although land was assigned with strategic and not commercial objectives in mind and was often of mediocre quality, the Army nonetheless constituted one of the earliest and most effective means by which land in the colonies was accessed by Gaels. From this perspective the importance of the Seven Years' War cannot be underestimated. Calculations of the number of Highlanders emigrating to the colonies prior to 1760 suggest a total of

40. S.R.O., Campbell of Barcaldine Papers, GD 170/3158; S.R.O., Gillanders of Highfield Papers, GD 427/302/6; GD 427/304/4.
41. S.R.O., Maclaine of Lochbuie Papers, GD 174/1348; S.R.O., Campbell of Barcaldine Papers, GD 170/3158; S.R.O., Breadalbane Muniments, GD 112/11/1/4/34.

approximately 3,000. If accurate, then the influx of three Highland regiments, consisting of at least several thousand men in total, represented a crucial shift in the scale and depth of the region's contact with the North American empire. This new level of interaction was cemented by the settlement of Highland soldiers and officers from 1763 onwards. By virtue of a proclamation in 1763, captains received 3,000 acres, subaltern officers 2,000 acres and ordinary soldiers 50 acres.[42] The pattern of these settlements varied substantially from isolated parcels of land, such as the three grants totalling 2,000 acres awarded to Lieutenant Henry Munro in Georgia in 1764, to concentrated block grants involving whole regiments. Over a period of just eight months from July 1764, for example, 27,600 acres north of Ticonderoga in New York were awarded to the officers and non-commissioned officers of the 42nd and 77th Highland Regiments. Though total fatalities in the three Highland regiments serving in America had been considerable (one estimate is of around 800 men), they cannot account for the fact that fewer than one in five men returned to the Highlands in 1763 (see Appendix 5). This suggests that a substantial number of Highland soldiers chose to take up the option of being accommodated in the colonies.[43] The amount of land involved in the settlement of military units expanded significantly when again instituted at the end of the American Revolutionary War, largely because such grants made provision for the immediate dependants of the soldiers themselves. Government stipulated that on top of the regulatory 100 acres for every individual soldier, his wife and children each added another 50 acres to the final total. This provision for immediate kin made military resettlement policies particularly apposite for Highlanders in light of their tendency to emigrate in large family groups (see Appendix 6). The result was that military emigrants were responsible for the creation of substantial new settlements. The demobilisation of four provincial battalions in what was later to become Upper Canada, for instance, involved 122 officers, 1,684 rank-and-file and over 1,656 women and children, making a total acreage of 256,000. Settlement of the 2nd battalion of the 84th Highland Emigrant Regiment along the Nine-Mile River in Nova Scotia involved an eventual total of 81,000 acres.[44] Highlanders often formed a substantial minority of such personnel: in St John's Isle, for example, a 1787 list of 301 disbanded soldiers included 35 Gaels. Similarly, in Nova Scotia the spring of 1784 saw the registering of claims by ex-military Highland personnel totalling over 19,800 acres. In Quebec, meanwhile, soldiers and their families made up over one in three of the

42. T.M. Devine, 'Landlordism and Highland Emigration', p. 89; J. Redington (ed.), *Calendar of Home Office Papers, 1760–65* (London, 1878), p. 304.
43. P.R.O., C.O. 5/1134, pp. 235–238; S.R.O., F.E.P. E769/91/69(1–2); J.S. Keltie, *A History of the Scottish Highlands, Highland Clans and Highland Regiments*, vol. 2 (Edinburgh, 1875), pp. 346, 454–7, 465.
44. P.R.O., C.O., 217/35, ff. 74–5; B.L., Haldimand Papers, Add Ms 21826, ff. 62–3; S.R.O., Maclaine of Lochbuie Papers, GD 174/2154/15.

850 loyalist Gaels domiciled in the province by the autumn of 1784: they were entitled under settlement regulations to an approximate total of 34,500 acres[45] (see Appendix 6).

Military settlement thus created relatively large, concentrated centres of Highland landownership in North America. These prefabricated communities represented a major landmark in the development of trans-Atlantic Highland networks, and in the emergence of 'chain emigration' from the region. Again, what little correspondence from rank-and-file soldiery survives, suggests that such personnel assisted the flow of information and gossip about America back into the relatively isolated Scottish Highlands. The substantial number of Highland military officers either settled or stationed in North America played an especially crucial role in this flow of information. The Reverend William Thom, who attempted to counter negative landlord propaganda respecting conditions in the colonies, saw the officer class as vital in this respect. From as early as 1763, when details emerged in the Scottish press of their involvement in land settlement schemes on St. John's Isle, it was understood that it was in the financial interest of such annuitant officers to encourage emigration in an effort to enhance the productivity and overall value of their new property. This economic motive formed the basis for the subsequent high-profile involvement of military officers in the emigration process, and explains why, in 1769, Captain Cameron of Glendessary negotiated with tacksmen from Macleod's estate in Skye regarding the purchase of land in St. John's Isle.[46] In the case of a party of emigrants from the Grant estate in Strathspey in 1774 this initial military connection was fundamental:

> A letter . . . from Lieutenant James Grant at New York . . . gives . . . the most favourable accounts of the country he is in, and wishes much that James and family was to go out there, as he says, he is sure he would do extremely well, for himself and family. I think it a very lucky circumstance for James, that Lieutenant James is before him, as he is a very proper man to get information of such lotts of land as are to be disposed of.[47]

In 1785 the respected commentator John Knox noted that a similar process had re-emerged after the interruption of the war, and that the new military settlements were again exerting migratory influence on the north of Scotland. He firmly believed that 'the Highlanders who served in the American war, being by royal proclamation, entitled to settlements in that country, were

45. P.R.O., C.O., 217/59, ff. 134–5, 161, 165–74; C.O. 700/Nova Scotia/50; C.O. 700/Nova Scotia/54; C.O. 700/Nova Scotia/67.
46. *Edinburgh Evening Courant*, 23 March 1763; D.C.M., 1/855/6. See also S.R.O., Maclaine of Lochbuie Papers, GD 1/1003/156; GD 174/2177/10; A.E. Stamp (ed.), *Journal of the Commissioners for Trade and Plantations, 1768–1775* (London, 1937), p. 170.
47. W. Thom, *op. cit.*, p. 10; S.R.O., Gillanders of Highfield Papers, GD 427/206/7; S.R.O., Seafield Muniments, GD 248/226/2/17.

desirous that their kindred and friends should partake of their good fortune'.[48] The settlement of soldiers from Breadalbane in the province of New Brunswick, for example, provided an initial precedent that ensured the maritime colonies emerged as the chosen destination for further civilian emigration from Highland Perthshire. An especially conspicuous example of the type of 'chain emigration' sparked by new military settlements was the large-scale departure from Knoydart of over 500 people led by Lieutenant Angus MacDonnell of Sandaig, formerly of the 71st Highland Regiment. The fact that MacDonnell was already entitled to land was obviously important in motivating his own leadership; more generally, the generous treatment of loyalists meant that upon their arrival in Quebec the emigrants admitted candidly that they were 'in expectation of grants out of the waste lands of the Crown'. The decision of Quebec's governor to settle them in precisely this manner sent a powerful and positive signal to those contemplating emigration from the Highlands. An investigation in October 1790 into the motives of recently arrived Eigg and Arisaig emigrants revealed the trans-Atlantic 'pull' effect of provincial land policy. They admitted that, 'having heard from their friends & relations settled in the upper parts of this province that upon removing to this country they would be able to obtain portions of the waste land of the Crown contiguous to them, they were glad to embark for Canada'.[49]

The influence of military officers was not, however, limited to the immediate aftermath of each conflict. Equipped with a 'safety net' of land in the colonies, individuals such as Lieutenant Hugh Fraser of the 78th Highland Regiment returned in the 1760s to the annexed estate of Lovat, only to become involved in the organisation of emigration in 1773 once economic and tenurial conditions deteriorated rapidly. Such actions demonstrate how Highland officers were often confident and at ease in assessing opportunities and risks on both sides of the British Atlantic world. The actions of Lieutenant Allan Stewart, again of Fraser's 78th Regiment, typify this approach as well as the fact that the migratory influence of military settlements often had a long germination period, and became especially important when poor conditions in the Highlands activated a search for alternative opportunities. The introduction of sheep into Appin by 1775, therefore, witnessed Stewart depart with 70 dependants determined upon 'settling in the lands granted him by the government at the end of the last war'.[50] Yet the knowledge of military officers with respect to opportunities and conditions in

---

48. S.R.O., Maclaine of Lochbuie Papers, GD 174/1348; S.R.O., Campbell of Barcaldine Papers, GD 170/3158; John Knox, *A View of the British Empire more Especially Scotland: with some Proposals for the Improvement of the Country and the Extension of its Fisheries and the Relief of the People* (London, 1785), p. 127.
49. M.E. Vance, loc. cit., pp. 49–50; M. McLean, op. cit., p. 118; P.R.O., C.O. 42/11, f. 145; C.O. 42/72, f. 57; C.O. 42/82, ff. 15–20.
50. S.R.O., F.E.P. E769/91/162, 229, 315(1); P.R.O., T. 47/12, ff. 119–20.

North America meant they emerged as important initial facilitators of emigration to a wide range of destinations, not just to areas of military settlement. Half-pay officers were thus conspicuous in organising emigration from Urquhart and Coigach in 1774, Breadalbane in 1785, Appin in 1791, Locheil and Glenelg in 1792, and South Uist in 1803. This sequence confirms how officers remained an important element in emigration from the region until the early 1800s, by which time an intricate web of trans-Atlantic Highland networks had firmly established itself.[51]

Ultimately, however, military emigration must not be viewed as a one-way street, simply expediting the flow of emigrants in a westerly direction. The influence of military settlements also reached back over the Atlantic and gave substantial leverage to ex-military personnel in their domestic negotiations with landlords. It was the soldiers who were not prepared to settle in the colonies who made the most complex impact upon the region. In 1783 Lord Alexander Macdonald of Sleat gave orders that men from the 76th Macdonald Regiment who had refused their entitlement to land in British North America be accommodated instead on his Skye estate with tenant allotments of one penny rating. Not only were these soldiers a major consideration within the estate's tenurial structure during the 1780s, but Macdonald, by promising never to remove them from their farms, generated a tangle of settlement and congestion problems so complex that military personnel who had served in America still formed a complicating factor in the wholesale estate reorganisation of 1801.[52]

Such situations were compounded by the fact that Highland soldiery quite deliberately used their offer of land in the colonies as a bargaining chip to gain better settlement conditions at home. In February 1763 young men from Assynt wrote from America to the estate factor, Alexander Mackenzie of Ardloch, offering to take tacks at a 5% annual increase until the rents on each farm were 25% above their original level; in return, they asked for tacks of forty to fifty years. While admittedly under only very specific and limited conditions, military status clearly gave Highlanders a relatively strong negotiating position. A similar situation was evident upon the Perthshire estates of the fourth Earl of Breadalane in the aftermath of the American Revolutionary War. In 1785 it was noted that some soldiers were considering emigrating back to Canada in the light of what they felt were unacceptable conditions of tenure. As John Campbell of Achallader related:

> I was authorised to give them hopes, on their return, everything else being equal of preference to others . . . If they knew that your Lordship

51. M. McLean, *op. cit.*, pp. 122–23; S.R.O., Seafield Muniments, GD 248/226/4/11, 43; GD 248/369/4/9, 11; GD 248/1532, p. 37; S.R.O., F.E.P. E746/75/66(1); E746/113/35(1–2), 98; S.R.O., Breadalbane Muniments, GD 112/16/4/1/3; P.R.O., C.O. 42/12, f. 382.
52. C.D.T.L., GD221/4249/1; GD 221/5790; GD 221/5516/5/1; GD 221/4250/44; GD 221/676/4; GD 221/701; GD 221/694/4; GD 221/718/1.

wrote me to provide for them in Balleid [part of Achallader's own estate], they would look upon it as a proscription from any settlement on this estate, and would naturally turn their thoughts to Nova Scotia, where they were offered a 100 acres each, fifty more to such as were married, and fifty for every child they had, a years provision from the King, besides their arms and tools.[53]

In a tough negotiating stance very rarely associated with Highland tenantry, the ex-soliders had made it clear they wished to be able to choose between a variety of farms, as opposed to being assigned a particular holding. Failure on the landlord's part to offer them this choice would then entail their emigration back to Nova Scotia. Not only do their actions and those of the Assynt men reveal the rising social expectations of Highland soldiers but, more generally, they illustrate how Gaels astutely played imperial settlement policy off against their private landlords and how they had become surprisingly attuned to operating within, and taking what advantage they could, of Britain's Atlantic empire.

Government and Landlords, 1775–1815: A Patriotic Partnership?

Although military and imperial considerations often undermined landlord attempts to retain their populations, it remained the case that government was broadly in agreement with the proprietors. This common ground was to prove crucial in developing anti-emigration strategies for the region during the period from 1763 to 1815. Despite the growth in liberal, free trade ideas elsewhere in Britain by 1800, the region's place within the empire continued to be seen almost exclusively in mercantilistic terms.[54] This was largely owing to the culture of state intervention that grew up around the Highlands in the immediate aftermath of the '45, and which continued to be acceptable because the region's military importance meant it fell into the one area of society even free trade thinkers like Adam Smith conceded the state had an indisputable responsibility for – namely, defence of the realm.[55] It was certainly the case from the 1760s onwards that the economic future of the Highlands was merely one element in a more generalised debate on Scotland's overall commercial and social development. However, while certain issues were undoubtedly held in common with the rest of Scotland,

---

53. N.L.S., Mackenzie of Delvine Papers, Ms 1319, f. 41; S.R.O., Breadalbane Muniments, GD 112/16/4/1/3; GD 112/11/1/4/57.
54. J.M. Bumsted, *op. cit.*, pp. 45–6; A.J. Youngson, *After the 'Forty-Five* (Edinburgh, 1973), pp. 71 & 87.
55. A.V. Judges, 'The Idea of a Mercantile State', in D.C. Coleman (ed.), *Revisions in Mercantilism* (London, 1969), pp. 78–9; A. Smith, *An Inquiry into the Nature and Causes of the Wealth of Nations*, eds. R.H. Campbell & A.S. Skinner, vol. 2 (Oxford, 1976), pp. 689, 705–6; P. White, *Observations on the Present State of the Scotch Fisheries and the Improvement of the Interior Parts of the Highlands* (Edinburgh, 1791), p. 60.

the region's military reputation influenced discourse and analysis to an extent not evident elsewhere. Commentators like the Reverend John Walker, James Anderson and John Knox, as well as the Scottish press in general, condemned Highland emigration, justified retention of the region's population and called for direct state intervention primarily because of the Highlanders' proven utility as a martial race. Constant reference to military usefulness was deemed all the more necessary by such commentators given the Gaels' widely acknowledged lack of commercial and industrial skills which in the case of other emigrating populations, such as Northern Irish weavers, formed the basis of opposition to their departure.[56] An important consequence of this focus on military demography was that landlord policies in the Highlands came under unusually intense attack, not merely for dislocating populations – Lowland landlords were, after all, equally guilty in this respect – but also for implementing estate management strategies which directly threatened national security and defence. Improvement as practised in the Lowlands was considered beneficial and patriotic while in the Highlands it destroyed a vital sector of the nation's military resources, and was thus to some extent questionable on the very same patriotic grounds.[57] Indeed, policies that led to emigration were described by an adviser to the Sutherland family in 1788 as 'chargeable with the want of philanthropy and state policy'. Another commented that there existed

> unfavourable impressions as to the tendency of their conduct . . . Any proprietor resolved to enjoy the full value of his estate [found] that his conduct was deemed oppressive and unjust. When a populous valley was converted into sheep walks, the author of the change was held up as an enemy of the public, who, for a sordid interest, promoted the desolation of his country.[58]

56. Anon., *The Present Conduct of the Chieftains and Proprietors of Lands in the Highlands of Scotland towards their Clans and People Considered Impartially* (Edinburgh, 1773), pp. 6–7; J. Anderson, *An Account of the Present State of the Hebrides and Western Coasts of Scotland* (Dublin, 1786), xvii; J. Knox, *op. cit.*, iv–v; J. Walker, *An Economical History of the Hebrides and Highlands of Scotland*, vol. 1 (Edinburgh, 1808), pp. 43–5; *Caledonian Mercury*, 6 September 1775, 5 April 1792; *Scots Magazine* vol. 36 (Edinburgh, 1774), pp. 221, 345.
57. T.C. Smout, 'Problems of Nationalism, Identity and Improvement in Later Eighteenth Century Scotland', in T.M. Devine (ed.), *Improvement and Enlightenment* (Edinburgh, 1989), pp. 15–18; *Scots Magazine*, vol. 36 (Edinburgh, 1774), p. 346; *Caledonian Mercury*, 4 January 1775; Anon., *A Letter to the Lord Advocate of Scotland* (Edinburgh, 1777), p. 7; J. Knox, *op. cit.*, p. 127; S.R.O., Gillanders of Highfield Papers, GD 427/207/9; N.L.S., Sutherland Papers, Dep. 313/725, meeting 20 November 1773.
58. J. Walker, *op. cit.*, vol. 2, p. 412; N.L.S., Sutherland Papers, Dep. 313/979/14; S.R.O., Seafield Muniments, GD 248/1529, letter 31 March 1801, Sir James Grant-Robert Dundas; T. Douglas (Selkirk), *Observations on the Present State of the Highlands with a View of the Probable Causes and Consequences of Emigration* (Edinburgh, 1806), p. 130.

Improvement, and even the migration it engendered, were seen in the Lowlands primarily in terms of an exercise in proprietary rights and entrepreneurial endeavour, all the more justifiable as both served to strengthen, not weaken the state. In the Highlands, the same economic criteria undoubtedly applied; the crucial difference, however, was the unusually high level of state interest and concern in the process and the extent to which it was felt Highland landlords needed to adopt specialised strategies which balanced the patriotism of commercial improvement with that of retaining a valued reservoir of military manpower.

Any real basis for such a distinctive, regionally adjusted approach to improvement was ultimately possible only because landlords themselves, especially in areas of the North-West where the labour-intensive kelp economy predominated, were extremely anxious to maintain high levels of population. Even in interior, eastern districts of the Highlands like Cromdale, Kingussie and Moy, where labour-intensive industries were absent, population decline in the range of 19–31% between the 1750s and 1790s gave some ground to the fears of landlords like Sir James Grant that the region was haemorrhaging tenantry at an unacceptably rapid rate. They feared the result would be labour problems in the short term and an imbalance between population levels and available commercial opportunities in the longer term.[59] If actually motivated by somewhat different concerns, both government and landlords were anxious for some form of solution to the emigration problem in the early 1770s. For several interconnected reasons the issue of military manpower proved central to this search for an anti-emigration policy. Landlords understood that any emphasis on their part on the need to retain Highlanders for military purposes helped confirm their patriotic credentials, which tended to be questioned whenever their role in sparking emigration was highlighted. Furthermore, in both 1775 and most obviously in 1803 during the campaign for the Passenger Act, emphasising the national interest in the form of protecting military resources allowed Highland landlords to disguise their own commercial interests. Most crucial of all, however, was the fact that landlords knew such an emphasis played upon the particular military concerns of the state, making it all the more likely that government would intervene and tackle the issue directly. The military dimension became part of the lobbying language of a special interest group attempting to influence the fiscal-military state into acting favourably on its behalf. Expectation amongst Highland landlords that government would intervene upon mercantilistic grounds and legislate against emigration was evident almost as soon as noticeable, large-scale departures commenced in the 1760s. The omens appeared favourable when in October 1773 Lord Chief Justice Thomas Miller began monitoring emigrant numbers. Partly

---

59. J. Hunter, *The Making of the Crofting Community* (Edinburgh, 1976), pp. 24–5; D.J. Withrington and I.R. Grant (eds.), *The Statistical Account of Scotland*, vol. 17 (Wakefield, 1979), lii; S.R.O., Seafield Muniments, GD 248/244/4/2.

because of this evidence of interest at Westminster, Highland lairds began to assume that emigration would be prevented by legislation. Similarly, in 1774 the Earl of Seaforth requested that soldiers be sent to Lewis in an effort to forcibly prevent his tenantry from leaving.[60] The fact that populations with a track record of military disaffection appeared to be emigrating into another part of the empire on the brink of rebellion did, without doubt, cause a significant degree of anxiety in official circles. Nonetheless, government remained deeply sceptical of both the utility and legality of direct intervention. A request in April 1775 by Inverness-shire proprietors that government tackle the issue was ignored until, finally, on 23 August 1775, Parliament declared America in armed rebellion. War allowed the state to exercise its authority in matters relating to defence of the realm and, on 4 September 1775, Henry Dundas banned emigration from Scottish ports; it is indicative of the altogether different scale and reasoning behind state intervention in Scotland that such a ban did not appear to have been instituted in England.[61]

The banning of emigration in 1775 was an unprecedented act of state intervention, more important for what it said about how contemporary elites envisaged the region than for its actual impact on departures – a point, moreover, that applies equally to the Passenger Act. In a Treasury report that constitutes the single most important summary of the state's relationship with the Highlands during the era of first-phase Clearance, Dundas set out his reasons for banning emigration and, more importantly, the remedial policies he felt were vital if a long-term solution to the problem was to be found.[62] Dundas's ideas revolved around two key points and served as the foundation for government policy in the region for the following thirty years. First, military service was the issue that primarily underpinned interaction between government and the region. Second, in order to combat emigration a partnership was envisaged between Highland landlords and London. In return for implementing estate policies that assisted the retention of population, government would guarantee financial support to landlords by awarding them lucrative regimental commissions or other forms of imperial patronage. Of course to preserve population simply for the good of the state was to expect landlords to act outwith the normal economic concerns of their class, and would have been a wholly unrealistic proposition if not matched by a willingness on the part of government to divert state finance into the region. As it was, several features of the arrangement led to its eventual failure. First, it assumed that the Highlands could maintain a level of involvement in the army that could justify disproportionate government spend-

60. N.L.S., Sutherland Papers, Dep. 313/725, meeting 30 November 1773; B.A.M., Box 54/5/39–40; N.L.S., Mackenzie of Delvine Papers, Ms 1487, f. 160; S.R.O., Gillanders of Highfield Papers, GD 427/207/11, 15–16; GD 427/11/7; GD 427/207/18–19; R.A. Roberts (ed.), *Calendar of Home Office Papers, 1773–1775* (London, 1899), p. 219.
61. P.R.O., S.P. 54/45, ff. 165, 172a; S.R.O., Seafield Muniments, GD 248/509/1/48–49x; GD 248/244/4/2, 12–14; B. Bailyn, *op. cit.*, p. 54.
62. I. Adams & M. Somerville, *op. cit.*, pp. 137–38; M. Fry, *loc., cit.*, p. 66–7.

ing in the region. Second, and most crucial, no effort whatsoever was made to regulate the actions of landlords; indeed, it was accepted that 'it is impossible for a moment to think of restraining the owners of lands in the free and absolute disposal of them'. In reality this meant that the partnership was largely one-sided, with landlords simply relying on state assistance when their own estate management regimes induced mass emigration.[63] Nonetheless, its obvious weaknesses do not mean that the kind of partnership envisaged for the Highlands should be dismissed instantly. Its importance lies rather in the fact that by providing an up-to-date justification for the maintenance of tenantry, it was in part responsible for the forty-year time lag between the landlords' adoption of commercial land practices and their eventual decision to abandon the idea of a numerous estate population. Though certainly never instrumental in preventing departures on a large scale, the patriotic partnership can be seen as one explanation of the intermittent and cyclical pattern that characterised the region's emigration experience from 1760 to 1815.

Co-operation between the state and Highland proprietors got off to a good start. During the American Revolutionary War major landlords received a disproportionate amount of military patronage. Another central plank in this alliance was the disannexation of estates forfeited in 1746; indeed, this had commenced prior to the war when Simon Fraser of Lovat received his father's estate on the understanding that he 'give small farms at low rents . . . to stop emigrations' – a policy which, ironically, he did not pursue on the estate of Lovat itself but implemented instead on his other, recently purchased estate of Morar.[64] This was tacit recognition on the part of government that its own efforts to introduce improvement had failed, and that, for the future, economic progress in the region was best implemented by private landowners with a certain element of state support. Total disannexation eventually occurred in 1784; yet government had in fact earlier demonstrated its commitment to the retention of Highland population. As it suffered its last major eighteenth-century subsistence crisis, a report to the Commons in May 1784 highlighted that the Highlands required assistance of £74,679. Although relief was intended primarily to prevent starvation in the short term, its aim in the longer term was the avoidance of an upturn in emigration. In all, Westminster spent £17,700 – equivalent to nearly 25% of the region's entire needs. Furthermore, this total did not include the deliberate maintenance of Highland fencible regiments upon full pay in order to lessen the impact of hundreds of demobilised men returning to stricken areas.[65] In

63. S.R.O., Melville Castle Muniments, GD 51/52/2.
64. *Caledonian Mercury*, 14 February 1774. I am grateful to Dr. Rob Clyde for this reference. For Fraser's tenurial strategy in Morar for 'preserving the ancient inhabitants of this country as a nursery for the army', see S.R.O., Fraser-Macintosh Collection, GD 128/32/3.
65. Parliamentary Papers, 1846, XXVII, *Documents Relative to the Distress in Scotland 1783*, pp. 501, 509–10; N.L.S., Sutherland Papers, Dep. 313/3499; A.U.L., Gordon Military Papers, Ms 2284/35.

assessing the development of the Highlands during the first phase of Clearance, this culture of anticipated state intervention should not be underestimated. As late as 1817 proprietors in the North-West called upon government to meet obligations brought upon it by the population's heavy involvement in state service. One landlord argued: 'The claim on government is much strengthened by the fact that a considerable part of the population never contributed anything to the advantage of the proprietors, though furnished a great number of excellent seamen and soldiers to government' and that '. . . it is to be kept in view that there is not only a great surplus population in these islands, but a very large proportion of it are totally unconnected with the landholders, that is to say chiefly the individuals returning from public service'.[66]

The years immediately after the defeat in America witnessed the creation of various mechanisms that put what was, after all, an informal arrangement upon a more secure footing. In 1786 Dundas unsuccessfully attempted to represent proprietary interests by securing a permanent ban upon emigration from the British Isles. The foundation of the British Fisheries Society and a 1785 parliamentary report on that industry were evidence that government intended giving practical backing to the pro-population stance of landlords. In 1787 further evidence of the benefits that could accrue to the region's elite through close ties with the state came in the form of two new Highland regiments destined for India, and the East India Company's subsequent promotion of subscriptions for the British Fisheries Society which yielded an eventual donation of £6,000. Above all, the formation of the Highland Society in early 1784 should be seen as the creation of the lobbying organisation that represented the landlord side of the patriotic partnership.[67] Even as the new century arrived and emigration again appeared in the region, there was evidence that the underlying military rationale behind government involvement in the region was still a potent factor. The successful attempt by Highland landlords to obtain a ban on emigration in 1801–3 has already been highlighted as convincing proof of their ability to influence the pre-reformed legislature of Great Britain.[68] Indeed, the Passenger Act campaign was in many ways the apogee of the landlords' use of the patriotic partnership. By June 1801 the Highland Society had begun to question how renewed emigration might be tackled. On 3 July a committee was formed, and its opening statements illustrate how patriotism was to prove vital in legitimising the ban. It proposed that support be sought from Frederick, Duke of York: by which means it hoped to ally their cause with an important national

66. A.U.L., Material Relating to British Fisheries Societies, Ms 2015; Ms 2023.
67. S.R.O., Gillanders of Highfield Papers, GD 427/3066; A.U.L., Material Relating to British Fisheries Society, Ms 960; Ms 962; N.L.S., Adv. Ms 20.5.5., p. 2; S.R.O., Maclaine of Lochbuie Papers, GD 174/1329/28; S.R.O., RH4/188/1, pp. 38–41; J. Dunlop, *The British Fisheries Society, 1786–1893* (Edinburgh, 1978), pp. 20, 23–5.
68. E. Richards, loc. cit., vol. 2, p. 207; J. Hunter, loc. cit., pp. 23–25.

military figure. On 21 January 1802 the Society voted to send its first report to the administration of Henry Addington. Immediately after, and again in order to emphasise its patriotism, the meeting's next vote was to thank the 42nd Highland Regiment for its part in the Egyptian campaign, the outcome of which, many believed, had been vital in saving the empire in India and in bringing Napoleon to the peace table.[69]

By February 1802 initial contacts had seemed promising, yet there remained deep-seated fears amongst proprietors that government would fail to respond sufficiently. This explains several features of the anti-emigration campaign. First, Society members felt that the report needed 'to be touched with gentle hands': polite phraseology for avoiding the impression that commercial self-interest motivated the outcry against emigration. In this respect the issues of poor trans-Aatlantic shipping conditions and military recruitment played the same role – namely, of diverting attention from the kelping agenda. Second, the prominent Highland lairds on the Society's committee on emigration were Sir James Grant, Fraser of Farrline and Grant of Rothiemurchus. The low profile of the large kelping landlords in the official campaign reveals a sensitivity to charges of private gain at the expense of legal rights of movement within the empire. Moreover, the government's attitude suggested that this sensitivity was warranted. The Peace of Amiens was signed in March 1802; yet at the end of the same month the Home Secretary, Thomas Pelham, informed Ranald MacDonnell of Glengarry that the administration, while considering legislation desirable, did not think it legally possible. This official reluctance simply meant that landlords became all the more convinced that the military dimension was the one sure method of guaranteeing action at Westminster.[70]

This is evident in the second Society report sent to London on 9 July 1802. Even more than the first, its terminology was that of empire and the state. The aim of the Society, the report noted, was not the accumulation of private property and wealth, 'but the extension of productiveness and enlargement of the population of the Highlands which would be a boon to the wealth and efficient strength which constitute the greatness of the British empire'. It stressed the revenue that would accrue as well as the contribution 'in a still greater degree than at present to its naval and military force'.[71] The tendency to make population the primary concern reveals the extent to which demography, as much as commercial progress, dominated debate on the Highlands' economic development. As it was, the government was still not persuaded to act. Indeed, in mid-November 1802 it refused to impose additional tariffs on foreign kelp. This was despite the fact that from as early as September 1801, landlords such as Macdonald of Sleat had noted

69. S.R.O., RH 4/188/2, pp. 44, 443, 498–505 and 523.
70. S.R.O., RH 4/188/2, p. 443; RH 4/188/4, f. 38; S.R.O., RH 2/4/218, f. 151; RH. 2/4/222, f. 167.
71. S.R.O., RH 4/188/2, p. 531.

that if the industry continued to be unprofitable, then the populations it sustained would need to emigrate. In all, the campaign of 1801–2 demonstrated the limitations of government action in peacetime. In May 1803 war broke out again; and in an illustration of the connection between emigration and war the Passenger Act was passed in June 1803. Conflict, as already noted, allowed government intervention on grounds of national defence. The whole context of the emigration debate thus altered with the recommencement of hostilities. Selkirk highlighted this when he noted that 'In a period of great and imminent national danger, the reflection may occur, as it has in fact, to men whose opinions deserve the highest respect that any exclusive attention to commercial improvement may lead to pernicious consequences'.[72]

The final push for legislation was articulated in a third report by the Society as well as in the conclusions of Thomas Telford in November 1802. This third report continued to emphasise the patriotic dimension and listed the government's priorities. The army and navy came first, then agricultural improvement, then fishing, and finally kelp. The nature of the war made the prevention of emigration all the more urgent. The early years of the Napoleonic conflict were, from the British point of view, defensive. Contemporary military theory stressed that defensive war required more men: indeed, the legislation that established the first national census stressed how defence naturally required more manpower reserves.[73] Again, the Highland Society emphasised the region's martial abilities in order to tie in with national defence concerns. Defence in Britain meant, first and foremost, the navy. The Society, under the leadership of the fifth Duke of Argyll, commenced a fund of £1,000 to train West Highland gentry for the navy. Thus the seafaring populations of Gaeldom could be drawn into Britain's single most important military sector. This tactic was also applied to the army. On 24 June 1803, as the Passenger Act worked its way through Parliament, the Society's whole meeting concentrated upon recruitment. As a result, the meeting opened a subscription 'for encouraging a certain description of young men then preparing for emigrating to America to enter regiments of the line or the navy'.[74]

The orchestrated campaign of the Society was paralleled by more general attempts to portray emigration as retarding military effectiveness. Throughout 1801 Sir James Grant, in his capacity as Lord Lieutenant of Inverness-shire, highlighted the loss of men from volunteer companies while, more generally, it was argued that emigration agents were 'crimps' who manipulated dislike of the militia to generate dangerous levels of disaffection.[75] This

72. C.D.T.L., GD 221/4180/15; T. Douglas, *op. cit.* p. 76.
73. J.E. Cookson, *The British Armed Nation, 1793–1815* (Oxford, 1997), pp. 45, 96; L. Colley, *op. cit.* 289.
74. S.R.O., RH 1/188/2, pp. 16, 27, 546, 643.
75. S.R.O., Seafield Muniments, GD 248/3410/10/11; GD 248/1530, p. 40; S.R.O., Melville Castle Muniments, GD 51/52/4.

suggests that while the issue of humanitarian concern has traditionally been seen as the smoke screen used by landlords to divert attention from their real commercial agenda, the recruitment and defence question clearly lay at the very heart of attempts to first bring about and then legitimise the Passenger Act.

A natural corollary of this reliance on the military issue was the expectation that the state would act in a proactive manner and provide employment opportunities for those denied the option of departing for North America. This in turn explains the particular importance attached in the Highlands to the fencible and volunteer establishments. From their very inception in 1794, estate advisers like Colonel John Macleod of Talisker noted that volunteer units would be ideal in preventing emigration. Ranald Macdonald of Ulva argued that the social problems of under-employment and partial redundancy which were expressed in the form of emigration could be ameliorated by creating a new military role for the region's numerous tenantry. In North Uist, Lieutenant Ewan Macdonald of Griminish argued that problems of private estate management such as over-population and lack of vacant tenancies could be solved by creating a large number of local volunteer companies.[76]

In essence, volunteering was seen in the Highlands less as a British defence mechanism and more as a form of state social provision, ideally suited to addressing the area's structural socio-economic problems. Such responses to the opportunities thrown up by the proliferation of defence forces in the Revolutionary and Napoleonic period show clearly that Highland elites yielded to nobody in their ability to colonise the fiscal-military state and turn it to their own particular advantage. This statist approach is mirrored in a real appreciation of the impact of regular military pay, however poorly it compared with civilian wages. According to the tacksman of Kyles Bernera in North Uist, such companies helped 'tenants to pay their rents and reconcile emigrants to their native country'. Likewise, several commentators pointed to the loss of the £5 per annum in volunteer pay as a major contributory factor in the sudden upturn in emigration during the short period of peace between 1801 and 1803. This explains why the disbandment of volunteers in the spring of 1802 was widely criticised as a counter-productive cost-saving exercise that simply stimulated further losses in valuable population. In December 1802 Sir James Grant argued that although the reduction of the volunteers had been an acceptable policy for Scotland as a whole, their somewhat different social role in the North of Scotland meant that their demobilisation had prompted the re-emergence of large-scale emigration.[77]

76. S.R.O., Melville Castle Muniments, GD 51/1/1986; GD 51/52/2, 5–7; S.R.O., Seafield Muniments, GD 1526, letter 16 September 1794; GD 248/1527, letter 29 November 1796, Lieutenant Ewen Macdonald-Grant; GD 248/1531, pp. 107–8
77. C.D.T.L., GD 221/815; S.R.O., Maclaine of Lochbuie Papers, GD 174/1426/60; S.R.O., Melville Castle Muniments, GD 51/52/4; S.R.O., Seafield Muniments, GD 248/1530, pp. 104–6; GD 248/1531, pp. 109–110; GD 248/1532, pp. 1–2.

The Military and Highland Emigration, 1763–1815   199

Similar sentiments lay behind requests in 1801 by companies in Skye and Strathspey for their services to be continued, despite the forthcoming peace. When in April 1803 volunteer units were again established, offers from Arisaig, Sleat and the Small Isles were forwarded with the recommendation that approval would stem the depopulation of these areas. Adding to these calls for a regionally adjusted use of government employment was Lord Advocate Robert Dundas, who attempted in August 1803 to get fencible regiments, as opposed to a compulsory militia, restored as the primary defence force in the Highlands.[78]

Running in parallel, therefore, with the public work schemes, such as the Caledonian Canal set up in the aftermath of the Passenger Act, was a less high-profile push from the localities for the implementation of a recruiting policy that dovetailed official defence needs with the elite's desire to stem emigration. It was, above all, on the Island of Skye that state service in the form of volunteering was most obviously developed as an anti-emigration mechanism and as the means of mitigating the effects of landlordism. In 1803 the island presented 30 offers to raise local units – 3,200 men in all. Because it was anxious to restrict the growth of volunteering in order that other forms of recruitment deemed more efficient could produce enough men, the government stated that it would only allow volunteer numbers equivalent to six times the county quota for militia men. In Skye this resulted in only 400 men being approved as volunteers in the initial re-mobilisation of 1803 – less than half the 811 men who had served prior to 1802. The result was a storm of petitioning from Inverness-shire's M.P. Sir Charles Grant, Sir James Grant the Lord Lieutenant and lairds like Lieutenant-Colonel Alexander Macdonald of Lyndale, all asking for an increase in the number of companies in Skye. Lyndale highlighted the fact that there were over 570 people who had intended emigrating from Skye but who had been prevented by the introduction of the Passenger Act. Eventually, in late September 1803, despite the government's attempts to minimise volunteer expansion, a new Skye battalion of 500 men was approved, only to be followed in January 1804 by further concessions allowing an additional 20 men per company in the pre-existing Skye units.[79] In all, this strategy of linking state employment to the prevention of emigration was a noticeable success, and tangible proof of the material benefits that could arise from fostering a close partnership with government. The result was that Inverness-shire's volunteer establishment expanded by 26%, or 700 men – all of whom were enrolled in the western areas most associated with emigration.

Yet the government's willingness to focus military employment quite deliberately upon regions susceptible to population loss was extremely

78. S.R.O., RH 2/4/88, f. 243; S.R.O., Seafield Muniments, GD 248/1530, pp. 135–7, 152; GD 248/1532, pp. 126–7, 178–80; GD 248/1533, pp. 27, 65.
79. S.R.O., Seafield Muniments, GD 248/1532, pp. 220, 237, 308; GD 248/1533, pp. 65, 108–9, 163–4, 287; GD 248/1534, pp. 36–39, 85; GD 248/1535, pp. 21–2.

short-lived. As recruiting mechanisms adapted to the altogether different scale and duration of the war against France, so the idea of approving military units merely on the basis of particular social requirements was rendered untenable. Instead, compulsory recruitment was introduced with a view to supplying the line forces with regular and assured quotas of recruits from militia regiments. Under these arrangements 'the coercive power of the state ought to apply equally to every part of the Kingdom; and as the arable are capable of maintaining more men than the grazing districts, the operation of such a law ought to bear upon them in proportion'.[80] One immediate result of the change in British recruiting methods was that local, part-time military employment, proportionally a far more important element of the Highland economy than in other developed areas of Scotland, went into rapid decline from 1808 onwards. In that year it was decided that the British volunteer establishment of over 1,300 individual corps was to be replaced with only 270 local militia battalions, directly controlled and financed by the state rather than through local elite or proprietary influence. In Inverness-shire over 1,150 men were left surplus after the creation of these new units. Thereafter, these men found their volunteer units were progressively run down and denied clothing allowances or lucrative periods on permanent service. It was the same Sutherland: in 1804 volunteering provided part-time but secure employment for over 1,000 men, but by 1812 the local militia battalion stood at only 400 men, prompting one estate official to bemoan the drift of military policy. 'I am sorry we are restricted to 400, as many fine lads offering their services were reluctantly rejected.'[81] From a Highland perspective, therefore, the emergence of systematic forms of compulsory recruitment meant that the kind of state employment opportunities that had formed one element of the patriotic partnership were actually curtailed by the state itself. Indeed, although commercial and estate management policies were primarily responsible for the increasing reluctance of Gaels to enter military service, the state itself was involved in abolishing the particular forms of local military employment that had maintained living standards and the overall economic viability of large sections of the region's population. The new forms of recruiting policy introduced by the British state between 1803 and 1812 had the same effect as the landlords' adoption of commercial pastoralism inasmuch as both accentuated the redundancy of Highland tenantry.[82]

The policy of levying recruits in proportion to population was crucial in that it lowered the economic value of Highland populations at a time of

80. J.E. Cookson, *op. cit.*, pp. 116–118; J. Robertson, *A General View of the Agriculture of the County of Inverness* (London, 1808), pp. 331–332n.
81. J.E. Cookson, *op. cit.*, pp. 87–9; S.R.O., Seafield Muniments, GD 248/1537, pp. 156–61, 215, 386, 408; GD 248/1538, pp. 167, 170–1, 176–7; N.L.S., Sutherland Papers, Dep. 313/747/18; Dep. 313/3277/4; Dep. 313/3289/3, 9; Dep. 313/3290/4.
82. J. Prebble, *op. cit.*, pp. 100–1.

ongoing realignment in elite attitudes towards maintaining large numbers of tenantry. As a prominent theorist who wished to revise accepted thinking, which saw a numerous tenantry as a sign of patriotic responsibility and commercial productivity, Thomas Douglas, fifth Earl of Selkirk was conscious that the single most damaging accusation against his promotion of emigration was that it had a decidedly negative effect upon Britain's military strength. Indeed, Selkirk conceded that he had finalised his emigrationist theories prior to the outbreak of war in 1793. However, given the premium on military manpower and the region's reputation in that particular regard, he had postponed publication of his ideas. Aware that 'among the effects of emigration there is none that has been more lamented than the loss of that valuable supply of soldiers which the public service has hitherto derived from the Highlands', Selkirk understood the need to directly address this military dimension. It is surely no coincidence that in 1808 he published a pamphlet espousing a type of universal recruiting system that mobilised men equally across the United Kingdom and created the huge force necessary to rival the French level of war commitment. Though Selkirk's method differed from that actually introduced by the government, both versions avoided reliance on any particular area and, instead, produced an overall number of men that made the contribution of the northern region only a small, insignificant percentage. In effect, recruiting methods were increasingly put in place that undermined the army's need to rely on the Highlands to the extent it had done in the past. Above all, by demonstrating the region's demographic insignificance, and the reality that the Highlander was but a small part of a much larger national effort, Selkirk helped remove the allegation that emigration could 'militate against the best interests of [the] country'.[83] In doing so, he, perhaps even more immediately than Thomas Malthus, was vital in furthering the process whereby Highland elites reversed their anti-emigration stance during the decade or so after 1803.

Conclusion

The issue of military strength and recruiting productivity lay at the centre of the debate on Highland depopulation during the period of first-phase Clearance. The region's distinctive links with the imperial British military were paradoxical in that they served to expedite emigration through military settlement while simultaneously providing justification for efforts to retain Highlanders in the region for future use as soldiers. Not only did military land grants in 1763 and 1783 constitute an important staging post in the development of trans-Atlantic contacts, but the Gaels' use of this sector of public policy raises wider questions regarding the nature of the Highland

---

83. T. Douglas, *op. cit.*, pp. 6, 63–78; T. Douglas, *On the Necessity of a More Effectual System of National Defence and the Means of Establishing the Permanent Security of the Kingdom* (London, 1808), pp. 17–25.

Diaspora in this period. Attention has usually focused on the backward-looking, 'conservative', peasant mentality exhibited by emigrants, emphasising the process as simply indicative of a wider inability on the part of the region's population to adapt to inclusion within the empire. However, that the army often, in effect, subsidised emigration from the area calls into question the idea that Highlanders were simply incapable of envisaging and implementing positive responses to imperial opportunities in the same way, as say, their Lowland counterparts. That many Highlanders relied upon finding enterprise opportunities and social advancement within the framework of state employment and military re-settlement in the colonies, as opposed to the private, entrepreneurial avenues of the tobacco or sugar trade does not detract from the fact that they were obviously capable of constructing specialised strategies designed to derive material benefits from British imperialism.[84]

Ironically, the state formed an equally important part of the landlord response to mass emigration. Burdened with chronically under-capitalised tenants and poor land, Highland proprietors found that their efforts to initiate improvements produced alarming levels of emigration that, in turn, sparked hostile external assessment of their actions. Under these circumstances landlords responded positively to overtures by government officials like Dundas who suggested a partnership whereby they would reap the benefits of military and colonial office in return for the state's use of their tenantry. This regionally adjusted approach to the containment of emigration not only facilitated the commercial exploitation of tenantry through various labour-intensive industries, but had the additional benefit of allowing landlords to broaden the underdeveloped economy by including a significant element of state employment. Thus, while a desire on the part of later eighteenth-century Highlands landlords to retain large numbers of tenantry can undoubtedly be explained in part as a cultural hangover from the days of clanship, it was also the result of an entirely contemporary and rational strategy for furthering commercial progress.[85] Government-sponsored schemes to curtail emigration, such as canal and road building, certainly had little real effect, although we should remember that volunteering in the region was used by governments for the same purpose and to much better effect, not least because it was applied directly to localities like Skye most immediately affected by population loss. This suggests that the influence of the state may have been greater than previously supposed. Yet it was through its influence with the landlords, the only true dictators of conditions on the ground, that the fiscal-military state made its significant impact on Highland emigration. Although perhaps indirectly, the state and its military

84. E. Richards, 'Scotland and the Uses of the Atlantic Empire', pp. 92–5; J.M. Bumsted, *op. cit.*, p. 46; A.I. Macinnes, *Clanship, Commerce and the House of Stuart, 1603–1788* (East Linton, 1996), p. 232.
85. E. Richards, *A History of the Highland* Clearances: *Agrarian Change and the Evictions, 1746–1886*, vol. 1, pp. 145–6.

interests formed a major element in the wider debate on Highland emigration, and this in turn resulted in a strategy that represented the nearest British equivalent to the type of interventionist attitude seen in Europe towards the social consequences of agrarian improvement.[86] However, in the longer term such a strategy was partly responsible for the seesawing in approaches to the issue of Highland demography. Both government and landlords exhibited this mentality, which, in turn, ensured the excessive retention of population and, later, their subsequent removal in an equally excessive over-compensation. Indeed, the whole concept of a patriotic partnership during the period 1775–1815 served merely to make the emigration experience of the Highlands more extreme than it might otherwise have been.

---

86. T.M. Devine, 'Social Responses to Agrarian "Improvement": the Highland and Lowland Clearances in Scotland', in R.A. Houston & I.D. Whyte (eds.), *Scottish Society, 1500–1800* (Cambridge, 1989), pp. 150–52.

CHAPTER SEVEN

Military Service and British Identity in the Highlands, 1746–1815

The nature and extent of Highland identification with Britishness in the last half of the eighteenth century up until Waterloo has been closely associated with the region's military contribution to the British army. The reasons for this particular link are twofold. First, wider British identity itself is generally taken to have received a substantial stimulus from the prolonged series of wars with Catholic continental states that punctuated the period from 1688 to 1815. The overwhelmingly alien and invariably hostile 'others' of France and Spain served as a rallying point for a sense of common Protestantism which not only bridged the mutually suspicious religious traditions of Presbyterianism and Anglicanism, but also slowly, over time, became the foundation for an exclusivist British nationalism. The unprecedented scale of the French Revolutionary and Napoleonic Wars saw this connection between military conflict and identity formation achieve an altogether new dynamism and depth. As the French put concepts of nation and citizenship at the heart of military service motivation so, in reply, British elites consciously sought to expose the population and the mass of armed volunteers to ideas of wider loyalty, beyond village, county or even older centres of national allegiance such as Scotland. This process of replacing historic and mutually antagonistic Scottish and English chauvinisms had already been expedited by disproportionate Scots involvement in a system of imperial spoils which expanded considerably through the acquisition and subsequent defence of colonial territory and trade. Commercial profits arising from this state-led aggression against foreign markets not only provided the practical buttressing for Britain's military-economic power, but also heightened its attractiveness to certain groups, including many Scots, who otherwise would not have found the new nation necessarily deserving of their loyalty. In both an ideological and material sense, therefore, war underpinned the development of British identity as a whole, and ensured that the definition of its constituent parts and their exact degree of Britishness was often, though by no means exclusively, measured by evidence of military participation and loyalty.[1]

1. L. Colley, *Britons: Forging the Nation, 1707–1832* (London, 1992), pp. 56, 70–71, 83, 125–127, 365–68; P.J. Marshall, 'A Nation defined by Empire, 1755–1776', in A. Grant & K. J. Stringer (eds.), *Uniting the Kingdom? The Making of British History* (London, 1995), p. 209.

The second, more specific link between army service and the Highlands' sense of Britishness arose from the fact that the militarism inherent in concepts of Britain had particularly strong if somewhat distinctive credentials within the region. Large-scale and disproportionate recruitment in the period after Culloden, especially in the form of Highland regiments, has traditionally been seen as perhaps the single most obvious symptom of the region's increasingly British status, and, indeed, of a supposedly farsighted and philanthropic desire on the part of political leaders such as William Pitt the Elder to find a productive and worthwhile role for Gaeldom within the Union. Involvement in the army certainly facilitated the rehabilitation and reconciliation of prominent Jacobite families such as the Frasers of Lovat, and the Mackenzies of Cromartie and Seaforth, as well as the Camerons of Locheil and Macphersons of Cluny. High-profile regiment-raising during the Seven Years War and against American colonists not only demonstrated their commitment to the Hanoverian state, parliamentary supremacy and authoritarian imperialism, but also ensured the return of family properties forfeited in the late 1740s through the Jacobite delinquency of their predecessors.[2] Moreover, the mass enlistment of rank-and-file Gaels within the army is also taken to have assisted a more general reassessment of the Highlander's status within British society. Whereas in 1745–6 the Gaels were confirmed in Lowland Scottish and English opinion as barbaric, alien, and non-British to the extent of actively co-operating with the national enemy, by 1815 their record of military service ensured that the Highland soldier emerged as the morally untainted and exemplary defender of Britain, its constitution and empire.[3]

Yet however well established this link between British identity and Highland military service appears in theory and in practice, it should not be accepted uncritically. First, emphasis on the rehabilitation of a select number of Jacobite families, while certainly providing concrete evidence of elite reconciliation with Britain's political establishment, cannot really serve, as it often has done, as an argument that the region's British identity received a major stimulus and firm framework within which to develop. Beyond that specific example there are more fundamental questions. Ideas of what, exactly, 'military service' entailed surely need clearer and more careful definition. Enlistment in the regular line regiments, for instance, should not be equated simply with what was, after all, the British military machine's largest area of expansion – the home defence establishment, more particularly the volunteer corps of 1794–1808. This demarcation between local and

2. D.M. Henderson, *Highland Soldier: A Social Study of the Highland Regiments, 1820–1920* (Edinburgh, 1989), p. 51; B. P. Lenman, *The Jacobite Clans of the Great Glen, 1650–1784* (Edinburgh, 1984), pp. 179, 202, 208.
3. T.M. Devine, *Clanship to Crofters' War: The Social Transformation of the Scottish Highlands* (Manchester, 1994), pp. 91–93; M. Fry, *The Dundas Despotism* (Edinburgh, 1992), pp. 137–9; R. Clyde, *From Rebel to Hero: The Image of the Highlander, 1745–1830* (East Linton, 1996), pp. 150, 176–177.

imperial service needs to be applied particularly to Scotland, where the cult of the line regiment, especially the Highland regiment, has tended to dominate ideas of what British military service actually entailed. Furthermore, this shift in focus makes the link between Britishness and armed service seem far less straightforward in two particular ways. First, it inevitably detaches involvement in the army from particular spheres of operation, such as Ireland and the empire as a whole, which were more obviously linked to a 'British' context, and, instead, places the whole issue of military enlistment within a more parochial and less obviously national framework. Second, the argument that mass volunteering was vital in generating a genuinely widespread sense of Britishness has, itself, not gone unchallenged. Alternative perspectives have emerged which highlight the local motivations that, more often than not, underlay apparently selfless commitment to Britain's defence. A prominent dynamic within English urban volunteering, for example, was a desire on the part of town elites to demonstrate their growing political, economic and social importance to established and largely rural county oligarchs.[4]

Critical analysis of service motivation, therefore, raises the fundamental question of just how far being part of the various sectors of Britain's military machine made the Gael seem more British to non-Gaels, and, more importantly, how far such disproportionate involvement was symptomatic of a genuine identification with the idea of Great Britain on the part of ordinary Highlanders. Highlighting the often implicit social and economic particularisms which shaped the contours and pattern of military service constitutes a more realistic and less deterministic method of understanding the exact relationship between the army and the Highlands' identity or identities. We need, also, to place military service within a broader socio-economic context. For example, beyond attempting to explain the apparent collapse of recruitment in the region in the early 1800s as largely symptomatic of Highland Clearance, there has been a tendency to compartmentalise the military theme and define its impact on Highland identity in isolation from other major political, economic and social forces operating within the region.[5] The weakness of this approach is that it neglects the possibility that additional factors which served to confirm the British character of the Highlands, such as Improvement and Protestantism, may not in fact have operated alongside recruitment or indeed with each other in a particularly synchronised, or even complementary, way. The various ideas of geography, rural romance and social development which increasingly shaped Lowland

---

4. For a particularly useful revision of the argument on military service and identity, see J.E. Cookson, *The British Armed Nation* (Oxford, 1997), pp. 7–8, 10; J.E. Cookson, 'The English Volunteer Movement of the French Wars, 1793–1815: Some Contexts', in *The Historical Journal*, vol. 32 (1989), pp. 878–9.
5. E. Richards, *A History of the Highland Clearances: Agrarian Change and the Evictions, 1746–1886*, vol. 1 (London, 1982), pp. 141–157; R. Clyde, *op. cit.*, pp. 88, 172–73.

and English attitudes to the region, were, themselves, highly contradictory – representing in fact 'a combination of opposites'.[6]

This suggests that directly equating Highland involvement in the nation's armed forces with Britishness cannot be assumed to be an entirely convincing or coherent argument. To assess the impact of the Highlanders' participation within the military sphere it is important not only to contrast recruitment with other contemporaneous social and cultural developments, but also to understand how the issue of the Gaels' identity involved two distinct perspectives, external and internal. Thus, while considerable attention has focused on how Lowland Scotland and England began to see the Highlander and the Highlands as somehow British, this in itself is insufficient. Attempts must also be made to understand whether Gaels themselves identified in any sense with Britain and how, if at all, their military service was evidence of this process.

Evangelical Presbyterianism, Militarism and Britishness

The interaction of evangelical Presbyterianism with military service and commercial improvement in supposedly engendering a sense of British identity within the region points to the need for a more cautious approach when endowing Protestantism with 'nation-forging' properties. Initially, Protestantism's central role in the formation of Britishness seems entirely convincing. The largely passive but unmistakably hostile reaction of central Lowland Scotland in 1745 to Charles Edward Stuart's religious convictions mirrored that of England, and represented only one particular example of the genuine antipathy felt by the majority of Scotland's population towards Catholicism. The mobbing sparked by the prospect of Roman Catholic relief in 1778, for example, actually began in Scotland, and if not on the scale of the Gordon riots in London was just as indicative of ongoing and deep-seated anti-Catholic sentiment.[7] However, this idea of a 'common Protestantism' binding Scotland and England together has been criticised for failing to take sufficient account of the different religious opinions that existed north of the border. The obvious divide between Presbyterianism and Anglicanism may indeed have mattered little when confronted with the power of Catholic or atheistic revolutionary France, yet there remains little evidence that a majority of Scottish Presbyterians ever abandoned their distinctly suspicious attitude towards the nature of English church government. Opposition to the 1712 Patronage Act, for instance, remained widespread in every sense of the

6. For a useful discussion of the various strands within Highlandism and, indeed, within the concept of Improvement itself, see P. Womack, *Improvement and Romance: Constructing the Myth of the Highlands* (Edinburgh, 1989), p. 3; C.W.J. Withers, 'The Historical Creation of the Scottish Highlands', in I. Donnachie & C. Whatley (eds.), *The Manufacture of Scottish History* (Edinburgh, 1992), p. 152.
7. M. Fry, *op. cit.*, pp. 76–7.

word: geographic, social and chronological. Even the highly 'emulative patriotism' of North Britishness, with its conscious enthusiasm for increased assimilation with England, was, nevertheless, characterised to an extent by ongoing Scottish particularism as a direct result of such Presbyterian concerns.[8]

Within this context the rise of evangelicalism in the Highlands can be seen to have helped shape external attitudes towards the region and, moreover, how Highlanders themselves formulated their own particular perspectives of Britain. Yet the growth of evangelical Protestantism was by no means inevitable or indeed consistent across the North of Scotland. The region remained largely unaffected by the Secessions of 1739 and 1761; while the ongoing presence of local Catholic and Episcopalian majorities demonstrated that even established Presbyterianism, with distinct advantages over dissenting evangelicalism, had nevertheless failed to establish anything like complete control.[9] However, the preaching practices of many evangelical ministers and dissenters in particular, which placed deliberate emphasis on lay individuals disseminating the gospel within the home, were undoubtedly attuned to conditions in large, thinly populated Highland parishes. Aside from this practical point, their religious message undoubtedly found special resonance within communities already breaking up under the pressures of socio-economic change, rent increases, tenurial innovation, and large-scale recruitment and emigration. In an age of cultural bewilderment and alienation, with traditional social relationships collapsing or suffering under elite indifference, evangelicalism's emphasis on the need for dedicated pastoral attention from ministers and lay religious elites must have seemed particularly attractive. The decline of the tacksman's social role as local manager and go-between undoubtedly stimulated the desire for alternative leadership.[10] The widespread disgust of tenantry in Urquhart in 1773 at their minister's self-confessed unwillingness to catechise their children was probably born in part of this search for new active, local leadership. Similarly high expectations were also apparent throughout Argyllshire in 1797 when the Relief Church minister the Reverend Niel Douglas criticised established

---

8. The most convincing feature of the argument that common Protestantism did not necessarily serve as a unifying force for Scotland and England is the fact that Scottish historians who disagree over the nature of Scottish identity in this period nevertheless agree on this particular point. See R.J. Finlay, 'Caledonia or North Britain?: Scottish Identity in the Eighteenth Century', in D. Brown, R.J. Finlay and M. Lynch (eds.), *Image and Identity: The Making and Re-making of Scotland through the Ages* (Edinburgh, 1998), p. 151; C. Kidd, 'North Britishness and the Nature of Eighteenth Century British Patriotisms', in *Historical Journal*, vol. 39 (1996), pp. 362–65, 377.
9. R. Clyde, *op. cit.*, pp. 57–59.
10. T.M. Devine, *Clanship to Crofters' War*, pp. 103–4. For a particularly detailed description on how *Na Daoine* ('The Men') operated effectively in local communities, see Alexander Stewart, *An Account of a Late Revival of Religion in a part of the Highlands of Scotland* (Edinburgh, 1800), pp. 20–27.

ministers for failing to impart much-sought-after religious instruction and comfort.[11]

Evangelical ministers and dissenting lay preachers thus found many, though by no means all, Highland districts receptive to their particular brand of gospel message. Their preaching, however, raises questions about the extent to which evangelical Protestantism promoted a truly British vision of the region. For example, it served to undermine the Gaels' traditional adulation of martial deeds. Conventional poetry, such as that of Duncan Ban Macintyre, continued to exult in the valour and honour of military conflict but found increasing competition in the spiritual emphasis of the evangelical poets. To the latter, the battle was now for the soul and victory in the form of personal redemption and salvation. Highland evangelicalism can be said to have constituted an increasingly powerful local counter-culture to the Lowland and English image of the Gael as an enthusiastic British warrior.[12]

Committed spiritual leadership could also bring military service and evangelicalism into direct conflict. The anti-Erastian expectations of many congregations ensured a certain tension over the participation of ministers in obviously secular activities. As the search for personal grace and salvation formed the ultimate focus of evangelical teaching, so involvement in worldly affairs on the part of ministers became increasingly unacceptable in some quarters. This is significant, given the overall administrative importance of ministers within rural communities in general. Intimation from the pulpit constituted one of the primary means whereby the dictates of estate policy were actually passed on to the population at large: indeed, this role of estate messenger may have alienated local populations and paved the way for adherence to evangelical teachings.[13] More specifically, with the eclipse of the tacksman, ministers formed an increasingly vital element in persuading communities to co-operate with the recruiting demands of their landlords. In 1756, the minister of Ruthven in Badenoch offered the men of his congregation one guinea to join the Highland regiment. In 1778 the Reverend Thomas Ross of Kilmonavaig conducted negotiations between local recruits and the fourth Duke of Gordon; while in the parish of Laggan warnings of eviction were issued from the pulpit in response to the Duke's lack of success there.[14]

11. S.R.O., Seafield Muniments, GD 248/226/2/91 & 93; N. Douglas, *Journal of a Mission to Parts of the Highlands of Scotland in Summer and Harvest, 1797* (Edinburgh, 1799), pp. 14–15.
12. A. Macleod (ed.), *The Songs of Duncan Ban Macintyre* (Edinburgh, 1952), p. 569; R. Clyde, *op. cit.*, pp. 86–89.
13. For the importance of ministers in implementing estate management on the estates of Lovat, Coigach and Assynt during the 1760s and 1770s, see S.R.O., F.E.P. E769/79/39; E769/91/163(1); E746/113/23(1) & 24; N.L.S., Fletcher of Saltoun Papers, Ms 17589, f. 88; N.L.S., Sutherland Papers, Dep. 313/1106/ unnumbered letter dated Dunrobin, 2 January 1773, James Sutherland to John Mackenzie of Delvine; N.L.S., Mackenzie of Delvine Papers, Ms 1485, f. 70.
14. *Scots Magazine*, vol. 18 (Edinburgh, 1756), p. 196; S.R.O. Gordon Castle Muniments, GD 44/25/7/21/2; GD 44/27/12/13/3.

Nor were these isolated incidents. The synod of Argyll during 1759, the ministers of Kilmoraick in 1757, Barvas in 1779, Abernethy, Duthill, Urquhart and Killin in 1793 and Appin in 1804 were all involved either in compiling lists of suitable men, persuading individuals to enlist, or warning of eviction for failure to comply.[15]

The intimate involvement of many Church of Scotland ministers in a process that invariably aroused deep local hostility and apprehension was often considered highly inappropriate at best. When the minister of Killean in Argyll tried to persuade his male parishioners to enlist in the new Scottish militia, 'the people were struck with the contrast of his officiating a little before in the name of the King of Heaven, and now acting, as some of them expressed it, the part of a recruiting sergeant to an earthly king'.[16] Such criticisms illustrate how the shift towards personal religion often entailed the emergence of a strong element of indifference towards secular issues and concerns. As a result, participation in the regular army was fundamentally reassessed and increasingly frowned upon for corrupting 'pious' young men through drink or sexual promiscuity.[17] Such considerations also led ministers and lay preachers into non co-operation with the process of local recruitment – as was the case in Kildonan during the 1750s. Conscription and impressment raised even more explicit objections: in a typically radical manner, Douglas criticised enforced military service in the militia; while the Cowal preacher, the Reverend Donald McArthur, was himself pressganged in 1804 for preaching against conscription and naval impressment.[18]

This element of anti-militarism represented only the most obvious instance where the role of religion in the Highlands could conflict with other factors which supposedly promoted the British character of the region. In areas where a strong evangelical tradition had taken root, the issue of local landlords appointing parish ministers over the heads of congregations could prove extremely emotive. Alienation caused by the presentation of a minister in Golpsie was felt by the factor to have helped induce emigration. Similar

15. S.R.O., Campbell of Stonefield Papers, GD 14/146; S.R.O., F.E.P. E769/91/163(1); S.R.O., Gillanders of Highfield Papers, GD 427/217/25; S.R.O., Seafield Muniments, GD 248/465/unnumbered letter, Abernethy, 14 May 1793; GD 248/683/3/ letter Castle Grant, 14 April 1793; GD 248/1526, Inverness, 26 July 1794, Alexander Baillie Esq. of Dochfour-Sir James Grant; S.R.O., Campbell of Breadalbane Muniments, GD 112/11/4/2/33(1–3); S.R.O., Campbell of Ballaveolin Papers, GD 13/6/420.
16. N. Douglas, *op. cit.*, p. 73.
17. More perhaps in hope than from experience, ministers often laid the blame for instances of V.D. in their parishes upon demobilised local soldiers; more generally, military service was viewed as having a corrosive effect on morals. See D.J. Withrington & I.R. Grant (eds.), *The Statistical Account of Scotland*, vol. 17 (Wakefield, 1981), p. 118; vol. 13 (Wakefield, 1976), p. 454.
18. S.R.O., F.E.P. E721/6, p. 114; N.L.S., Mackenzie of Delvine, Ms 1487, f. 142; N. Douglas, *op. cit.*, p. 145; D.E. Meek, 'The Preacher, the Press-gang and the Landlord: the Impressment and Vindication of the Rev. Donald McArthur' in *Scottish Church History Society*, vol. 25 (1994), pp. 275, 282.

objections in 1774 in another parish were so intense that it was noted: 'Rogart is likely to be a very disagreeable settlement. Twelve are all who concur with the presentation and the people threaten, I am assured, either to emigrate or become seceders from us'.[19] Riots or opposition occurred in Stratherrick in 1766, Rogart in 1774 and Clyne in 1777, and it was felt by elites that such disputes proved that populations were infected with 'religious madness' and that 'a popular call . . . [was] a dangerous expedient as it would be making the people of consequence'.[20] Rejection of landlord authority and rights of property (in an *ancien régime* sense the right to present a minister amounted to property) by Highlanders on religious grounds contrasted strongly with their reputation as a politically illiterate, ignorant but consequently wholly reliable peasantry. While this presumption of political immaturity had helped establish the image of the Highlanders as loyal and trustworthy, their involvement in Presbyterian evangelicalism, however limited, helped to counter this impression. Indeed, it was a measure of the British establishment's genuine apprehension over the country's internal security that it often saw in evangelicalism an insidious form of seditious activity.[21] Preaching methods which worked well in large Highland parishes were, from the authorities' point of view, suspicious if not actually subversive. Family worship or prayer meetings within the home led by non-local itinerant lay preachers could easily be construed as secretive, conspiratorial and seditious. The fourth Earl of Breadalbane complained to the Lord Advocate in 1804 that missionary activity on his Highland estate in Perthshire took the form of 'secret meetings which it is supposed is for political purposes'.[22] Lay preachers were portrayed as undermining the authority of established ministers – and thereby the whole hierarchical order of society. To many contemporary observers some of the effects of evangelical religion were distinctly negative: the enthusiasm and zeal of its devotees, as well as the often emotional and highly charged nature of spiritual conversion, seemed to mirror the revolutionary madness and fanaticism of France. Thus an evangelical minister from Moulin in Ross-shire, the Reverend Alexander Stewart, noted how 'the sentiments and language of our people are much misrepre-

19. J. MacInnes, 'The Origin and Early Development of "The Men"', in *Records of the Scottish Church History Society*, vol. 8 (1944), p. 26; N.L.S., Mackenzie of Delvine Papers, Ms 1485, f. 158; Ms 1487, f. 160.
20. S.R.O., Seafield Muniments, GD 248/371/4/19; N.L.S., Mackenzie of Delvine Papers, Ms 1485, ff. 179–81, 243, 262, 266. For formal opposition to a presented minister in Lochalsh in 1770, see S.R.O., Gillanders of Highfield Papers, GD 427/201/4, 12–13; GD 427/213/13.
21. J.A. Haldane, *Journal of a Tour Through the Northern Counties of Scotland and the Orkney Isles, in Autumn 1797* (Edinburgh, 1798), pp. 41–2, 46, 48.
22. S.R.O., Breadalbane Muniments, GD 112/74/872/1. For hostility felt by Breadalbane towards evangelical activity on his estate, see M.E. Vance, Emigration and Scottish Society: The Background of Three Government Assisted Emigrations to Upper Canada, 1815–1821 (University of Guelph Ph.D., 1990), pp. 57–8.

sented, and are the object of much wonder, and ridicule, and invective in other places'.[23] The fact was that evangelical religion, most especially during the Revolutionary and Napoleonic era, was open to some damning if particularly crude misinterpretations. According to one observer, evangelical endeavour was, 'something at bottom that may be hostile to government... their plan is hostile in tendency'.[24]

It can of course be argued that unusually radical preachers like Douglas and the Haldane brothers generated equally untypical and inaccurate impressions, and that evangelical Presbyterianism did not in fact involve any serious rejection of or disaffection towards late eighteenth-century Britain. It was certainly the case that Douglas and others within the Relief Church were especially vociferous in their opposition to patronage, military conscription, and politics in general. However, it was also the case that most evangelical and dissenting movements in Scotland were politically conservative and supportive of the British establishment, especially given the atheism of revolutionary France.[25] This is all fair and accurate as far as it goes, but fails to address the fact that commentators quite deliberately highlighted the anti-militarism and the supposedly seditious character of evangelical and dissenting religion. That to do so was inaccurate or unfair is entirely beside the point; it was the impression created as a result of such misrepresentations that ultimately mattered.

To outside observers, then, evangelical religion in the Highlands presented a somewhat confusing and not altogether satisfactory means of gauging the region's relationship with the rest of the country. It is also the case that evangelical Presbyterianism contributed to the particular way in which Gaels rejected certain crucial aspects of British identity. Its influence in this context arose from the fact that evangelical theology and concepts of British nationhood both attached crucial importance to the ideal of wealth, albeit for diametrically opposite reasons. In seeking to emphasise their own specific objections to patronage, and to underline the supreme importance they attached to the individual's search for spiritual salvation, Presbyterian evangelicals drew upon biblical criticisms of man's greed and the ungodly nature of worldly riches. In doing so they fundamentally queried 'the elevation of rank, extent of wealth, authority and influence'.[26] In 1797 the Reverend Douglas was asked by Argyll gentry if he had preached that 'all

23. A. Stewart, op. cit., p. 30.
24. D.J. Brown, Henry Dundas and the Government of Scotland (University of Edinburgh, Ph.D., 1989), p. 170; G. Mitchell, Remarks upon a Publication entitled, Journal of a Tour Through the Northern Counties of Scotland and the Orkney Isles, in Autumn 1797 (Aberdeen, 1799), v; N.L.S., Melville Papers, Ms 53, pp. 80–1.
25. E. Vincent, 'The Responses of Scottish Churchmen to the French Revolution', in Scottish Historical Review, vol. 73 (1994), pp. 205–9. For Haldane's anti-Paine position, see J.A. Haldane, op. cit., p. 40.
26. N.L.S., Mackenzie of Delvine Papers, Ms 1485, f. 276; N. Douglas, op. cit., p. 18.

patrons and great people' would be thrown out of their castles and estates and then cast into hell. While denying he had uttered such sentiments, Douglas added that he had in fact praised the fifth Duke of Argyll for maintaining the religious rights and social status of his tenantry, and that he hoped 'the Great might be led to copy his example, and be admonished by the fate of their brethren in a neighbouring nation, who had been driven from their stately dwellings, and divested of their possessions'.[27]

Given the crucial role assigned to rampant Francophobia in unifying the disparate parts of the nation, Douglas's use of events in France to chastise those who seemed to turn religion into property clearly underlines how certain strands of Presbyterianism cannot simply be assumed to have reinforced Britishness. This deliberate denigration of worldly wealth, moreover, stood in stark contrast to the ideology that equated Britain with commerce, material riches and affluence. In fact, representations of Britain went so far as to marry the Protestant religion to the business of making money; by such means Britain was promoted and affirmed as the new Israel, a chosen land and people whose unique prosperity was protected by and indicative of God's favourable intervention and concern.[28] The issue of lay patronage, therefore, was merely symptomatic of a wider critical appraisal by the evangelicals of Britain's materialistic value system. Indeed, evangelical religion may have proved popular in many areas of the Highlands precisely because of its explicitly 'non-British' interpretation of the actual value of material wealth. It was, after all, the desire to increase their income and confirm their British status that had led Highland landlords to the improvements and rent increases which had generated unprecedented levels of emigration from the region after 1760. There is also little doubt that the subsequent reaction to these economic changes often entailed intense disillusionment and alienation, which militated against the development of Britishness. Conventional arguments that British identity rested securely upon a hatred of the French and an appreciation of Britain's ability to provide a relatively secure and prosperous livelihood for its subjects are flatly contradicted as far as the Highlands are concerned by Allan Macdougall's **'Song to the Lowland Shepherd'**:

> They have been flung to the fringe of privilege
> away from the patrimony of their grandfathers;
> we would love the French to come
> to chop the heads of the Lowlanders.[29]

It is not hard to imagine the appeal of a religious movement that emphasised the pointless nature of secular wealth and the likelihood of damnation for the

---

27. N. Douglas, *op. cit.*, p. 62.
28. L. Colley, *op. cit.*, pp. 31–33.
29. D.E. Meek, *Tuath is Tighearna: Tenants and Landlords* (Edinburgh, 1995), p. 187.

rich if they did not repent of their sins. Thus, while elite ideology could claim Israel was reborn in an improved and wealthy Britain, Gaels could stress the unbiblical nature of their landlords' obsession with money and gain. In an Islay poem from 1775, **A Song between Dugald and Donald**', the idea of Britain as the new Israel was explicitly rejected:

> Your friends who departed under sail
> Have arrived safe and well
> In the land of excellence
> Where there is balminess and warmth
> Which the Almighty has bestowed upon us
> In order to take us from Egypt
> In which we are in pain.
>
> ... In Babylon the Children of Israel were better off
> Than we are presently in our land.
> We are like sheep without a shepherd
> Being scattered on every side.[30]

The accusation that the Highlands were now no better than Egypt or Babylon reveals how Gaels deployed their own religious imagery to communicate their lack of identification with the idea of Britain and their justification for departing for the 'country of milk and honey',[31] the real new Israel of the North American colonies. Indeed, the general issue of emigration, which was so crucial to external impressions of the region, was often tied to evangelical religion in a negative way. Landlords and established ministers criticised 'the mischief done by seditious teachers', who disseminated a religious message which tended to 'unsettle the minds of the people very much', introducing new ideas and 'mental derangement' into communities which in turn increased the likelihood of emigration. This link, real or misrepresented, between evangelicalism and population loss was especially damaging given the widespread belief that emigration was detrimental to Britain's defence interests. Again, evangelicalism was seen to conflict with British perceptions of the region's military utility, and was thus implicitly tainted as treasonable in effect if not in intention. Such negative interpretations paralleled the notion that Highland emigration was in a sense an incomprehensible, almost wilful, repudiation of the very idea of an improved Britain. Thus, in 1802, Alexander Irvine noted that 'It is a singular phenomenon in the history of Britain, that so many citizens should leave the most favoured province.

---

30. 'A Song between Dugald and Donald, in which the poor plight of the Gaels, who are forced to leave their own land, is revealed'. From A. & D. Stewart's collection, 1804. I am particularly grateful to Professor Donald Meek of the Celtic Department, University of Aberdeen, for this reference.
31. W, Matheson (ed.), *The Songs of John MacCodrum* (Edinburgh, 1938), p. 201. For evangelicalism's role in the region, see also J. Hunter, *The Making of the Crofting Community* (Edinburgh, 1976), pp. 96–97.

Emigration shows either an increase in knowledge, change in manners, impatience of restraint, a revolutionary spirit'.[32]

Criticism of the landlords' pursuit of excessive wealth and its effect on population was never of course solely, or indeed generally, dependent on evangelical Presbyterian belief: concepts of *duthchas*, for instance, provided an equally cogent and more readily available framework within which Gaels could construct their particular censures of landlordism and improvement.[33] What is nonetheless true, however, is that 'Protestantism' in the Highlands did not automatically operate to promote identification with Britishness. Instead, it served alongside and, indeed, was increasingly to replace concepts of clanship as an alternative channel through which Gaels could express their own distinctive dissatisfaction with the new British socio-economic order.

British Perceptions of the Highlander: the Unimproved Soldier

Nowhere does the potential for internal tension between the central strands making up the idea of Britishness find better expression than in the economic reasons underpinning government and wider British society's justification for disproportionate military recruitment in the Highlands. Whereas in the late 1740s and early 1750s the issue was still seen, especially by senior figures like Cumberland, primarily in terms of countering Jacobite disaffection, by the the time of the Seven Years War the rationalisation of Highland recruitment had changed significantly in character. Increasingly, the focus was on the minimal value of Highlanders within the economy of Scotland and the United Kingdom as a whole. This new emphasis was symptomatic of widespread concerns beyond the region about the effect of mass mobilisation upon increasingly sophisticated economies. During the Austrian War of Succession, for example, it was generally understood that Scotland had lost almost 10,000 men,[34] creating an understandable apprehension that such drains on manpower might affect the country's labour market, in spite of its undoubted structural under-employment and slack. More fundamentally, war served to heighten existing concern in Scottish intellectual circles over the impact and consequences of undiluted improvement. By 1759 an intense debate had emerged in Edinburgh clubs like the Select Society over the relationship between the development of a mercantile economy and the supposed decline

---

32. M.E. Vance, loc. cit., p. 59; N.L.S., Melville Papers, Ms 57, p. 1; S.R.O., Seafield Muniments, GD 248/1530, Inverness-shire Lord Lieutenancy Letter Book, 1801–1802, p. 52; A. Irvine, *An Inquiry into the Causes and Effects of Emigration from the Highlands* (Edinburgh, 1802), pp. 54, 155.
33. A.I. Macinnes, 'Scottish Gaeldom: The First Phase of Clearance', in T.M. Devine (ed.), *People and Society in Scotland, 1760–1830*, vol. 1 (Edinburgh, 1988), p. 72.
34. N.L.S., Minto Papers, Ms 11001, f, 16; Ms 11014, f. 121; A. Grant, *A Dissertation on the Chief Obstacles to the Improvement of Land and Introducing Better Methods of Agriculture throughout Scotland* (Aberdeen, 1760), pp. 38–9.

in Scotland's military prowess. This was a question which genuinely vexed those who saw trade and the empire as truly indivisible, yet also understood the need to defend that empire and the material wealth and progress that it secured. Intellectuals and prominent Scottish politicians throughout 1759–63, and again in 1776 and the early 1780s, highlighted the need for a national militia in order that the country not only defend its material progress, but indeed reclaim its traditional martial ethos. By contrast, manufacturing developments and improved agriculture were highly labour-intensive, and the prospect of a militia soaking up manpower reserves raised concerns and objections among politicians, social theorists and commercial men alike. The debate was characterised from the start by a polarisation of differing British patriotisms: between those asserting the patriotic nature of a militia and those who argued that the pursuit of military strength must avoid crippling equally important commercial activity through policies whereby 'the labourer must be taken from his plough and the manufacturer from his loom'.[35]

In contrast to the deep divisions over recruitment's role in Lowland and English society, opinion was all but unanimous over the very different condition of the Highlands. Not only did the '45 and the occupation of Scotland by the Jacobites vividly demonstrate the supposedly superior military capacity of the Highlands over the Lowlands, but Enlightened thinking itself also drew attention, in a new and fundamental way, to the region's military potential. With society's development now conceptualised as various stages in a logical progression, from savage primitiveness through feudalism with its concomitant militarism to a modern, specialised commercial society, so the Highlands was increasingly envisaged as remaining within the second, militaristic phase of development. Thus Adam Ferguson described the northern population as 'a people regardless of commercial arts' but who were thus more naturally disposed to indulge in warlike activity.[36] Certain strands of Enlightenment thinking, therefore, provided a cogent intellectual framework which addressed commercial concerns by highlighting Highland militarism as a surrogate defence mechanism for wider Scottish

---

35. J. Robertson, *The Scottish Enlightenment and the Militia Issue* (Edinburgh, 1985), pp. 69, 76, 86–89; P. Womack, *op. cit.*, pp. 40–42; *Answers to the Queries addressed to the Serious Consideration of the Public* (n.d., 1760); J. Bell, *Reasons Against a Militia for Scotland* (Edinburgh, 1783), p. 4; J. Russell, *Correspondence of John, fourth Duke of Bedford*, vol. 2 (London, 1842), p. 393. For details of the proposed Scots Militia of 1759–60, see B.L., Leeds Papers, Egerton Ms, 3433, ff. 256–62; A. Allardyce, *Scotland and Scotsmen in the Eighteenth Century*, vol. 1 (Edinburgh, 1888), p. 335.
36. Anon., *Political Observations Occasioned by the State of Agriculture in the North of Scotland* (n.p., 1756), pp. 6–7 16; A.J. Youngson, *After the 'Forty-Five: The Economic Impact on the Scottish Highlands* (Edinburgh, 1973), pp. 10–14. For evidence of textile manufacturers' relief at the failure of the 1776 Scottish Militia Act, see N.L.S., Mackenzie of Delvine Papers, Ms 1407, ff. 90, 99; B.A.M., Box 65/2/57.

society. Yet, in so doing, it entrenched real and imagined differences between the region and the rest of the country as opposed to highlighting any possible similarities. Thus in 1760, at the height of the first militia controversy, a pamphlet defending Lord Advocate Robert Dundas of Arniston noted that in opposing the militia scheme and acquiescing in William Pitt's desire to use the Highlands exclusively for line regiments, Dundas had clearly demonstrated both an astute understanding of the distinctive condition of Highland society and a patriotic appreciation of Lowland Scotland's commercial needs:

> Did he not, in the midst of the factious cry, *Arm, Arm, Arm,* save our infant manufactures, and put parliament in mind of what has been so long the object of every true Scottish patriot. Did he not, to preserve the military glory of our nation, so justly dear to Scotsmen, give check to a measure that would have wholly destroyed the Highland battalions.[37]

Such sentiments were a direct result of the fact that Lowland and English opinion, and, indeed, local Highland elites seeking military commissions, chose to stress the idea that the region simply did not have any real industrial or commercial sector which could be damaged by excessive loss of labour. Given the emergence of kelping, weaving, spinning and seasonal migration, this was of course a serious misrepresentation. Nonetheless, this particular argument continued to be deployed through the American Revolutionary War and the French wars of 1793–1815. James Small from Callander in Highland Perthshire noted in January 1776 that two additional battalions were 'rather an advantage than a loss to the country, I mean the Highlands, for there is little or no trade or manufactures . . . They are not only the best troops for that country [the American colonies], but they can be easiest spared'.[38] Nor were such sentiments simply the preserve of those who, like Small, were seeking a commission. In early 1778 the Reverend John Walker, who could and did claim some expertise on the region, again exemplified the rationale of political economy underlying Highland military service. His arguments clearly demonstrate that, far from stimulating positive, external British perceptions of the Highlands, the recruiting issue tended in fact to emphasise the region's poverty-stricken and unimproved nature. In a report to the government he noted:

> The Highland counties contain a greater number of men fit for the field, than has ever been fully known. The proportion of men fit for the army is much greater than anywhere else in the kingdom. It is almost equal to

---

37. Pitt's objection to the Scottish militia was that it would prove popular with Highlanders and so ruin a proven recruiting basin for the regular army. See N.L.S., Minto Papers, Ms 11001, f. 63; Anon., *The Public Catechised: or a Few Cool Questions to the People* (n.p., 1760?).
38. B.A.M., Box 65/2/2. For a petition from Caithness highlighting how regiments were especially practical, given that Highlanders were 'inured to industry', see H.R.A., 1: 1/1, Caithness Commissioners of Supply, petition 6 December 1775.

the number of fighting men. For except a few gentry, none of the inhabitants are placed by their circumstance above the life of a common soldier. It is fortunate, too, upon the present emergency, that whatever number of soldiers may be drawn from the Highlands, it cannot in any sensible degree, affect the agriculture, manufactures, or trade of the Kingdom.[39]

This type of thinking, which essentially ghettoised the region commercially and confirmed its status as little more than an imperial-military reservation, calls into question the extent to which military recruitment in the region was in fact motivated by a charitable desire to rehabilitate Jacobite families. It suggests, rather, that the policy was essentially constructed around a fundamental appreciation of the greater economic value of Lowland and English society. Moreover, such notions extended up to the very highest levels of the British political nation and invariably surfaced when the issue of recruiting in the Highlands was discussed. In November 1775, whilst justifying the new 71st Highland Regiment of Simon Fraser of Lovat, William Wildman, Lord Barrington, the Secretary of War, informed the House of Commons of the poor national recruitment levels that had made resorting to the North of Scotland all but inevitable. He denied opposition claims that the majority of Britons had qualms about fighting their fellow Protestant colonists, and stressed, instead, the commercialised and full-employment nature of Britain itself. Living standards had risen, as had wealth-generating opportunities in the form of an expanding manufacturing and commercial economy. This made the army a poor employment option for most of the population. Barrington's argument was supported by evidence of wage disparity. Within Lowland Scotland wages for relatively low-paid day labourers were around 9d per day in 1773; while by the harvest of 1778 such labourers were paid at least 1 shilling per day. Both levels certainly contrasted favourably with the 6d per day paid to both soldiers and Highland day labourers.[40] In early February 1778 the Secretary explicitly confirmed to the House that it was the commercially backward nature of the Highlands which had prompted the government's decision to raise new regiments there. Countering queries as to why an offer by Welsh gentry to raise a regiment had not received permission whilst six new battalions had been assigned to Highland chiefs, he pointed out that

39. P.R.O., S.P. 54/47, f. 79. Exactly the same portrayal of the Highlands was evident in a Scottish pamphlet of the same year which noted: 'If the fear of disturbing the manufactures restrained the conductors of the war from thinking of new levies in England or the Low countries of Scotland why did they not avail themselves . . . of the Highlands of Scotland, where there are no manufactures'. See N.L.S., Anon., *A Letter to His Grace The Duke of Buccleuch on National Defence. To which is Added a Postscript Relative to Regiments of Fencible Men Raising in Scotland* (Edinburgh, 1778), p. 18.
40. J. Almon (ed.), *The Parliamentary Register*, vol. 3 (London, 1776), pp. 130–1; S.R.O., Court of Session Productions, C.S. 96/1401, Farm Journal Book of Rosehall Farm; S.R.O., Seafield Muniments, GD 248/49/3/5; GD 248/50/1/5.

the administration felt Welsh manpower was too valuable to be sent abroad in large numbers – an assertion later given practical credibility when, in August of the same year, labourers from the Principality refused to seasonally migrate into Shropshire to assist tenant farmers with their harvest for fear of army conscription.[41] Barrington's parliamentary defence of Highland recruitment in February 1778 did not so much reveal government thinking on the matter as simply rivet existing metropolitan assumptions regarding the region's high military profile and its lack of diversified commercial activity. Just as Scottish pamphlets stressed how Highland elites and gentry were 'proud and indigent' – and thus peculiarly motivated to seek army commissions – so the Secretary of War, in perhaps the single most illuminating if cynical comment on how the region was actually perceived by British elites in this period, stressed how the lack of improvement, paradoxically, enhanced the military value of the Highlands to Britain as a whole. Thus he argued that the North of Scotland could afford, and indeed required, large drains of manpower given that its 'women are more fruitful than the soil'.[42]

This confirms that one of the underlying reasons why British governments continued, despite rapidly changing socio-economic conditions within the region, to depend so heavily on the Highlands was that some of the arguments used to justify recruitment were undoubtedly characterised by economic rationalism. The emphasis on a numerous, underemployed and therefore poverty-stricken population re-emerged strongly during the 1790s when, in February 1797, Henry Dundas and Frederick, Duke of York, backed plans for the mobilisation of 16,000 Highlanders in 'clan' levies. The timing of these proposals, coming as they did after sustained fencible recruiting and immediately prior to balloting for the Scottish militia, points to a continuing desire on the part of government to place excessive recruiting expectations on the region in order to alleviate more damaging social dislocation elsewhere. The preamble to the 1797 scheme again reveals how the recruiting issue merely reflected impressions of the lack of commercial development in the region:

> From the ordinary avocations of the Highlanders in general, it is obvious that no equal number of men in any one district of the Kingdom, can be employed with as little injury to agriculture and manufactures.[43]

41. J. Fortescue (ed.), *The Correspondence of King George III*, vol. 4 (London, 1928), p. 2; *The Parliamentary History of England from the Earliest period to the year 1803*, vol. 19 (London, 1814), p. 686; *Glasgow Mercury*, 12 February and 24 August 1778.
42. N.L.S., Anon., *A Letter to His Grace The Duke of Buccleugh on National Defence*. p. 18; *The Parliamentary History of England from the Earliest Period to the Year 1803*, vol. 19 (London, 1814), p. 687.
43. S.R.O., Macpherson of Cluny, GD 80/938/3; N.L.S., Melville Papers, Ms 6, f. 157; Ms 45, pp. 35–6; Ms 1048, f. 3; Ms 14838, f. 182; B.A.M., Box 59/4/18, 98; Bundle 353/unnumbered manuscript on 1797 plan.

Although never implemented in 1797, and, indeed, ignored in June 1803 when resurrected in a similar form,[44] the plan suggests that large-scale Highland recruiting during the post-Culloden period had more to do with distinctly negative or at least unflattering impressions of the region than with any conscious acknowledgement of its essentially British character. Indeed, if such involvement in the military was predicated along lines which emphasised the lack of employment and trade, then army service actually served to perpetuate and highlight the profoundly non-British character of the region. After all, commerce, the pursuit of material wealth, and the uniquely prosperous condition of the country's peasantry and urban artisans all combined to form a central shibboleth defining British society and identity. Conversely, significant stress was placed on the fact that poverty and economic backwardness were generally indicative of conditions on the continent, where Catholic superstition and arbitrary rule ensured that the mass of the population lived in relative penury. This 'cult of trade' in British thinking also stressed how merchants and those who otherwise contributed to the material wealth of the nation, such as agricultural improvers, were, at the very least, as important as the admirals and generals who exemplified the element of militarism within the country's perception of itself. Above all, the pursuit and accumulation of wealth were deemed highly patriotic in that they furnished the necessary building blocks for British military and, above all, naval strength.[45]

Given this perspective, it is possible to place an entirely different interpretation upon the widespread association of Highland military service with retarded commercialism. Indeed, disproportionate recruitment seemed explicitly to expose the region's distinct lack of other, vitally important 'British' virtues and characteristics. The belief that it was economic wealth and improvement that guaranteed British liberty and freedom, for instance, helps to explain why some commentators felt that the sheer scale of the Highlanders' involvement in the army somehow confirmed their arbitrary motivation, if not alien status. Certain Scots who strongly supported the American colonists clearly felt that the loyalty of Scotland, and the Highlands in particular, to the British cause was coloured by excessive, poverty-stricken militarism and a casual indifference to hallowed constitutional niceties. James Boswell thus noted in 1783 that Parliament's rights of taxation and concerns for legitimate political authority had not been particularly relevant factors north of the Border, and that the war 'was almost universally approved of in Scotland, where due consideration was had of the advantage of raising regiments'.[46] While over-simplifying political attitudes in Scotland

44. S.R.O. RH 1/2/521, 'Plan to Raise Twenty Thousand Men from Scottish Highlands, 1803'.
45. L. Colley, *op. cit.*, pp. 33–35, 58–62, 69–72; J.E. Cookson, *British Armed Nation*, pp. 22–3.
46. J. Boswell, *A Letter to the People of Scotland on the Present State of the Nation* (Edinburgh, 1783), p. 4.

and the Highlands during the period of the American Revolutionary War, Boswell's comments do underline how real ambiguities and counter-interpretations could and indeed did run through perceptions of large-scale Highland military service. In a conflict dominated by the rhetoric and ideology of liberty and property – a very 'English' war in many respects – it was easy to see the alien characteristics of commercial underdevelopment, poverty and arbitrariness underpinning disproportionate Highland recruitment. By such means, Highland soldiers could be easily portrayed, not as a Britons, but as foreigners. When in August 1775 rumours of Fraser's new battalion began to circulate, it was noted that 'the force of the country will now be exerted to the utmost. Scotch Highlanders, Irish Papists, Canadians, Indians etc. will all in various shapes be employed'.[47]

Equating Highlanders with Irishmen, Canadians and Indians was not, however, entirely typical. Although wholly negative attitudes to Highland soldiery were common enough within the thirteen colonies and sporadically manipulated by marginalised M.P.s like John Wilkes, such examples should not be seen as representing mainstream British impressions of the region.[48] Apart, perhaps, from certain instances during the war in America such as the February 1778 Norfolk county petition against Highland regiments signed by 5,400 people,[49] military service did not appear to generate a comprehensively non-British image of the Highlands. However, this should not be taken to mean that recruitment did, after all, confirm the genuinely British identity of the region. Rather, the 'British' and the 'alien' interpretations are overly simplistic, and fail to take account of the contradictions and tensions which Highland military service imposed upon the region's identity. The fact that Highlanders were grouped with such obviously non-British, yet imperial peoples, is particularly telling and informative. It suggests that Highland military service during this period widely corresponded with a 'provincial' and imperial perception of the region, rather than a strictly 'core' British identity. Changes in public policy help to illustrate the distinction, and how it was possible to appreciate a community's imperial status without necessarily considering it wholly British. The 1774 Quebec Act signified to many concerned observers that an increasingly authoritarian regime in London seemed prepared to use alien Catholic populations of French extraction as a military resource against the liberties and rights of Protestant American colonists. Thus the legislation represented, along with Highland military service and attempted Catholic relief in Ireland, an identifiable trend in

---

47. W.B. Donne (ed.), *The Correspondence of King George III with Lord North from 1763–1783*, vol. 1 (London, 1867), p. 258.
48. For images of Highlanders in the colonies and in Parliament, see N.L.S., Fletcher of Saltoun Papers, Ms 16694, f. 213; Ms 16714, f. 77; *Caledonian Mercury*, 14 August 1776; 15 and 19 February 1783. I am grateful to Dr R. Clyde for these *Caledonian Mercury* references. W.B. Donne (ed.), *op. cit.*, vol. 2, p. 97; J. Almon (ed.), *op. cit.*, vol. 3 (London, 1776), pp. 130, 428; vol. 8 (London, 1778), p. 13.
49. *Parliamentary History of England*, vol. 19 (London, 1814), pp. 759–69.

metropolitan government towards the pragmatic reassessment and utilisation of certain provincial societies within a larger imperial context. Whereas the Canadians' preference for Catholicism and French legal institutions would have been unacceptable within a purely domestic 'British' framework, their loyalty was such that acceding to their forms of government undoubtedly held some attractions if viewed from the important perspective of imperial defence. The same general but crucial point was equally true of Ireland's substantial pool of Catholic manpower and the Highlands' own reservoir of 'unimproved' peasantry.[50] That certain distinctive features of provincial societies, which were undesirable and alien from the perspective of the British core, could nevertheless be wholly desirable from a broader imperial empire raises doubts as to whether the Empire served to unify and assimilate or, instead, to perpetuate the reality and perception of regional particularism. In the case of the late eighteenth-century Highlands there is a strong argument for the latter. The contrast between Gaeldom's unimpressive commercial profile and its military utility was such that many felt certain 'non-British' aspects of its society should be preserved. Over-reliance on the very manpower that had so threatened the country less than twenty years earlier, for instance, meant that by 1760 Scottish gentry felt the country's patriotic improvement agenda was being deliberately sacrificed, and that in London 'Scotland is looked upon and must be reserved as the fund for recruiting the army'. John Knox expressed similar sentiments in 1785, noting that 'it seems a political maxim with many persons, that the Highlands of Scotland are to be considered merely as a nursery for soldiers and seamen . . . and that to facilitate the business of recruiting, it is expedient to keep them low'.[51] It is easy to see how Highlanders could be viewed as having more in common with other provincial peoples who did not qualify for full British status either in respect of religion, commercial wealth or a consequent lack of appreciation of liberty and freedom of property.

The incompatibility of the twin British 'patriotisms' of improvement and recruitment illustrates this particular point. Stressing the patriotic nature of agricultural change in the Highlands not only mirrored the ideology of a

50. *Scots Magazine*, vol. 36 (Edinburgh, 1774), pp. 301–5; S.J. Connolly, 'Varieties of Britishness: Ireland, Scotland and Wales in the Hanoverian State', in A. Grant and K.J. Stringer (eds.), *op. cit.*, p. 203; R.K. Donovan, 'The Military Origins of the Roman Catholic Relief Programme of 1778', in *Historical Journal*, vol. 28 (1985), pp. 83 and 90; S.R.O., Correspondence of Sir James Montgomery, RH 4/56/40, 'Governor James Murray's report on Quebec province, 1765'; D. Milobar, 'Quebec Reform, the British Constitution and the Atlantic Empire, 1774–1775', in P. Lawson (ed.), *Parliament and the Atlantic Empire* (Edinburgh, 1995), p. 82. For a specific reassessment of clanship, see S.R.O., Seaforth Muniments, GD 46/6/35.
51. N.L.S., Fletcher of Saltoun Papers, Ms 16714, f. 123; J. Knox, *A View of the British Empire, more Especially Scotland: with some Proposals for the Improvement of that Country and the Extension of its Fisheries and the Relief of the People* (London, 1785), p. 133.

commercially superior Britain, but also played a vital role in justifying the elite's pursuit of larger incomes while simultaneously weakening the basis for any protest. The fifth Duke of Argyll's proposals in 1775 for tenurial change and a woollen manufactory at Inveraray were held up as examples of 'patriotic' endeavour which stood in direct contrast to the actions of many other landlords.[52] To improve, therefore, was to confirm one's British credentials in a cultural sense as much as to increase one's profits in a material one. Yet such patriotic rhetoric had altogether different connotations during wartime. Few, if any, means of demonstrating commitment to the United Kingdom surpassed that of regiment raising. Thus Sir John Sinclair of Ulbster, who justified improvement through the language of patriotism, found himself confronted with somewhat different expectations. In 1794 Sinclair found his rhetoric had come home to roost in the form of a prime-ministerial request for a regiment. Sinclair was taken aback and declared that he was no soldier; however, in the circumstances it was all but impossible for him to refuse.[53] Furthermore, from the 1770s Highland landlords found that the region's reputation as a military reservoir allowed criticisms of their commercial policies to be couched in similarly patriotic terms: after all, it was surely less than patriotic to undermine a proven and cheap supply of vital military manpower.[54] This conflict of expectations was evident in the answer of John Campbell, third Earl of Breadalbane, to a request in June 1759 for men from his estate:

> It is impossible for me to answer your Lordship's questions, what men I can raise and in what time, for I have for many years taken great pains in that part of the country where my interest lies to bring peoples' minds from the thought of arms to that of industry and Improvement . . . for several years [I] pursued a wrong plan, thinking it for the service of the government and for my own advantage, by removing all idle people out of my estate.[55]

52. S.R.O., Seafield Muniments, GD 248/49/2/8; *Edinburgh Advertiser*, 3 January 1775; D. Loch, *Essays on the Trade, Commerce, Manufactures and Fisheries of Scotland*, vol. 1 (Edinburgh, 1778), pp. 147–48.
53. T.C. Smout, 'Problems of Nationalism, Identity and Improvement in later Eighteenth Century Scotland', in T.M. Devine (ed.), *Improvement and Enlightenment* (Edinburgh, 1989), pp. 15–18; I.H.M. Scobie, 'The Caithness Fencibles and a Recruiting Card of 1799', in *Journal of the Society of Army Historical Research*, vol. 6 (1927), pp. 6, 97.
54. W. Thom, *Informations concerning the Province of North Carolina, Addressed to Emigrants from the Highlands and Western Isles of Scotland* (Glasgow, 1773), pp. 6, 11; Anon., *The Present Conduct of the Chieftains & Proprietors of Lands in the Highlands of Scotland towards their Clans and People Considered Impartially* (1773), p. 5; J. Knox, *op. cit.*, p. 121; J. Macdonald, *A General View of the Agriculture of the Hebrides or Western Isles of Scotland* (Edinburgh, 1811), p. 118.
55. B.L., Hardwicke Papers, Add Ms 35450, ff. 262, 285.

Breadalbane was arguing that he faced two distinct and, to his mind at least, conflicting ideas of Britishness. Moreover, these differing concepts of the British identity of the region by no means remained in equilibrium. As the army shifted towards professional and non-proprietorial recruiting from the mid-1790s, so any patriotic justification for retaining Highland populations for military reasons was largely extinguished. The result was that by the early 1810s the British ideology of commercial endeavour was unfettered by conflicting military expectations of the region and given greater precedence and prominence, at least by Highland elites. This new climate ensured that the old association between the region's militarism and its lack of economic development now, ironically, began to serve as justification for clearance. In 1810 the Ross-shire improver, Sir George-Stuart Mackenzie, noted that:

> Notwithstanding its being inconsistent with the liberty enjoyed by Britons, with common justice, with sound policy, that the Highland proprietors alone, of all others in the empire should be deprived of the benefit of an improved system of rural economy, and condemned to poverty in order to provide recruits for the army; yet this is the sum and substance of all the outcry against emigration.[56]

Underlying Mackenzie's emphasis on the right of 'Britons' to improve their property was the implication that Highlanders had remained unimproved and were essentially redundant. Furthermore, the Gaels' high-profile military service actually helped to foster this negative image. British society saw soldiering as peculiarly suited to those who were simply unable or unwilling to work in the civilian economy. The absence of hard, continuous labour was believed to characterise the soldier's life and provide one of its few attractions.[57] It is clear how such perceptions could easily begin to count against those closely associated with soldiering once circumstances changed in 1815. 'Laziness' and 'indolence' were increasingly highlighted as innate characteristics of the Highlander during the mid-nineteenth century.[58] If nothing else, this underlines how the Gael's presence within the eighteenth-century British army only ever offered a partial and, ultimately, ineffective basis for a truly rounded and sustainable belief in his British identity.

---

56. G.S. Mackenzie, *A General Survey of the Counties of Ross and Cromarty* (London, 1810), pp. 297–299.
57. J. Cookson, *British Armed Nation*, p. 100. For negative perceptions of soldiering, see D.J. Withrington and I. R. Grant (eds.), *The Statistical Account of Scotland*, vol. 9, pp. 623–6; vol. 11, p. 47; vol. 13, p. 50.
58. J. Hunter, *The Making of the Crofting Community* (Edinburgh, 1976), p. 38; E.A. Cameron, 'Embracing the Past: The Highlands in Nineteenth Century Scotland', in D. Brown, R.J. Finlay and M. Lynch (eds.), *op. cit.*, p. 209.

The Volunteers, Britishness and Local Identity

If disproportionate Highland military service made a more ambiguous impression on external observers, especially over the longer term, than has previously been assumed, then it also remains far from clear whether such involvement in the country's armed forces produced a new and heightened sense of Britishness amongst Gaels themselves. An obvious criticism of the argument which links Highland soldiers to the development of British identity within the region is its excessive concentration on regular line regiments. From at least 1766, with William Pitt the Elder's speech regarding Highland recruitment, the nature of the Gaels' military service has usually been viewed within an explicitly imperial context.[59] This particular perspective derives from the desire of contemporary Scots to demonstrate either their loyalty to or equality within the empire. The enthusiastic praise heaped on the 42nd Highland Regiment in 1801 after the British army's victory at Alexandria, for example, formed part of a national resurgence in confidence which saw Scottish military personnel like Sir John Moore and Sir Ralph Abercrombie praised as imperial warrior-heroes on a par with any from south of the Border.[60] Throughout the rest of the nineteenth century hagiographic regimental histories, aimed at a self-assured and self-congratulatory imperial audience, reinforced the tendency for the Highlands' military contribution to be seen almost exclusively in terms of the regular army. This is however a severe distortion of actual service patterns and totally neglects the growth in Scotland's home defence forces from 1759. Whereas in the Seven Years War only two (Argyll and Sutherland) battalions out of twelve were raised for service within Scotland, by the Revolutionary and Napoleonic wars 21 of the 31 new 'Highland' regiments were non-regular, fencible units.[61]

Moreover, the emergence of volunteering as a large-scale form of military service has until recently been almost totally neglected. This is all the more surprising given its scale and popularity north of the Border. It is worth stressing this point: enthusiasm for volunteering in Scotland, and the Highlands in particular, stands in marked contrast to the often genuine dislike of regular army service. Whether Gaels did or did not willingly enlist in the line and fencible regiments raised by their landlords has formed a controversial but ultimately sterile argument within wider debates about the eighteenth- and early nineteenth-century Highlands. Despite some attempts to defend

---

59. R. Clyde, *op. cit.*, pp. 152–9; D.M. Henderson, *op. cit.*, pp. 5–17. For evidence that Highlanders had become particularly identified with imperial endeavour, see S.R.O., Seafield Muniments, GD 248/49/2/23; D. Duff, *Scotland's War Losses* (Glasgow, 1947), p. 12.
60. S.R.O., RH 4/188/2, p. 443; J.E. Cookson, *British Armed Nation*, pp. 149–50.
61. For an index of the Highland regiments, though many were in fact only nominally Highland, raised during the period from 1725–1815, see J. Prebble, *op. cit.*, pp. 497–501.

crude Victorian assertions regarding the Gael's overwhelmingly positive attitude towards regular soldiering, this stereotype has been thoroughly discredited and the coercive power of landlords substituted in its stead.[62] Indeed, Gaels seemed prepared to expend substantial amounts of their relatively limited capital to avoid certain forms of military service, undermining claims that their disproportionate profile within the army arose from an inability or unwillingness to pay for substitutes or fines. As demonstrated earlier with respect to the Breadalbane estate, families were often forced to expend significant sums on unofficial bounties for substitutes destined for their landlord's levy, which accordingly reduced their ability to pay militia or conscription fines. Yet despite their undoubted difficulty in paying such sums, the vast majority of fines in Perthshire for failure to supply quotas for the Army of Reserve were paid, not by Lowland parishes, but by the largely Highland districts of Balquhidder, Weem, Dull and Killin. Similarly, a petition of 1807 by inhabitants of the Highland parish of Kenmore revealed that in order to avoid militia service the population had paid the equivalent of nearly 15% of their annual rent. Appendix 4, which relates to naval fines for 1795–6, confirms this pattern of substantial outlay, demonstrating that Highland counties tended, if anything, to be at the top end of those fined for failing to supply men.[63]

While the role of social ambition in reconciling recruits and their families to the prospect of military service should not be underestimated, it is clear that many went to significant financial lengths to avoid conscription and that, generally, Gaels were reluctant rather than willing recruits within the British army.[64] The same cannot, however, be said of volunteering. Across Scotland as a whole, highly localised armed service proved noticeably more popular than in England. While constituting only 15% of the British population, Scotland accounted for over 36% of Britain's entire volunteer force in 1797. By 1806, even allowing for changes in pay and service

62. For a more traditional analysis, see D.M. Henderson, *op. cit.*, pp. 20–1. For emphasis on the landlord's social leverage, see R. Clyde, *op. cit.*, pp. 175–6; J. Prebble, *op. cit.*, pp. 104–5; E. Richards, *op. cit.*, vol. 1 (London, 1982), pp. 141–46.
63. J.E. Cookson, *op. cit.*, pp. 101, 107–8 and 128; S.R.O., Irvine Robertson Series, GD 1/53/103; S.R.O., Maclaine of Lochbuie Papers, GD 174/1410/206; GD 174/638; S.R.O., Breadalbane Muniments, GD 112/52/588/1; GD 112/9/2/2/3; GD 112/52/592/7.
64. Examples are too numerous to list comprehensively, but the following references give a good chronological and geographic spread: B.L., Hardwicke Papers, Add Ms 35450, f. 40 [1745]; N.L.S. Fletcher of Saltoun Papers, Ms 16605, ff. 48–54 [1745]; N.L.S., Murray Erskine Collection, Ms 5079, f. 60 [1756]; S.R.O., Campbell of Barcaldine Papers, GD 170/1534 [1759]; S.R.O., Gordon Castle Muniments, GD 44/47/3/2/88 [1778]; S.R.O., Gillanders of Highfield Papers, GD 427/303/1 [1778]; S.R.O., Seaforth Papers, GD 46/17/3/unnumbered letter dated Highfield, 17 June 1793; S.R.O., Seafield Muniments, GD 248/683/63 [1793]; N.L.S., Sutherland Papers, Dep. 313/1115/57 [1799]; S.R.O., Maclaine of Lochbuie Papers, GD 174/926 [1795]; GD 174/1480/15–16 [1803].

conditions and the mass arming of England in response to the invasion scares of 1798 and 1803, the number of Scottish volunteers stood at 52,337– still 15.9% of the United Kingdom's whole force. The underlying social reasons for this disproportionate Scottish contribution also appear to have differed markedly from those in England. South of the Border volunteering was closely associated with municipal politics and identities; yet given its much smaller, albeit rapidly expanding urban base, this cannot satisfactorily serve as an explanation for Scottish responses. This is even more obviously the case if seen from a Highland perspective, especially given the lack of any convincing explanation of why Lowland towns could surpass the region as a recruiting ground for regulars but not for volunteers.[65] There is little doubt that volunteering in the region was particularly disproportionate, and that it constituted the single largest avenue for later eighteenth-century Highlanders to gain any real experience of the British state. By October 1803 Inverness-shire's volunteer establishment stood at 3,440 men; in Skye alone in 1806 there were 1,090 volunteers while in Sutherland there were 1,190. National figures reveal that in proportion to their respective populations these local units were significantly more popular in the North than elsewhere in Scotland. The counties of Argyll, Inverness, Ross, Cromarty, Sutherland and Caithness, for instance, had a population of 255,993 in 1801 – 15.9% of Scotland's as a whole: yet the same counties had raised 11,336 volunteers – or 19.1% of the Scottish total.[66]

Above all, though, it is the sharp contrast evident between these high volunteering levels and the numbers enlisted in the regular army through the recruiting acts of the early 1800s that underlines the lack of enthusiasm for overseas British service. Both the Army of Reserve Act of 1803 and the Additional Act of 1804 were designed to get men accustomed to military service in a militia form so that they would then more readily enlist in the regular army. Neither act involved the coercive power of Highland landlords, which could so often account for high levels of participation; in this respect they serve as a particularly good litmus test of attitudes towards local or British military service. These recruiting returns call into question common assumptions regarding Scotland's, but most especially the Highlands', enthusiasm for military service. Under the Army of Reserve Act each of the three kingdoms was assigned a particular quota of men. England raised

65. J.E. Cookson, *The British Armed Nation*, pp. 128, 140; J.G. Kyd (ed.), *Scottish Population Statistics* (Edinburgh, 1952), pp. 23, 82–3. Note that Inverness, as the only town in or near the Highlands, was comprehensively outperformed by rural districts, especially the west coast and islands. See S.R.O., Seafield Muniments, GD 248/1527, Inverness-shire Lord Lieutenancy Letter Book, 1796–97, unnumbered letter dated Inverness, 31 January 1797; GD 248/1535, Inverness-shire Lord Lieutenancy Letter Book, 1804, pp. 289–90.

66. S.R.O., Seafield Muniments, GD 248/1534, Inverness-shire Lord Lieutenancy Letter Book, 1803–1804, p. 240; Marquis of Cambridge, 'The Volunteer Army of Great Britain, 1806', in *Journal of the Society of Army Historical Research*, vol. 13 (1931), pp. 114–72.

93.7% of its quota – 29% having volunteered to extend their services into the army. In Ireland 81.9% of the quota was reached, with a respective volunteering total of 21.9%: Scotland raised 92.2% of its required total, admittedly higher than Ireland's, but only 17.5% volunteered. Likewise, even allowing for the fact that Scotland's population was only 30% of Ireland's, the number of men volunteering for the army from the Scottish militia during the period 1809–1813 was proportionately much less – 2,843 compared to 18,670 – equivalent to only 15% of Irish recruitment rates.[67] Totals for the Additional Act shown in Table 21, which include a county breakdown to distinguish the response of the Highlands, confirm that, if anything, the region had an even greater distaste for extended 'British' service than Scotland as a whole.

Table 21. Men Raised in England, Ireland and Scotland under the Additional Act and Enlisting in the Regular Army, June 1804–December 1805[68]

Area	Total Recruited	Enlisting for army service	%
England	4,979	1,864	37.4
Ireland	3,562	926	25.9
Scotland	989	247	24.9
Highlands	194	23	11.8

These figures all suggest that we need to distinguish quite carefully between various *types* of military service before making generalised statements about the warlike Highlander. Clearly, patterns of military service, far from demonstrating the Highlanders' sense of Britishness, actually demonstrate the persistence of a pervasive and dominant sense of localism within the region.[69] This is further strengthened by the fact that cycles of volunteering in the region appear to have had a rather incidental correlation with the wider British context. For example, it was the French invasion crisis of 1798 that actually generated the majority of Britain's volunteer establishment during the French Revolutionary War, increasing its numbers by 112% from 54,600 to 116,000 men. In Inverness-shire, however, the majority of volunteer companies had appeared prior to the invasion scare, and only 45.8% of its establishment emerged during the period of the invasion threat. The county's cycle of response was not therefore motivated primarily by wider national considerations; rather, the chronology underlines the somewhat

67. For populations of Scotland and Ireland, see M. W. Flinn (ed.), *Scottish Population History* (Cambridge, 1977), p. 302; K.H. Connell, *The Population of Ireland, 1750–1845* (Oxford, 1975), pp. 5 and 25; J.W. Fortescue, *op. cit.*, pp. 295, 309.
68. S.R.O., RH 4/158/1/237, ff. 256–8. Highlands = Caithness, Sutherland, Ross & Cromarty, Inverness and Argyll.
69. L. Colley, *op. cit.*, pp. 294–5.

Military Service and British Identity in the Highlands 229

paradoxical point that over-representation within the British military could in fact indicate non-national concerns.[70]

Indeed, whether Highland communities were as overly committed to British defence as might appear to be the case from their volunteering performance is certainly open to question, given the more immediate if strictly pragmatic local reasons for involvement. The rapid recruitment of Fraser of Lovat's battalion from January to March 1757, for example, was assisted by the emergence of famine conditions in the region; likewise, in 1776 Ewan Macpherson of Cluny benefited from a dearth in Badenoch while enlisting men for the 71st Highland Regiment.[71] Military employment as a response to adverse economic conditions certainly influenced the pattern of volunteering at the end of the century. In July 1799, at a time when government had refused to accept any more offers of service, Sir James Grant, Lord Lieutenant of Inverness-shire, informed Henry Dundas that an additional five proposals had arrived from Skye and that 'there are a number of young fellows offering themselves dayly'. However, these potential companies were in no way linked to invasion fears, as Britain had in fact gone back onto the offensive, but rather can be viewed as a logical local response to the failure in cattle prices and high meal costs in the Highlands at the time.[72]

Apart, then, from its limited attraction as a strategy born of economic hardship, the reasons why volunteering proved so popular in the Highlands remain far from clear. It is testimony to the low esteem in which the regular army was held by Highland populations that they were, to begin with, suspicious even of the volunteering process. Confusion over the exact nature of military enlistment was rife in light of the government's decision in 1794 to extend the operational requirements of Scotland's fencible regiments. Not surprisingly, many felt that volunteering was nothing more than a new device to entice them into full-time army service. In Skye, for example, men refused to sign the 'enrolments from a mistaken notion that it is making them soldiers or otherwise not understanding it'. The biggest worry amongst Highland populations, however, was that prolonged military activity would curtail their ability to complete other profitable or necessary labour tasks. In March 1804, while explaining the reluctance of Inverness-shire volunteers to commit themselves to 40 days full-time service, Sir James Grant conceded that 'this being seed time, when the necessary agricultural operations for the year must be carried on, will most likely retard the offers in some degree'.[73]

70. J.E. Cookson, *op. cit.*, p. 71; S.R.O., Seafield Muniments, GD 248/1529, Inverness-shire Lord Lieutenancy Letter Book, 1798–1800, pp. 3, 42–5, 440–41.
71. S.R.O., F.E.P. E769/91/3; S.R.O., Gordon Castle Muniments, GD 44/47/2/75(2).
72. S.R.O., Seafield Muniments, GD 248/1529, Inverness-shire Lord Lieutenancy Letter Book, 1798–1800, pp. 208, 252, 260, 275–6, 321.
73. For examples from Skye, Barra and Badenoch, see S.R.O., Seafield Muniments, GD 248/1526, Inverness-shire Lord Lieutenancy Letter Book, 1794–96, unnumbered letter Inverness, 26 July 1794, Alexander Baillie-Sir James Grant; unnumbered letter Castle Grant, 19 October 1794, Sir James Grant-Duke of Portland; GD 248/1530, Inverness-shire Lord Lieutenancy Letter Book, 1801–1802, p. 44; GD 248/1535, Inverness Lord Lieutenancy Letter Book, 1804, pp. 213–4.

Yet volunteering was in fact characterised by certain basic features which alleviated these concerns, thereby making it particularly appealing for Highland populations. First, after January 1799, enrolling as a volunteer removed liability from balloting for the militia, though not necessarily from army conscription measures such as the 1803 Army of Reserve Act. This exemption proved to be a substantial incentive and, moreover, as with the Rum and Lyndale companies in 1806–7, helped influence the offers of individual companies to extend their range of service. A willingness to serve in any area of Britain should not therefore be taken to mean identification with or sympathy for Britishness. It was, rather, just as likely to be evidence of the genuine dislike of conscription traditionally associated with the region's population, or an attempt to ensure the unit's survival in the longer term by increasing its utility and attractiveness to central government.[74] Second, the level of commitment required by involvement in such companies was, initially at least, extremely limited. During 1794 and 1797, for instance, when Colonel John Macleod of Talisker and Sir James Grant finalised proposals for volunteer corps in Skye and Strathspey, the marching distance was set at a maximum of five and ten miles respectively.[75] Typically, units met once or twice a week (at a rate of one shilling per day) within their own parish for training, discipline and drill. By situating part-time military service firmly within an estate or parish context, volunteering did not entail relative neglect of the other civilian employments that were vital in supporting the living standards of the population. It could of course be argued that too much localism can be read into volunteer service, and that the British component was in fact more important than might at first seem the case. It was certainly true from 1798 onwards, and especially after the revival of the volunteers a year after their disbandment in 1802, that companies came under severe government pressure to extend the range and duration of their services to include regional military districts and, indeed, the whole of Britain in the event of an actual invasion.[76] Although permanent service did indeed become

---

74. Those volunteering prior to August 1803 were exempted from liability for army conscription but only if the company agreed to serve across the whole military district. See J.W. Fortescue, *The County Lieutenancies and the Army, 1803–1804* (London, 1909), pp. 27, 59, 198; L. Colley, *op. cit.*, pp. 294, 300; J.E. Cookson, *The British Armed Nation*, pp. 9, 74; S.R.O., Seafield Muniments, GD 248/1533, Inverness-shire Lord Lieutenancy Letter Book, 1803, pp. 52–56, 249; GD 248/1536, Inverness-shire Lord Lieutenancy Letter Book, 1804–1808, pp. 259–60, 372–4.
75. S.R.O., Seafield Muniments, GD 248/1526, Inverness-shire Lord Lieutenancy Letter Book, 1794–96, unnumbered letter, dated Castle Grant, 16 September 1794, Sir James Grant-Duke of Portland; S.R.O., Seafield Muniments, GD 248/1527, Inverness-shire Lord Lieutenancy Letter Book, 1796–1797, unnumbered letter, Castle Grant, 20 March 1797, Sir James Grant-Duke of Portland.
76. For changes in volunteer conditions of service, see J.E. Cookson, *The British Armed Nation*, pp. 80–81; S.R.O., Melville Castle Muniments, GD 51/1/897; GD 51/1/900/2; GD 51/1/905/2; GD 51/1/986.

an increasingly prominent feature of local military activity, this did not necessarily clash with the immediate concerns of rural communities. Rather, periodic instances of full-time service secured additional and increased levels of state pay, and, furthermore, were usually timed to coincide with periods of underemployment within the region itself. Sutherland companies, for instance, were notified in 1805 that, if at all possible, they would be called out of their parishes between the months of October and July. Commanders also allowed married men to temporarily remove themselves in order to remain behind and manage their farms. By avoiding the crucial harvest period and concentrating service during the traditionally slack months of the agrarian year, even extended-service volunteering proved popular in the region not because it reflected a concern for British security but rather because it was in effect nothing more than a form of state-subsidised seasonal migration.[77]

Reaction to the disbandment of volunteer units and the transfer of their manpower into new militia companies in 1808 confirms that it was the local and part-time nature of these levies that attracted Highlanders in such numbers. In October 1808, after the Act instituting the new local militia battalions had been passed in Parliament, Francis Humberston-Mackenzie, Earl of Seaforth and Lord Lieutenant of Ross-shire, found that his Kintail, Lewis and Glensheal tenantry objected strenuously to the change in their conditions of service. In the Black Isle, men refused to enrol in the new militia battalion, while the Wester Ross companies complained vociferously about the amount of time now required away from their homes. Even a distance of twenty-four miles proved highly controversial – suggesting that concern for wider county, never mind British, affairs was all but absent. By December, Seaforth had become severely embarrassed at his failure to persuade volunteers to switch to the new arrangements, especially given his earlier assurances to London that two new militia battalions could easily be created in Ross-shire.[78]

Yet in highlighting the often deep dislike of Gaels for regular or extended forms of service it is important not to under-estimate just how attractive localised, part-time military activity could be in relatively underdeveloped rural areas with rising rents and limited, unreliable earning opportunities. A particular feature of volunteering, for instance, was the flexible and accommodating nature of its service requirements. In order to ensure that the various labour-intensive if somewhat sporadic tasks such as kelping and peat cutting, which formed a central feature of estate economies in the region, were completed, training or mobilisation was often temporarily delayed or

77. N.L.S., Sutherland Papers, Dep. 313/3280/1; Dep. 313/3283/30; Dep. 313/746/, f. 32. For similar seasonal offers of service in the months after seed planting, see S.R.O., Seafield Muniments, GD 248/1535, Inverness-shire Lord Lieutenancy Letter Book, 1804, pp. 238, 278, 294; S.R.O., Maclaine of Lochbuie Papers, GD 174/1426/49.
78. S.R.O., Seaforth Muniments, GD 46/17/16, letters 5, 15, 21, 25 October and 1 November 1808.

rescheduled. Once integrated with local work patterns, often by means of evening drill, such companies were widely accepted as particularly useful in complementing and supplementing established sources of Highland income.[79] During 1794–95, landlords and officers in North Uist, Skye and Kinlochleven pushed for permanent pay as a means of arousing enthusiasm for local military service. Likewise, when the volunteers were disbanded in April 1802, the government was made fully aware of the particular importance attached to such income, and its central role in persuading Highlanders to participate in national defence.[80] The surprisingly high proportion of rent that could be answered for by means of volunteer earnings has already been noted in Table 17. There can be little doubt that in an area lacking the variety of income sources evident in the Lowlands, one of the overriding attractions of local state service was that it constituted an additional and relatively reliable profit-making activity. Large-scale volunteering in the region was in fact grounded in immediate estate and materialistic concerns, and not a wider appreciation of national issues.

Of course it can be quite legitimately argued that an overwhelmingly local agenda did not necessarily prevent British sentiment from determining volunteer patterns in the region. It is certainly simplistic to assume that Gaels were incapable of demonstrating wider notions of Britishness or adopting a complex sequence of 'concentric loyalties'. Gaelic poetry confirms that military service, most obviously in the regulars, exposed Highlanders to a whole series of issues as diverse as the growing importance of Prussia and the defence of the American and Indian empires. This also suggests, however, that involvement in the army did not necessarily serve to generate an exclusively or even predominantly 'British' outlook, especially if what is meant by Britain is an ever closer domestic Anglo-Scottish union as opposed to the wider empire. Indeed, it is possible to argue that rather than military service engendering a sense of Britain, it actually served to reinforce, modernise and entrench local identity. Thus, while Gaelic poetry that celebrated victory at Quebec in 1759 could conceive of Britain only through a 'primitive feeling of loyalty' to George II, its central emphasis was actually on 'the warriors of the Rough Bounds'.[81] Likewise, verses that appeared to demonstrate a very British hatred of the French, as in Duncan Ban Macintyre's *Song to the Earl of Breadalbane* or *Song of the Gazette*, attached their

79. S.R.O., Breadalbane Muniments, GD 112/74/859/19; S.R.O., Seafield Muniments, GD 248/1536, Inverness-shire Lord Lieutenancy Letter Book, 1804–1808, pp. 341, 372–4; S.R.O., Melville Castle Muniments, GD 51/1/905/2.
80. S.R.O., Seafield Muniments, GD 248/99/1/6–7, 9, GD 248/192/2/27; GD 248/1530, Inverness-shire Lord Lieutenancy Letter Book, 1801–2, pp. 104–6; GD 248/1531, Inverness-shire Lord Lieutenancy Letter Book, 1802, pp. 109–110.
81. For a description of crude, underdeveloped patriotism which centred on the King and military matters, see T.C. Smout, 'Problems of Nationalism, Identity and Improvement in later Eighteenth-Century Scotland', p. 3; W. Matheson (ed.), *The Song's of John MacCodrum*, p. 57; T. Swinton (ed.), *The Poetry of Badenoch* (Inverness, 1906), p. 479.

priorities very much to the celebration of, and latent rivalry between, the districts of Glenorchy and Glenfalloch, or, alternatively, the high social status of soldiering when compared with other occupations in poor rural communities.[82]

Agrarian and local concerns were clearly important factors in the Gaels' attitude to military service. In light of this it is perhaps possible to offer an alternative interpretation of how volunteering was perceived in the region. There has been a somewhat romanticised and largely unconvincing tendency, born of over-concentration on the regulars, to see in Highland battalions a definite continuity of the clan regiments of pre-1745 society.[83] Yet by being particularly sensitive to agrarian needs and accommodating the ultimate priority of farming and the estate economy, it was the distinctly less romantic or high-profile volunteers that came closest of all British military arrangements to actually replicating Highland clanship's military ethos and practice.[84]

82. A. Macleod (ed.), *The Song's of Duncan Ban Macintyre* (Edinburgh, 1952), pp. 369, 379.
83. D.M. Henderson, *op. cit.*, p. 5; P. Womack, *op. cit.*, p. 45.
84. For a particularly helpful account of clanship's military ethos and priorities, see A.I. Macinnes, *Clanship, Commerce and the House of Stuart, 1603–1788* (East Linton, 1996), pp. 168–170.

Conclusion

In the Scottish Highlands the years between 1715 and 1815 were a period of transition during which the region's entire social and economic structure was irredeemably altered. Scholars have for some time stressed how before and especially after the battle of Culloden the military dimension to Highland society was fading in importance and that forces of commercialism had emerged as the dominant dynamic within the region.[1] Yet however much the whole era of first-phase clearance tends to be summarised in terms of commercial, Highland landlordism, the period was also characterised by unprecedented state involvement, most noticeably in the form of military recruiting. As elsewhere in Britain and Ireland the intrusion, if usually through local agencies, of the state into even the most isolated localities was driven by international war. In the hundred years between Sheriffmuir and Waterloo, for example, the United Kingdom was at war for forty-three: furthermore, this total does not include such small colonial conflicts as those in North America in 1754–56 and India in 1790–92. Indeed, it is ironic that when compared to the earlier and supposedly more militarised era of clanship, war was probably as much if not more of a factor shaping the new post-Culloden Highlands.

This helped ensure that the supposed demise of militarism after 1746 simply did not occur, and that levy activity was in fact to intensify over the succeeding decades, if in an altogether different form. That the region's dependence on warlike endeavour was now state-sponsored as opposed to private, clan-based military activity should not detract from its scale and depth, nor from the fact that it encompassed many different areas of Highland society. By a variety of different measurements the number of people with a direct involvement in military activity increased after 1745 rather than decreased. The region's political representatives, for example, were closely associated with the British military. An estimate of Members of Parliament serving as military officers in the 1770s suggests that the overall British ratio was approximately one in eight. The profile of Scottish M.P.s shows that a much larger number – one in five – were involved in the military. However, of the seventy-eight M.P.s representing the Highland counties of Caithness, Sutherland, Ross and Cromarty, Inverness-shire and Argyll, as well as the region's burghs, during the years between 1747 and 1815, thirty-six – or nearly one in two – were connected with the armed

---

1. M. Gray, *The Highland Economy, 1750–1850* (Edinburgh, 1957), pp. 56–9.

forces.[2] These figures mirror the pattern evident in Table 1, which shows that the Highland electorate was the most militarised in Scotland. Even within the institutions which sprang up as a result of the social and economic integration of the region's landowning class, such as the Glasgow Highland Society and the Highland Society of London, the same close connection with the military is evident. In 1783 over one member in three of the London Society was in the military.[3] Nor was this militarisation simply a characteristic of the elite. Though estimates for the number of rank-and-file Highlanders in British army service vary considerably and should be treated with caution, the scale of recruitment in the region is immediately striking. One particularly prominent feature is its extremely specialised nature: Highlanders were overwhelmingly involved in the land as opposed to the naval service. Despite suggestions by Sir John Sinclair of Ulbster that eight Gaelic-speaking ships of the line could be formed from the west coast's estimated reserves of 5,000 fishermen, the senior service never consciously adjusted its methods of enlisting to cater for regional characteristics.[4] These specific contours to the region's involvement in Britain's military machine are evident from Appendix 1 which shows how Highland parishes were the most heavily recruited areas in Scotland. In obvious contrast, by 1815 only one port in the Highlands, Tobermory, was in the top ten of Scottish sea towns in terms of the annual value of naval Greenwich pensions received by its inhabitants and those of its hinterland (see Appendix 3). While the region's contribution to the navy was small in comparison to the sea ports and coastal burghs of Scotland, which were intensely press-ganged,[5] the Old Statistical Account of Scotland, written largely during the mass mobilisations of the 1790s, provides eloquent testimony to the almost omnipresent status of army recruitment in Highland localities. One in three parish ministers in Ross-shire alluded to recruiting, while in Argyllshire it was nearly one in two. In Caithness, meanwhile, 70% of parish ministers recorded some aspect of military levying: likewise, of the twelve island parishes making up Inverness-shire's western seaboard, nine recorded some aspect of such activity.[6] Highland involvement in the British

2. R. Sedgwick (ed.), *The House of Commons, 1715–1754*, vols. 1–2 (London, 1970); L. Namier and J. Brooke (eds.), *The House of Commons, 1754–90*, vols. 2–3 (London, 1964); R.G. Thorne (ed.), *The House of Commons, 1790–1820*, vols. 3–5 (London, 1986); B.J. Broomfield, 'Some One Hundred Unreasonable Parliamentary Men – A study in Military Representation in the Eighteenth Century British Parliament', in *Journal of the Society for Army Historical Research*, vol. 39 (1969), pp. 94–6.
3. *The Scheme of the Erection of the Glasgow Highland Society* (Glasgow, 1760?); S.R.O., Seafield Muniments, GD 248/179/3/25x.
4. For discussion of the naval use of Gaelic manpower, see S.R.O., RH 4/158/1/2; RH 4/203/2/5(2).
5. N.L.S., Minto Papers, Ms 11014, ff. 41–42; *Caledonian Mercury*, 8 and 10 May 1790.
6. D.J. Withrington & I.R. Grant (eds.), *Old Statistical Account*, vols. 8, 17–20 (Wakefield 1979–83).

army easily surpassed the levels of manpower mobilised during the Jacobite era. Contemporary estimates for the Seven Years War period of 1756–63, for example, put the region's involvement at around 12,000 men – almost the same number as were mobilised in 1715, easily the largest of the Jacobite uprisings. Despite exaggerated suggestions that perhaps as many as 70,000 Highlanders served in the various regular, fencible and militia units raised during the French Revolutionary and Napoleonic Wars, more conservative estimates which include the volunteers nonetheless still point to totals ranging from 48,000 to around 37,000 men.[7] Given that the region's population stood at between approximately 250,000 and 300,000 during the last half of the eighteenth century, even the lower, more realistic estimates still represent a remarkable level of manpower drain into the army. Albeit the Highlands were in no way an officially instituted military reserve comparable to the Irish establishment, these levels of recruitment ensured that contemporaries routinely envisaged the region as something akin to a recruiting reservation.[8] In certain respects the Highlands assumed a function not dissimilar to other European peripheries or former frontier areas. Austrian deployment of Croat populations in distinct military establishments, for example, not only mirrored the tactic of the Highland regiment, but a similar equation of military service with commercial underdevelopment was likewise applied to both regions by their respective governments.[9]

Central to any understanding of why recruitment took the form it did in the Highlands is the fact that metropolitan perceptions of the region throughout the whole 1715–1815 period were remarkably inaccurate and increasingly anachronistic. Clanship and the range of its functions had been subject to such a degree of polemic and political misrepresentation, especially in the years from 1715–1750s,[10] that it is perhaps unsurprising that eighteenth-century governments exhibited a considerable level of ignorance and, more importantly, reliance on local agents for their understanding of the area. One of the most important factors dictating the region's relationship

7. S. Johnson, *A Journey to the Western Islands of Scotland* (London, 1984), p. 104; E. Richards, *A History of the Highland Clearances: Agrarian Change and the Evictions 1746–1886*, vol. 1 (London, 1982), p. 148; A.I. Macinnes, 'Scottish Gaeldom: The First Phase of Clearance', in T.M. Devine and R. Mitchison (eds.), *People and Society in Scotland, 1760–1830*, vol. 1 (Edinburgh, 1988), p. 83; J.E. Cookson, *The British Armed Nation, 1793–1815* (Oxford, 1997), p. 129.
8. Anon., *A Letter to a Noble Lord Containing a Plan for Effectually Uniting and Sincerely Attaching the Highlanders to the British Constitution and Revolutionary Settlement* (London, 1748), pp. 29–30; N.L.S., Fraser Collection, Ms 1034, f. 104, 'Observations on the North of Scotland, particularly the Island of Skye'; *Caledonian Mercury*, 24 October 1791; J. Macdonald, *A General View of the Agriculture of the Hebrides or Western Isles of Scotland* (Edinburgh, 1811), pp. 552–4.
9. M. Duffy, *The Army of Maria Theresa: The Armed Forces of Imperial Austria, 1740–1780* (London, 1977), pp. 84–89.
10. A.I. Macinnes, *Clanship, Commerce and the House of Stuart, 1603–1788* (East Linton, 1996), pp. 164–9, 171, 180–1.

with the British fiscal-military state was that the latter failed to recognise the decline and extinction of clanship, and instead retained remarkably traditional views regarding its military nature and function. This was to some extent evident prior to the 1745 uprising when, as a result of large-scale military campaigning on the continent during the Austrian War of Succession, government figures like Tweeddale and Robert Dundas encouraged chiefs like Macpherson of Cluny to exploit traditional clan ties to keep order in the region, thereby freeing regular troops for use as reinforcements in Flanders. Access to clan manpower, as much as a desire to rehabilitate Jacobites, became the rationale behind the government's disproportionate use of the region during the Seven Years' War, and again during the 1775–1783 conflict. Crucially, each successive recruiting drive masked the reality of profound economic change, and instead powerfully reinforced government misconceptions about clanship's continuing vitality. Thus, as late as 1797, arguably the single most powerful fiscal state in Western Europe believed it was still possible to mobilise Highland manpower in clan levies.[11]

The irony that as clanship imploded in the Highlands its influence was maintained at the very metropolitan centre which had been historically opposed to its existence, raises important questions with respect to the '45. It has become an accepted interpretation of Highland history that the final Jacobite uprising had little or no long-term impact on the development of the region. While an examination of the last Jacobite uprising from a socio-economic perspective justifies the view that it was largely irrelevant, this ignores its impact upon the political and governmental centre.[12] The '45 gave a practical demonstration of Highland militarism which, in turn, distorted British recruiting strategy for the following fifty-five years. It is difficult therefore not to come to the conclusion that the longer-term impact of the '45 on the Scottish Highlands has been seriously under-estimated. Outwith the region, it was seen as convincing proof of the northern population's innate bellicosity; and it is ironic that Jacobitism was the advert for Highland society that in effect stimulated its involvement within the empire in the specialised form of proprietary regiments.

British governments remained misinformed about the changes in the socio-economic structure of the Highlands largely because its agents in the region, the landlords themselves, had no reason to apprise the political centre of clanship's rapid decline and extinction; indeed, the opposite was the case. Given that the state still believed in clanship and awarded regimental commissions on that basis, there were practical and even lucrative reasons why landlords would continue to generate an impression of sustained local and kin-based power. In this sense clanship was still a crucially important factor

---

11. J.E. Cookson, *op. cit.*, pp. 137–38.
12. A.I. Macinnes, 'Jacobitism', in *History Today*, vol. 34 (1984), p. 29; T.M. Devine, *Clanship to Crofters' War: The Social Transformation of the Scottish Highlands* (Manchester, 1994), pp. 30–1.

for even the most commercially motivated of landlords, but now as a lobbying mechanism to expedite state and imperial colonisation rather than as a means for organising and protecting their local, autonomous power. Perhaps the greatest success for later eighteenth-century Highland landlords (from their perspective, at least) was not the imposition of commercial policies that increased estate revenues; rather, it was the successful pursuit of these policies alongside an equally successful ability to conceal from London the reality of clanship's effective extinction. The result was that the British state devised its recruiting policies for the Highlands as if clanship was still the supreme social arrangement. In the development of the region during the era of first-phase clearance clanship formed the framework of later eighteenth-century imperial government's understanding of the Scottish Highlands.

The British state's willingness to create distinctive recruiting arrangements centred upon what was perceived as the chiefs' clan power, points to an alternative analysis for the effects of large scale war upon the eighteenth century Highlands. Traditionally, regiment raising and the whole process of imperial conflict have been viewed as producing greater government centralism and a stronger identification amongst previously particularist societies with the idea of a Greater Britain. Yet the idea that war resulted in government reaching out from the centre to more fully assimilate peripheries has by no means gone unchallenged. 'Provincial' interests were as likely to reinvent themselves and become agents of the state, thereby manipulating its authority for their own ends and reinforcing their own status.[13] Highland landlords, through their manipulation of the metropolitan centre's belief in clanship, constitute a particularly high-profile and successful Scottish example of this process. Moreover, to justify excessive rewards of patronage landlords needed to distinguish themselves from their competitors: this they did by deliberately emphasising the uniqueness, both real and imaginary, of the Highlands. This raises an intriguing question as to the impact of the scramble for imperial posts and offices. While such rewards undoubtedly helped engender a new sense of Britishness at one level, a more subtle, indirect consequence was that the Highlands continued to be differentiated, as much as assimilated.

Indeed, it has recently been argued that the strain of large-scale conflict meant that the fiscal-military state was never in fact primarily concerned with centralising internal, domestic arrangements. Thus, rather than the orthodoxy that war and empire led to greater unity, it has been suggested that the diversion of government resources and attention into imperial expansion resulted in a process of domestic 'disengagement' by the political centre.[14] The belief of British governments that clanship could be re-deployed as a recruiting

---

13. J.E. Cookson, *op. cit.*, pp. 4–5, 7, 67.
14. J. Innes, 'The Domestic Face of the Fiscal-Military State: Government and Society in Eighteenth-Century Britain', in L. Stone (ed.), *An Imperial State at War: Britain from 1689–1815* (London, 1994), pp. 97–101.

mechanism for the empire was part of this process. It would explain, for example, why, after a determined if misdirected state assault upon its legal and military basis in 1747, William Pitt the Elder, when faced with unprecedented global war in 1757, sanctioned the use of kin association to obtain manpower from the Highlands. Indeed, the struggle for imperial supremacy was to witness, time and again, British governments encourage the military aspects of Highland society within the empire while striving simultaneously to undermine these characteristics within the region itself. Thus it was that the state enforced draconian disarming legislation while positively encouraging the settlement of armed Highlanders in areas as diverse as Georgia in 1735 and Quebec in 1784. Recruiting in the region was merely the most high profile, domestic symptom of this complex and ambiguous process. The global military effort to sustain British imperialism led in some instances, not to further integration, but to a distinct downgrading of assimilative tendencies within the United Kingdom itself and an active promotion of distinctiveness on contested imperial frontiers. Ultimately, recruiting may well be summarised as having taken the Highlands two steps forward towards a firmer sense of Britishness while simultaneously taking the region two steps back.

The impact of recruitment can be applied in a wider sense to Scotland's position within the British Union. Archibald Campbell, third Duke of Argyll's manipulation of the metropolitan need for military manpower is undoubtedly a classic example of how the disengagement process applied to Scotland as a whole. The 1745 uprising had seen the removal of Scotland's official manager and a determination on the part of key Westminster figures to ensure that Argyll did not automatically fill the vacuum and become a new Secretary of State for Scotland in all but name. However, with the arrival of war in May 1756 central government chose to disengage from the running of Scotland and, instead, looked to Argyll to fulfil the very role of manager that had aroused metropolitan hostility towards him in the first place. Indeed Argyll and, later, Dundas's efficient mobilisation of military manpower suggests that political management in Scotland can be seen as a form of 'provincial' response to empire. The end result was that both managers to some extent justified the idea that Scotland should have some distinct, though unofficial, political arrangement which furthered Scottish loyalty to Westminster while simultaneously providing Scots with access to state offices and patronage. No longer having, like court managers of the later seventeenth century, to control the Parliament in Edinburgh, managers like Argyll and Dundas had in effect evolved to better suit the realities of imperial politics, constituting the semi-official lobbying agent for Scots.[15] In contrast to the Irish Lord Lieutenant, their nearest British islands equivalent, Scottish

---

15. D. Szechi & D. Hayton, 'John Bull's Other Kingdoms: The English Government of Scotland & Ireland', in C. Jones (ed.), *Britain in the First Age of Party* (London, 1987), pp. 246–52; M. Fry, *The Dundas Despotism* (Edinburgh, 1992), pp. 308–9.

managers may well have found that the lack of a Parliament that might otherwise have continued to dominate their relationship with both metropolitan authorities and local political elites, meant they were better able to concentrate upon strategies that facilitated Scots colonisation of the wider empire. This is reflected in the fact that Argyll's supervised expansion of Highland regiments during the Seven Years War amounted to the first large example of government patronage since the Union which specifically catered for Scots. Comparisons of Ireland and Scotland, meantime, have emphasised that while the former retained its Parliament, though in a decidedly subservient relationship to Westminster, the latter's civic institutions were so distinctive as to avoid colonisation by large numbers of Englishmen. This meant that, after the Union, Scotland's political elite still did not face anywhere near the same level of competition for posts within their own country as experienced by Irishmen.[16] This suggests that the British-Highland military may have been doubly significant for Scots in that, first, it was clearly an avenue of imperial patronage where competition from other nationals within the British islands would be minimal, though by no means absent altogether. Second, and even more importantly, Highland regiments demonstrated to Scots that inclusion within the empire did not mean they would be restricted only to those areas of Church, Law and University which had been all but ring-fenced for them by the legislation of 1707. Crucially, from a Scots perspective, Highland regiments pointed to the logic that the wider empire, as distinct from the fully assimilated United Kingdom envisaged in the concept of North Britain, offered a safer, less competitive route to material wealth and equality with the English.[17]

Yet however innovative and sophisticated Scottish political elites proved themselves to be in formulating responses to the opportunities presented by the fiscal-military state and imperial expansion, it is nonetheless true that Highland military recruitment was based upon an essentially negative view of the region. Thus, an argument in support of excessive reliance upon Highland manpower was that it protected vital commercial and manufacturing sectors of the wider British economy from dislocation, labour shortages, wage inflation and decreased profitability. This supports the argument that the region experienced some form of 'internal colonialism', and that its economic development was organised merely to protect the core economies of the rest of the United Kingdom. The internal colonialism thesis is that areas like the Scottish Highlands with underdeveloped economies evolved along complementary, not competitive lines. Moreover, in order to find a market niche, the Highland economy developed in the form of 'highly specialised

16. F.G. James, *Ireland in the Empire, 1688–1700* (Cambridge, Mass, 1973), pp. 155–56; S.J. Connolly, 'Varieties of Britishness: Ireland, Scotland and Wales in the Hanoverian State', in A. Grant and K.J. Stringer (eds.), *Uniting the Kingdom? the Making of British History* (London, 1995), pp. 201–2.
17. C. Kidd, 'North Britishness and the Nature of Eighteenth Century British Patriotisms', in *The Historical Journal*, vol. 39 (1996), pp. 362–4.

export economies'.[18] Viewed in a negative light, recruiting can, arguably, be summarised as representing just such an economy; alternatively, in a positive sense, it can be see as a 'provincial' response which sought the most effective means of addressing the particular socio-economic conditions prevailing in the region at the time. From this perspective the process of internal colonisation is inverted and state revenue in the form of army commissions for the Highland elite, Chelsea pensions and volunteer companies for the tenantry is redirected for use on the periphery. In this way military employment can be envisaged as simply one of the specialised economies that emerged from the region's inclusion within the empire – Gaeldom's equivalent of Glasgow's tobacco trade. Moreover, becoming tied, into such a distinctive relationship with the fiscal-military state suggests that if one elite group in the British islands could be described as a Junker or service caste it was as much Highland landlords as members of the protestant Irish landowning class.[19]

Recruitment was also part of the broader picture of Highland economic development in this period in that it was evidence of an over-reliance on one or two staple industries or export trades in raw, primary materials, be it cattle, kelp, sheep or manpower. This in turn suggests that recruitment was indicative of a quite different, divergent pattern of imperialism in the Highlands. At one level, the financial importance of military employment in the region points to the fact that, unlike large areas of the United Kingdom which found both commercial diversity and depth through imperial expansion, the effect of inclusion within the empire in the case of the Highlands was an underwriting of economic underdevelopment and a subsequent over-reliance on one or two highly specialised economies. Yet the North of Scotland's experience of and reaction to the British Empire was quite different in another, equally fundamental respect. Thus, while the supposedly less peripheral, Lowland parts of Scotland constructed and identified their economic interests with other 'provincial' areas of the empire, most notably the North American colonies and the West Indies, the Highland response ironically placed a much greater emphasis on identifying with and relying upon the metropolitan centre and the fiscal-military state in particular.[20]

18. M. Hechter, *Internal Colonialism: The Celtic Fringe in British National Development, 1536–1966* (London, 1975), p. 81. For a more recent re-assertion of the internal colonialism theory, see E. Richards, 'Scotland and the Uses of the Atlantic Empire', in B. Bailyn and P. D. Morgan (eds.), *Strangers within the Realm: Cultural Margins of the First British Empire* (London, 1991), pp. 92–5.
19. T.G. Fraser, 'Ireland and India', in K. Jeffery (ed.), *An Irish Empire?: Aspects of Ireland and the British Empire* (Manchester, 1996), p. 78; J.M. Mackenzie, *Empires of Nature and the Nature of Empires: Imperialism, Scotland and the Environment* (East Linton, 1997), p. 65.
20. A. Calder, *Revolutionary Empire: The Rise of the English-Speaking Empires from the Fifteenth Century to the 1780s* (London, 1998), pp. 285–6, 357; N.C. Landsman, 'The Provinces and the Empire: Scotland, the American Colonies and the Development of British Provincial Identity', in L. Stone (ed.), *An Imperial State at War: Britain from 1689 to 1815* (London, 1994), pp. 260–1.

Paradoxically, therefore, by contrast with the often misguided and obsolete perceptions that prompted the state's decision to recruit in the Highlands, the motives which prompted landlord involvement with the British military represented a rational and pertinent 'regional imperialism' that was designed to answer distinctive socio-economic realities. While the commercialised nature of Highland recruiting has traditionally been emphasised in order to demonstrate the severe alienation it caused amongst the region's population, such an interpretation is equally important in seeking to explain why elites continued what might otherwise have seemed an increasingly outmoded and obsolete practice.[21] The opposite was in the fact the case: through the medium of military levying Highland proprietors accessed state finances that had the additional benefit of remaining relatively stable while also, crucially, complementing other estate-based sources of revenue. Yet while the motives of landlords were characterised by their new commercial attitudes, the interaction between recruitment and Highland tenantry is far more ambiguous. Despite the historiographic orthodoxy that military recruitment was the method whereby Highlanders defended their traditional rural communities against landlord-inspired change, detailed examination of estate records and, more importantly, the stated aims of recruits themselves, suggest a somewhat different interpretation.[22] Recruiting did undoubtedly delay sheep farming on the Gordon, Seaforth, Glengarry and Sutherland estates during the period 1775–1800; however, this needs to be contrasted with the fact that levying also undermined the established social structure. Recruitment was socially corrosive because of its selective nature. Given that landlord motivation was entrepreneurial, recruitment was designed to complement, not to damage, estate economies. The result was that those who had the least input in terms of rent productivity were targeted as a priority. However, this strategy also meant that Highland recruits were unrepresentative of the hierarchical and complex social structure evident within the pre-clearance *baile*. This underlying contrast, between an essentially heterogeneous Highland society and military recruits drawn excessively from one or two estate groups, was to have significant social consequences. By promising land to personnel from backgrounds that were traditionally landless or largely landless in character, military levying put additional pressure upon a landholding system already experiencing considerable stress. Thus, far from protecting traditional social structures, recruitment helped to focus land hunger on established tenurial arrangements on estates as diverse as Lochtayside and Skye. Indeed, such was the level of demand legitimised by the process that even seven years after the end of the Napoleonic wars, in March 1822, Maclaine of Lochbuie noted regarding a neighbour's estate: 'Every

---

21. J. Prebble, *Mutiny: Highland Regiments in Revolt, 1743–1804* (Harmondsworth, Middlesex, 1975), p. 95.
22. R. Somers, *Letters from the Highlands* (Glasgow, 1848), pp. 22–3: J. Prebble, *op. cit.*, pp. 96–101.

vacancy on Lochnell's estate is I may engage, ten deep to old soldiers and other followers'.[23] One consequence of this type of pressure was that it facilitated the destruction of the tacksman while stimulating the development of subdivision and the emergence of a new lesser tenantry. Crofting can in fact be directly linked to British military levying because demobilisation produced periods of especially acute demand for land. Division of tenant holdings, already occurring on a piecemeal basis to support the kelp industry, became something of an estate management imperative in order that the settlement needs of soldiers and those they displaced could be met. Moreover, crofting can also be traced directly to the ambition of lower Highland tenantry as articulated in the form of recruiting promises. In areas as far apart as Netherlorne and North Uist this social trend, far from uniting estate populations, often led to systematic attempts by returning soldiery to evict established tenantry. Thus, while undoubtedly a testimony to the coercive power of Highland landlordism, military service also exacerbated internal tensions within the mass of the population and ensured that the emergence of crofting was characterised in part by the settlement of certain tenantry through the eviction and downward social mobility of others.[24]

There is another aspect to recruitment, besides its role in the development of crofting, which allows it to be compared directly with kelping – namely its relatively short lifespan. For all the romantic praise heaped on Highland regiments as the embodiment of an ancient martial tradition, it is important to note the relatively short space of time during which large-scale recruitment for the British army was actually practised in the region. Only sixty years separate the first Highland regiment, the 42nd Black Watch, from the last unit raised by proprietary means, the 93rd Sutherland Highlanders. Because recruitment in the region centred upon serving the needs of the army on an *ad hoc* basis, usually during periods of acute imperial crisis, it was vulnerable to the development of more systematic, fully professionalised methods of obtaining men. Furthermore, because the form of recruiting most successfully practised in the region relied upon civilian, proprietary power, it was susceptible to criticism from British military elites who disliked what they perceived as the preferential promotion of non-army personnel. As a result of these tensions over the nature and composition of the army, recruiting did not prove in the longer term to be a particularly stable form of regional economic activity – again, similar to kelping. Thus, from the late 1790s onwards, as governments increasingly recruited by ballot and parish quotas, proprietary levying was not only highlighted as an inefficient and costly method of recruiting but, indeed, was rendered unnecessary. Yet by denying landlords the possibility of enlisting men for rank, these developments removed what had been a crucial financial prop for post-clanship Highland society. The possibility that their populations might prove the means of

23. S.R.O., Maclaine of Lochbuie Papers, GD 174/1633/3.
24. J. Hunter, *The Making the Crofting Community* (Edinburgh, 1976), p. 15.

obtaining military office and revenue had to some extent justified the concept of a numerous tenantry to many Highland proprietors. This suggests that while ultimately forced to do so by the scale of the French wars, it is nonetheless the case that changes in British recruiting policy actually increased the redundancy of Highland populations, and so the eventual likelihood of their clearance.

Yet in a way the arrival of professional forms of recruiting was merely symptomatic of a wider evolution in the British state that had serious implications for the Highlands given the nature and limitations of its own particular integration within the empire. So much of the region's economic activity by 1815 revolved around the concept of a mercantilist, fiscal-military state which protected, often by aggressive military means, British manufactures and commerce within a protectionist imperial framework. The dramatic increase in kelp prices during the era of Napoleon's Continental System, for example, was perhaps the main, key factor that kept whole communities in the north-west Highlands economically viable. Cattle, likewise, increased in value as a direct result of, amongst other things, Britain's inordinately large navy. However, in 1815, with the end of what can be seen as a prolonged conflict with Spain and, most especially, France for imperial primacy, Britain's need for such an aggressive fiscal-military state was much reduced. In its place there emerged a *laissez-faire* polity with decidedly less interventionist tendencies and which slashed military spending.[25] The resounding British victory at Waterloo, by removing any immediate need for the type of state and 'big government' which the Highlands had come to overly rely upon as part of its own approach to empire, proved in many ways to be a greater, far more fundamental reverse for the region than Culloden.

---

25. J.E. Cookson *op. cit.*, pp. 246–7; P. Harding and P. Mandler, 'From "Fiscal-Military" State to Laissez Faire State, 1760–1850', in *Journal of British Studies*, vol. 32 (1993), pp. 46–8, 52–3.

APPENDICES

Appendix 1: Recruitment Levels, from Old Statistical Account of Scotland

County	Parish/District	Male Population	Date[s]	No recruited	Ratio
Sutherland	Kildonan	286#	1775–83	102	1:3
Sutherland	Reay	1,228	1778–83	175	1:7
Inverness	Kilmallie & Kilmonavaig	6,088*	1756–63	750	1:8
Argyll	Tiree	1,184	1775–83	120	1:10
Fife	Crail	738	1775–83	72	1:10
Renfrew	Kilbarchan	762	1790s	70	1:11
Argyll	Tiree	1,184	1793	100	1:12
Wigton	Stranraer	1,050*	1778	80	1:13
West Lothian	W. Queensferry	505*	1790s	35	1:14
Argyll	Ardnamurchan	2,126	1793–5	139	1:15
Ross	Lochalsh	640	1793	40	1:16
Argyll	Dunoon	1,683*	1775–83	90	1:19
Kincardine	Nigg	497	1775–83	24	1:21
Caithness	Thurso	1,573	1793–4	70	1:22
Stirling	Campsie	800	1790s	35	1:23
East Lothian	Prestonpans	936	1775–83	40	1:23
Aberdeen	Aberdour	609	1775–83	27	1:23
Shetland	Standsting	630	1790s	24	1:26
Angus	Craig	639	1775–83	24	1:27
Inverness	Urquhart	2,355*	1793	80	1:29
Lanark	Hamilton	2,303	1778	60	1:38
Argyll	Rum	443*	1793	11	1:40
Angus	Kirriemuir	2,190	1775–83	52	1:42
Ross	Avoch	622	1775–83	13	1:48
Argyll	Kilfinichen & Kilviceuen	3,002*	1775–83	60	1:50
Argyll	Kilfinichen & Kilviceuen	3,002*	1793	56	1:54
East Lothian	Whittingham	296	1775–83	4	1:74
Lanark	Cadder	842	1790s	11	1:77
Moray	Dyke & Moy	728	1793	8	1:91
Shetland	Delting	1,504*	1790s	16	1:94
Fife	Leuchars	1,620*	1790s	14	1:116
Roxburgh	Linton	383*	1790s	3	1:128
Dumfries	Johnstone	293	1790s	2	1:147
Ayr	Kilwinning	2,360*	1790s	12	1:197
Shetland	Unst	1,998*	1790s	10	1:199
Angus	Edzell	470	1791	2	1:235
Orkney	S. Ronaldsay	1,426*	1790s	5	1:285

Note: * denotes total population only, so ratio in these areas underestimated by approximately one half. # = Kildonan includes males of military age only. D.J. Withrington and I. R. Grant (eds.), *The Statistical Account of Scotland*, vols. 2–20 (Wakefield, 1973–83). Highland average = 1: 24: Lowland average = 1: 83.

Appendix 2: Chelsea Pensioners residing in Scottish Counties, Ireland and England, 1770

County	Population [1775]	Chelsea Pensioners	Ch. P. per Population
Midlothian & Edinburgh	89,094	724	1: 123
Nairn	5,694	30	1: 189
Inverness	63,929	270	1: 237
Caithness	22,215	88	1: 252
Lanark	80,559	330	1: 244
Stirling	40,798	124	1: 329
Sutherland	20,774	52	1: 400
Ross & Cromarty	47,654	117	1: 407
West Lothian	16,829	39	1: 432
Moray	30,010	69	1: 434
Aberdeen	113,315	259	1: 437
Dunbarton	13,857	29	1: 478
Ayr	59,268	112	1: 529
Berwick	23,906	45	1: 531
Banff	40,409	74	1: 546
Clackmannan	9,003	16	1: 563
Argyll	60,849	107	1: 569
Angus	68,593	118	1: 581
Dumfries	41,934	70	1: 599
Roxburgh	31,392	50	1: 627
Wigton	16,466	26	1: 633
Perth	121,612	166	1: 732
Renfrew	26,620	34	1: 783
Kinross	4,889	6	1: 814
East Lothian	29,709	31	1: 958
Fife	80,970	83	1: 975
Kirkcudbright	21,205	7	1: 3,029
Bute	6,866	2	1: 3,433
Orkney & Shetland	38,751	7	1: 5,536
Kincardine	24,346	2	1: 12,173
Scotland	1,395,500	3,087	1: 452
England & Wales	6,899,000	10,391	1: 663
Ireland	3,584,000	2,055	1: 1,744

Note: Figures for Chelsea Pensioners drawn from S.R.O., Grant of Monymusk Papers, GD 345/1249. County populations are drawn from 1755 figures shown in the introduction to D.J. Withrington and I.R. Grant (eds.), *The Statistical Account of Scotland*, vols 2–20 (Wakefield, 1973–83). National population totals are drawn from G. Holmes and D. Szechi, *The Age of Oligarchy: Pre-Industrial Britain, 1722–1783* (London, 1993), pp. 345 & 350.

Appendix 3: Greenwich Pensions paid in Scottish Ports, 1815

Burgh	Population (1790s)	Naval Pension (1815)	£ pension per person
Lerwick	903	£446	1: 2
Anstruther	1,000	£199	1: 5
Kirkcaldy	2,607	£658	1: 3
Port Glasgow	4,036	£714	1: 6
Tobermory	300	£51	1: 6
Kirkwall	2,000	£276	1: 7
Leith	13,841	£1,851	1: 7
Dunbar	1,200	£147	1: 8
Bo'ness	2,613	£297	1: 9
Greenock	14,299	£1,118	1: 13
Montrose	5,194	£399	1: 13
Alloa	2,941	£218	1: 13
Ayr	3,871	£231	1: 17
Campbeltown	4,985	£292	1: 17
Aberdeen	24,493	£1,061	1: 23
Stornoway	1,340	£57	1: 23
Stranraer	1,602	£56	1: 29
Rothesay	2,607	£81	1: 32
Dundee	22,500	£692	1: 33
Inverness	5,107	£142	1: 36
Prestonpans	1,492	£36	1: 41
Wigton	1,032	£18	1: 57
Oban	586	£10	1: 59
Kirkcudbright	1,641	£25	1: 66
Perth	19,871	£288	1: 69
Port Patrick	512	£4	1: 128
Fort William	1,200	£6	1: 200

Note: Greenwich pension figures drawn from P.R.O., Scottish Commissioners of Customs Accounts, T. 47/21. Population figures from D.J. Withrington and I. R. Grant (eds.), *The Statistical Account of Scotland*, vols. 2–20 (Wakefield, 1973–83).

Appendix 4: Fines for Naval Quota Deficiencies, Scottish Counties, 1795–6

County	Population	Fine	£ fine per population
Kirkcudbright	26,707	£1,400	1: 19
Sutherland	22,681	£1,170	1: 19
Dunbarton	18,728	£925	1: 20
Roxburgh	32,391	£1,400	1: 23
Moray	27,549	£1,150	1: 24
Dumfries	53,589	£2,125	1: 25
Caithness	24,802	£975	1: 25
Argyll	73,412	£2,713	1: 27
Lanark	151,234	£5,375	1: 28
Nairn	5,979	£200	1: 30
Banff	41,889	£1,225	1: 34
Kincardine	26,799	£750	1: 36
Clackmannan	8,693	£225	1: 38
Ross & Cromarty	56,386	£1,455	1: 39
Aberdeen	113,315	£2,575	1: 44
Inverness	70,491	£1,350	1: 52
Perth	126,411	£2,350	1: 53
Wigton	20,993	£350	1: 60
Stirling	48,428	£400	1: 121
Ayr	73,511	£450	1: 163
Fife	87,224	£25	1: 3,490

Note: Figures drawn from S.R.O. Exchequer Papers, E 208/9/1 and D.J. Withrington and I. R. Grant (eds.), *The Statistical Account of Scotland*, vols. 2–20 (Wakefield, 1973–83).

Appendix 5: Recruitment and Demobilisation Rates, West-Highland Seaboard, 1756–63

District	No. of Fighting men	Recruited in 1756–63	%	Men returned after demobilisation	% of those recruited
Lewis	1,331	170	12.7	34	20
Harris	430	118	27.4	14	11.8
North Uist	381*	60	15.7	–	–
S. Uist & Benbecula	441*	100	22.6	–	–
Barra	230*	31	13.4	6	19.3
Islay	1,068	c. 500	46.8	–	–
Skye	2,248	c. 500	22.2	–	–
Glenelg	363	100	27.5	–	–
Canna	114	14	12.2	3	21.4
Coll	238	40	16.8	–	–
Tiree	202	57	28.2	12	21
Mull	1,057	350	33.1	50	14.2
	8,103	2,040	25.1	–	–

Note: Figures from M.M. Mackay (ed.), *The Rev. Dr. John Walker's Report on the Hebrides, 1764–1771* (Edinburgh, 1980).

Appendix 6: Military and Loyalist Emigrants, Quebec Province, 1784

Township	Total Population	Highlanders & %	Males & %	Females & %	Children & Servants	Soldiers & family & %
Chaleur Bay	129	31 (24%)	11 (35.4)	4 (12.9%)	16 (51.6%)	0
Sorel	316	25 (7.9)	7 (28%)	6 (24%)	12 (48%)	24 (96%)
Montreal	617	54 (8.75)	18 (33.3)	10 (18.5%)	26 (48%)	37 (68.5%)
Chambly	66	1 (1.5%)	1 (100%)	–	–	1 (100%)
St. Johns	375	27 (7.2%)	6 (22.25)	7 (25.9%)	14 (51.8%)	12 (44.4%)
Lachine Point	207	40 (19%)	7 (17.5%)	12 (30%)	21 (52.5%)	19 (47.5)
Mullie	90	33 (36.6%)	15 (45.4)	6 (18.1%)	12 (36.3%)	13 (39.3%)
1st Township	456	340 (74.5)	93 (27.3)	64 (18.8%)	183 (53.8)	28 (8.2%)
2nd Township	517	107 (20.6)	36 (33.6)	22 (20.5%)	49 (45.7%)	46 (42.9%)
3rd Township	75	6 (8%)	3 (50%)	–	3 (50%)	5 (83.3%)
4th Township	202	26 (12.8%)	10 (38.4)	4 (15.3%)	12 (46.1%)	0
5th Township	177	12 (6.7%)	5 (41.6%)	1 (8.3%)	6 (50%)	9 (75%)
6th Township	166	40 (24%)	18 (45%)	6 (15%)	16 (40%)	29 (72.5)
7th Township	228	12 (5.2%)	3	2	7 (58.3%)	12 (100%)
8th Township	182	9 (4.9%)	4 (44.4%)	1 (11.1%)	4 (44.4%)	7 (77.7%)
Cataragui N° 1	220	1 (0.4%)	1 (100%)	–	–	1 (100%)
Cataragui N° 2	416	34 (8.1%)	14 (41.7)	5 (14.7%)	15 (44.1%)	0
Cataragui N° 3	580	19 (3.2%)	14 (73.6)	4 (21%)	1 (5.2%)	17 (89.4%)
Cataragui N° 4	240	–	–	–	–	–
Cataragui N° 5	299	33 (11%)	24 (72.7)	2 (6%)	7 (21.2%)	33 (100%)
Total	5,558	850 (15.2)	290 (34.1)	156 (18.1)	404 (47.5)	293 (34.4)

Note: Figures from B.L. Haldimand Papers, Add Ms 21828, ff. 29–151.

Bibliography

MANUSCRIPTS
Aberdeen University Library

Material Relating to British Fisheries Society – Mss 960, 962, 2015, 2023.
Gordon Military Papers – Ms 2284.

British Library

Egerton Mss, Ms 929, 'Memorial on Nova Scotia'.
Haldimand Papers, Add Mss 21826, 21828.
Hardwicke Papers, Add Mss 35447–51, 35509–10.
Holland House Papers, Add Mss 51375, 51378, 51429.
Leeds Papers, Egerton Mss, Ms 3433.
Letter Book of John Calcraft, Add Ms 17493.
Liverpool Papers, Add Mss 38192, 38342.
Newcastle Papers, Add Mss 32687, 32707, 32712–15, 32717, 32727, 32736–37, 32854, 32857, 32859–62, 32864, 32869–70, 32890–91, 32995–97, 33047, 33049.

Glasgow City Archives

TD 132, Records of Messrs George Kippen, John Glasford & Co., TD 132/48.
TD 219, Campbell of Succoth Papers, TD 219/10.

Glasgow University Business Records Centre

J.A. & J.L. Campbell & Lamond, W.S., UGD 37/2/1–2.

Glasgow University Library

Campbell of Inverneil Papers.

Highland Regional Archive

Caithness, Cromatry & Sutherland Commissioners of Supply Papers.

Mitchell Library

British Army Lists, 1740–1784.

National Library of Scotland

Adv. Ms 20.5.5., Manuscript on Improvement of North West Highlands (1784?).
Culloden Papers, Ms 2968.
Fletcher of Saltoun Papers, Mss 16511, 16513, 16615, 16517–19, 16591, 16593, 16596–97, 16604–5, 16609–10, 16626, 16630–31, 16677, 16690–94, 16696, 16698, 16708–10, 16714, 16716–17, 16725, 16728, 17505–6, 17522, 17563–4, 17589–90.
Fraser Collection, Ms 1034, 'Observations on the North of Scotland, particularly the Island of Skye.'
Letter Book of Lord George Beauclerk, Ms 13497.
Mackenzie of Delvine Papers, Mss 1136, 1140, 1143, 1149, 1171, 1238, 1284, 1314, 1319, 1327, 1367, 1407, 1461, 1483–85, 1487.
Melville Papers, Mss 4–6, 45, 53, 57, 1048, 1054, 1070, 3834; Miscellaneous Melville Papers, Mss 14838, 19578.
Minto Papers, Mss 11001, 11002, 11005, 11009, 11014, 11015, 11017, 11035.
Minutes of Tutors of Maclaine of Lochbuie, Ms 20758.
Miscellaneous Small Collections, Ms 3638.
Murray Erskine Collection, Ms 5079.
Stuart-Stevenson Papers, Ms 8250.
Yester Papers – Mss 7045, 7054–58, 7060–66.
Sutherland Papers – Dep. 313; Joass Accession 10225.

John Rylands Library

Bagshawe Muniments, B. 5/1.

Private Collections

Blair Atholl Muniments.
Clan Donald Trust Library, Macdonald of Sleat Papers.
Dumfries House, Loudon Papers.
Dunvegan Castle Muniments.

Public Record Office

P.R.O. Chatham Papers, 30/8/18, 33, 240 & 242.
Colonial Office: C.O. 5/115, 1134.
                   C.O. 42/11–12, 16, 24, 72, 82, 94, 316–17.

```
                    C.O. 43/10.
                    C.O. 217/56-7, 59-60, 103-4.
                    C.O. 226/5, 7-8.
                    C.O. 700/Nova Scotia/50, 54, 67.
State Papers:       S.P. 41/27.
                    S.P. 54/45-7.
Treasury Papers:    T. 47/12 & 21.
War Office:         W.O. 1/617, 972-5, 977-79, 991, 993, 995-8, 1002.
                    W.O. 4/101-3.
                    W.O. 120/5, 7, 14-18.
                    W.O. 123/113, 115.
```

National Archives of Scotland (formerly Scottish Record Office (S.R.O.))

Abercairny Muniments – GD 24
Abercromby of Forglen & Birenbog – GD 185
Breadalbane & Gavin of Langton Papers – RH 4/196
Boyle of Shewalton Papers – GD 1/481
Campbells of Balliveolin – GD 13
Campbells of Stonefield – GD 14
Campbells of Jura – GD 67
Campbells of Barcaldine – GD 170
Campbells of Breadalbane – GD 112
Campbells of Dunstaffnage – GD 202
Clerk of Pencuick – GD 18
Craigie of Glendoick Papers – GD 1/609
Cunningham/Graham Muniments – GD 22
Court of Session Productions – C.S. 96/1401, Farm Journal Book of Rosehall Farm; C.S. 96/3108, 'Log Book of Campbeltown registered vessel '*The Peggy*'.
D. Murray–Rose Papers – GD 1/400.
Descriptive Roll of 93rd Highlanders – RH 2/8/99
Exchequer Records – E 208/9/1.
Forfeited Estate Papers – E721–E788
Fraser-Mackintosh Collection – GD 128
Gillanders of Highfield Papers – GD 427
Gordon Castle Muniments – GD 44
Grant of Monymusk – GD 345
Highland Society Sederunt Books – RH 4/188/1–4
Home Office Domestic Entry Books – RH 2/4/218–222, 313, 318
Irvine-Robertson Series – GD 1/53/103.
Kennedy of Dalquharran Papers – GD 27
Loch Muniments – GD 268
John Macgregor Collection – GD 50
Mar & Kellie Papers – GD 124

Mackay of Bighouse – GD 87
Mackenzie of Coul – GD 1/1149
Mackenzie of Seaforth Muniments – GD 46
Maclaine of Lochbuie Papers – GD 174
Macpherson of Cluny – GD 80
Melville Castle Muniments – GD 51
Methven Collection, Letter Books of William Macdonald, GD 1/8/17–18
Miscellaneous Broadstairs Papers – GD 1/616
Mitchell Collection, RH 2/5/12.
Sir James Montgomery Papers, RH 4/56/40
Montrose Muniments, GD 220
Papers Relating to Robert Craigie of Glendoick – GD 1/609
Plan to Raise Twenty Thousand Men from the Scottish Highlands, 1803 – RH 1/2/251
Robertson of Straloch Papers – GD 1/90
Seafield Muniments – GD 248
Scrymgeour/Wedderburn Muniments – GD 137
Society of Antiquaries Collection – GD 103
Steuart of Dalguise Muniments – GD 38
Townshend Papers – RH 4/56/11–12; RH 4/98/1
Trustees of Manufactures & Fisheries – NG 1/1/16, 113; NG 1/3/8

CONTEMPORARY NEWSPAPERS & PERIODICALS

Caledonian Mercury
Edinburgh Advertiser
Edinburgh Evening Courant
Glasgow Mercury
London Gazette
The Scottish Highlander and North of Scotland Advertiser
The Scots Magazine

CONTEMPORARY COMMENTARIES

Anderson, J., *An Account of the Present State of the Hebrides and Western Coasts of Scotland* (Dublin, 1786)
Anderson, J. *The Interest of Great Britain with regard to her American Colonies Considered* (London, 1784)
Anon., *A Letter to a Noble Lord Containing a Plan for Effectually Uniting and Sincerely Attaching the Highlanders to the British Constitution and Revolutionary Settlement* (London, 1748)
Anon., *Political Observations Occasioned by the State of Agriculture in the North of Scotland* (n.p., 1756)
Anon., *Answers to the Queries Addressed to the Serious Consideration of the Public* (n.d., 1760)

Anon., *The Public Catechised; or a Few Cool Questions to the People* (n.p., 1760?)

Anon., *The Scheme of the Erection of the Glasgow Highland Society* (Glasgow, 1760?)

Anon., *The Present Conduct of the Chieftains and Proprietors of Lands in the Highlands of Scotland Towards their Clans and People Considered Impartially* (Edinburgh, 1773)

Anon., *A Letter to the Lord Advocate of Scotland* (Edinburgh, 1777)

Anon., *A Letter to His Grace The Duke of Buccleuch on National Defence. To which is Added a Postscript Relative to Regiments of Fencible Men Raising in Scotland* (Edinburgh, 1778)

Bell, J., *Reasons Against a Militia For Scotland* (Edinburgh, 1783)

Boswell, J., *A Letter to the People of Scotland on the Present State of the Nation* (Edinburgh, 1783)

Brown, R., *Strictures and Remarks on the Earl of Selkirk's Observations on the Present State of the Highlands* (Edinburgh, 1806)

Dalrymple, J., *Letters from Sir John Dalrymple to the Right Honourable Lord Viscount Barrington* (London, 1779)

Douglas, N., *Journal of a Mission to Parts of the Highlands of Scotland in Summer and Harvest, 1797* (Edinburgh, 1799)

Douglas, T. (5th Earl of Selkirk), *Observations on the Present State of the Highlands with a View of the Causes and Probable Consequences of Emigration* (Edinburgh, 1806)

Douglas, T. (5th Earl of Selkirk), *On the Necessity of a More Effectual System of National Defence and the Means of Establishing the Permanent Security of the Kingdom* (London, 1808)

Ferguson, A., *A Sermon Preached in the Erse Language to His Majesty's First Highland Regiment of Foot* (London, 1746)

Grant, A., *A Dissertation on the Chief Obstacles to the Improvement of Land and Introducing Better Methods of Agriculture throughout Scotland* (Aberdeen, 1760)

Haldane, J.A., *Journal of a Tour Through the Northern Counties of Scotland and the Orkney Isles, in Autumn 1797* (Edinburgh, 1798)

Irvine, A., *An Inquiry into the Causes and Effects of Emigration from the Highlands* (Edinburgh, 1802)

Johnson, S., *A Journey to the Western Islands of Scotland* (London, 1984)

Knox, J., *A View of the British Empire more Especially Scotland: with some Proposals for the Improvement of that Country and the Extension of its Fisheries and the Relief of the People* (London, 1785)

Loch, D., *Essays on the Trade, Commerce, Manufactures and Fisheries of Scotland*, vol. 1 (Edinburgh, 1778)

Macdonald, J., *A General View of the Agriculture of the Hebrides or Western Isles of Scotland* (Edinburgh, 1811)

Mackenzie, G.S., *A General Survey of the Counties of Ross and Cromarty* (London, 1810)

Macleod, D., *Gloomy Memories in the Highlands of Scotland versus Mrs. Harriet Beecher Stowe's Sunny Memories* (Glasgow, 1892)

Mitchell, G., *Remarks upon a Publication entitled, Journal of a Tour Through the Northern Counties of Scotland and the Orkney Isles, in Autumn, 1797* (Aberdeen, 1799)

Robertson, J., *A General View of the Agriculture of the County of Inverness* (London, 1808).

Somers, R., *Letters from the Highlands* (Glasgow, 1848)

Stewart, A., *An Account of a Late Revival of Religion in a part of the Highlands of Scotland* (Edinburgh, 1800)

Stewart, D., *Sketches of the Character, Manners and Present State of the Highlanders of Scotland*, 2 vols. (Edinburgh, 1822)

Thom, W., *Informations Concerning the Province of North Carolina, Addressed to the Emigrants from the Highlands and Western Isles of Scotland* (Glasgow, 1773)

Walker, J., *An Economical History of the Hebrides and Highlands of Scotland*, 2 vols. (Edinburgh, 1808)

White, P., *Observations upon the Present State of the Scotch Fisheries and the Improvement of the Interior Parts of the Highlands* (Edinburgh, 1791)

PRINTED PRIMARY SOURCES

Adam, C.E. (ed.), *View of the Political State of Scotland in the Last Century* (Edinburgh, 1887)

Adam, R.J. (ed.), *John Home's Survey of Assynt* (Edinburgh, 1960)

Adam, R.J. (ed.), *Sutherland Estate Management, 1802–1816*, 2 vols. (Edinburgh, 1972)

Almon, J. (ed.), *The Parliamentary Register or History of the Proceedings & Debates of the House of Commons* (London, 1775–83)

A. Smith, *An Inquiry into the Nature and Causes of the Wealth of Nations*, eds. R.H. Campbell and A.S. Skinner, vol. 2 (Oxford, 1976)

Cregeen, E.R. (ed.), *Argyll Estate Instructions: Mull, Morvern and Tiree, 1771–1805* (Edinburgh, 1964)

Dalrymple, J. (ed.), *Memoirs of Great Britain and Ireland from the dissolution of the last parliament of Charles II until the sea battle of La Hogue*, vol. 2 (London, 1773)

Donne, W.B. (ed.), *The Correspondence of King George III with Lord North from 1768–1783*, vol. 1 (London, 1867)

Duff, R.H., *Culloden Papers* (London, 1815)

Ferguson, J. (ed.), *The Scots Dutch Brigade in the service of the United Netherlands, 1572–1782* (Edinburgh, 1899)

Fortescue, J. (ed.), *The Correspondence of King George III*, vols. 3–4 (London, 1928)

Fraser, W., *The Chiefs of Grant*, 2 vols. (Edinburgh, 1883)

Grant, F.J. (ed.), *Commissariat Records of the Isles: Register of Testaments* (Edinburgh, 1902)
Gray, J.M. (ed.), *Sir John Clerk of Penicuik* (Edinburgh, 1892)
Hayter, T. (ed.), *An Eighteenth Century Secretary at War: The papers of William Viscount Barrington* (London, 1988)
H.M.C., *Laing Manuscripts*, vol. 2 (London, 1925)
Journal of the House of Commons, vols. 37–38 & 40 (London, 1803)
Kyd, J.G. (ed.), *Scottish Population Statistics* (Edinburgh, 1952)
MacArthur, M.M. (ed.), *Survey of Lochtayside, 1769* (Edinburgh, 1936)
Mackay, M.M. (ed.), *The Rev. Dr. John Walker's Report on the Hebrides, 1764 and 1771* (Edinburgh, 1980)
Macleod, A. (ed.), *The Songs of Duncan Ban Macintyre* (Edinburgh, 1952)
Macleod, R.C., *The Book of Dunvegan*, vol. 2 (Aberdeen, 1939)
Matheson, W. (ed.), *The Songs of John MacCodrum* (Edinburgh, 1938)
Miller, A.H. (ed.), *Scottish Forfeited Estate Papers, 1715–1745* (Edinburgh, 1909)
The Parliamentary History of England from the Earliest Period to the Year 1803, vols. 13–15 & 19 (London, 1813–14).
Paton, H. (ed.), H.M.C., *Polywarth Manuscripts, 1725–80*, vol. 5 (London, 1961)
Redington, R.J. (ed.), *Calendar of Home Office Papers, 1760–65* (London, 1878)
Roberts, R.A., (ed.), *Calendar of Home Office Papers, 1770–1775*, vols. 1–2 (London, 1881 & 1899)
Russell, J. (ed.), *Correspondence of John 4th Duke of Bedford*, vol. 1 (London, 1842)
Sixth Report of the Royal Commission on Historical Manuscripts (London, 1877)
Stamp, A.E. (ed.), *Journal of the Commissioners for Trade and Plantations, 1768–1775* (London, 1937)
Statutes at Large from the Twentieth Year of the Reign of George II to the Thirtieth Year of King George II (London, 1769)
Swinton, T. (ed.), *The Poetry of Badenoch* (Inverness, 1906)
Warrand, D. (ed.), *More Culloden Papers*, vols. 1–5 (Inverness, 1930)
Wills, V., *Statistics of the Annexed Estates, 1755–56* (Edinburgh, 1973)
Withrington, D.J. and Grant, I.R. (eds.), *The Statistical Account of Scotland*, vols. 2–20 (Wakefield 1973–83)
Yorke, P.C. (ed.), *The Life and Correspondence of Philip Yorke Lord Chancellor Hardwicke*, vol. 3 (Cambridge, 1913)

PARLIAMENTARY PAPERS

Parliamentary Papers, 1841, *First Report of the Select Committee on Emigration (Scotland)*.

Parliamentary Papers, 1846, XXVII, *Documents Relative to the Distress in Scotland, 1783.*
Parliamentary Papers, 1884, XXXII–III, XXXV, *Report of H.M.'s Commissioners into the Condition of the Crofters and Cottars in the Highlands and Islands of Scotland.*

SECONDARY SOURCES
BOOKS & ARTICLES

Adam, M.I., 'The Highland Emigration of 1770', in *Scottish Historical Review*, vol. 16 (1919)

Adams, I. and Somerville, M., *Cargoes of Despair and Hope: Scottish Emigration to North America, 1603–1803* (Edinburgh, 1993)

Allardyce, A., *Scotland and Scotsmen in the Eighteenth Century*, vol. 1 (Edinburgh, 1888).

Anderson, O., 'The Role of the Army in Parliamentary Management during the American War of Independence', in *Journal of the Society for Army Historical Research*, vol. 34 (1956)

Ayling, S., *The Elder Pitt: Earl of Chatham* (London, 1976)

Bailyn, B., *Voyagers to the West: Emigration from Britain to America on the Eve of the Revolution* (London, 1986)

Bailyn, B. and Morgan, P.D. (eds.), 'Introduction', in *Strangers within the Realm: Cultural Margins of the First British Empire* (London, 1991)

Barker, T.M., *Army, Aristocracy, Monarchy: Essays on War, Society, and Government in Austria, 1618–1780* (New York, 1982)

Bayly, C.A., *Imperial Meridian: The British Empire and the World, 1780–1730* (London, 1989)

Beckett, T., 'The Augmentation of the Army in Ireland, 1767–69' in *English Historical Review*, vol. 96 (1981)

Black, J., 'Foreign Policy and the British State, 1742–1793', in J. Black (ed.), *British Politics and Society from Walpole to Pitt* (London, 1990)

Black, J., *Pitt the Elder* (Cambridge, 1992)

Brewer, J., *The Sinews of Power: War, Money and the English State, 1688–1783* (London 1989)

Brewer, J., 'The Eighteenth Century British State: Contexts and Issues' in L. Stone (ed.), *An Imperial State at War: Britain from 1689–1815* (London, 1994)

Brock, W.R., *Scotus Americanus* (Edinburgh, 1982)

Broomfield, B.J., 'Some One Hundred Unreasonable Parliamentary Men – A Study in Military Representation in the Eighteenth Century British Parliament', in *Journal of the Society for Army Historical Research*, vol. 39 (1969)

Brown, D.J., 'Nothing but Strugalls and Corruption': The Commons' Elections for Scotland in 1774', in C. Jones (ed.), *The Scots and Parliament* (Edinburgh, 1996)

Brown, K.M., 'From Scottish Lords to British Officers: State Building, Elite Integration and the Army in the Seventeenth Century', in N. Macdougall (ed.), *Scotland and War, AD 79–1918* (Edinburgh, 1991)

Browne, J., *History of the Highlands and of the Highland Clans*, vols. 3–4 (Glasgow, 1838).

Browning, R., *The Duke of Newcastle* (London, 1975)

Bruce, A., *The Purchase System in the British Army* (London, 1980)

Bullion, J.L., 'Securing the Peace: Lord Bute, the Plan for the Army, and the Origins of the American Revolution', in K.W. Schweizer (ed.), *Lord Bute: Essays in Re-interpretation* (Leicester, 1988)

Bulloch, J.M., *Territorial Soldiering in the North East of Scotland during 1759–1814* (Aberdeen, 1914)

Bumsted, J.M., *The People's Clearance: Highland Emigration to British North America, 1770–1815* (Edinburgh, 1982)

Burgoyne, F., *Historical Record of the 93rd Sutherland Highlanders* (London, 1883)

Caird, J.B., 'The Creation of Crofts and New Settlement Patterns in the Highlands and Islands of Scotland', in *Scottish Geographical Magazine*, vol. 103 (1987)

Calder, A., *Revolutionary Empire: The Rise of the English-Speaking Empires from the Fifteenth Century to the 1780s* (London, 1998)

Cambridge, Marquis of, 'The Volunteer Army of Great Britain, 1806', in *Journal of the Society of Army Historical Research*, vol. 13 (1931)

Cameron, E.A., *Land for the People?: The British Government and the Scottish Highlands, c. 1880–1925* (East Linton, 1996)

Cameron, E.A., 'Embracing the Past: The Highlands in Nineteenth Century Scotland', in D. Brown, R.J. Finlay and M. Lynch (eds.), *Image and Identity: The Making and Re-making of Scotland through the Ages* (Edinburgh, 1998)

Campbell, R.H., 'The Scottish Improvers and the Course of Agrarian Change', in L.C. Cullen and T.C. Smout (eds.), *Comparative Aspects of Scottish and Irish Economic and Social History, 1600–1900* (Edinburgh, 1977)

Cavendish, A.E.J., *An Reismeid Chataich* (published privately, 1928)

Checkland, S.G., *Scottish Banking: A History, 1695–1973* (Glasgow, 1975)

Clark, J.C.D., *The Dynamics of Change: The Crisis of the 1750s and English Party Systems* (Cambridge, 1982)

Clayton, T.R., 'The Duke of Newcastle, the Earl of Halifax and the America origins of the Seven Years' War', in *Historical Journal*, vol. 24 (1981)

Clive, J. and Bailyn, B. 'England's Cultural Provinces: Scotland and America' in *William and Mary*, vol. 9, 3rd series (1954)

Clough, M. & Richards, E., *Cromartie: Highland Life, 1650–1914* (Aberdeen, 1989).

Clyde, R., *From Rebel to Hero: The Image of the Highlander, 1745–1830* (East Linton, 1995)

Colley, L., *Britons: Forging the Nation, 1707–1837* (London, 1992)
Connell, K.H., *The Population of Ireland, 1750–1845* (Oxford, 1975)
Connolly, S.J., 'Varieties of Britishness: Ireland, Scotland and Wales in the Hanoverian State', in A. Grant and K. J. Stringer (eds.), *Uniting the Kingdom? The Making of British History* (London, 1995)
Cookson, J.E., 'The English Volunteer Movement of the French Wars, 1793–1815: Some Contexts', in *Historical Journal*, vol. 32 (1989)
Cookson, J.E., *The British Armed Nation, 1793–1815* (Oxford, 1997)
Cregeen, E.R., 'The Tacksmen and their Successors: A Study of Tenurial Reorganisation in Mull, Morvern and Tiree in the Early Eighteenth Century', in *Scottish Studies*, vol. 13 (1969).
Cregeen, E.R., 'The Changing Role of the House of Argyll in the Scottish Highlands', in N.T. Phillipson and R. Mitchison (eds.), *Scotland in the Age of Improvement: Essays in Scottish History in the Eighteenth Century* (Edinburgh, 1996)
Cullen, L.M., 'Scotland and Ireland, 1600–1800: Their Role in the Evolution of British Society', in R.A. Houston & I.D. Whyte (eds.), *Scottish Society, 1500–1800* (Cambridge, 1989)
Devine, T.M., 'The Emergence of the New Elite in the Western Highlands and Isles, 1800–60', in T.M. Devine (ed.), *Improvement and Enlightenment* (Edinburgh, 1989)
Devine, T.M., 'Social Responses to Agrarian "Improvement": The Highland and Lowland Clearances in Scotland', in R.A. Houston & I.D. Whyte (eds.), *Scottish Society, 1500–1800* (Cambridge, 1989)
Devine, T.M., 'Landlordism and Highland Emigration', in T.M. Devine (ed.), *Scottish Emigration and Scottish Society* (Edinburgh, 1992)
Devine, T.M., *Clanship to Crofters' War: The Social Transformation of the Scottish Highlands* (Manchester, 1993)
Devine, T.M., *The Transformation of Rural Scotland: Social Change and the Agrarian Economy, 1660–1815* (Edinburgh, 1994)
Devine, T.M., 'The Making of a Farming Elite? Lowland Scotland, 1750–1850', in T.M. Devine (ed.), *Scottish Elites* (Edinburgh, 1994)
Dickson, P.G.M., *Finance and Government under Maria Theresa, 1740–1780, vol. 2: Finance and Credit* (Oxford, 1987)
Dodgshon, R.A., *Land and Society in Early Scotland* (Oxford, 1981)
Dodgshon, R.A., 'Pretense of Blude' and "Place of thair duelling": The nature of Scottish Clans, 1500–1745', in R.A. Houston and I.D. Whyte (eds.), *Scottish Society, 1500–1800* (Cambridge, 1989)
Dodgshon, R.A., 'Strategies of Farming in the Western Highlands and Islands prior to Crofting and the Clearances' in *Economic History Review*, vol. 46 (1993)
Donovan, R.K., 'The Military Origins of the Roman Catholic Relief Programme of 1778', in *Historical Journal* vol. 28 (1985)
Duff, D., *Scotland's War Losses* (Glasgow, 1947)
Duffy, C., *The Army of Frederick the Great* (London, 1974)

Duffy, M., *The Army of Maria Theresa: The Armed Forces of Imperial Austria, 1740–1780* (London, 1977)

Dunlop, J., *The British Fisheries Society, 1786–1893* (Edinburgh, 1978)

Dunn-Pattison, R.P., *History of the 91st Argyll Highlanders* (London, 1910)

Dwyer, J. and Murdoch, A., 'Paradigms and Politics: Manners, Morals and the Rise of Henry Dundas, 1770–1784', in J. Dwyer, R. A. Mason and A. Murdoch (eds.), *New Perspectives on the Politics and Culture of Early Modern Scotland* (Edinburgh, 1982)

Ferguson, W., 'Dingwall Burgh Politics and the Parliamentary Franchise in the Eighteenth Century', in *Scottish Historical Review*, vol. 38 (1959)

Finlay, R., 'Caledonia or North Britain?: Scottish Identity in the Eighteenth Century', in D. Brown, R.J. Finlay and M. Lynch (eds.), *Image and Identity: The Making and Re-making of Scotland through the Ages* (Edinburgh, 1998)

Flinn, M.W., 'Malthus, Emigration and Potatoes in the Scottish North West, 1770–1870', in L.M. Cullen and T.M. Devine (eds.), *Comparative Aspects of Scottish and Irish Economic and Social History, 1600–1900* (Edinburgh, 1977)

Flinn, M.W,, *Scottish Population History: From the 17th Century to the 1930s* (Cambridge, 1977)

Fortescue, J., *A History of the British Army*, vols. 3–5 (London, 1902)

Fortescue, J., *The County Lieutenancies and the Army, 1803–1804* (London, 1909).

Fraser, T.G., 'Ireland and India', in K. Jeffery (ed.), *An Irish Empire? Aspects of Ireland and the British Empire* (Manchester, 1996)

Fry, M., *The Dundas Despotism* (Edinburgh, 1992)

Gilbert, A.N., 'Military Recruitment and Career Advancement in the Eighteenth Century', in *Journal of the Society of Army Historical Research*, vol. 57 (1979)

Gilles, W.A., *In Famed Breadalbane* (Perth, 1938)

Grant, I.F., *The Macleods: The History of a Clan, 1200–1956* (London, 1959)

Gray, M., *The Highland Economy, 1750–1850* (Edinburgh, 1957)

Guy, A.J., 'The Irish Military Establishment, 1660–1776', in T. Bartlett and K. Jeffery (eds.), *A Military History of Ireland* (Cambridge, 1996)

Hanham, H.J., 'Religion and Nationality in the Mid-Victorian Army' in M.R.D. Foot (ed.), *War and Society: Historical Essays in Honour and Memory of J.R. Western, 1928–1971* (London, 1973)

Harding, P. and Mandler, P., 'From 'Fiscal-Military' State to Laissez-Faire State, 1760–1850', in *Journal of British Studies*, vol. 32 (1993)

Harding, R.H., 'The Growth of Anglo-American Alienation: The Case of the American Regiment, 1740–1742', in *Journal of Imperial and Commonwealth History*, vol. 17 (1989)

Hayton, D., 'Constitutional Experiments and Political Expediency, 1689–

1725', in S.G. Ellis and S. Barber (eds.), *Conquest and Union: Fashioning A British State, 1485–1725* (London, 1995)

Henderson, D.M., *Highland Soldier: A Social Study of the Highland Regiment, 1820–1920* (Edinburgh, 1989)

Hechter, M., *Internal Colonialism: The Celtic Fringe in British National Development, 1536–1966* (London, 1975)

Hill, J.M. *Celtic Warfare, 1595–1763* (Hampshire, 1993)

Holmes, G. & Szechi, D., *The Age of Oligarchy: Pre-industrial Britain, 1722–1783* (London, 1993)

Hopkins, P., *Glencoe and the End of the Highland War* (Edinburgh, 1986)

Hunter, J., *The Making of the Crofting Community* (Edinburgh, 1976)

Ingrao, C.W., *The Hessian Mercenary State: Ideas, Institutions, and Reform under Frederick II, 1760–1785* (Cambridge, 1987)

Innes, J., 'The Domestic Face of the Fiscal-Military State: Government and Society in Eighteenth-century Britain', in L. Stone (ed.), *An Imperial State at War: Britain from 1689–1815* (London, 1994)

Jackson, R.V., 'Government Expenditure and British Economic Growth in the Eighteenth Century: Some Problems of Measurement', in *Economic History Review*, vol. 43 (1990)

James, F.G., *Ireland in the Empire, 1688–1700* (Cambridge, Mass, 1973)

Jones, C., 'The Military Revolution and the Professionalisation of the French Army under the Ancien Régime', in M. Duffy (ed.), *The Military Revolution and the State* (London, 1980)

Judges, A.V., 'The Idea of a Mercantile State', in D.C. Coleman (ed.), *Revisions in Mercantilism* (London, 1969)

Keltie J.S., *A History of the Scottish Highlands, Highland Clans and Highland Regiments* (Edinburgh, 1875)

Kidd, C., *Subverting Scotland's Past: Scottish Whig Historians and the Creation of an Anglo-British Identity* (Cambridge, 1993)

Kidd., C., 'North Britishness and the Nature of Eighteenth Century British Patriotisms', in *Historical Journal*, vol. 39 (1996)

Landsman, N.C., 'The Provinces and the Empire: Scotland, the American Colonies and the Development of British Provincial Identity', in L. Stone (ed.), *An Imperial State at War: Britain from 1689 to 1815* (London, 1994)

Landsman, N.C., 'The Legacy of the British Union for the North American Colonies: Provincial Elites and the Problem of Imperial Union', in J. Robertson (ed.), *A Union for Empire: Political Thought and the British Union of 1707* (Cambridge, 1995)

Leneman, L., *Living in Atholl: A Social History of the Estate, 1685–1785* (Edinburgh, 1986)

Lenman, B.P., *Jacobite Clans of the Great Glen, 1650–1784* (London, 1984)

Lenman, B.P., 'Militia, Fencible Men and Home Defence, 1660–1797', in N. Macdougall (ed.), *Scotland and War, AD 79–1918* (Edinburgh, 1991)

Lenman, B.P., 'Scotland and Ireland, 1742–1789' in J. Black (ed.), *British Politics and Society from Walpole to Pitt, 1742–1789* (London, 1990)

Lloyd, E.M., 'The Raising of the Highland Regiments in 1757', in *English Historical Review*, vol. 17 (1902)

Lynch, M., *Scotland: A New History* (London, 1992)

McDowell, R.B., 'Colonial Nationalism and the Winning of Parliamentary Independence, 1760–1782', in J.W. Moody and W.E., Vaughan (eds.), *A New History of Ireland: Eighteenth Century Ireland, 1691–1800*, vol. 4 (Oxford, 1986)

McDowell, R.B., *Ireland in the Age of Imperialism and Revolution* (Oxford, 1991)

Macinnes, A.I., 'Jacobitism' in *History Today*, vol. 34 (1984)

Macinnes, A.I., 'Repression and Conciliation: The Highland Dimension, 1660–1688', in *Scottish Historical Review*, vol. 55 (1986)

Macinnes, A.I., 'Scottish Gaeldom: The First Phase of Clearance', in T.M. Devine and R. Mitchison (eds.), *People and Society in Scotland, 1760–1830*, vol. 1 (Edinburgh, 1988)

Macinnes, A.I., 'The Impact of the Civil Wars and Interregnum: Political Disruption and Social Change within Scottish Gaeldom', in R. Mitchison and P. Roebuck (eds.), *Economy and Society in Scotland and Ireland, 1500–1939* (Edinburgh, 1988)

Macinnes, A.I., 'Land Ownership, Land Use and Elite Enterprise in Scottish Gaeldom: from Clanship to Clearance in Argyllshire, 1688–1858', in T.M. Devine (ed.), *Scottish Elites* (Edinburgh, 1994)

Macinnes, A.I., *Clanship, Commerce and the House of Stuart, 1603–1788* (East Linton, 1996)

Macinnes, J., *Brave Sons of Skye* (Edinburgh, 1899)

MacInnes, J., 'The Origin and Early Development of "The Men"', in *Records of the Scottish Church History Society*, vol. 8 (1944)

Mackay, J., *The Reay Fencibles* (Glasgow, 1890)

Mackintosh, C.F., *Antiquarian Notes* (Inverness, 1897)

Mackenzie, A., *A History of the Highland Clearances* (Glasgow, 1966)

Mackenzie, J.M., *Empires of Nature and the Nature of Empires: Imperialism, Scotland and the Environment* (East Linton, 1997)

Mackenzie, T.A. and Ewart, J.S., *Historical Records of the 79th Queen's Own Cameron Highlanders* (London, 1887)

Mackenzie, W.C., *Simon Fraser, Lord Lovat: His Life and Times* (London, 1908)

McKerral, A., 'The Tacksman and his Holdings in the South West Highlands' in *Scottish Historical Review*, vol. 26 (1947)

MacLean, M., *The Raising of the 79th Highlanders* (Inverness, 1980)

McLean, M., *The People of Glengarry: Highlanders in Transition, 1745–1820* (London, 1991)

McLynn, F.J., *The Jacobite Army in England* (Edinburgh, 1983)

Marshall, P.J., 'A Nation Defined by Empire, 1755–1776', in A. Grant and

K. J. Stringer (eds.), *Uniting the Kingdom? The Making of British History* (London, 1995)

Meek, D.E., 'The Preacher, the Press-gang and the Landlord: the Impressment and Vindication of the Rev. Donald McArthur', in *Scottish Church History*, vol. 25 (1994)

Meek, D.E., *Tuath is Tighearna: Tenants and Landlords* (Edinburgh, 1995)

Menary, G., *The Life and Letters of Duncan Forbes of Culloden* (London, 1936)

Middleton, R., 'The Recruitment of the British Army, 1755–1762', in *Journal of the Society of Army Historical Research*, vol. 68 (1989)

Milobar, D., 'Quebec Reform, the British Constitution and the Atlantic Empire, 1774–1775', in P. Lawson (ed.), *Parliament and the Atlantic Empire* (Edinburgh, 1995)

Mitchison, R., 'The Government of the Highlands, 1707–1745', in N.T. Phillipson, and R. Mitchison (eds.), *Scotland in the Age of Improvement: Essays in Scottish History in the Eighteenth Century* (Edinburgh, 1996)

Morgan, V., 'Agricultural Wage Rates in Late Eighteenth Century Scotland', in *Economic History Review*, vol. 24 (1970)

Murdoch, A., *'The People Above': Politics and Administration in Mid-Eighteenth Century Scotland* (Edinburgh, 1980)

Namier, L. and Brooke, J. (eds.), *The History of Parliament: The House of Commons, 1754–1790*, vols. 2–3 (London, 1964)

O'Donovan, J., 'The Militia in Munster, 1715–78', in G. O'Brien (ed.), *Parliament, Politics and People: Essays in Eighteenth Century Irish History* (Dublin, 1989)

Olson, A.G., *Making the Empire Work: London and the American Interest Groups* (Harvard, 1992)

Parker, A.W., *Scottish Highlanders in Colonial Georgia: the Recruitment, Emigration and Settlement at Darien, 1735–1748* (Athens, Georgia, 1997)

Prebble, J., *Mutiny: Highland Regiments in Revolt, 1743–1804* (Harmondsworth, Middlesex, 1975)

Richards, E., *A History of the Highland Clearances*, vols. 1–2 (London 1982–85)

Richards, E., 'Scotland and the Uses of the Atlantic Empire', in B. Bailyn and P. D. Morgan (eds.), *Strangers within the Realm: Cultural Margins of the First British Empire* (London, 1991)

Riley, P.W.J., *The English Ministers and Scotland, 1707–1727* (London, 1964)

Robertson, J., *The Scottish Enlightenment and the Militia Issue* (Edinburgh, 1985)

Robson, E., 'The Raising of a Regiment in the American War of Independence', in *Journal of the Society of Army Historical Research*, vol. 27 (1949)

Scobie, I.H.M., 'The Caithness Fencibles and a Recruiting Card of 1799', in *Journal of the Society of Army Historical Research*, vol. 6 (1927)

Scobie, I.H.M., 'The Independent Companies of 1745-7', in *Journal of the Society of Army Historical Research*, vol. 20 (1941)
Scott, H.M., *British Foreign Policy in the Age of the American Revolution* (Oxford, 1990)
Sedgwick, R. (ed.), *The House of Commons, 1715-1754*, 2 vols. (London, 1970)
Semple-Mackenzie, J., 'Bygone Recruiting in Skye', in *Journal of the Society of Army Historical Research*, vol. 18 (1939)
Seton, B., 'Recruiting in Scotland, 1793-94', in *Journal of the Society of Army Historical Research*, vol. 11 (1932)
Shaw, J.S., *The Management of Scottish Society, 1707-1764* (Edinburgh, 1983)
Sherrard, O.A., *Lord Chatham: Pitt and The Seven Years War* (London, 1955)
Shy, J., *Towards Lexington: The Role of the British Army in the Coming of the American Revolution* (Princeton, 1965)
Simpson, J., 'Who Steered the Gravy Train, 1707-1766', in N.T. Phillipson, and R. Mitchison (eds.), *Scotland in the Age of Improvement: Essays in Scottish History in the Eighteenth Century* (Edinburgh, 1996)
Simpson, P., *The Independent Highland Companies, 1603-1760* (Edinburgh, 1996)
Smith, A.M., 'State Aid to Industry – An Eighteenth Century Example', in T.M. Devine (ed.), *Lairds and Improvement in the Scotland of the Enlightenment* (Glasgow, 1978)
Smith, A.M., *Jacobite Estates of the Forty-Five* (Edinburgh, 1982)
Smout, T.C., 'Scottish Landowners and Economic Growth, 1650-1850', in *Scottish Journal of Political Economy*, vol. 11 (1964)
Smout, T.C., 'The Landowner and the Planned Village in Scotland, 1730-1830', in N.T. Phillipson and R. Mitchison (eds.), *Scotland in the Age of Improvement: Essays in Scottish History in the Eighteenth Century* (Edinburgh, 1996)
Smout, T.C., 'Problems of Nationalism, Identity and Improvement in later Eighteenth Century Scotland', in T.M. Devine (ed.), *Improvement and Enlightenment* (Edinburgh, 1989)
Speck, W.A., *The Butcher: The Duke of Cumberland and the Suppression of the '45* (Caernarfon, 1995)
Stigger, P., 'Recruiting for Rank in 1764, 1804 and 1857', in *Journal of the Society of Army Historical Research*, vol. 70 (1992)
Sunter, R.M., *Patronage and Politics in Scotland, 1707-1832* (Edinburgh, 1986)
Szechi, D. & Hayton, D., 'John Bull's Other Kingdoms: The English Government of Scotland and Ireland', in C. Jones (ed.), *Britain in the First Age of Party* (London, 1987)
Thorne, R.G. (ed.), *The House of Commons, 1790-1820*, vols. 3-5 (London, 1986)

Tullibardine, Marchioness of, *A Military History of Perthshire* (Perth, 1908)

Vincent, E., 'The Responses of Scottish Churchmen to the French Revolution', in *Scottish Historical Review*, vol. 73 (1994)

Womack, P., *Improvement and Romance: Constructing the Myth of the Highlands* (Edinburgh, 1989)

Wills, V., 'The Gentleman Farmer and the Annexed Estates: Agrarian Change in the Highlands in the Second Half of the Eighteenth Century', in T.M. Devine, (ed.), *Lairds and Improvement in the Scotland of the Enlightenment* (Glasgow, 1978)

Wilson, P.H., *War, State and Society in Würtemberg, 1677–1793* (Cambridge, 1995)

Withers, C.J., 'The Historical Creation of the Scottish Highland', in I. Donnachie & C. Whatley (eds.), *The Manufacture of Scottish History* (Edinburgh, 1992)

Youngson, A.J., *After the 'Forty-Five: the Economic Impact on the Scottish Highlands* (Edinburgh, 1973)

Youngson, A.J., *The Prince and the Pretender: Two Views of the '45* (Edinburgh, 1996)

THESES

Brown, D.J., Henry Dundas and the Government of Scotland (University of Edinburgh Ph.D., 1989)

Carpenter, S.D.M., Patterns of Recruitment of the Highland Regiments of the British Army, 1756–1815 (St. Andrews University M.Litt. Thesis, 1977)

Ferguson, K.P., The Army in Ireland from the Restoration to the Act of Union (Trinity College, Dublin Ph.D., 1980)

Hayes, J.W., The Social and Professional Background of the Officers of the British Army, 1714–1763 (University of London M.A. Thesis, 1956)

McGilvray, East India Patronage and the Political Management of Scotland, 1720–1774 (Open University, Ph.D., 1989)

Vance, M.E., Emigration and Scottish Society: The Background of Three Government-Assisted Emigrations to Upper Canada, 1815–1821 (University of Guelph Ph.D., 1990)

Western, J.R., The Recruitment of the Land Forces in Great Britain, 1793–99 (Edinburgh University Ph.D., 1953)

Index

A Song Between Dugald and Donald, 214
Aberarder, estate of, recruitment from, 140
Abercrombie, Sir Ralph, imperial war hero, 225
Abernethy, 7
   minister of involved in recruitment process, 210
Acadians, French, in Nova Scotia, 57
Achachar, lands of, 158
Achaglean, 95
Achalader, *see* Campbell, John, of Achalader
Achiltibuie, 96
Achnamaddy, farm, 124
Achnashine, 153
Achtrichtan, farm of, 160
Addington, Henry, 76, 196
   administration of aided by Henry Dundas, 53
   military polices of alienate Highland landlords, 74
Admiralty, First Lord of, *see* Dundas, Henry
Airlie estates, protected by Cluny's watch scheme, 38
Alexandria, British victory at, 225
America,
   access of colonists to army patronage in, 22, 182
   Anglo-Spanish frontier in, 183
   as 'land of milk and honey' to evangelical Gaels, 214
   British defeat in, 195
   British territorial expansion in, 66, 88, 138, 178
   character of Earl of Loudon's army in, 24
   colonies in, Pitt's military policy towards, 47, 182
   Franco-American alliance in, 59
   Franco-British tensions in, 46
   Highland landownership in, 187
   Highlanders to be deployed in, 57
   immigration to, 178, 181
      directed away from USA, 181
   raising of provincial regiments in, 22, 24
   rebellion in, 193
      impact of on emigration policies, 193
   relationship between military and colonial authorities in, 179
   resettlement of loyalists in, 183
   role within Empire, 178
   Scottish perceptions of empire in, 178
   state patronage in, 178
American War of Independence *or* American Revolutionary War, 5, 55, 59, 62, 66–67, 68, 77, 118, 156, 169, 177, 217, 221
   balance of professional and proprietorial recruitment for, 71
   deployment of Highland regiments in, 59
   deployment of mercenaries by British in, 66, 68
   implications of absence of Scottish manager during, 54
   recruiting proposals for, channelled through Dundas, 53
   recruitment of Highland regiments for, 61, 65, 68, 73, 75, 112, 122, 131, 142, 147
   sheep-farmers in Argyll bankrupted by, 135
   stimulates credit drain, 136
Amiens, Peace of, 128, 196
Anderson, James, condemns emigration, 191
Anglicanism, 204, 207
Annexed Estates, Board of, 77, 82, 89, 98–99, 101, 112
   'civilising' role of, 89
   Commissioners of, 80, 81, 85, 97
   criticisms of, 77
   impact of Seven Years War on policies of, 83–84
   membership of, 80
   policies of, 78, 81–84, 89–93, 95, 97, 98, 100, 101, 112
      encouragement by of commercial development on west coast, 97–98
      failure of, 92–94
      implications of for depopulation and eviction, 83, 90, 243
      long-term consequences for on Highlands, 94
      orders removal of subtenants, 95, 99
      proposes foundation of planned villages, 81, 91, 99
   regulation by, of tack terms, 86
   role as recruiter and resettler of military personnel, 77–78, 80, 83, 85–86, 87–90, 98, 101
      costs of resettlement, 92
      resettlements by of demobilised sailors and soldiers, 89, 91, 92, 94, 99, 112; *see also* Campbell, John, of Lochend
Annexing Act, 78, 80
   objectives of, 82
   opposition to at bill stage, 79
Appin,
   estate, 107
      disposal of, 79
   minister of involved in recruitment process, 210
Ardeonaig, tenants in, recruitment amongst, 114
Ardnahua, farm, 124
Ardshiel, forfeited estate, 175
argathelians, political faction, 13, 17, 32, 46
   control of military patronage, 48, 49, 50
      reinforces management system of, 56
   hostility to squadrone, 27
Argyll, 37, 111, 112, 115, 139, 141, 235
   agricultural colonists from, 87, 160
   Breadalbane estates in, 125, 126
      policy of overpopulation on, 126
      removal of improving tenants on, 122
   rents from, 118
   droving trade in, 176

duke of, see Campbell, Archibald; Campbell,
            John (bis)
    recruitment by, 61, 131
    emergence of crofting in, 99, 164, 243
    fencible regiment, 102, 107, 137
    heritors, 107
    militia, 102
    sheep-farmers in bankrupted by American war,
            135
    Synod of, involvement of in recruitment process,
            210
    tacksmen in, 78, 170
    volunteer establishment in, 227
Arisaig, emigration to Canada from, 188
Army of Reserve Act, 227, 230
Assynt,
    army pensioners in, 150
    dismantling of large tacks in, 170
    reports to Napier Commission in, 5, 150
    social profile of emigrants from, 172
Atholl,
    adoption of clan-based system of property
            protection in, 37
    Aeneas MacDonnell of Glengarry's watch in, 37
    dukes of, see Murray, James
    4th, government pressure on to recruit, 61
    allied with Argyll, 51
    benefits to, of raising Highland regiments, 31
    challenge Argyll's control of patronage
            system, 49
    chamberlain of duke of, 19
    proposals by for formation of regular
            regiments from companies, 25
    recruitment capability of, 61, 63, 143
    supports role of manager in award of
            patronage, 55
Auchaneich, farm, 158
Austria,
    army of, 66
    Croat service in, 236
    Hanoverian policy towards, 26
    subsidies from, to British military, 47
Austrian War of Succession, 26, 42, 215, 237
    as catalyst for 1745 Jacobite rising, 26

Badenoch, 133, 142, 148, 170
    Duke of Gordon to assume responsibility for
            peace and security in, 38
    inter-clan rivalries in, 33
    reorganisation of tacksman farms in, 171
    resistance to recruitment amongst tacksmen in,
            155, 156
baille, 158
Baillemore, crofting community at, development
            of, 110, 111
Ballavicar, farm, broken up into crofts, 112
Ballephail, farm subdivided for crofts, 165
Ballimartin, farm subdivided for crofts, 165
Balnagown-Coul dispute, 17–18
Balquhidder, 226
Barcaldine, see Campbell, John
Barnyards, 86, 87
Barrington, Lord, see Wildman, William
Barrisdale, see MacDonnell, Coll
    consolidation of tenancies at, 95
    development of crofting at, 97
    resettlement of demobilised men at, 91
Barvas, minister of involved in recruitment
            process, 210

Beaich, farm, 176
Beauclerk, Lord George, Commander-in-Chief in
            Scotland,
    excluded from army patronage by Argyll, 50
Beauly, 81
Bedford, Duke of, see Russell, John
Benderloch, 174
Bibiscally, 96
Black Isle, resistance to militia service in, 231
Black Watch, 28, 75, 107, 145, 243
Blair Atholl, 7, 143
Blairliargan, development of crofts at, 111
Bland, General Humphrey, Commander-in-Chief
            in Scotland, 83
    observations on improvements in Highlands and
            issue of depopulation, 83, 90
Blarichirn, farm, 158
Blarmore, development of crofts at, 111
Board of Annexed Estates, see Annexed Estates
Bochoil, farm, 124
Bonawe furnace, 97
Borelandbog, 91
Borhogie, farm, 158
Boswell, James, 220, 221
Braddock, Lieutenant-General Edward,
    annihilation of Ohio expedition led by,
            46
Brae Atholl, plans to seize prominent Jacobites in,
            21
Braes of Glenorchy, 174
Breachachie, farm of, 158
Breadalbane, Earls of, 61; see also Campbell, John
    3rd Earl of, 55
    government pressure on to recruit, 61, 104
    hostile relationship with House of Argyll, 102
    seek links and patronage opportunities with
            fiscal-military state, 132
Breadalbane estates, 97, 99, 101, 107, 110, 114–
            115, 119–120, 123, 126, 130, 143,
            163, 170, 174
    demographic trends on, 115, 119–120, 126–127
    emigration from, 189
    ground officers on, 114
    improvement on, 102–103, 104, 108, 114, 125,
            126–128
    Jacobite threat to, 106–107
    military emigration from, 188
    recruitment on, 102, 106, 110, 112, 113–115,
            116–119, 120, 226
    based on rental value, 107
    for Black Watch, 107
    government, 106
    Jacobite, 106
    tenantry resistant to, 107, 121, 226
    reorganisation of, 125–127, 175
    tenurial profile of, 119–120, 166
    subtenure, 120
Breadalbane Fencibles, 72, 73, 113–114, 138
    half-pay officers in, 72
    men from recruited into line regiments, 113
    mutiny of, 113
    recruit profile of, 115, 143
    refuse deployment in Ireland, 73, 113
Britain,
    commercialism of, 218
    commitment in to military forces, 65–66
    diplomatic isolation of, consequences for
            military potential of, 66
    emphasis on naval strength of, 66

European policy of, 26, 66, 113
imperial expansion of,
　anti-emigration policies towards, 179, 181, 190, 192–193
　demographic problems consequent on, 178, 181
　Scottish responses to, 56, 75, 76, 178, 182, 238
naval and mercantile policy of, 88
peace negotiations with France and Spain, 88
Scottish factionalism as threat to, 43
war with France, 88, 113
war with Spain, 17, 26, 88
British army, 9
attitudes in towards distinctive regional contributions to, 24, 60
Borders, Scottish, Loudon proposes formation of regiment in, 50
bounties, 144, 145, 146, 226
campaigns in Bengal, 9
campaigns in Flanders, 26, 47
campaigns in North America, 9, 46, 47
clan gentry, exploitation by of opportunities in, 30, 31, 139
centralisation and regulation of, 20
commissions in, see commissions, military
economic attractions of service in for substantial Highland tenants, 86
elites, attitudes of, 23
　towards Gaels, 56
　towards Irish, 23
employment prospects in, 218
English regiments, 30
　commanded by Scots, 30
　Highlanders serving in, 30
　recruitment of, 69
expansion of, 36, 54
fencible regiments in, 54, 59, 60, 73, 111, 113, 115, 122, 133, 194, 198, 199, 225, 229
　award of, 54
　officers, status of, 74
　service of in Ireland, 73
German Protestant battalions in, 46
Hanoverian mercenaries in, 47
Hessian mercenaries in, 47, 66, 67, 68
Highland regiments, 1–2, 3, 4, 6, 8, 10, 12, 15, 22, 25, 26, 30, 31, 46, 47, 48, 49, 56–57, 58, 65, 68, 73, 75, 84, 131, 140, 205, 236, 240
36th Highland regiment, 174
42nd Highland regiment (Black Watch), 6, 28, 47, 75, 145, 173, 185, 186, 196, 225, 243
　Lord John Murray, colonel of, 62, 145
43rd Highland regiment, 24–25, 34
54th Highland regiment, 29, 32, 106
57th Highland regiment, 174
71st Highland regiment, 63, 72, 176, 185, 188, 218, 229
73rd Highland regiment, 72, 145
74th Highland regiment, 54, 72, 110, 185
　Dundas influence over appointments to, 54
76th Highland regiment, 72, 147, 189
77th Highland regiment, 68, 186
78th Highlanders, 56, 68, 141, 145, 161, 188
　2nd battalion and recruitment for rank, 73
　Seaforths, 72

79th Highland regiment and recruitment for rank, 73
84th Highland Emigrant regiment, 186
88th Highland battalion, 93
89th Highland battalion, 93
92nd Highlanders, Dundas prevents disbandment of, 56, 73
93rd Sutherland Highlanders, 4, 7, 141, 147, 150, 159, 243
　pensioners from, 150
100th Highland regiment, 145–146
Black Watch, see 42nd Highland regiment
Breadalbane Fencibles, 72
and Cape Breton expedition, 57
characterisation of, 6, 84, 205
Chelsea Pensioners from, 150
as clan levies, 84–85, 141, 143, 144, 233, 237
commanded largely by traditionally non-Jacobite families, 61
demobilisation of, 68, 74, 88, 90, 91, 92, 93, 95, 99, 150, 157, 163, 164, 194, 243
　emigration associated with, 89, 164, 186, 198–199
　re-enlistment after, 89
deployment of in French Revolutionary war, 59
deployment of in North America, 46, 59
development of from Independent Companies, 15, 20, 24, 25–26, 27, 29
Dunbartonshire Fencibles, 140
employed in attritional conflicts, 56–57
Egyptian campaign, 196
formation of promoted by Argyll, 50, 56
Gaelic personnel profile of, 22–23, 24, 150
Grant Fencibles, 72, 115
　recruitment profile of, 115
half-pay officers, 62, 68, 72, 94, 148, 172, 177
　economic role of, 148, 154, 172
　emigration of, 189
　facilitate recruitment, 68
　re-enter service, 172–177
historiography of, 1–2, 5, 6, 84
influence of clanship on, 39, 40, 41, 42, 59, 61–62, 104
Lovat's, 59, 61, 84
Lowland Scottish recruitment into, 65
military service in, as counter to Jacobitism, 31, 32, 61
Montgomery's, 59
　remissions of pay from to kin in Scotland, 152
mutinies of, 9, 113, 182
negative impact on recruitment of planned overseas service by, 28, 29
Northern Fencibles, 144
officer profile of, 50, 61–62, 71, 73, 143
potential Jacobitism in, 30
professionalising of, 65, 69, 72, 73, 243
proprietary, 4, 9, 12, 59, 69, 73, 84, 177, 237, 243
　see Fraser, Simon; Mackenzie of Seaforth
Reay Fencibles, 7
recruitment of, 57, 58, 59, 70, 73, 76, 105, 113, 116, 121, 122–123, 130, 131, 132, 133, 144, 238
　as patriotic endeavour, 223

costs of, 70, 75, 107–108, 116–118, 144, 146, 158–159
  facilitated by role of clan chiefs as officers in, 63, 68
  government policy regarding, 61, 65, 106
  Jacobite prisoners into, 57
  liability for based on rental value of estate, 107, 110
  occupation profile, 143
  political pressures behind, 105
  socially specific, 144
  Whig clans, 25, 140
 sent to India, 49, 195
 service of in Flanders, 22, 26, 34, 36
 urban Scottish recruitment into, 65
 Wade recognises need for, 23
historiography of, 65
influences of German militarism on, 69
Irish in, 4, 23, 24, 67–68
  anti-Catholic recruitment policy of regiments, 23, 24
  Catholic, 67
  dispersal of into non-Irish regiments, 24
  officer profile of regiments, 23, 24, 50
  overseas service, attitudes towards, 67
  'Protestant interest' in, 23, 67
  raised by Irish parliament, 23, 67
  recruiting of refused, 60
  recruitment costs of, 70
  regiments sent to American war, 46, 66, 67, 68
 land for service policies of in North America, 183
 Lowland regiments, 30
  Highlanders serving in, 30
  recruitment of, 59, 69
 mercenaries in, 66
  from Duchy of Wurtemburg, 66
  Hanoverian, 47
  Hessian, 47, 66, 67, 68
  limitations in use of, 66
  Russian, 66
 militias, relationship with, 74; see also militia
 Naval tradition in Britain, impact on, 66
 officer class,
  half-pay, 71, 94, 148, 154, 172, 177, 189
  profile of, 65, 69, 73, 154
  professionalism of, 69, 73, 243
  rank of linked to recruitment ability, 70, 71
  settlement of, implications for small tenantry, 96–97
 organisational trends in, 65, 69
 patronage in, 19, 22–23, 27, 29, 32, 39, 43, 46, 47, 53, 58, 61, 72, 105, 128
  government direction of, 61
  impact of on Scotland's semi-autonomous status, 42
  justifications for disproportionate Highland elite access to, 63, 238
  negative aspects of, 34
  reinforces Scottish particularism, 42, 238
 presence in Highlands, 7
 professionalising of, 65, 69, 72, 73, 224, 243
 promotion structure within, 69–70, 71
 provincial regiments of, raised in America, 22
 recruiting, 1, 2–3, 4, 7, 9, 11, 12, 41, 69–70, 102–105, 106, 107, 112, 119–120, 121, 123–126 passim, 130, 131, 132, 133, 158–159

ancien régime methods of, 65
as social purgative, 108
changes in policy towards, 69–70, 74, 105, 107
costs of, 70, 107–108, 116–118, 144, 146
decline of, in Highlands, 42
for rank, 69, 71–73, 138, 145, 176
impact of French Revolutionary and Napoleonic wars on, 73
 in Highlands, 73
impact of Seven Years War on, in Highlands, 44, 75
in Highlands, 41, 58–59, 75, 102, 109, 110, 113, 116, 132
incompatibility of with improvement policies, 102, 104, 110, 111, 121–122, 129
liability for based on estate rental value, 107, 110
loss of estate manpower through, 105, 107, 108–109, 114, 118, 142, 155, 156
occupation profile, 143
professional, 70, 76, 243–244
proprietary, 69, 70, 73, 74, 76, 84, 105, 158, 237, 243
unregulated, 55
regimental histories of, 6–7, 225
regular regiments in,
  award of, 54
  relationship with American colonial authorities, 179
  relationship with Independent companies, 20
  role of in assimilating Scots and Highlanders into British state, 9, 10, 12
  scale of, 66
Scots in, 4, 29, 50
Scots-Dutch brigade, officers from transfer into British army, 61
service in as social ladder, 87
service in as reinforcing mechanism for local identity, 232
socio-economic context of military service, 206
standing force, 66
structure of, 65, 67
subsidised by Austrians and Dutch, 47
Swiss battalions in, 46
unpopularity in Scotland of extended regular service in, 227
volunteer units, formation of, 55, 205, 225, 241
  British sentiment underlying, 232
  disbandment of, 231, 232
  importance of wages from, 232
  local economic concerns behind, 232
  manpower transferred to militias, 231
  popularity of in Scotland, 225, 226–227
  replicates clanship ethos and practice, 233
  Welsh gentry, offers of recruitment by, 60, 218–219
British Fisheries Society, 195
British-Highland military establishment, 32, 36, 240
 commissions in, 39
 justifications for disproportionate Highland elite access to, 63, 238
 patronage of, 48, 238, 240
 expansion of, consequent on warfare, 50
 formation of, 29, 40, 49, 206
 government recruitment policy, 61, 65, 75
 institutionalisation of as part of standing army, 64–65

lobbying of, 62–63
  and manipulation of image of Highland militarism, 63
  overseas service, focus on, 29, 30, 39
  paradoxical character of, 49
  relationship with clanship, 58, 59, 60
British identity, development of, 204–233 *passim*
  absence of characteristics of in Highlands, 220
  as new Israel, 213
    rejection of concept by evangelicals, 214
  Francophobia as stimulus for, 213
  Highland identification with, 207, 230
  inherent militarism of, 205
  nationalism, 204
  polarisation of manifestations of, 216, 222, 224
  rejection of elements of by Gaels, 212
  role of Protestantism in, 207, 209, 215
  underpinned by war, 204
British state,
  absolutist nature of, 132, 221
  assimilation of Scotland into, 9–10, 13–14, 39, 222, 238
  attitudes of to provincial identities, 221–222, 238
  changing recruitment practices, impact of in Highlands, 42
  development of *laissez-faire* ideology in, 244
  fiscal-military, 9–10, 59, 64, 128, 132, 138, 202, 237, 238, 240, 241
    Highland colonisation of, 59, 64, 132, 137–138, 145, 150, 166, 198, 238, 240, 242, 244
    interventionist tendencies of, 128, 202–203, 234, 244
  historiography of formation of, 9–10, 41, 132
  ideal of wealth in, 212, 220
  ideology of commercial endeavour in, 224
  imperial expansion of, 36, 40, 41, 56, 66, 75, 88, 221
    consequences of for military, 66, 75, 88
    incorporation of provincial identities through, 221–222, 238
  imperial vision of, 10
  military-economic power of, 204
  military establishment of, in Scotland, 14, 15, 29–30, 41
    as source of regionally specific patronage, 14, 19, 22–23, 238
  negative image of soldiering in, 224
  patronage opportunities in, 132, 238
  political centralism in, 49
  relationship of core with periphery, 169
  role of Henry Dundas in, 53
  scale of military machine in, 132
  wars of, Scottish attitudes towards, 44–45
Brogaig, farm, 151
Buchanan, Stirlingshire,
  gentry and tenants of and lobby for Independent companies, 15
Bunchgavy, 96
Burgoyne, General John, 185

Caithness,
  Lord Lieutenancy of, 39
  recruitment in, 235
  volunteer establishment in, 227
Calcraft, John, regimental agent, 48
Caledonian Canal, 199
Callander, 81

Callechan, consequences of loss of sheiling lands at, 125
Cameron, Charles, of Lochiel, 63, 131
Cameron, Major Allan, of Erracht, 72
Camerons of Glendessary, 19
  ambush Mackenzies at Locharkaig, 19
  cattle-raids by Macphee kinsmen of, 19
  feud with Mackenzies, 19
Cameron, Captain, of Glendessary, involved in emigration schemes, 187
Cameron of Glen Nevis, introduction of sheep onto estates of, 160
Cameron of Locheil, 8, 17, 32
  Charles Cameron of, *see* Cameron, Charles, of Lochiel
  disputes with MacDonnells, 17
  estates of, prominence of half-pay officers on, 148
  gains commissions on Lovat's battalion, 84
  government pressure on to raise men, 61
  government retains all mineral rights on estates of, 32
  Jacobitism of, 17, 205
  relationship of, with Cluny Macphersons, 33
Cammuscross, 164
  division of into crofts, 165
Campbell, Lieutenant-Colonel Alexander, 174
Campbell, Alexander, captain in 74th Highland regiment, 110
Campbell, Major Allan, re-enters full-time military service, 174
Campbell, Archibald, Earl of Ilay, 3rd Duke of Argyll, 16, 31, 34, 37, 42, 43, 45, 46, 47, 51–52, 53, 105, 106
  alliance with Pelhams, 28, 44
  and annexed estates, 79
  associate of Henry Fox, 45
  association with Highland recruitment, 48, 75, 102, 239–240
  calls for his support of watch companies, 37
  consequences for of '45, 43
  controls lucrative imperial patronage, 49
  distrusts Earl of Tweeddale, 27
  and establishment of Highland companies, 28
  exercises patronage over military commissions, 27, 33, 34, 42, 45, 47, 48, 49–50, 51, 53, 55, 103, 105
    extends to rank of field officer and colonel, 50, 103
  management role of,
    as recruiter, 102, 103, 105, 240
    in Scotland, 45–46, 50, 51–52, 55, 103, 239
    linked to military patronage, 52, 55, 105
    more limited role in Lowlands, 50
  military backing of for Hanoverian state, 103, 239
  political enmity of with Earl of Marchmont, 51
  positive effects of war on position of, 46–47, 48
  post-'45 hostility towards, 43, 46, 49
  promotes formation of Highland regiments, 50, 84, 239–240
  and Highland fencibles, 50
  raises militia, 106
  relationship with 1st Duke of Newcastle, 44, 48
  relationship with Sir Robert Walpole, 48
  secretary of, observation on officer profile of Lord Cathcart's West Indies force, 29
  suspects political alignment of Clan Fraser, 31

unofficial status as 'minister for Scotland', 42, 46, 52, 55
willingness of to accommodate suspected Jacobites within military establishment, 34
Campbell, Archibald, of Achalladder, factor on Breadalbane estates in Perthshire, 110, 121
Campbell, Archibald, of Easdale, promises land for recruitment, 123, 124
Campbell, Archibald, of Inverneil, MP in Dundas interest, 54
Campbell, Lieutenant Archibald, 95
Campbell, Archibald, of Stonefield, 31–32
  calls for formation of new Independent companies, 28
Campbell clan,
  of Breadalbane, hostility of towards Argyll, 51
  disproportionate control of military patronage by, 34
  domination of Highlands by, 27, 43, 49
  impact of '45 on domination of Highlands by, 43
Campbell, Captain Colin, of Carwhin, promises land for recruitment, 123
Campbell, Captain Colin, of Glenfalloch, military income of, 138–139
Campbell, Colin, of Glenure, 37
Campbell, David, of Glenlyon, promises land in return for military service, 123
Campbell, Duncan, of Glenure, 55, 104, 174
  involvement of in sheep-farming, 135
  military levy from estates of based on rental value, 107
  seeks military patronage for family, 55, 174–175
Campbell, Sir Duncan, of Lochnell, 18
Campbell, James, of Inverawe,
  major in 42nd Highland Regiment, 47
  to raise battalion for American war, 46
Campbell, John, 2nd Duke of Argyll, 14
  military career of, 49
  political alliance with Duncan Forbes of Culloden, 27
  supports Union bill, 14
Campbell, John, 5th Duke of Argyll, 74, 174–175
  former Commander-in-Chief in Scotland, 55
  leads Highland Society, 197
  petitioned for patronage, 174–176
  political inactivity of, 55
  raises Western Fencibles, 142
  refuses to lobby for commissions, 55
  re-organisation of tenurial pattern of estates of, 165, 223
  presented as 'patriotic', 223
Campbell, John, 1st Earl of Breadalbane,
  proposes scheme for military deployment of clansmen, 25
Campbell, John, 2nd Earl of Breadalbane, 37
  levies cess to finance prosecution of thieves, 37
Campbell, John, 3rd Earl of Breadalbane, 55, 102–105, 106, 108, 113–114, 116–117, 120–121, 123, 124–125, 175, 223
  as counterpoise to argathelian dominance of Scotland, 102
  'Britishness', 224
  debarred from Board of Annexed Estates, 80
  deprived of military patronage, 103
  estates of utilised as source of recruits, 102, 113–120 passim

military backing of for Hanoverian state, 103
obtains command of regiment in French revolutionary war, 113, 114, 116
offers to recruit on Perthshire estates, 103
  government rejects offer, 104
  seeks control of commissions arising therefrom, 103
petitions for support for resettlement projects, 97
promises land or benefits for recruitment, 123–124
recruitment costs of, 116–118
subjected to pressure to recruit, 61, 103, 104–105
targets recruitment, 109, 114, 116–117
Campbell, John, 4th Earl of Breadalbane, 74, 126, 128, 138, 189
  alienated by disbandment of Fencibles, 74
  emigration from estates, of military personnel, 189
  improvement of estates by, 126–127, 128
  investigates condition of estates, 126
  opponent of Dundas, 54
  suspicious of missionary activity, 211
Campbell, John, 4th Earl of Loudon, 24, 179
  army of in America, 24, 47
  commands 54th Highland regiment, 29, 33, 106
  Campbell domination of military commissions under, 34
  recruitment for, 31, 57, 106
  men from regiment to be settled in Nova Scotia, 57, 183
  proposes formation of Borders regiment, 50
Campbell, John, Lord Glenorchy, 107; see also Campbell, John, 3rd Earl of Breadalbane
  calls for formation of new Independent companies, 28, 37
  clansmen of, implicated in cattle raids against Macintyres, 37
  recruitment by, 106
  re-deploys clansmen to curb cattle-raiding, 37
Campbell, John, Lord Lorne, 52
  unofficial 'minister of Scotland', 52
Campbell, Colonel John, of Mamore, commands English regiment, 30
Campbell, Colonel John, 93
Campbell, Lieutenant-Colonel John, of Barbreck, commands 74th Highlanders, 110
Campbell, Lieutenant John, of Ardtettle, tacksman, 122
Campbell, John, of Achallader, reports to 4th Earl of Breadalbane on re-emigration of military personnel, 189–190
Campbell, John, of Barcaldine, 174
Campbell, John, of Lochend, factor on Breadalbane Argyll estates, 111, 112, 125, 126
Campbell, Lord Frederick, 55
Campbell, Major Mungo, 175
Campbell, Patrick, eldest son of Duncan Campbell of Glenure, career of, 175–176
Campbell, Major Robert, of Finab, 106
Campbell of Barcaldine and Glenure,
  enters Highland military in response to socio-economic change, 174, 177
  political manoeuvrings of linked to military patronage, 175

Index

takes tack of farms on Breadalbane and Argyll estates, 174
Campbell of Cawdor, urged to join Macpherson of Cluny's watch scheme, 38
Campbeltown, settlement of demobilised personnel at, 91, 94
  impact of on local labour market and economy, 94
Canada,
  Catholicism in, 222
  emigration to, 182
  French legal institutions in, 222
  resettlement of American loyalists, 183
Canadian fencibles, formation of linked to colonial policy, 182
Cape Breton, 181
  expedition to as military exile for Highland companies, 57
  lieutenant governors of ordered to discourage emigration to, 179
Carie, farm, 124
Carnochroy, 95
Carteret, Earl of, *see* Granville, John
Carwhin, 121
Cathcart, Charles, 8th Lord Cathcart, 29
  commands expedition to West Indies, 29
  grants commissions to Scots cadets from line regiments, 29–30
cattle trade and farming, development of, 111, 118, 125, 134, 170, 173, 244
Ceilvellich, 110
cess, levy of to finance prosecution of thieves, 37
Charles Stuart, Jacobite Pretender, 35, 43, 61, 207
Chelsea pensioners, 89, 150, 241
Chisholm, estate tenantry of, 63
Clan-Chattan, political divisions of, 33
clanship, 13
  as lobbying mechanism, 64
  as mechanism for control of Highlands, 35–36, 37, 38, 40, 64
  chiefs, role of as regimental officers facilitates recruitment, 63–64, 68, 143
  decline of, 41, 58, 59, 60, 63, 64, 75, 115, 131, 139, 237
  destruction of as government policy, 14
  feuding, 16
  government attitudes to and perceptions of, 36, 39, 57, 58, 59–60, 62–63, 64, 71, 75, 77, 78, 236, 238
  influence of on government recruitment policy, 42, 59–60, 61, 75, 238
  judicial functions of, 35
  levying power of, 140–141, 237–238
  manipulation of image of, 63, 64
  manpower potential of, 16, 25
  militarism of, traditional, 61, 63, 115, 142, 145, 202, 237
    as basis for Highland involvement in army, 61–62, 104, 130, 132, 166, 238
    perceived negative impact on land use and tenurial efficiency, 77, 78, 121
    relationship of with Hanoverian military structure, 15, 36, 39, 40, 41, 57, 58, 59, 60, 62–63, 130, 238
  role of, 41, 154, 236
  supposed Jacobitism of, 58
Clark, John, tenant of Campbell of Easdale, 124
Clerk, Sir John, of Penicuik, 81

views on socio-economic condition of Highlands, 81
Cluny, *see* Macpherson, Ewen
Coiash, farm, divided into crofts, 112
Coigach, barony of, 87
  annexed estate, 87, 94
  displaced small tenants in settled on crofts, 96, 97
  emigration from, 189
  fishermen settled in, 96
  settlement of half-pay officers in, 96
colonia, 91
commissions, military, 30, 32, 39, 55, 59–60, 72, 86, 103, 105, 109, 142, 172, 218, 237, 241
  access to for independent peers denied by Henry Dundas, 54
  argathelians' control of, 29, 32, 42, 43, 48, 51
  as items of political patronage, 14, 19, 22–23, 27, 29, 42, 48, 51, 56, 105
  clan influence over, 39, 237
  difficulties in filling, 28
  domestic,
    as counter to Jacobitism, 32, 39
    as source of patronage, 30, 31, 238
  lack of co-ordination in deployment of, 33, 55
  overseas,
    as counter to Jacobitism, 31, 32, 39
    as source of patronage, 30, 31, 238
  rescinding of, 32
  selected use of, 32–33
congestion, consequent on removal of sub-tenants, 96
Cope, General John, 33, 106
Corrie, 96
Corriecainloch, watch at pass of, 38
Corrieconallie, lands of, 158
Coul, *see* Mackenzie, Sir Alexander
Court of Justiciary, 17
Court of Session, 15, 33
Craigie, Robert, Lord Advocate, 22, 37, 38
  and army patronage, 22–23, 28, 34
  relationship with Duncan Forbes, Lord President, 27
Crannich, 121
credit banking, 136
Crimean War, 3
crofting,
  development of, 108–127 *passim*, 151, 164–165, 166, 168, 243
  pressures for creation of by displaced tenantry, 112, 126–127
Cromartie, Earl of, *see* Mackenzie, George
Cromarty,
  resettlement of demobilised men at, 91
  volunteer establishment in, 227
Cromdale, 7, 192
Crubinmore, farm, 158
Culcairn, *see* Munro, George
Culloden,
  battle of, 8, 26, 49, 56, 63, 75, 78, 79, 80, 155, 205, 234, 244
    devastation of land following, 107
    estates of, protected by Cluny's watch scheme, 38
    role of battle in demise of clanship, 58–59, 234
Cumberland, Duke of,
  advocates cannon-fodder policy towards Highlanders, 57

objects to raising of Highland battalions, 46
opposition of to annexation bill, 79, 80
supports raising of Highland battalions, 47, 84, 215

Dalmally, 114
Dalrymple, John, 2nd Earl of Stair, squadrone politician,
  Commander-in-Chief of British army in Flanders, 34, 49
  controls distribution of commissions in forces, 34
  mounts challenge to Argyll control of patronage, 49
  orders 43rd Highland regiment onto Continent, 34
Dalttiack, scarcity of labour in due to military recruitment, 86
Debrisay, Thomas, Lieutenant Governor of St.John's Isle, 179
  instructed not to encourage emigration, 179
Deskford, Lord, see Ogilvy, James
Dingwall, election of provost at, 18
  Munro of Culcairn's soldiers interfere in, 18
disarming legislation, 27, 35, 36, 38, 57, 78, 239
  recruitment into army of those found guilty under, 57
Dornie, 96
Douglas, Rev. Neil, Relief Church minister, 212
  criticisms of established ministers, 208–209
  hostile to enforced military service, 210
Douglas, Thomas, 5th Earl of Selkirk, 197, 201
  raises new fencible regiment for service in Canada, 182
Drumfearn, lands of, 163
Drumfour, lands of, 158
Drummond, John, of Quarrell, financier, 30
  political uses of patronage in East India Company by, 30
Duachy, farm, 122
Duart, 176
Duirinish, enlistment from Macleod estates of, 140
Dull, 226
Dunbartonshire Fencibles, 140
Dundas, Henry, 43, 53–54, 55–56, 74, 76, 113, 180, 219, 229, 239
  anti-emigration policies of, 180, 181, 193, 195
  control of Scottish MPs by, 53, 54
  denies commissions to independent peers, 54
  development of power of, 53
  management policies of, 56, 239
  policy of recruitment under 'clan chiefs', 60, 64, 219
  political offices held by:
    First Lord of the Admiralty, 53
    Lord Advocate, 53
    President of the India Board, 53
    Secretary of War, 53
  relationship with Henry Addington's administration, 53
  relationship with William Pitt the Younger, 53, 64
  rapprochement with Portland Whigs, 54
  represents Scottish landed interest within Union, 52
  rise linked to recruitment for American War, 53
  unofficial status as 'minister for Scotland', 42, 46, 52, 53, 239
  use of patronage as instrument of political management, 56
  military, 42, 51, 53, 54, 56, 202
  wider influence of in Britain and empire, 53
Dundas, Robert, of Arniston, Solicitor-General, Lord Advocate, 27, 36, 37, 38, 39, 216, 237
  calls for restoration of fencible regiments, 199
  criticises use of clanship as mechanism for judicial management in Highlands, 35
  opinion of on Independent companies, 28
  opposes militia scheme, 218
  supports policy of watch commissions, 37
Dunmore, Lord, see Murray, John
Dutch Republic,
  Highlanders serving in armies of, 7
  Scots-Dutch Brigade and defence of Dutch Republic, 21, 29, 57
  control of commissions in by Tweeddale, 29
  officers from transfer into British army, 61
  subsidies from, to British military, 47
duthcas, 215
Duthil, 7
  minister of involved in recruitment process, 210

Easdale slateworks, 97, 124
East India Company, as source of patronage, 30, 173, 195, 238
East Indies, service in, 127
East Tullochean, 122
Easter Bunchgavy, sub-tenants of, 87
Edderachylis, wage increases in, 156
Edinburgh, 16, 17, 18, 19, 121, 239
  clubs in, 215
  Independent companies in garrison of, 20
  perceptions of Highlanders of government in, 19–20, 25
Eigg, emigration to Canada from, 188
elections, 54, 105
  management of, by Argyll, 51, 105
  management of, by Henry Dundas, 51
  role of military patronage in, 51
  Sutherland (1761), 51, 105
electorate, military personnel amongst, 106
Elgin, watch scheme in, 38
Elliot, Sir Gilbert, MP for Selkirk, 82
  improver, appointed to Board of Annexed Estates, 82
emigration, 3, 75, 147, 163, 168, 169, 171, 177–178, 179, 182, 183, 188, 191, 194, 198, 201, 202
  banning of, 180, 193, 195
  'chain', 187, 188
  civilian, 188
  colonial governors support, 180
  consequences of for availability of labour, 192
  government opposition to, 179–180, 182, 190–191, 192–193, 194, 195, 197, 199, 202–203
  historiography of, 168–169
  impact of on military strength, 201
  imperial context of, 168
  imperial settlement policies, 169
  improvement policies stimulate, 191–192
  landlords,
    abandon opposition to, 201
    opposition to, 190, 192–193, 195, 196–197, 199

Index

linked to military service, 182, 183–184, 185, 186–188, 189, 201
  associated with land settlement for Highlanders, 184, 185, 186–188, 201
  of officer class, 186–189
  encourage emigration, 187, 188–189
  half-pay officers, 189
  relationship to evangelical religion, 214
  seasonal, 231
  social profile of emigrant groups, 171–172, 179, 187
  state interest in process, 169
  stimulated by demobilisation, 198
  'tacksman oppression' as factor in, 171
  volunteer service promoted as alternative to, 199, 202
  war, relationship with, 197
England,
  anti-Catholic attitudes of, 207
  perceived dependence of on Scotland for military manpower, 44–45
  recruitment quotas in, 227–228
Episcopalianism, 13, 208
Erskine, James, Lord Grange, Lord Justice Clerk, 15, 16
eviction, 82–83, 146, 149, 166, 243
  historiography and portrayal of, 146

Fanblair, 87
Farquhar, Robert, of Seathraw, settlement of demobilised personnel on estates of, 94
Farquharson clan, Jacobitism of, 33
Farr, 153, 172
Fencible Regiment of the Isles, 147, 163, 164
  enlistment terms, 147, 164
fencible regiments, 54, 59, 60, 73, 111, 113, 115, 122, 133, 140, 152, 194, 198, 219, 225, 229
  as alternatives to emigration, 198
  demobilisation of, 164
    linked to emigration, 198–199
  deployed in Ireland, 73, 113, 147
  officers in, status of, 74
Ferguson, Adam, military chaplain, 6, 216
feudal superiorities,
  renewal of as instrument of patronage, 32
  renewal of on estates of forfeited families, 32
Findlater, Lord, see Ogilvy, James
Fir-Tacsa, see tacksmen
fishing,
  consequences for industry of impressments into Navy, 90
  linked with crofting, 96, 98
  Parliamentary Report on, 195
  settlements, 92, 96, 97
Flanders,
  Highland regiment in, 22, 26
  Independent companies serve in, 20
  war in, 25, 26, 28, 34, 47, 237
Fletcher, Andrew, Lord Milton, secretary to Duke of Argyll, 23, 29, 59, 105
  and annexed estates, 79, 90
  'King's Cottagers' on, 90
  refuses son a commission in Highland regiment, 23
  response to collapse of Kincardineshire fishing industry, 90
Fletcher, Henry, son of Andrew, Lord Milton, 23
  seeks commission in Highland regiment, 23

Florida, colonisation of, 180
Fontenoy, battle of, British defeat at, 29
  consequences of defeat at for Highland recruitment, 29
Forbes, Duncan, of Culloden, Lord Advocate, 21, 29, 31, 33, 79
  attempts to influence Macphersons, 33
  cautions against use of Independent companies against Jacobites, 21
  intermediary between earls of Tweeddale and Ilay, 27
  Lord President, 21, 58
  policy of towards forfeited estates, 79
  political alliance with 2nd Duke of Argyll, 27
  proposes formation of new regular Highland battalions, 25–26, 27
  proposes system of local watch commissions, 37
Forbes, Captain John, of New, factor on Lovat and Cromarty estates, 94, 96
Fox, Henry, Secretary of State for the Southern Department, 45
  associate of Argyll, 45
Fox-North coalition, 53
France, 132, 204
  alliance with Americans, 59
  atheism in Revolutionary France, 207, 212
  Catholicism in, 207
  concepts of nation and citizenship in linked to military service, 204
  Hanoverian policy towards, 21, 26, 27
  Highlanders serving in armies of, 7
  peace negotiations with Britain and Spain, 88
  planned invasion of Scotland by (1744), 27
  recruitment for army of in Scottish Highlands, 21
  scale of, 22
  supports Jacobite campaigns in Scotland, 26
  war against, 26, 46, 65, 71, 73, 88, 244
Fraser clan,
  Jacobitism of, 205
  relationship of, with Cluny Macphersons, 33
  suspect political loyalties of, 31
Fraser gentry,
  excluded from domestic patronage, 31
  proposed role of as commanders of regular battalions, 25
Fraser, Captain Hugh, 95–96
  improvement of lands by, 96
Fraser, Lieutenant Hugh, organises emigration from Lovat estate, 188
Fraser, James, of Foyers, 31
  fails to secure commission in Independent company, 31
  Jacobitism of, 31
  rejects commission in Jamaica, 31
Fraser, Lieutenant James, requests farm of Glenconvinth and removal of smaller tenants, 96
Fraser, John, lieutenant, tacksman of Knockchoilim, 87
Fraser, Simon, lieutenant, tacksman of Fanblair, 87
Fraser, Simon, of Lovat, 7, 15, 31, 44, 47
  conflict with Grant of Glenmoriston, 37
  employs kin network as instrument for local management, 37
  failure of to implement disarming policy, 35
  joins Jacobites, 33
  loses commission, 18, 32, 33, 35
  memorials to George I, 18

military manpower available to, 33
raises independent companies, 7
uses independent companies to intimidate voters, 18
Fraser, Simon, younger, 70, 138
and 71st Highland regiment, 63, 176, 185, 218
and 78th Highland regiment, 141
commands Highland battalion, 47, 70, 84, 138, 142
controls appointments to commissions in battalion, 48
kinship with Norman Macleod of Dunvegan, 138
negative reactions to appointment of, 58
petitions for restoration of Lovat estate, 82, 142, 194
raises regiment, 59, 61, 68, 70, 84–85, 86, 138, 141, 142, 184, 221, 229
economic factors behind, 229
proprietary status of, 59
Fraser, of Farraline and Ardochy, 30, 196
Frederick of Prussia, 66
French Revolutionary War, Highland regiments deployed in, 59

Gaels,
attitudes of to regular soldiering, 225–226, 233
attitudes of to volunteering, 226, 231–232, 233
avoidance of military service by, 226, 231
characterisation of, 6, 11, 191, 224
culture of, 6, 205, 209
development of British identity, 207, 209, 212, 224, 225
alienation from, 214, 215, 232
expectations of, 2, 190
identity, 207
involvement of in British imperial service, 30, 150, 224
recruitment of, 4, 7, 9, 11, 12, 56, 58, 149
romanticisation of, 1–2
status and rights of, 3
Gage, Thomas, Commander-in-Chief in North America, 62
requests Highland reinforcements, 62
Garden, Alexander,
calls for abandonment of traditional agricultural practices, 97
settlement of demobilised personnel on estates of, 93
Garden, Francis, settlement of demobilised personnel on estates of, 94
George I, king of Great Britain, 18
George II, king of Great Britain, 21, 26, 232
policy of severing Scottish trade and commercial links with parts of Europe, 21
'primitive loyalty' of Gaels to, 232
George III, king of Great Britain,
opposition of to raising of new regiments, 71
and professionalism of army, 70, 243
and raising of Highland battalions, 46, 64, 70
Georgia, Highlanders introduced as soldier-settlers, 183, 239
Germany, deployment of Highlanders in, 105
Gilchrist, Dugald, Sutherland estate factor, 157
Gillanders, George, of Highfield, factor in Stornoway, 156
Glasgow, 121, 146
Earl of Home rumoured to be raising battalion in, 46

English regiment deployed in, 17, 21
Malt Tax riots in, 17
tobacco trade, 241
Glasgow Highland Society, 235
Glasvein, farm, 151
Glencripesdale, farm, 176
Glenduror, farm, 175
Glenelg,
emigration from, 189
social profile of emigrants from, 171
Glenfalloch, rivalry of with Glenorchy, 233
Glengarry estate, loss of tenant land to recruits on, 164
Glenlivet, 144
Glenmoriston,
land in lying waste, 107
Lovat accused of failing to disarm clansmen in, 35
wage increases in, 156
Glenorchy,
Breadalbane estates in, 101, 108, 111, 112, 117, 122, 124
impact of recruitment on, 112, 122, 124
rents from, 107
Campbell tenantry in to form private watch companies, 37
Lord, see Campbell, John
rivalry of with Glenfalloch, 233
Glenquaich, establishment of crofts in for demobilised soldiers, 110
Glensheal, Mackenzie estates of, 136, 137, 160
attempted sale of, 160–161
concessions to tenantry on in return for enlistment, 160
recruitment from, 161
resistance to militia service in, 231
Glenshira, Campbell tenantry in to form private watch companies, 37
Glen Tilt, 7, 143
Golspie, emigration from stimulated by presentation of minister, 210
Gordon, ducal house of,
control of regiment by, 51
divided political allegiances of, 32, 34
estates,
presented as natural recruiting ground, 63
reconstruction of tenurial pattern of, 158, 170
fencible regiment of, 158
sub-tenantry recruit in, 158
hostility of to Argyll, 51
recruitment capability of, 61
rivalry of with Macphersons in Badenoch
Gordon, Duchess of, 157
Gordon, Duke of, see also Gordon, Alexander; Gordon, George
importance of half-pay officers on estate of, 149
Laggan rental of, prominence of half-pay officers in, 148
resistance of senior tenants of to recruitment, 155, 156
Gordon, of Fyvie, attempts of, to gain control of regiment, 55
Gordon, Alexander, 4th Duke of,
attempts of, to gain control of regiment, 54
forges patronage link with fiscal-military state, 133
introduction of sheep-farming on estates of, 160
losses of estate manpower to, 142

Index

raises battalion of fencibles, 133, 144, 160
  negotiations for, 209
Gordon, George, 3rd Duke of Gordon, 38, 54
  to assume reponsibility for peace and security of Badenoch and eastern Highlands, 38
Gordon, Lord Adam, military career of assisted by Argyll, 51
Gordon, Lord Charles,
  Hanoverian sympathies of, reduce Jacobite recruiting success amongst Gordons, 34
  receives military commission, 32, 34
Gordon, Lord Lewis, recruiting for Jacobites hampered by Hanoverian sympathies of brother, 34
Gordon, Sir Robert, of Gordonstoun,
  calls for formation of new Independent companies, 28
  supports Macpherson of Cluny's watch scheme, 38
Gordon, Lieutenant Robert, tacksman, 172
Gordon, William, 16th Earl of Sutherland, 57
Gordon, William, 17th Earl of Sutherland,
  raises fencible regiment, 143
  recruitment strategy for, 143
  relationship with Argyll, 51
Gordon, William, of Achorachan, military assessment on lands of, 144
Gordon riots, 207
Gower, Lord, 166
Graham, James, of Glengyle, agrees fee to keep watch in Highland Stirlingshire, 38
Grange, Lord, see Erskine, James
Grant, clan, 7, 30
  estates of, 7
  military manpower of, 7
  of Glenmoriston, 37
  service in Independent companies, 30
Grant Fencibles, 72
  half-pay officers in, 72
  refuse deployment in Ireland, 73
Grant, Sir Archibald, of Monymusk, 57, 81
  resettlement by of demobilised soldiers, 89
Grant, Sir Charles, MP for Inverness-shire, 199
Grant, Sir James,
  conference of tenantry of with Lochaber MacDonnells, 36
Grant, Sir James, of Grant,
  association of with Henry Dundas, 53, 54, 74
  encourages settlement of army pensioners, 151
  estate management policies of, 133, 140, 141, 151, 166
  opposed to emigration, 192, 196, 198
  failure of to secure control of battalion, 55
  lord lieutenant of Inverness, 197, 229
  military income of, 138
  proposes volunteer force in Strathspey, 230
  raises fencible regiment, 73, 115
    demobilisation of, 74
    recruitment profile of, 115
  rentals, significance of military personnel in, 173
  value to of brother's regiment, 137
Grant, Lieutenant John, to enlist former Jacobites for service in India, 57
Grant, John, of Tullochgrubin, tacksman, 170
Grant, Sir Ludovick, of Grant, resettlement of demobilised soldiers by, 89
Grant of Rothiemurchus,
  membership of anti-emigration committee of Highland Society, 196

urged to join Macpherson of Cluny's watch scheme, 38
Grant-Colquhoun, Captain James,
  commands independent company in Atholl, 19
  kinship of with Macgregors, 19
Granville, John, 1st Earl of Carteret, favourite of George II, 26
  European policy of and implications for British army, 26
grassum, soldiers offered by small tenants as form of, 144
Gray, Robert, tacksman in Assynt, 172
Grenville, George, 52
Groam, 86
Gualachullian, crofts at, 111
Guest, Lieutenant-General Joshua, 36

Haldane, Rev., evangelical minister, 212
Haldimand, General Frederick, Commander-in-Chief in Quebec, 183
Hardwicke, Lord Chancellor, 37, 47, 83, 102, 103
  exerts political pressure on Earl of Breadalbane, 104
  identifies recruiting potential of Breadalbane estates, 102
  opposes colonel's commission for Lovat, 58
  seeks to limit argathelian power, 47
Hay, John, 4th Marquis of Tweeddale, Secretary of State for Scotland, 18, 38, 237
  control of military commissions by, 29
  distrust of Ilay, 27
  military policy under, 28, 36
  resigns, 44
  weakness of control of Scotland, 27
Hay, Thomas, brother of Marquis of Tweeddale, 28
Highland clearances, 1, 3, 11
  first phase of, 195, 201, 234, 238
  historiography of, 3, 11, 12; see also Mackenzie, Alexander
  and military recruitment, 3–4, 5, 6, 11, 12
  Sutherland, 3
'Highland problem', 15, 20, 22, 24, 78
Highland Society,
  anti-emigration policies of, 195–197
  foundation of, 195
  seeks support of Frederick, duke of York, 195–196
Highland Society of London, 235
  military membership of, 235
Highlanders,
  as imperial frontiersmen, 183
  assimilation of into British state, 9, 10, 11, 15, 68, 206, 228, 238
  characterisation of, 6, 11, 19–20, 116, 205, 211, 224, 228, 238
  deployment of in North America, 46, 183
  emigration of, 180, 190
  favoured in military patronage, 23, 24, 29, 238
  Hanoverian, 14, 57
  manipulation by of Lowland perception of Highland disorder, 17–18, 58
  militarism of society of, 7, 8, 16
  government attitudes towards, 36, 61–63
  mutinies of, 9, 182
  non-British images of, 221
  presentation of as foreigners, 221
  possession of military equipment by, 7, 16
  potential Jacobitism of, 16

proposed disarming of, 16, 27, 35, 57, 58, 239
recruitment of,
  proprietary, 69, 237
  rationale behind, 25, 29, 40, 43, 57–58, 61, 187–188
role as soldier-settlers in Georgia, 183
romanticisation of, 1–2
serving in foreign armies, 7, 21, 22, 29
  link with economic hardships at home, 21–22
volunteering, enthusiasm for, 226–227, 228
  as experience of British state, 227
warfare of, 8–9, 16
Hints Towards a Plan for Managing the Forfeited Estates, 89, 90
Holm, planned crofting community at, 98
Holy Roman Emperor, *see* Joseph II
Home, Henry, Lord Kames, 178
Home, William, 8th Earl of Home, ally of Argyll, 46
  rumoured to be raising battalion in Glasgow, 46
Houghary, farm subdivided for crofts, 165
Humberston-Mackenzie, Francis, Earl of Seaforth, 231
  award of regiment to, 54, 137
  debts of, 136
  Dundas secures colonelcy of 78th Highlanders for son of, 56
  governorship of Barbados, 137
    value of pension from, 137
  kelp rents of, 137
  opponent of Dundas, 54
Hume, Hugh, 3rd Earl of Marchmont,
  opponent of Argyll, 51, 58
  recruitment by, 136
  refused permission to raise regiment, 59
  requests state assistance, 136
Humphrey Donaldson & Co, creditors of Earl of Seaforth, 137

Idrigill, subdivided into crofts, 165
Impress Act, 85
Improvement, 77–81, 85, 90, 96, 98, 116, 126, 127, 128, 133, 141, 144, 191–192, 194, 202, 206, 213, 215
  associated with depopulation and eviction, 82–83, 125, 243
  'Britishness' of, 223
  complexities of, 80
  function of in state context, 192
  government policy towards, 99
  incompatibility of with large-scale recruitment, 102, 104, 110, 111, 121–122, 128, 129, 165
  linked to grant of tacks on annexed estates, 87, 96
  meaning of in Highland context, 80–81
  resistance to, 157
Inch, farm, 160
Inchberry, 86
Inchree, sub-tenantry at, 158
Independent Companies, 7, 13–14, 17, 18, 19, 20, 22, 24, 27, 28, 35, 40, 60, 140
  as recruiting nurseries for Highland regiments, 28
  award of commissions in, 19, 27, 60
  calls from gentry for development of, 28
  'civilising', effects of, 19
  deployed to prevent foreign recruiting in Highlands, 22

  deployment of in local property disputes, 19, 28, 37, 38
  detachments of stationed in Ross-shire, 18
  development of Highland regiments from, 15, 20, 22, 24–25, 29, 30, 40
  as extension of Hanoverian state in the Highlands, 19, 20, 21, 22, 39
  functions of, 14, 15, 19, 20, 21, 22, 24, 28, 35, 36
  in Wade's Edinburgh garrison, 20
  intelligence gathering role of, 35
  negative aspects of, 18–19, 20
  negative impact on recruitment of overseas deployment, 28, 29, 35
  pre-Union, 15
  proposed regimental structure of, 20, 25
  re-constituted as 43rd Highland regiment for Spanish war (1739), 24–25, 26, 30
  role of and regularisation in Wade's Scottish command, 20, 21, 24, 27
  scale of, 14, 36
  serve with regular army in Flanders, 20, 22, 28
  service in as stepping-stone to regular commission, 30
  suspected Jacobitism of captains in, 30
  used to intimidate voters, 18; *see also* Dingwall, election of provost at, *and* Nairn, by-election at
India,
  as source of patronage, 30, 74, 138
  Board of Control, presidency of, *see* Dundas, Henry
  British territorial expansion in, 66, 196
  commissions in Highland units sent to, supervised by Argyll, 49
  deployment of German mercenaries in, 66
  Highland companies raised for expedition to, 57, 195
India House, 54
Inverallen, 7
Inverary, woollen manufactory at, 223
Invercauld, estates of protected by Cluny's watch scheme, 38
Inverguseran, sub-tenant of, aspirations to social improvement through enlistment, 164
Inveriananmor, 111
Inverness, Cope marches to, 33
Inverness-shire,
  Grant estates in, 115
  introduction of sheep-farming in, 160
  recruitment activity in, 235
  volunteer establishment in, 227, 228
Inversheal, single-tenant farm, 161
Inveruie, 81, 92
Ireland, 3, 76, 206
  attitudes to overseas military service in, 67
  Catholic manpower reserves of, 222
  Commander-in-Chief in, 49
  contribution of to British imperialism, 1, 67
  'establishment' in, 23, 50, 66, 67, 236
  control of patronage in peacetime, 50
  fencible regiments deployed in, 73, 113, 147
  institutionalised patronage base in, 50
  Lord Justice of, 23
  Lord Lieutenant of, 23, 67, 239
    control of military patronage by, 23, 49–50, 175
    grants commissions to non-Irish clients, 50
    loses control over Irish regiments serving outwith Ireland, 50

Index

parliament in, 10
proposed deployment of Hessian mercenaries in, 67
Protestants in, martial traditions of, 41
recruitment from, 4, 67, 68
  economic consequences of, 67
  quotas, 228
  regiments from deployed in American war, 46, 68
  regiments raised in and paid for by Irish parliament, 23
  relationship with Westminster, 76
Irvine, Alexander, 214–215
Islay, labour shortages in, 156
Isle Martin, fishing and crofting at, 96

Jacobitism, 7, 9, 13, 14, 15, 16, 29, 31, 43, 58, 131
  decline in, 32
  and Episcopalianism, 13
  increased Highland involvement in imperial strategies as consequence of, 40, 60, 215
  militant, 20
  overseas commissions as means of countering, 31, 60
Jacobite Risings, 27
  French support for, 26–27
  of 1715, 11, 13, 36, 78, 131, 236
    conciliatory policies following, 78–79
  of 1745, 6, 8, 11, 12, 13, 20, 22, 26, 35, 39, 42, 43, 50, 56, 57, 61, 75, 78, 106, 140, 237
    absence of Independent companies as contributory factor in, 20
    and Austrian War of Succession, 26
    impact of on Campbell political dominance, 43
    influence of on government recruitment policy, 42, 58, 75, 87, 102
    influence of on perceptions of Highland problem, 78, 237
    military levy during, 41–42, 106
    origins of, 39
    recruitment during, 107, 236
    reveals flaws in Scottish governmental system, 43
    role of 54th Highland regiment in suppression of, 29
  socio-economic impact of, 237
Jacobites,
  arming of, security concerns over, 30
  clan support for, 32, 35, 41, 131, 140
  deployment of clan manpower against, 35
  growing divisions in previously Jacobite families, 32
  in Brae Atholl, 21
  in Lochaber, 21
  political animosity towards forfeited families, 78
  recruitment by, 107
  rehabilitation of through British military service, 41, 47–48, 60, 131, 205, 218, 237
  restricted ability of to recruit in Inverness-shire, 35
  serving in foreign armies, 21
Jamaica, negative attitude of Highland gentry towards military commissions in, 31
Johnstone, George, governor of West Florida, promotes immigration, 180

Joseph II, Holy Roman Emperor, 66
  limits British recruitment within his territory, 66
Jura, settlement of army pensioners on, 151

Kaimes, Lord, estate management policies of, 133, 178
kelp industry, 98, 118, 130, 134–135, 138, 141, 148, 192, 196, 217, 243
  prices, 244
  problems of, 134–135, 196–197
    emigration as consequence of, 197
  promotes excessively subdivided crofts, 130, 166, 243
  rents from, 137
  stimulates demographic growth, 118
Kenmore, petitioners in seek to avoid militia service, 226
Kennedy, John, factor on Breadalbane's Perthshire estate, 123–124
Keppoch, see MacDonnell, Captain Ranald, 62
Kerr, John, 1st Duke of Roxburghe, 37
Kildonan,
  emigrants from, social profile of, 172
  enlistment from, 140, 159
  minister opposes recruitment in, 210
  people of, 4–5
Kilearn, Stirlingshire,
  gentry and tenants of and lobby for Independent companies, 15
Killean, minister of, hostility to his recruitment efforts, 210
Killin, 114, 226
  minister of involved in recruitment process, 210
Kilmoraick, involvement of minister in recruitment process, 210
Kilmuir, 151
  economic status of half-pay officers in, 148
kin network,
  as defence mechanism, 39
  as instrument for local management, 36–37, 38
  as recruitment mechanism, 239
Kincardineshire, collapse of fishing industry in, 90
'King's Cottagers' scheme, 90, 91, 95
Kingussie,
  economic status of half-pay officers in, 148
  population decline at, 192
Kinloch Rannoch, 81
Kinlochleven, 232
Kintail,
  cattle-raiding into, 19
  Mackenzie estates in, 136, 137, 160
    preferential leases offered to recruits on, 161
    recruitment from, 161, 185
    reorganisation of, 171
    resistance to militia service in, 231
Kintomey, farm, 153
Kintyre, costs to of failure to provide recruits, 108
Knockchoilim, 86
  tacksman of, 87
Knocknairy, 86
Knox, John,
  condemns emigration, 191
  observations by on military emigration policies, 187, 222
Knoydart, 81
Kyle of Sutherland, watch on, 38
Kyles Bernera, tacksman of, view of on importance of military pay to local economy, 198

Kilytrie, development of crofts at, 111, 118–119
Laggan,
  economic status of half-pay officers in, 148
  minister issues warnings of evictions, 209
Letterfour, 163
Lettoch, 86
Lewis,
  development of crofting in, 97–98
  failure of droving credit in, 134
  fishing settlement on, 94, 97
  internal colonisation in, 94
  kelp industry on, 134–135
  Mackenzie estates on, 136–137, 143, 146
    attempts to prevent emigration from, 193
    recruits from, 146
    rentals, 170
  reorganisation of, 171
  reports to Napier Commission in, 5
  resettlement of demobilised sailors and soldiers on, 94, 97–99 passim
  resistance to militia service in, 231
  rumour of Russian arms landed in (1725), 17
Lindores, Lord, requests military commission, 48
Lismore, 107
Little Garth, 86
Liverpool, transport of arms from to Skye, 35
Livingston, Gilbert, of Seil, Breadalbane tenant, 124
Lochaber, 7, 17, 142, 158, 160
  plans to seize prominent Jacobites in, 21
  tacksmen responsible for bounties of men levied in, 144
Lochalsh, Mackenzie estates of, 136, 170
  enlistment costs on, 144
Locharkaig, ambush at, 19
Lochawside, 124
Lochbroom, report on established fishing in, 96
Lochbuie, 153, see also Maclaine, Murdoch
Locheil, emigration from, 189
Lochend, see Campbell, John, of Lochend
Lochgarry, men from selected for recruitment, 140
Lochnell, estate of, 243
Loch Ness, 143
Lochshin, watch at east end of, 38
Loch Tay, 125, 126
Lochtayside,
  Breadalbane estates on, 101, 106, 107, 118, 124, 127
  over-crowding in, 112
  tenancies on divided in favour of military personnel, 109, 126
London, 16, 19, 26, 27, 51
  moneyed interests in, 132
  perceptions of Highlanders by government in, 19–20, 25, 61, 75
  weak wartime administrations in, consequences of, 53
Lord Advocate, see Craigie, Robert; Dundas, Henry; Forbes, Duncan
Lord Justice Clerk, see Erskine, James
Lord Lieutenancies, role of, 39
Lord President, see Forbes, Duncan
Lorne,
  Breadalbane estates in, 101, 108
  commercial developments in, 97
  development of crofting in, 97–98
  resettlement of demobilised sailors and soldiers in, 98–99

Lorne, Lord, see Campbell, John
Lothian, estate management policies in, 134
Loudon, earl of, see Campbell, John
Lovat, see Fraser, Simon, Lord Lovat
Lovat estate,
  annexed, 84, 188, 194
  emigration from, 188
  interaction of improvement and recruitment in, 84–85, 95
  recruitment from, 85, 87, 98
  resettlement of demobilised men at, 91
    disruption on caused by, 94, 95, 98
Lower Fernoch, 111
Luing, island of, estate management policies on, 111

MacArthur, Rev. Donald, Cowal preacher, pressganged for preaching against conscription, 210
MacCrown, Hugh, sergeant, receives grant of farm, 122
Macdonald, Lieutenant, seeks sheep-farm in Glensheal, 161
Macdonald, Lord,
  breaks terms of lease for enlistment agreements, 147
  crofting on estates of, 151–152
  petition to by army pensioners, 151
  rental value of Skye estates of, 149, 164
Macdonald, Lord Alexander, of Sleat, 64
Macdonald, Sir Alexander,
  breaks up large tacks into multiple holdings, 171
  settles returning soldiers on, 189
  government pressure on to recruit, 61
  receives military commission, 32, 34
  seeks links and patronage opportunities with fiscal-military state, 132
Macdonald, Lieutenant-Colonel Alexander, of Lyndale, 199
Macdonald, Donald, army pensioner, 151
Macdonald, Lieutenant Ewan, of Griminish, 198
Macdonald, Sir James, of Sleat, impact of recruitment on estate revenues of, 107
Macdonald, John, of Clanranald,
  creditors of, 138
  gains commissions in Lovat's battalion, 84
  recruitment on estates of, 63
Macdonald, Norman, soldier, son of tenant in Kilmuir, 164
Macdonald, Ranald, of Ulva, 198
Macdonald, William, pensioner of 93rd Sutherland Highlanders, 4
Macdonald of Glencoe,
  enlistments from, 140
  Jacobitism of, 140
MacDonald of Glengarry, recruiting potential of estates of, 63
Macdonald of Morar, gains commissions in Lovat's battalion, 84
Macdonald of Sleat, 8, 163, 196–197
  anti-argathelian attitude of family, 34
  committed to Loudon's rgiment in 1745, 35
  divided political allegiances within family of, 32
  feud with Macleods of Dunvegan, 8
  offered regiment, 59
  recruitment capability of, 61
  recruitment linked to grant of leases, 147, 159, 162, 163–164

Index

settlement of pensioners on estate of, 151, 189
successful use of military patronage system by, 34
MacDonnell, Aeneas, of Glengarry, watch service of in Atholl, 37
MacDonnell, Alexander, tenant of Inch, recruiting for Duke of Gordon, 160
MacDonnell, Lieutenant Angus, of Sandaig, leads emigration from Knoydart, 188
MacDonnell, Lieutenant Archibald, 95
MacDonnell, Coll, of Barrisdale, 19
  blackmail operations of, 19
  control of independent company, 19
MacDonnell, Ranald, of Glengarry, 161–162, 196
MacDonnell, Captain Ranald, of Keppoch, offers to raise men for American Revolutionary War, 62
MacDonnell of Glengarry, 164
  gains commissions in Lovat's battalion, 84
  offers to sell estate to Crown, 79
MacDonnell of Lochaber, 17, 32
  conference of with Grants, 36
  disputes with Camerons, 17
  Jacobitism of, 17, 33
MacDonnells of Lochgarry,
  Jacobitism of, 39
  recipients of army patronage, 39
Macdougall, Allan, *Song to the Lowland Shepherd*, 213
Macgregor, James, factor in Strathspey, 133
Macgregors, of Rannoch Moor, 19
Macintyre clan, 37
Macintyre, Duncan Ban, poetry of, 209, 232
  Song to the Earl of Breadalbane, 232
  Song of the Gazette, 232
Mackay, Donald, 3rd Lord Reay, 79
  proposes inalienable annexation of forfeited estates, 79
Mackay, George, MP for Sutherland, 51, 79
Mackay, James, Sutherland tacksman, 156
Mackay of Bighouse, Strath Halladale estates of, 163
Mackenzie clan,
  conflict with Cameron/Macphees, 19, 38
  demand assistance of Independent company soldiers in Kintail, 19
  and election at Dingwall, 18
  former Jacobitism of, 17
  divisions within, over issue of, 32
Mackenzie of Cromartie,
  annexed estates of, 87
  levying and resettlement of military personnel on, 87–88
  demonstrates loyalty in military command during American wars, 61
  former Jacobitism of family, 205
Mackenzie of Fairburn, 19, 161
Mackenzie of Lentron,
  house destroyed by Camerons, 19, 38
  supervises local kin-based protection scheme, 38
Mackenzie of Seaforth, 72, 73, 98, 159; *see also* Humberston-Mackenzie
  debts of, 136–137
  estates of, 136–137, 160–161
  instructed to appoint half-pay officers to his regiment, 72
  Jacobitism of, 205
  military income of, 138

opposes emigration, 193
recruitment from estates of, 140, 144–145, 146
resistance to from senior tenants, 155
seeks grant of regiment, 64
sells commission to brother-in-law, 137
Mackenzie, Sir Alexander, of Coul, Whig and argathelian, 17, 18
dispute with Munros and Rosses, 17, 18
Mackenzie, Major Alexander, of Belmaduthie, 137
Mackenzie, Alexander, of Ardloch, Assynt estate factor, 189
Mackenzie, Alexander, of Fairburn, 37–38
supervises local kin-based protection scheme, 38
Mackenzie, Alexander, half-pay ensign, 153
Mackenzie, Alexander, 3
The History of the Highland Clearances, 3
Mackenzie, George, 3rd Earl of Cromartie,
estranged through failure to secure commissions in Loudon's battalion, 34
Mackenzie, Lieutenant George, of Gairloch, half-pay officer returning to service, 173
Mackenzie, James Stuart, 52
Mackenzie, John, Lord Macleod,
kinsman of Henry Dundas, 54
MP, 54
raises battalions for India service, 54
Mackenzie, Dr John, 94, 98
develops crofting on Mackenzie estate, 98
Mackenzie, Kenneth, Lord Macleod, offers commission to Norman Macleod, 145
Mackenzie, Kenneth, of Seaforth, 18, 57, 59, 94, 131
settlement of demobilised personnel on lands of, 92
Mackenzie, Roderick, naval doctor, 179
Mackenzie, Lieutenant Simon, tenancy of at South Langwell, 97
Mackerchar, Duncan, crofter at Tommachrocher, enlists, 124
Mackinnon family, Lovat requests ensigncy in line regiment for, 31
Mackintosh clan, 7
divided political allegiances of, 32
rivalries of with Macphersons in Badenoch, 33
Mackintosh, Aeneas, receives military commission, 32
company deserts to join wife's Jacobite regiment, 33
Mackintosh, Captain William, of Crathiemor, tacksman, re-enters military service, 173–174
Mackintosh of Balnespick, estates of, labour shortages on, 156
Maclaine, Archibald, of Lochbuie,
loses estate manpower through enlistment, 142
Maclaine, Murdoch, of Lochbuie, 242
involvement in sheep-farming, 135
military income of, 137, 138
quartermaster of Argyll Fencibles, 137
recruitment from estates of, 146, 152, 159, 162
intimidatory nature of, 159
into Dunbartonshire Fencibles, 140
operation of system, 146, 147
remissions of pay by soldiers to kin on estates of, 152
McLean, Lieutenant Colonel Allan, of Torloisk, raises Highland regiment of emigrants, 184
Maclean clan, divided political allegiances of, 32

McLean of Coll, occupation profile of recruits from estates of, 143
Maclean of Duart, 8
Maclean of Torloisk, estranged through failure to secure military commissions for sons, 34
Macleod clan, declining Jacobitism of, 32
Macleod, Lord, *see* Mackenzie, John
Macleod, Lord, of Cromartie, 63
Macleod of Dunvegan, 8, 19, 35; *see also* Macleod, Colonel Norman
   at battle of Worcester, 8
   committed to Loudon's regiment in 1745, 35
   disarmed tenantry of in Glenelg, 19
   feud with Macdonalds of Sleat, 8
   requests government protection and arms, 35–36
   senior tenants resist recruiting drives by, 155
   successful use of military patronage policy amongst, 34
   supports Macpherson of Cluny's watch scheme, 38
Macleod of Macleod, 140
   estate recruitment by, 140
   remissions of pay from soldiers to kin on estates of, 152
Macleod, Donald, 3
   Gloomy Memories, 3
Macleod, Donald, army pensioner, 151
Macleod, Colonel John, of Talisker, 198, 230
Macleod, John, son of Norman Macleod of Dunvegan, receives commission, 34
Macleod, Norman, of Dunvegan, colonel, 5, 21–22, 31, 43, 63–64
   basis of estate economy of, 134
   career, 137–138, 145
   debt of, 138
   estates of, 138
   eviction by of former soldiers, 5
   manpower reserves of estates, 145
   promises Macdonald of Sleat access to Campbell military patronage, 34
   receives military commissions, 32, 64, 138, 145
      promotions linked to provision of recruits, 64, 138, 145
   recruitment of tenantry by, 145, 146, 159
   rental income of, 134, 138
   serves in India, 138
   susceptibility of to overtures of co-operation from government, 34
Macleod, Patrick, of Geanies, lieutenant, 72
   promoted to captain, 72
MacNeill of Barra, gains captaincy in Lovat's battalion, 84
Macphees, kinsmen of Cameron of Glendessary, 19
   cattle-raids by into Kintail, 19
Macpherson clan,
   divided political allegiances of, 32
   former Jacobitism of, 205
   rivalries of with Gordons and Mackintoshes in Badenoch, 33
Macpherson, Andrew, of Benchar, Badenoch tacksman, 132–133
Macpherson, Alexander, tacksman, 158
   attempts to improve lands, 158
Macpherson, Major Duncan, of Cluny, recruiter for Lovat, 184

Macpherson, Ewan, of Cluny, recruits regiment during famine period, 229
Macpherson, Ewan, of Cluny, receives military commission, 32, 33, 237
   blackmail operations of, 38
   exposed position of, 33
   joins Jacobites, 33, 39
   offers to raise private watch company, 38
   support for amongst Highland gentry, 38
   recipient of army patronage, 39
   relationship with Frasers and Camerons, 33
Macpherson, Captain John, of Bellachroan, 149
Macpherson of Killihuntly, scheme for pacification of Highlands, 20
Mains of Lovat, 86
Malt Tax riots, 17, 21
Malthus, Thomas, 201
Mansfield, Earl of, *see* Murray, William
Marchmont, Earl of, *see* Hume, Hugh
Martin of Letterfinlay, development of sheep-farming by, 160
Meikle Portclair, 86
Menzies, Sir Robert, recruitment on estates of, 63
Merse, estate management policies in, 133
militias, 53, 57, 71, 73, 74, 106, 199, 200, 219, 230, 231
   as means of reclaiming national martial ethos, 216
   decline of, 200
   intellectual arguments in favour of, 216
   loss of tenantry to, 107
   patriotic nature of, 216
   pay, contribution of to economy, 153
   transfers from to line regiments, 74, 227–228
Miller, Thomas, Lord Chief Justice, monitors emigrant numbers, 192
Milns of Kimoraick, 86
Milton, Lord, *see* Fletcher, Andrew
ministers,
   authority undermined by lay preachers, 211
   involvement in recruiting process, 209–210
   local leadership of, 208–209
   non-cooperation with recruitment process, 210
   roles as estate messengers, 209–210
Monaltry, 94
Moniack, 86, 87
Montgomery, Archibald, 11th Earl of Eglinton, 47
   commands new Highland battalion, 47
   controls appointments to commissions in battalion, 48
   raises regiment, 59, 152
Monymusk, settlement of Chelsea pensioners at, 89
Moore, Sir John, 225
Moray, Grant estates in, 115
Moray, watch scheme in, 38
Morvern, 176
Mountstuart, Lord, *see* Stuart, John
Moy, population decline at, 192
Mull, 176
   enlistment from, 142
   into Dunbartonshire Fencibles, 140
   into Western Fencibles, 142, 146
Mulroy, clan fight at, 7
Munro clan, 17
   dispute with Sir Alexander Mackenzie of Coul, 17
Munro, Captain George, of Culcairn, 17, 18
   commands independent company, 17
   uses company to intimidate voters, 18

Index

Munro, Lieutenant Henry, receives land grants in Georgia, 186
Murray, Lord George, Jacobite commander, 31
Murray, James, 2nd Duke of Atholl, 19, 105, 106, 132, 141–142
  debarred from Board of Annexed Estates, 80
  enthusiasm of for raising Independent companies, 28
  relationship with Rannoch Moor Macgregors, 19
  seeks aid of Alexander Robertson of Strowan, 37
  seeks links and patronage opportunities with fiscal-military state, 132
Murray, John, 4th Duke of Atholl, 136
Murray, John, 4th Lord Dunmore, 61
  former page-in-waiting to Charles Edward Stuart, 61
  highlights recruiting potential of Highland estates, 63
  refused regiment, 61
Murray, Lord John, 72
  colonel in 42nd Highland regiment, 62, 105–106, 145
  MP for Perthshire, 105
  supported by 3rd Earl of Breadalbane, 106
  offers lieutenant-colonel's commission to Norman Macleod, 145
  proposed recruitment by on Menzies and Clanranald estates, 63
  secures military commission, 31
  seeks command of second battalion, 62
Murray, John, of Strowan,
  candidate in Perthshire election, 106
  supported by Atholl and Argyll, 106
Murray, William, 1st Earl of Mansfield, political influence of, 52
Murray-Keith, Robert, 93, 107
Murray-Macgregor, Sir John, of Landrick, reports on condition of Breadalbane estate, 127, 128

Nairn, by-election at, voters intimidated by Fraser of Lovat's soldiers, 18
Napier Commission, 5, 148, 150
Napoleon,
  Continental System, 244
  peace negotiations with, 196
Napoleonic Wars, 65, 197, 225, 242
naval commissions,
  patronage of contolled by Henry Dundas, 53
Navy,
  demobilisations from, 90–92
  pensions, 235
  recruitment from Highlands, 197, 235
  scale of, 244
Netherlorne, 97, 112, 118, 121, 124, 125, 127
  Breadalbane estate rentals in, 107
  settlement of demobilised personnel on Breadalbane estates in, 97, 124, 243
  creation of crofts for, 109, 243
New Brunswick,
  creation of, 181
  military emigration to, 188
New Tarbat, 81, 91, 92, 94
New York,
  policy of land for military service in, 184
  settlement of former soldiers in, 185
Newcastle, 1st Duke of, 45, 76, 79
  alliance with William Pitt, 45
  attitude to management of Scotland, 44
  relationship with Argyll, 45–46, 47, 48, 52
  uses Scottish military high command to support Argyll's enemies, 49
Nine-Mile River, demobilised soldiers settle along, 186
North, Lord, 63
  attitude to Scottish politics, 54
North Britain, emulative patriotism of, 208
North Carolina,
  policy of land for military service in, 184
  Scottish emigration to, 182
North Langwell, 96
North Uist, 232
  contribution of army pay to estate income in, 153
  recruitment in,
    density of, 163
    linked to development of crofts, 165, 243
  requests for land in, 162, 243
  settlement of half-pay officers in, 149
Northern Department, control of Scottish business by, 52
Northern Fencibles, 144, 158
Nova Scotia, 180–181, 182, 185
  demobilised soldiers settle in, 186
  emigration to from Breadalbane estates, 190
  French Acadians in, 57
  Governor instructed to discourage emigration to, 179–180
  men from Loudon's regiment to be settled in, 57

Oban, farm, 122
Ogilvy, James, Lord Deskford, anti-argathelian, 45
3rd Earl of Seafield, 89
  resettlement of demobilised sailors and soldiers by, 89, 91, 92, 94
Ogilvy, James, Lord Findlater, opponent of Argyll, 58
Ohio expedition, annihilation of, 46
Old Statistical Account, 148, 155, 235
  records presence of Highland recruitment, 235

Park, development of crofting at, 98
Parr, John, governor of Nova Scotia, favours emigration, 180–181
Passenger Act, 180, 182, 192, 193, 195, 197, 198, 199
patriotism and the British ideal,
  agricultural change, patriotic nature of, 178, 191, 222–223
  'British' virtues, absence of in Highlands, 220
  'Britishness', measures of, 204
  commercial development, presented as patriotic ideal, 178, 191, 192, 217, 224
  depopulation, anti-patriotic presentation of, 3, 191, 194, 223
  Dundas and patriotism, 217
  differing British patriotisms, polarisation of, 216, 222
  emulative patriotism of North Britain, 208
  estate reorganisation in terms of, 191, 223
  improvement as patriotic activity, 191, 222, 223
  landlords, identification of with patriotic ideals, 192, 195, 196, 197
    activities of Highland Society, 195–197
    militia service within, 216
  patriotic partnership, 190–201 *passim*, 203

recruitment as patriotic endeavour, 169, 222, 223
  justifications for extinguished, 224
  retention of reservoir of military manpower, 192
  Scots expressions of loyalty to Empire, 224
patronage,
  access to, for American colonists, 22
  access to in Highlands, 22, 30–31
  civil, 29, 48
  domestic, 30
    exclusion of Frasers from, 31
  East India Company, 30
  imperial, 30, 31, 44, 49, 76, 238
    devolutionary and centralising impact of, 49, 238
    financial significance of to Highland landlords, 137, 193–194, 202
    impact of on Scotland's semi-autonomous status, 42
    use of, to undermine disaffection, 30
  military, 19, 22, 27, 29, 32, 39, 42, 44, 47, 53, 58, 61, 64, 72, 85, 103, 128, 193–194, 238
    Argyll's control of, 48, 50, 103
    Dundas's use of, 53, 54, 193, 202
    financial significance of to Highland landlords, 137, 193–194, 202, 238
    government direction of, 61
    impact of on Scotland's semi-autonomous status, 42
    justifications for disproportionate Highland elite access to, 63, 193–194, 238
    limitations of, 32, 34
    reinforces aspects of Scottish particularism, 42, 238
    role in electoral politics, 51
    selected use of, 32
    political uses of, 30, 193
    renewal of terms of feudal superiority as instrument of, 32
Patronage Act, 207
Peinmore, 163
Pelham, Henry, Secretary to the Treasury, 44, 79
  relationship with Archibald, 3rd Duke of Argyll, 44
Pelham, Thomas, Home Secretary, 196
Perth, estates of, 84
  resettlement of demobilised men on, 91, 93
Perthshire,
  Argyll, political influence of in, 51, 105
  Army of Reserve, 226
    fines for failure to supply quotas to, 226
  Breadalbane estates in, 108–118 passim, 122, 125, 126, 170
    development of sheep-walks on, 125
    costs of recruitment in, 118
    disaffected families in, 30
    election in, 105, 175
    record of loyalty in, to British state, 104
    reluctance in to recruit, 104
    Scots-Dutch recruitment in, 21
Pitt, William,
  abandons use of Hessian mercenaries, 68
  alliance with Duke of Newcastle, 45
  anti-Argyll stance, 45, 48
  blue water policies of, 47
  seeks role for Gaels within British Union, 205, 225, 239

supports domestic recruitment policies, 47, 52, 68, 205, 218, 225, 239
Pitt, William, the younger,
  relationship with Henry Dundas, 53, 64, 180
poetry, Gaelic, 2, 209, 232
  anti-French tone of, 232
Porteous Riots, 18
Portland, Duke of, administration of, 54
Portsoy, 89
Presbyterianism, 204, 207, 208
  evangelical,
    Highlanders' involvement in, 211
    negative aspects of, 211
    producing shift towards indifference to secular issues, 210
    non-British character of, 213
    questions state ideal of wealth, 212–213, 214
    seditious nature of, 211–212
  interaction of with militarism, 207
  suspicions of Anglicanism, 207
President of the India Board of Control, see Dundas, Henry
Presmucherarch, farm, 158
Prestonpans, battle of, 8
Protestantism,
  and wealth generation, 213, 215
  nation-forging properties of, 207, 209
  promotion of 'Britishness' by, 215
Prussia, 66, 132, 232
  Frederick of, 66
  recruitment for army of in Scottish Highlands, 21

Quakers, involvement of in colonisation, 183
Quebec, 183
  Act, 221
  emigration to, 181, 188
  settlement of demobilised soldiers in, 186–187, 239
  victory at celebrated in Gaelic poetry, 232
Queensberry, Duke of, refused permission to raise regiment, 59

Rannoch,
  company troops in, 37
  Moor, Macgregors of, 19
Reay,
  estate, arrears of rent on, 134
  Fencibles, 7
  Lord, proposed as Lord Lieutenant of Caithness, 39
  military power of, 39
  service of clansmen of in Scots-Dutch brigade, 39
Relich, 87
Relief Church, 208, 212
Riddroch, 96
Rive, 96
Robertson, Alexander, of Straloch, offers to raise men for American Revolutionary War, 62
Robertson, Alexander, of Strowan, 37
Robertson, Duncan, of Drumachuine,
  estranged through failure to secure senior ranking commission, 34
  promised military commission, 32
  secures lands of Strowan with assistance of Forbes of Culloden, 33, 34
Robertson, Robert, Breadalbane estate surveyor, 121, 126, 127

Index

Rogart, opposition in to presentation of minister, 210
Ross family, 17
  dispute with Sir Alexander Mackenzie of Coul, 17, 18
  of Balnagown, 17
  of Pitcalnie, 17, 32
    Hanoverian sympathies of, 33
Ross, Malcolm, younger of Pitcalnie, receives military commission, 32
  joins Jacobites, 33
Ross, Rev. Thomas, minister of Kilmonavaig, conducts recruiting negotiations, 209
Ross of Mull, development of crofting on Argyll estates in, 164–165
Ross-shire, 18, 224, 235
  disaffected families in, 30
  independent company detachments stationed in, 18
  Ross and Munro interests in, 17
  volunteer establishment in, 227
Rothiemurchus, 7
Rough Bounds, warriors of, in Gaelic poetry, 232
Roxburghe, Duke of, *see* Kerr, John
Russell, John, 4th Duke of Bedford, opposition of to annexation bill, 79, 80
Russian mercenaries in British army, 66
Ruthven, 209

St. Clair, General James, 52
St. John's Isle, 187
  demobilised soldiers settle in, 186
  lieutenant governorship in, 181
  scale of Highland settlement in, 186
salt laws, 92
Saratoga, British defeat at, 59, 185
  impact of on Highland recruitment, 185
Scotland,
  anti-Catholic attitudes in, 13, 207
  anti-French attitudes in, 13
  assimilation of into British state, 9–10, 14, 56, 75, 238
  attitudes in towards Highlands, 45, 216
  attitudes in towards imperial war, 44–45, 56
  Borders of,
    abortive proposals for raising regiment in, 50–51
    absence of militarism in, 51
    influence of Earl of Marchmont in, 51
    limited development of imperial militarisation in, 50
    martial tradition in, 44
    similarities of to Highlands, 50
  consequences of '45 for relationship of with England, 44
  contribution of to British imperial military, 1, 2, 9–10, 56
  decline of military prowess of, 216
  factional politics in, 43
  flawed governmental system in, 43
  formation of volunteer military units in, 55
  Highlands of, 1–2, 11, 19–20, 31, 35, 40, 50
    agricultural change in, 3, 82–83, 86, 90, 99, 125, 128, 141, 154
      patriotic nature of, 222–223
    annexed estates,
      as experiment in social engineering, 77–79, 93
      changing tenurial structures of, 87, 89, 90, 96, 97, 98, 99
      consolidation of farms of, 86, 87, 89, 94, 95
      creation of croft holdings on, 90, 95, 96, 99
      disannexation of, 194
      failure of improvement policies on, 194
      long-term consequences of for Highlands, 94
      management of, 81–84, 89, 94, 96
      occupation profile of recruits from, 143
      removal of subtenantry on, 87, 94, 95, 96, 97, 99
      settlement of demobilised soldiers and sailors on, 91, 93, 94, 95, 99
      settlement of half-pay officers on, 96, 175
    anti-Erastianism, 209
    anti-militarism in, 210
    army pensioners in,
      contribution to local economies of, 150–151
      elite status of amongst small tenantry, 151
    assimilation of with British state, 9, 13, 14, 15, 39, 40, 59, 68, 202, 222, 238, 244
    attitudes towards, 22, 24, 40, 42, 190, 206–207, 216–218, 221, 236, 238, 242
    viewed as peripheral province, 42, 221
    'barbarity' of, 15, 16, 20
    Board of Annexed Estates in, 77; *see also* Annexed Estates Board
    British identity of, 204–210 *passim*, 220, 225
    Catholicism in, 208
    cattle-raiding in, 15, 17, 19, 28
      attempts to resolve, 36
    cattle trade, 111
    character of society in, 5, 6, 16, 20
    Chelsea Pensioners from, 150
    clanship and military service, 6, 7, 8, 11–12, 13, 15, 36, 40, 41, 59–60, 63, 75, 77, 78, 115, 116, 130, 139, 140–141, 202, 237
      as lobbying mechanism, 64
    collapse of clanship in, 7, 12, 13, 14, 41, 57–59, 60, 63, 115, 131, 139, 237
    colonial links of, 178, 186
    commercialising of, 147, 160, 169, 185, 200, 218, 234
      underdevelopment in, 218–220, 221, 222, 224, 241
    crofting in, 97, 99, 108–127 *passim*, 129, 151, 164–165, 166, 168, 239
    decline of military recruitment in, 42
    demobilisation, impact of, 80, 88, 90, 91, 92, 93, 95, 243
    depopulation in, 82–83
    development of British identity in, 21
    disarmament of, 20, 27, 35, 36, 57, 102, 239
    electorate in,
      aid management strategies of Argyll and Dundas, 51
      militarism of, 235
    elite in,
      as Junker or service caste, 241
      changing position of in British military, 74, 137
      economic dependence of on army, 75, 137–138, 139, 147–148, 172, 196, 202, 219
      financial insecurity of, 135–136

masks decay of clanship, 63, 64
militarisation of, 235
opposition of to emigration, 180, 196
recruitment by, 70, 75, 102–103, 142–143, 147
revenues from, 137, 138, 144–145, 148
trade estate populations for state office, 64, 244
utilised by Argyll for recruiting purposes, 51
emigration from, 3, 75, 147, 163, 168, 171; *see also* emigration
Episcopalianism in, 208
estates,
contribution of military pay to income of, 152–153, 154, 163, 198
importance of half-pay officers to economy of, 148–149, 151, 154, 172
as improvers, 149
management in, 11, 12, 64, 101, 125, 128–129, 133, 141, 142, 160, 162, 165, 168, 169; *see also* landowners
confused state of, 101, 125
linked to decline in recruitment, 42, 200
military levying from, 101, 104, 106, 107, 108–110, 114, 116–120 *passim*, 122–124, 126, 129, 130, 143–144, 145, 146, 156, 159, 164, 169
costs of, 157
resettlement of demobilised men, 164, 165
populations of, as recruiting resource, 130, 144, 145, 159, 160, 165, 192, 200, 202
rentals,
arrears of, 134
values of, 133, 163, 170
restructuring of tenurial patterns on, 158, 161, 163, 164, 165, 166, 170, 171, 172, 189
significance of half-pay officers on, 148
socio-economic role of, 130
tacksman and joint-tenant systems on, 130, 133, 157, 158
evictions in, 82–83, 146, 149, 166, 243
ghettoisation of, 40, 218
government policies in, 13–14, 16, 19, 21, 22, 24, 27, 29, 35, 36, 37, 47, 60, 68, 77–83, 99, 169, 190, 192, 193, 194, 199–200, 237–238, 242, 244
anti-emigration, *see* emigration
'civilising', 35, 89, 93
clan-based policy of property protection, 37, 38, 40
de-militarisation, 36, 57, 86, 102
incoherence of, 33, 34, 102
prevention of further disarmament, 36
public works schemes, 199, 202
re-arming disarmed clans, 35
recruitment, influence of '45 on government's policy towards, 42, 56, 58, 61, 102, 205
half-pay officers in, 148–149, 151, 172
emigration organised by, 189
re-enlistment of, 172
historiography of, 2–4, 7, 11
historiography of military service from, 5, 6, 7, 9–10
as imperial military reserve, 68

imperial role of, 42, 50, 56, 63, 75, 150, 202
implications for of professionalising of army, 69, 243
'improvement' in, 78, 80–81, 82, 83, 85, 87, 89, 98–99, 102–103, 104, 116, 125, 126, 127, 128–129, 133, 141, 165, 191–192, 202, 206, 213, 215
'Britishness' of, 223
link to recruitment, 101, 110, 111, 121, 129, 191
linked to grant of tacks on annexed estates, 87
resistance to, 157
independent companies in, 7, 13–15, 20, 21, 22, 24, 25, 29, 36, 39, 40
inter-clan tensions in, 33
Jacobitism in, 7–8, 13, 14, 20, 21, 31, 40
justice system in, 15–16, 39
labour shortages in, 86, 89
land use, 3, 5, 125
landowners in, 3, 4, 5, 11, 12, 64, 71, 76, 101, 128, 132
colonise army, 139
estate management policies of, 101, 108–111, 115–116, 122, 123, 125, 127, 128–129, 130, 136, 142, 143, 146, 148, 160, 162, 165, 168–169, 170, 172, 183, 191, 193–194
commercialism, 103, 111, 116, 118, 125, 126, 130, 145, 169, 185, 194, 198, 200, 238
linked with emigration, 168, 172, 191, 194
population retention, 183, 191, 192, 193, 198, 203
evictions by, 146, 168, 243
improvement by, linked to recruitment and emigration, 101, 111, 126, 129, 144, 165, 191, 202
involvement in kelp industry, 134–135
military entrepreneurship of, 103–104, 118, 132, 136, 139, 141, 142, 143, 144, 242
military levy, arrangements by for, 101, 104, 106, 107, 108–110, 114, 116–120 *passim*, 122–124, 126, 129, 130, 143–144, 145, 146, 156, 159, 165, 169, 185, 242
patronage, military and imperial, as source of income, 137–139, 193, 202, 237, 238, 242
property rights of, 211
relationship with tenants, 101, 114–115, 122–123, 128, 130, 139, 160
sheep-farming, 135, 161
socio-economic policies of linked to decline in recruitment, 42, 76, 103, 191, 200, 223
lawlessness in, 15, 16–17, 24
local protection schemes in, 37
mechanisms for control of, 35
militarisation of, 47, 58, 64, 147
militarism of, 51, 62, 102, 130, 131, 216, 220, 224, 234, 237
and clanship, 62–63, 78, 130, 132, 141, 142, 145, 165
and state and imperial service, 62, 63, 190, 205, 225, 237
military insurrection in, 15, 16–17

military potential of, 25, 29, 45, 60, 62, 65, 68, 139, 145, 169, 191, 197, 216, 222, 224, 236
manipulation of image of, 63, 197
military service from, 4–5, 7, 24, 28, 35, 40, 106, 145, 217, 227–228, 234
    linked to land, 145, 146–147, 162–165, 166, 185, 189, 242, 243; *see also* Breadalbane estates
    linked to wage increases, 156
MPs from, military backgrounds of, 234
Navy service in, 235
particularism of, 14, 15, 31, 36
perceived cultural distinctions of, 51
planned villages in, 77, 99
political disaffection of, 15, 22, 24, 31, 197
    influence of on opposition to emigration to America from, 193, 197
    relationship of to formation of British Highland military, 40
population of, 3, 4, 73, 89, 112, 114, 125, 127, 177–178, 191, 195
as 'problem' area, 15, 17, 20, 24, 78
Presbyterianism in, 208
Protestantism in, 206–215
recruitment for British army in, 3, 5, 6, 7, 9, 10, 11, 21, 28, 29, 40, 41, 48, 50, 51, 58, 60, 65, 68, 76, 80, 85, 87, 101, 102, 103, 104, 105, 109, 110, 112, 113, 115, 116, 118, 119–125, 126, 127, 128, 130, 131, 132, 133, 140, 144, 145, 158–159, 161, 162, 167, 169, 200, 201, 205, 207, 216, 217, 218, 219, 220, 223, 225, 227, 229, 234, 235, 238–239
    as economic strategy, 136, 141, 142, 144, 145, 148, 158, 159, 162, 163, 166, 241, 242
    as social purgative, 108, 162, 242
    centralised and politicised nature of, 102, 104, 106, 132, 238
    costs of, 70, 107–108, 116–118, 144, 146
    decline in, factors behind, 42, 60, 73, 76, 206, 223
    demographic patterns within, 108–112, 114, 116, 119–120, 122–123, 125, 142, 172, 242
    detrimental impact of, 103, 108–111, 114, 118–119, 121, 157
    during French Revolutionary and Napoleonic Wars, 73, 76, 112–113
    during Seven Years War, 44, 50, 59, 60, 75, 84, 131, 205, 215, 236, 237, 240
    government initiatives in, 102, 106, 244
    impact of on availability of labour, 86, 105, 107, 108–110, 114, 118, 142, 155, 156, 229
    occupation profile, 143
    positive impact of on Argyll's status, 48, 51
    produces wage inflation, 156
    proprietary, 69–70, 73, 74, 76, 105, 145–146, 158, 223, 237, 243
    quota system, 144, 158, 226, 227, 243
    'recruiting for rank', 69, 71, 72, 73, 138, 145, 176
    short-lived episode, 243
    social expectations arising from, 158, 159, 161, 162, 163, 164, 185, 190, 226, 242
    social profile of recruits, 86, 108–109, 116, 119–120, 121, 122, 123, 142–143, 154, 162, 165
recruitment for French army in, 21, 22
recruitment for Prussian army in, 21
reforming legislation in, 78
role of, as military reserve, 68, 73
role of central government in, 11, 16, 36, 42, 104, 234
seafaring tradition in, 197
similarities of to Borders, 50
socio-economic change in, 11, 14, 28, 40, 58, 60, 64, 77, 78–79, 82, 83, 86, 97, 98, 128, 131, 154, 155, 158, 168, 174, 176, 190, 196, 198, 208, 219, 237, 241
    appeal of evangelicalism in circumstances of, 208, 209
    linked to decline in recruitment, 42, 60, 131, 219, 223
    tenurial (in)security and military service, 5–6, 78, 85–86, 88, 108–122 *passim*, 123, 126, 127, 128, 147, 154, 157, 162–163, 164, 165, 167
    war as factor in shaping post-Culloden society in, 234
Highlandisation of culture in, 45
home defence forces in, 225
interaction of with British Empire, 10, 56
landlords, adverse effect of unregulated recruitment on economic position of, 55, 64
legal elite in, hostility of towards clanship, 36
Lowlands of,
    agricultural change in, 101
        leading role of landlords in promoting, 101
    disadvantaged in army patronage, 23, 59
    economic development of, 100, 139, 241
    economic links of with North American and West Indian colonies, 241
    estate management in, 101, 128
    hostility to Jacobitism and Catholicism, 207
    'improvements' in,
        as social and economic model for Highlands, 78, 81, 90, 99
        characteristics of, 81, 128
        government policy towards, 99
    policing role of Independent companies in, 15
    recruitment in, 50, 65, 84
North-East,
    disaffected families in, 30
    tenurial pattern in, 81–82
    unstable electoral politics in, 54
parliament in, 11
    MPs of lobby for raising of Independent companies, 15
patronage in, 29, 42, 44, 56, 58, 75, 76, 238
    Argyll's control of, 48
    impact of on Scotland's semi-autonomous status, 42
    reinforces aspects of particularism, 42
    Treasury control of, 44
political factions in, 13, 52; *see also* argathelians *and* squadrone
political management of, 43–45 *passim*, 50–52, 54, 55, 75; *see also* Campbell, Archibald, 3rd Duke of Argyll; Murray,

William, 1st Earl of Mansfield; Stuart,
    John, Lord Mountstuart
  attitudes to in, 56
  historiography of, 56
 semi-autonomous status of, 42
 Secessions in, 208
 sheriffs, conditions of tenure in, 58
 trade of with Continent, 21
  Hanoverian attempts to sever trade links, 21
 Treasury control of patronage in, 44
 volunteer service, 241
  attractions of to Highland populations, 230
  British sentiment within, 232
  disbandment of, 231, 232
  government pressure on to extend range and
    duration of service, 230
  importance of wages from, 232
  local economic concerns behind, 232
  manpower transferred to militias, 231
  popularity of, 225, 226–227, 229
  replicates clanship ethos and practice, 233
 wage levels in, 218
Scotophobia, 44, 53
Scots-Dutch Brigade, 21, 29, 57
 Mackay (Reay) involvement in, 39
 officers from transfer into British army, 61
Scottish Salt and Customs establishment, 48
 Argyll's control of appointments to, 48
Scullamus, 164
Seaforth, see Humberston-Mackenzie, Francis
 earls of, seek links and patronage opportunities
    with fiscal-military state, 132
 government pressure on to recruit, 61
Secretary of State for Scotland, see Hay, John, 4th
    Marquis of Tweeddale
Secretary of War, see Dundas, Henry
Seil, island of, estate management policy on, 111,
    112, 122, 124
Select Society, 215
Selkirk, Earl of, see Douglas, Thomas
Seven Years War, 44, 50, 76, 83, 87, 93, 103,
    157, 169
 impact of recruitment on estate incomes during,
    107
 military emigration during, 183, 185–186
 pattern of recruitment established during, 50,
    59, 75, 83, 225
 re-emergence of mass Highland recruitment
    during, 44, 60, 75, 84, 131, 205, 215,
    236, 237, 240
 stimulates credit drain, 136
Shaw, Lieutenant Daniel, offers to raise men for
    American Revolutionary War, 62
sheep-farming, 118, 125, 135, 137, 148, 159, 160
 emigration stimulated by, 188
 introduction of delayed by value of recruitment,
    160, 161, 242
 problems with, 135
Sheriffmuir, battle of, 12, 234
Simcoe, John Graves, Governor of Upper Canada,
    180, 181
 argues for increased emigration, 181
Sinclair, Sir John, government pressure on to raise
    men, 61
Sinclair, Sir John, of Ulbster, improver, 223
 proposes naval recruitment, 235
 requested to raise regiment, 223
Sinclair, Peter, sub-tenant on Breadalbane estate, 111
 son of, serving in fencibles, 111

Skye, 31, 148, 199, 232
 arms transported to from Liverpool, 35
 crofters in, 5
 development of fishing in, 97
 Hanoverian influence in restricts Jacobite
    recruitment in Inverness-shire, 35
 Macleod estate in, 5
 men from in Dutch service, 22
 prominence of half-pay officers on, 148–149
 reports to Napier Commission in, 5
 successful deployment of military patronage in,
    34
 volunteer establishment in, 227, 229
Small, James, 217
Solicitor-General, see Dundas, Robert, of Arniston
Sollitot, 163
South Langwell, fishing and crofting pattern at,
    96–97
South Uist, emigration from, 189
Spain, 17, 88, 178, 204, 244
 Britain declares war on, 24
 fears of invasion of Britain by, 25
 maritime and colonial nature of war with, 26
 peace negotiations with Britain and France, 88
Spanish War of Succession, recruitment during,
    107
 squadrone volante, political faction, 13, 26–27
 hostility to argathelians, 27
Stair, Earl of, see Dalrymple, John
Steuart, James, of Dalguise, 21
Stewart, Rev. Alexander, evangelical minister,
    211–212
Stewart, Lieutenant Allan, organises emigration
    from Appin, 188
Stewart, David, of Garth, 3, 6
 Sketches of the Character, Manners and Present
    State of the Highlanders of Scotland, 3
Stewart, John, of Invernahyle, 104
Stewart, Peter, provost of Campbeltown, 94, 97
 calls for abandonment of traditional agricultural
    practices, 97
Stewart of Appin,
 alienation of wadsetting rights on property of,
    32
 enlistment from, 140
 Jacobitism of, 140
Stewart of Ardsheal, estates of, 79
Stirlingshire, watch in, 38
Stornoway, wage increases in, 156
Strath, economic prominence of army pensioners
    in, 151
Strathavon,
 impact of recruitment on economy of, 156
 tacksmen responsible for bounties of men levied
    in, 144
Stratherrick,
 farms in recolonised from Argyll and Strathspey,
    87
 land in, lying waste, 107
 riots provoked by presentation of minister in,
    211
 subtenantry in, removed, 87, 96
Strathnaver, intimidatory recruiting in, 159
Strathspey,
 agricultural colonists from, 87
 economic status of half-pay officers in, 148, 149
 Grant rentals from, 137
 recruitment in, 140
 reorganisation of tacksman farms in, 171

Strelitz, 91
Stronmilchan, farm of, proposed subdivision of for military tenants, 111
Strowan, 91, 94, 95
  consolidation of tenancies at, 95
  recruitment from, 140
Stuart, John, Lord Mountstuart,
  lobbies for formation of militias, 53
  political influence of, 52–53
Stuart-Mackenzie, Sir George, improver, 224
Sutherland, 134, 139, 141, 143
  93rd Sutherland Highlanders, 4, 7, 141, 147, 155, 159, 243
    enlistment into linked to grant of leases, 147
    pensioners from, 150
  Clearances in, 3, 4, 147
    folk traditions relating to, 3
  Commissioners of Supply in, 38
    raise funds for watches, 38
  Earl of, see Gordon, William
  election in (1761), 51, 105
  estates,
    contribution of army pay to income of, 153
    enlistment from, 140, 158–159
    evictions from, 147, 243
    half-pay officers holding most valuable tenancies on, 149
    land on offered to demobilised men, 157–158
    rent arrears on, 134
    restructuring of tenurial patterns on, 157–158, 166, 170, 171, 172
  Elizabeth, countess of, 4, 54, 139, 141, 153, 172
    opponent of Dundas, 54
  family, 3
    raises proprietary regiment, 3, 141, 243
    recruitment by, 61, 131
      inactivity of senior tenants in support of, 155
      stipulations concerning land for service, 147
  fencible regiment, 51, 54, 73, 102, 140, 143, 147, 156
    demobilisation of, 157
    recruitment strategy for, 143
  George Mackay, MP for, 51
  run-down of volunteer military service in, 200
  volunteer establishment in, 227, 231
Sutherland, Captain James, estate factor, 172
Swedish East India Company, as military recruiter in Scottish Highlands, 21
Swordly, farm, 153

tacksmen,
  entering army, 86–87, 177
    re-entering, 172–174, 177
  erosion of status of, 86, 154, 158, 169–171, 177–178, 208, 243
  impact of recruitment on, 154–157, 158
  landlord hostility towards, 155, 170, 171
  military role, 154, 155
  'oppression' by, 171
  relationship with small tenantry, 158, 171–172
  responsibilities and role of, 154–155, 157, 171, 208
  role in emigration, 171, 172, 187
  tenurial security of, 78, 155, 170, 177–178
Taybridge, Independent company troops at, 37
Taymouth, 114

Telford, Thomas, 197
Thom, Rev. William, promotes emigration from Highlands, 187
Thomson, Alexander, improving tenant, 122
Ticonderoga, award of lands around to soldiers of 42nd and 77th Regiments, 186
Tiree, wage increases in, 156
Tobermory, value of naval pensions at, 235
Tommachrocher, croft, 124
Townshend, George, 4th Viscount Townshend, Lord Lieutenant of Ireland, 67
transhumance, calls for prohibition of, 97
Trotternish, 152
Trustees for the Improvement of the Manufactures and Fisheries, 157
Tullichglass, consequences of loss of sheiling lands at, 125
Tweeddale, Marquis of, see Hay, John

Ullapool, 81, 92, 96
Union,
  Act of, 8, 13, 14
  and nationalism, 13
  role of manager as barrier to complete Union, 56
  stimulates support for Jacobitism, 13
United States, threat to Canada from, 182
Urquhart,
  emigration from, 189
  enlistment from Grant lands of, 143
    socio-economic consequences of, 166
  minister of involved in recruitment process, 210
  reactions in to minister's reluctance to catechise, 208
  resistance to recruitment in, 155
  settlement of half-pay officers in, 149
  social profile of, 143
  wage increases in, 156

Wade, George, general, 16, 20, 23
  garrison policy of in Highlands, 27, 35
    collapse of, 35, 36
  and Malt Tax riots, 17, 21
  proposed regularising of Independent companies by, 21, 25
  removes clan weaponry, 35
wadset, 170
  alienation of capability to, 32
wadsetter class, 172
Wales, Marches of, martial tradition in, 41
Walker, Rev. John, 217
  condemns emigration, 191
Walpole, Sir Robert, prime minister, 24
  peaceful strategies of, 40
  relationship of with Earl of Ilay, 48
War Office, 48, 85, 113, 182
  petitions to, 63, 175
War, Secretary of, see Barrington, Lord; Dundas, Henry
wars,
  American Wars of Independence, 5, 55, 59, 62, 66–67, 68, 77, 118, 131, 156, 169, 177, 221
    balance of professional and proprietary recruitment for, 71, 243
    deployment of Highland regiments in, 59
    implications of absence of Scottish manager during, 54
    mercenaries deployed by British in, 66, 68

recruiting proposals for, channelled through Dundas, 53
recruitment of Highland regiments for, 61, 65, 73, 75, 112, 122, 142, 147
sheep-farmers in Argyll bankrupted by, 135
stimulate credit drain, 136
Austrian War of Succession, 26, 42, 215, 237
as catalyst for 1745 Jacobite rising, 26
British imperial, Scottish attitudes towards, 44–45, 46
French Revolutionary, 71, 73, 76, 106, 112–113, 198, 204, 225
invasion crisis of 1798, 228
stimulates credit drain, 136
Napoleonic Wars, 65, 73, 197, 198, 204, 225, 242
Seven Years War, 44, 50, 76, 83, 87, 93, 103, 157, 169
impact of recruitment for on estate incomes, 107
military emigration during, 183, 185–186
pattern of recruitment established during, 50, 59, 75, 83, 225
re-emergence of mass Highland recruitment during, 44, 60, 75, 84, 131, 205, 215, 236, 237, 240
stimulates credit drain, 136
Spanish War of Succession, recruitment during, 107
watch commissions,
as alternative to Independent companies, 37
organised by Macpherson of Cluny, 38
Waterloo, battle of, 12, 204, 234, 244
Waternish, enlistment from Macleod estates of, 140
weaving, 141
Weem, 26
West Indies,
Cathcart's expedition to, 29
economic links with Lowland Scotland, 241
negative attitude of Highland gentry towards service in, 31

Wester Borlum, scarcity of labour at due to military recruitment, 86
Wester Ross,
economic condition of, 173
introduction of sheep-farming in, 160
kin-based protection schemes in, 38
resistance to militia service in, 231
Western Fencibles, 142
Western Isles, elite tenantry in, 148
prominence of half-pay officers among, 148
Westminster, 16, 49, 240
concerns over emigration levels at, 193
factionalism at, 45, 76, 80
impact of on policy in Highlands, 80
flawed perception of Highland social structures at, 60, 236, 242
Scotophobia at, 44
Whigs, 16, 17, 30
clans, military recruitment from, 25
clan support for, 32
peers, 54
political divisions of, 29, 34
prominence of in Independent companies, 14
propaganda, 15
Whitehills, 89
Wildman, William, Lord Barrington, Secretary of War, 48–49, 58, 60, 103, 218, 219
Wilkes, John, MP, attitude to Highland soldiers, 221
William III, king, European policies of, 25
Worcester, battle of, 8
Wurtemburg, Duchy of, as source of mercenaries for British army, 66

York, Frederick, Duke of, 64, 69, 219
Commander-in-Chief, 69
military reforms of, 69
policy of, towards grant of new regular regiments, 64, 72
support of sought by Highland Society for anti-emigration policies, 195–196
Yorke, Philip, *see* Hardwicke, Lord Chancellor.